The China War Medal 1900 To The Royal Navy & Royal Marines

Compiled and Edited by
W. H. Fevyer & J. W. Wilson

ISBN 0 9481 3030 X

CONTENTS.

Appendix.

The following despatches published in the London Gazette refer to the operations in China.

INTRODUCTION

The medal roll for the Third China War to the Naval and Marine Forces is held at the Public Record Office under reference ADM 171-55. It will be noticed that a comparison between this roll and the roll for the Queen's South Africa Medal, where a recipient received both medals, can reveal inconsistancies in name or service number. To establish where the errors lie, and to correct them, would be impossible as one would need to check all the service records, and these are not all available at the Public Record Office. Therefore, we have transcribed the original handwritten records which were compiled at the time and were used for the naming and issuance of the medals. It should always be borne in mind that the rolls were kept not for researchers and collectors of the future, but as a record of the issuance of medals to recipients of proven entitlement and control of same.

Also included in this volume is a listing of the casualties compiled from various sources including:- Records held by the Ministry of Defence, The London Gazette, The Times, The Public Record Office etc., and we are confident that it is the most complete and detailed list published to date. Selected Despatches have been abstracted from The London Gazette to give the reader some indication of the role played by the Royal Navy and Royal Marines during the Boxer Rebellion.

Returned and duplicated medals have been listed in full and selected notes from the Roll have been included where considered appropriate. Medals presented by H.M. the King have been noted against individual names and also included is the list of recipients who received their medals from H.M. the King, as published in The Naval & Military Record of 13th March 1902.

The service numbers of the men have been included as an aid to further in-depth research as service papers are available at the Public Record Office as follows:

Royal Navy

Ratings	service numbers up to 165000	ADM 188 series
Commissioned officers		ADM 196 series

Royal Marines

Chatham Div.	service numbers up to Ch.14872	ADM 159 series
Portsmouth Div.	service numbers up to Po.11366	ADM 159 series
Plymouth Div.	service numbers up to Ply.11464	ADM 159 series
R.M.A.	service numbers up to RMA.9435	ADM 159 series
Officers		ADM 196 series

We trust that this companion volume to The Queen's South Africa Medal to the Royal Navy and the Royal Marines will be a useful addition to the book shelves of medal specialists, collectors and researchers.

W.H.F. 1985.

Periods for Entitlement to Bars & Medal.

Bar	Period for which entitled.
Defence of Legations	29th June 1900 to 14th August 1900
Taku Forts	17th June 1900
Relief of Pekin	10th June 1900 to 14th August 1900

Ship / Unit.	Period for which entitled.
H.M.S. Alacrity	10th June 1900 to 31st December 1900
H.M.S. Algerine	10th June 1900 to 13th November 1900
H.M.S. Arethusa	30th July 1900 to 31st December 1900
H.M.S. Aurora	10th June 1900 to 31st December 1900
H.M.S. Barfleur	10th June 1900 to 18th December 1900
H.M.S. Bonaventure	19th July 1900 to 31st December 1900
H.M.S. Centurion	10th June 1900 to 31st December 1900
H.M.S. Daphne	22nd June 1900 to 31st December 1900
H.M.S. Dido	21st July 1900 to 9th December 1900
H.M.S. Endymion	10th June 1900 to 17th November 1900
H.M.S. Esk	10th June 1900 to 31st December 1900
H.M.S. Fame	10th June 1900 to 18th December 1900
H.M.S. Goliath	25th August 1900 to 31st December 1900
H.M.S. Hart	1st July 1900 to 31st December 1900
H.M.S. Hermione	10th June 1900 to 31st December 1900
H.M.S. Humber	(10th June 1900 to 5th August 1900 (5th September 1900 to 25th September 1900 (16th October 1900 to 9th November 1900 (1st December 1900 to 19th December 1900
H.M.S. Isis	21st December 1900 to 31st December 1900
H.M.S. Linnet	14th June 1900 to 31st December 1900
H.M.S. Marathon	3rd August 1900 to 29th October 1900
H.M.S. Orlando	10th June 1900 to 31st December 1900
H.M.S. Peacock	17th June 1900 to 31st December 1900
H.M.S. Phoenix	10th June 1900 to 31st December 1900
H.M.S. Pigmy	1st July 1900 to 12th November 1900
H.M.S. Pique	30th June 1900 to 31st December 1900
H.M.S. Plover	(10th July 1900 to 10th August 1900 (17th September 1900 to 31st December 1900
H.M.S. Redpole	8th October 1900 to 31st December 1900
H.M.S. Rosario	24th June 1900 to 31st December 1900
H.M.S. Snipe	10th June 1900 to 31st December 1900
H.M.S. Terrible	21st June 1900 to 10th December 1900
H.M.S. Undaunted	19th June 1900 to 8th November 1900
H.M.S. Wallaroo	4th August 1900 to 31st December 1900
H.M.S. Waterwitch	10th June 1900 to 28th October 1900
H.M.S. Whiting	10th June 1900 to 31st December 1900
H.M,S. Woodcock	10th June 1900 to 31st December 1900
H.M.S. Woodlark	10th June 1900 to 31st December 1900
Legation Guard	10th June 1900 to 14th August 1900
North West Fort, Taku	30th June 1900 to 31st December 1900
Naval Depot, Wei-Hai-Wei	10th June 1900 to 31st December 1900
N.S.W. Naval Defence Force	7th August 1900 to 31st December 1900
S. Australia Naval Defence Force	7th August 1900 to 31st December 1900
Victorian Naval Defence Force	7th August 1900 to 31st December 1900
Royal Indian Marine Miscellaneous	(Period of entitlement not specified on roll (

H.M.S. ALACRITY.

H.M.S. Alacrity was a Despatch vessel of 1,700 tons and 250 x 32½ feet. Her armament consisted of 4 x 5 in and 4 x 6 pdr guns. The vessel was built by Palmer and launched on 28th February 1885. She was sold in September 1913 at Hong Kong.

Bars	*Total*	*Returned*	*Entitled*
TF & RP	*42*	*0*	*42*
TF	*8*	*0*	*8*
RP	*1*	*0*	*1*
None	*87*	*0*	*87*
	138	*0*	*138*

Notes:

Missing detail in the medal roll is indicated by the use of brackets; the spaces inside the brackets are not intended to indicate the exact amount of missing detail.

K - Medal presented by H.M. The King on 8th March 1902.

1 - This man is also on the medal roll of H.M.S. Centurion as entitled to a No Bar medal which was presented by H.M. The King.

Bars: TAKU FORTS, RELIEF OF PEKIN.

	Name	Rank	Number
	Bailey, W.J.	AB	199.727
	Bailey, W.R.	AB	186.195
	Barr, J.	Pte	Po1.970
	Bertie, J.	Pte	Ply7.990
	Bland, H.F.	Dom	355.053
	Browne, R.H.J.	St/Surgn	
	Burgess, G.F.	AB	171.381
	Burrows, G.	Sto	290.132
	Charrington, E.	Lieut	
	Clarke, G.	Pte	Po5.451
	Clarke, G.A.	Sto	281.931
	Cliff, W.J.	Ch/Sto	140.261
	Corbon, G.W.M.	AB	178.738
	Cradock, C.G.F.M.	Comdr	
	Dann, G.J.	AB	186.983
	Frogley, H.T.	PO1	137.998
	Griffiths, W.G.	Act/Ch/Sto	125.418
	Hayward, G.J.	L/S	155.619
	Hillier, E.J.	AB	183.431
	Howe, F.	Sto	143.707
	Jehan, H.D.	PO2	180.904
	Lea, H.	Sto	279.962
	Leggett, G.	Sto	158.751
	Lockley, J.G.	AB	159.215
	Longland, R.C.	AB	186.723
	McKenzie, G.	Sto	281.951
	May, W.S.	Gunr	
	Mitchell, P.H.	AB	171.144
	Morgan, T.	Sto	284.317
	Payne, H.W.	PO1	128.984
	Peacock, W.	AB	190.791
K	Randall, H.	PO1	147.447
	Rendle, W.	Pte	Po2.753
	Robb, T.J.	2/Yeo/Sig	151.259
	Robinson, E.	Pte	Ply7.989
	Shuttler, I.V.	PO1	155.528
	Stevenson, A.R.	AB	179.804
	Stratford, J.S.	AB	192.465
	Tilbury, L.	AB	183.122
K	Townsend, W.J.	AB	169.987
	Wingate, P.C.T.	3/Wrtr	341.103
	Witts, T.G.	Ord	192.466

Duplicate medals:

Name	Rank	Number
Clarke, G.	Pte	Po5.451 *
Witts, T.G.	Ord	192.466

* *Two duplicate medals issued.*

H.M.S. ALACRITY.

Bar: TAKU FORTS.

Denham, G.T.	Sto	152.591
Fry, A.J.	AB	178.641
Jordan, J.F.	AB	169.141
Keaton, E.J.	L/S	170.312
Macey, A.S.	Arm/Mte	152.920
Moore, R.E.	AB	193.109
Wood, A.E.	AB	143.542
Worth, J.	Sto	158.118

Bar: RELIEF OF PEKIN.

Wheeler, G.P.	Carp/Mte	145.705

NO BAR MEDALS.

Alderman, F.	Sto	282.932
Babey, T.	Sto	276.830
Baker, G.E.	L/Sto	160.002
Baldwin, A.	ERA	268.692
Bishop, P.	Sto	293.260
Black, J.	Sto	276.692
Bocock, R.H.	Sto.	283.172
Bramble, J.	Ch/Sto	128.329
Brockway, R.	Ch/Sto	100.085
Butland, J.R.	Sh/Cpl	128.971
Butler, C.	Ord	197.785
Button, J.	L/Sto	127.400
Callanan, W.	ERA	269.209
Cha Sing *alias* Jah Ning.	Capt/Std	
Chamberlain, H.E.	Sto	173.469
Choy Ah.	Sto	
Coad, W.	AB	170.395
Coleridge, G.E.	Act/Payr	
Collins, A.H.	Asst/Engr	
Corcoran, C.	AB	185.952
Cotton, T.F.	Ch/ERA	149.729
Davis, G.H.	Sto	153.806
Dawes, H.W.	Ord	197.212
Drennan, C.	Sto	276.824
Edwards, G.J.	Sh/Std	158.889
English, P.	Sto	(.755)
Evans, R.H.	L/Carp/Crew	342.689
Everett, F.	L/S	(8.451)
Fook Ah.	Pntr	
Forsyth, R.	Sto	277.789
Fraser, R.H.	Lieut	
Goyns, F.J.	2/Wrtr	168.933
Greenslade, F.G.	Sto	276.982
Hall, W.J.	Q/Sig	185.841
Harris, J.	Sto	175.421
Hicks, W.	Sto	276.672
Ho Ah.	Sto	
Hoar, R.	Pte	Ch5.369
Hodgson, H.E.	AB	192.459
Hoe Ah.	Dom	
Hon Ah.	Dom	
Hung Ah.	Sto	
Jones, J.A.	Sto	293.404
Kean Ah.	Dom	
Keene, J.B.	L/Sig	169.991
Kong Ah.	Dom	
Lewis, C.G.	Pte	Ply7.171
Ling Ah.	Sto	
Little, W.R.	PO1	138.985
Llewellyn, M.	Ch/Arm	127.973
Lovell, H.	AB	171.124
McDermid, T.	Pte	Ply8.886
McGregor, J.	AB	192.464
Martin, A.I.	ERA	269.157
Mernin, T.J.	AB	180.561
Miall, A.	Sto	277.210
Milmer, J.A.	L/Sto	143.029
Mobsby, H.	Pilot	
Mullins, G.	Pte	Po6.392
Mussell, J.	Sto	158.802
Newberry, T.	Sto	276.021
Opie, A.	Sto	286.480
Payne, J.W.	L/S	152.279
Peacock, D.	Ch/Engr	
Pemble, E.H.	Ch/PO	128.587 [1]
Ping Ah.	Sto	
Poate, T.P.	L/Sto	148.582
Presland, A.M.	Cpl	Po6.204
Prince, H.	Ord	190.748
Richards, S.	2/SBStd	350.411
Rooke, F.	AB	180.164
Sandle, A.	Ord	197.345
Sang Ah.	Sto	
Shawyer, J.	L/Sto	151.720
Shu Ah.	Sto	
Sing Ah.	Sto	
Son Ah.	Dom	
Stevens, J.	Sto	168.225
Stevens, W.	Sto	(283.2)
Symons, C.	Sig	(19 . 63)
Tearle, W.	ERA	269.205
Tin Sou.	Carp/Crew	
Ting Ah.	Capt/Cook	
Townsend, E.	PO1	139.101
White, F.H.	Pte	Po7.216
Wolfe, E.C.	Sh/Cook	158.898
Wood, A.E.	Lieut	

Duplicate medals:

Davis, G.H.	Sto	153.806
Hodgson, H.E.	AB	192.459

H.M.S. ALGERINE.

H.M.S. Algerine was a Sloop of 1,050 tons and 185 x 33 feet. Her armament consisted of 6 x 4 in and 4 x 3 pdr guns. The vessel was built in Devonport Dock Yard and launched on 6th June 1895. She was sold on 11th April 1919 as a salvage vessel.

Bars	*Total*	*Returned*	*Entitled*
TF & RP	*9*	*0*	*9*
TF	*95*	*1*	*94*
RP	*1*	*0*	*1*
None	*11*	*2*	*9*
	116	*3*	*113*

Notes:

Missing detail in the medal roll is indicated by the use of brackets; the spaces inside the brackets are not intended to indicate the exact amount of missing detail.

K - Medal presented by H.M. The King on 8th March 1902.

Bars: TAKU FORTS, RELIEF OF PEKIN.

Cackett, J.W.	AB	160.843
Chambers, A.S.	Lieut	
Courtis, E.G.	Gunr	
Duncan, G.	Lieut	
Godfrey, F.	AB	(176. 88)
Knight, S.	AB	168.115
Rogers, W.G.	AB	174.705
Speare, W.T.	AB	193.132
White, A.F.	Engr	

Bar: TAKU FORTS.

Adey, W.H.	L/S	106.778
Boland, W.	Carp/Crew	342.566
Brooks, D.	AB	185.926
Brown, F.H.	AB	184.541
Browne, J.	Sto	280.079
Burn, E.C.	Sto	291.752
Chan Ah.	Dom	
Clarke, J.	Pte	Ply9.443 K
Claypitt, S.D.	Ord	197.467
Cook, J.	Ch/Sto	121.130
Corber, S.S.	AB	163.298
Couch, A.C.	Pte	Ply3.227
Crews, W.J.	Ord	203.576
Crossan, J.	Sto	291.556
Curran, C.	Ord	203.572
Darlington, H.	Boy	199.445
Davies, J.	Pte	Ply5.219
Day, W.	PO2	147.138
Dimon, T.A.	AB	170.694
Dimond, F.	Pte	Ply5.807
Dodd, W.H.	Sto	280.954
Dolbear, S.W.	AB	161.022
Edgcombe, W.T.	2/Yeo/Sig	154.363
Edwards, T.	Sail/Mte	115.727
Evans, J.G.	L/Shpwrt	142.136
Fry, S.	AB	127.081
Furnaess, W.	Ord	197.949
Gibson, W.	SB/Attn	350.403
Guley, F.	AB	163.825
Hales, F.L.	PO2	127.090
Hargreaves, H.J.	Asst/Payr	
Hart, W.J.	Sto	281.423
Hemmens, A.	Sh/Cpl	118.276
Hill, A.L.	Ord	198.728
Hooper, W.	AB	156.796
Humphreys, E.	Sto	290.886
Iles, S.	Pte	Ply9.441
Jago, C.	AB	195.501
Jago, R.	Act/Ch/Sto	138.048
Jarvis, H.	AB	119.229
Jay Ah.	Dom	
Johnson, A.G.	Q/Sig	156.432
Johnston, M.	L/Sto	169.289
King, S.	Sto	283.056
Knight, G.H.	Ch/Sto	126.384
Lamping, F.	L/Cpl	Ply7.869
Larkworthy, F.	L/S	156.368
Lawrence, J.	L/Sto	154.927
Lee, W.	Sto	280.670

H.M.S. ALGERINE.

Bar: TAKU FORTS *continued.*

	Lytton, E.	Ch/PO	99.037
	Manning, F.	Sto	279.622
	Martin, P.	Ch/Carp/Mte	140.959
	Merrifield, J.H.R.	ERA	268.641
	Moy Ah.	Dom	
	Newman, H.	AB	192.370
	Newton, T.	PO1	139.164
	Norman, G.R.	Sto	165.874
	O'Brien, D.	AB	145.271
	Oliver, J.	AB	173.838
	Pascoe, J.	Shpwrt	342.917
	Pateyjohns, J.C.	Pntr	342.041
	Perrett, R.F.	PO1	147.869
	Phillips, F.	Pte	Ply8.707
	Pinn, C.H.	AB	145.277
	Pope, J.W.	Sto	291.747
	Ratel, P.G.	Pte	Ply9.444
	Reed, J.C.G.	Surgn	
	Rendle, W.R.	AB	133.666
	Ridge, A.W.	L/S	164.759
	Robinson, S.	Lieut	
	Rose, J.	Pte	Ply5.985
	St. John, E.S.	ERA	269.393
	San Ah.	Dom	
	Silvester, T.C.	Sh/Std	141.680
	Smale, A.	L/Sto	151.862
	Smith, C.E.M.	L/S	155.829
	Snowden, A.A.	Sig	191.701
	Stewart, R.H.J.	Comdr	
	Sweeney, P.	Sto	281.630
	Thomas, F.	L/Sig	162.913
	Thorne, R.	Sto	291.748
	Tucker, G.H.M.S.	PO1	150.790
	Vernon, J.R.G.	Ord	196.284
	Vincent, W.H.F.K.	Sergt	Ply5.091
	Wackley, R.M.	Arm/Mte	161.442
	Why Ah.	Dom	
	Willcox, H.J.	AB	178.938
	Wiltshire, H.W.	Ord	190.171
	Wise, T.W.	Pte	Ply9.442
	Wood, G.T.	2/Sh/Cook	152.531
	Woods, J.F.	Pte	Ply8.842
	Woolford, W.	Ord	203.573
	Wyatt, C.E.	Ch/ERA	141.579
	You Ah.	Dom	

Duplicate medals:

Name	Rank	Number
Brooks, D.	AB	185.926
Clarke, J.	Pte	Ply9.443
Crossan, J.	Sto	291.556
Dolbear, S.W.	AB	161.022
Hales, F.L.	PO2	127.090
Iles, S.	Pte	Ply9.441
Perrett, R.F.	PO1	147.869
Smith, C.E.M.	L/S	155.829

Returned medal:

Name	Rank	Number
Pope, T.C.	Ord	199.444

Bar: RELIEF OF PEKIN.

Name	Rank	Number
Stanton, J.W.W.	Surgn	

NO BAR MEDALS.

	Name	Rank	Number
	Bryant, A.J.	SB/Attn	131.889
	Chapman, G.A.	PO1	147.290
K	Cridland, W.	AB	168.091
	Cushney, E.C.F.F.	Pte	Ply7.170
	Howard, E.N.	Sto	294.183
	Jarrett, C.E.	AB	176.048
	Reed, W.	Sto	294.181
	Stewart, W.	Sto	281.623
	Thomas, W.J.	Ord	192.080

Returned medals:

Name	Rank	Number
Corben, C.	L/Sto	153.632
Hunt, E.D.	Comdr	

H.M.S. ARETHUSA.

H.M.S. Arethusa was a 2nd class Cruiser of 4,300 tons and 300 x 46 feet. Her armament consisted of 10 x 6 in guns. The vessel was built by Napier and launched on 23rd December 1882. She was sold on 4th April 1905 to Garnham.

Bars	*Total*	*Returned*	*Entitled*
None	*313*	*7*	*306*
	313	*7*	*306*

NO BAR MEDALS.

Name	Rating	Number
Adams, G.E.	Shpwrt	343.056
Agent, C.L.	PO2	135.879
Aitkenhead, W.G.	Pte	Ch3.572
Allen, T.	Sto	282.253
Allison, R.	Sig	197.527
Amis, L.W.	Ord	197.483
Attridge, W.R.	Sh/Std	148.165
Ballantyne, A.M.	Ord	198.046
Banks, A.G.	Dom	357.129
Barlow, W.	Gunr	
Barnes, F.	L/Sto	165.224
Bartlett, G.F.	Sto	291.386
Baster, W.H.	PO1	127.235
Bax, T.	Ord	192.089
Beeching, J.	L/Sto	155.237
Benton, W.	L/Sto	141.269
Blackie, J.B.	L/Carp/Crew	342.985
Blanks, T.A.	L/S	174.145
Bloomer, E.	Sto	279.171
Braddick, T.	Pte	Ply7.693
Breeze, A.P.	MAA	150.113
Bride, J.	Sto	146.743
Bristow, E.	Ord	190.485
Brodie, J.P.	Ch/ERA	121.633
Brooker, A.J.	Ord	187.350
Brown, D.	Ord	204.383
Brown, G.S.	AB	118.418
Brown, J.W.	Ch/Sto	143.956
Brown, W.	PO1	151.835
Browns, W.	Sto	290.220
Bruce, B.	Dom	357.885
Burgess, A.	Ord	195.061
Butler, F.A.	Asst/Engr	
Butterworth, H.	Lieut	
Cadwaladr, R.	Sto	288.433
Cain, A.	Cpl	Ch8.716
Capon, A.B.	Sto	282.755
Carpenter, F.W.	Pte	Ch8.209
Castle, C.	Sto	284.221
Catt, P.H.	Ord	198.317
Chase, J.J.	Sh/Cook	155.544
Christie, J.L.	AB	187.754
Clarke, R.	Dom	165.315
Clayton, J.	PO1	124.306
Clinton, J.J.	Sto	285.573
Clowes, J.	Yeo/Sig	151.744
Coleman, J.F.	PO2	170.658
Coley, A.	PO1	129.129
Colquitt, V.G.	AB	186.402
Compton, C.H.	Bugler	Ch9.616
Connor, E.	Ch/ERA	153.861
Cook, H.	Ord	192.495
Cooling, J.H.	Ord	198.582
Cooper, A.E.	L/S	164.789
Coughlan, D.	PO1	165.490
Cripps, E.G.	L/Sergt	Ch9.136
Croft, W.J.	Q/Sig	161.928
Crosbie, J.	Pte	Ch8.106
Crossfield, W.	ERA	269.716
Cummings, A.	Pte	Ch9.728
Cunningham, A.	Ord	197.290
Dalton, E.T.	Ord	197.428
Daniels, W.J.	Ord	197.598
Davis, C.W.	Arm/Crew	341.909
Davis, J.	SBStd	129.425
Day, C.W.A.	AB	188.966
Dear, E.J.	Pte	Ply8.714
Dickison, G.	Plmbr/Mte	341.003
Dobie, J.J.	Ord	189.955
Doble, C.H.	AB	178.685
Donovan, D.	Ord	196.681
Donovan, W.	Sto	285.335
Doswell, A.	Pte	Ch8.019
Duncan, T.C.	Sto	357.134
Easterbrook, G.	Pte	Ch5.722
Edwards, R.T.	Ord	204.197
Ellis, C.W.	Pte	Ch8.506
Eteson, S.	Sto	290.223
Fabian, W.C.	AB	179.703
Fawns, A.J.	Ord	195.770
Fawns, P.	ERA	268.592
Finney, T.W.	Sto	288.760
Fisher, J.J.	Ord	187.647
Fisk, H.J.	AB	188.417
Fletcher, W.G.	AB	191.467
Forbes, J.	Ord	199.695
Ford, E.	AB	185.252
Foster, A.	Ord	177.366

NO BAR MEDALS *continued.*

Name	Rank	Number
French, G.	Clerk	
French, J.	Ord	198.846
Frisbee, W.C.	Pte	Ch8.243
Froude, E.A.	ERA	170.125
Fu Ah.	Dom	
Garnett, R.	Ord	191.195
Gates, M.J.	Dom	356.819
Gethin, S.	Ord	204.365
Goddard, G.J.	Ord	196.352
Goddard, W.H.	Ord	196.569
Goodall, E.	Ord	203.827
Goodship, G.	AB	172.540
Grant, G.H.	AB	166.306
Green, A.J.	Ord	190.477
Green, S.	Sto	291.662
Greenstreet, W.J.	Arm/Crew	341.908
Grist, A.J.	Sto	282.814
Guilliard, P.	Ord	200.512
Hamer, R.R.	Asst/Payr	
Hannaford, J.F.	PO1	166.800
Harrington, D.	AB	173.357
Harris, A.J.	Ord	197.280
Harrison, F.	AB	168.970
Harryman, H.	Sto	291.387
Hathaway, R.	Pte	Ch7.766
Hawkins, A.A.	Pte	Ch8.678
Hay, J.	Ord	194.287
Hayward, C.E.	Sh/Cpl	122.287
Heath, J.F.	PO1	134.740
Hemmings, J.N.	Pte	Ch9.829
Henly, J.	Pte	Ch5.609
Hennessy, N.	Pte	Ch4.384
Henson, H.E.	AB	187.848
Herbert, B.A.	Sto	291.195
Hill, G.H.	L/S	175.488
Holder, G.S.	AB	154.330
Holmes, F.J.	Sto	282.593
Holmes, G.J.	Ch/Sto	120.727
Holt, H.	Sto	283.001
Howe, W.	Sto	286.703
Hughes, E.L.	Lieut	
Hughes, H.J.	AB	193.019
Hunt, E.H.	AB	167.282
Jackson, G.M.	Pte	Ch9.555
Jacobs, W.	Ord	192.592
James, C.J.	Ch/Engr	
Johnson, N.	AB	187.773
Johnston, R.	Arm	340.521
Jones, J.E.	Payr	
Jones, T.	Ord	202.955
Jones, W.H.	L/S	179.139
Joughin, T.	AB	187.833
Kelly, J.	AB	165.079
Kemp, A.	PO2	171.607
Kennett, F.J.	AB	171.792
Kent, W.V.	Sergt	Ch2.464
Kettlewell, W.H.	Ord	196.028

Name	Rank	Number
Kimber, W.	Ord	187.602
Kin Ah.	Dom	
King, H.	Ord	188.861
King, H.	Ord	204.372
Kiy, F.	AB	188.246
Knell, A.	L/Sto	154.823
Kop Ah.	Dom	
Lauch, P.	AB	190.987
Lawrence, A.	Ord	192.869
Lawrence, F.	Carp	
Lewis, W.J.	L/Shpwrt	342.644
Littlefield, W.H.	AB	183.287
Longridge, Rev. M.	Chaplain	
Lovett, C.H.	Pte	Po9.046
Lucas, W.T.	AB	184.308
Lynskey, J.	Sto	291.723
McAulay, N.	Ord	197.533
MacFarlane, G.W.	PO1	160.606
MacKay, J.E.	Ord	193.416
McKay, T.	Sto	287.489
Madge, J.G.	Ord	197.012
Maher, J.T.	Pte	Ch10.145
Main, D.C.	Sto	284.230
Male, F.A.	Sto	281.722
Mansel, C.P.	Lieut	
Mapleston, J.W.	Sto	290.210
Mathers, F.	Ord	197.606
Middlebrook, G.H.	AB	138.962
Mills, H.	Pte	Ch9.621
Mills, J.H.	PO2	139.417
Mitchell, F.	PO2	167.461
Moon, J.A.	St/Surgn	
Moore, C.D.	3/Wrtr	341.175
Moore, J.	Sto	290.213
Moore, W.S.	PO1	150.625
Moran, J.	Sto	283.478
Mortlock, W.	Ord	199.606
Mountford, W.R.	PO1	129.466
Muir, J.	Pte	Ch9.971
Murphy, W.	Sto	291.167
Murray, T.	AB	151.094
Nineham, H.	PO2	129.103
Nolan, R.J.	AB	191.215
Northmore, J.	Ch/Sto	142.650
Nudds, T.	Ord	196.960
O'Connor, D.	Cooper	140.653
O'Connor, M.	Act/Lieut	
O'Dea, P.	Sto	285.763
Oak, F.A.	Ord	200.667
Owen, C.	Pte	Ch7.486
Page, H.	L/Sto	168.421
Painter, H.	Sto	287.051
Pardoe, H.	AB	183.548
Parker, F.V.	PO1	154.010
Parker, T.W.	AB.	180.691
Payne, E.	AB	180.991
Pearce, T.A.	Engr	
Penny, E.	Bosn	
Percival, W.	Sto	282.082

NO BAR MEDALS *continued.*

Pert, C.H.	SB/Attn	350.450
Pick, A.	Sto	291.454
Pinder, F.	L/Sto	126.368
Pinkney, W.	Sto	284.872
Pollock, D.J.	AB	191.853
Poole, W.J.	Pte	Ch7.479
Pople, A.	Sto	282.811
Porteous, A.	Sto	290.039
Porter, L.E.	AB	179.047
Potter, A.	Ord	191.387
Prescott, J.	Ord	195.065
Preston, R.W.	Ord	197.574
Prew, A.J.	Q/Sig	198.604
Prior, A.G.	ERA	268.669
Prodger, J.	Ord	191.626
Pyatt, A.	Pte	Ch9.733
Quei Ah.	Dom	
Riches, J.	AB	162.215
Richmond, D.	Ord	200.974
Riddett, J.C.	Pte	Ch10.237
Rimmer, H.	AB	165.062
Robinson, G.H.	Ord	191.846
Rogers, E.	Sto	281.619
Rolfe, T.	PO1	146.700
Rombulow-Pearse, C.A.	Lieut	
Rook, J.	Sto	280.891
Rosher, J.G.	Sto	291.638
Rossiter, R.	Shpwrt	342.559
Royds, P.M.R.	Lieut	
Rugg, H.J.	AB	180.853
Rumsby, W.	Bosn	
Runacres, R.W.	Ord	196.000
Ruxton, A.E.	Lieut	
Satterly, W.A.	Ord	196.065
Senior, C.	L/S	170.761
Service, H.T.	Ord	204.366
Sewell, C.	AB	164.863
Sharpe, F.	Ord	200.760
Simpson, W.G.	Lieut(RMLI)	
Sisley, W.C.	Pte	Ch10.430
Skinner, H.	L/S	141.485
Small, H.	AB	179.124
Smerdon, F.J.	Pntr	341.891
Smith, A.	Ord	191.307
Smith, E.	Pte	Ch9.187
Smith, J.	Ord	196.961
Smith, S.F.	PO1	151.099
Smith, T.	Dom	41.758
Smith, W.	Cook/Mte	341.151
Snow, T.H.	AB	178.021

Sparrow, N.	Ord	197.262
Spencer, A.H.	AB	180.633
Spurrier, T.	Blksmth	341.075
Stapleford, W.G.	Dom	146.393
Startin, J.	Capt	
Stephens, A.	AB	180.774
Stevens, W.	Ord	190.978
Stirratt, A.	Ord	192.380
Stuart, J.	Sto	281.703
Syre, S.	Sh/Std/Asst	340.635
Tatum, T.W.	Ord	197.808
Taylor, T.	Sto	292.937
Tein Ah.	Dom	
Thompson, T.	Carp/Mte	340.640
Ting Qung.	Dom	
Todd, F.	Ord	200.199
Tom Ah.	Dom	
Triggs, E.	AB	180.789
Tucker, E.	Sto	282.602
Tuppen, P.L.	Sto	287.006
Tutton, E.H.	Sail/Mte	166.182
Twiner, F.H.	Sto	282.374
Tyler, E.A.C.	Sto	285.499
Wah Ah.	Dom	
Waldeck, F.	AB	185.963
Wallace, J.	Sto	282.825
Warrener, H.	L/Sig	183.338
Watkins, G.W.	PO1	131.476
Watt, J.	Sto	282.770
Wells, H.	Pte	Ch9.736
West, A.R.	Sto	291.377
Wheeler, S.W.	Sto	282.067
White, H.	Ord	191.746
White, J.	L/S	111.818
Whittard, H.	2/Yeo/Sig	158.216
Wicks, A.J.	Pte	Ch9.707
Williams, J.	Sto	286.966
Williams, W.	L/Sto	154.139
Willsher, W.	AB	185.332
Winter, G.	Sto	187.710
Wisdom, H.	Ord	204.205
Wood, G.	ERA	123.867
Woodcock, F.	L/Carp/Crew	342.807
Woodhouse, W.	Sto	159.443
Wottam, J.	L/Sto	277.974
Wotton, C.	Sig	195.740
Wright, C.	Sto	281.616
Wright, G.S.	AB	187.480
Wright, J.	L/Sto	129.399
Yeman, C.M.	Ord	204.210
Young, J.	AB	187.833
Yow Ah.	Dom	

NO BAR MEDALS *continued.*

Duplicate medals:

Amis, L.W.	Ord	197.483
Ballantyne, A.M.	Ord	198.046
Bloomer, E.	Sto	279.171
Clowes, J.	Yeo/Sig	151.744
Duncan, T.C.	Sto	357.134
Eteson, S.	Sto	290.223
Fawns, A.J.	Ord	195.770
Finney, T.W.	Sto	288.760
Gethin, S.	Ord	204.365
Hamer, R.R.	Asst/Payr	
Johnson, N.	AB	187.773
Northmore, J.	Ch/Sto	142.650
Nudds, T.	Ord	196.960
Tatum, T.W.	Ord	197.808

Duplicate medals - without issue no. on roll.

Pick, A.	Sto	291.454
Todd, F.	Ord	200.199
Woodhouse, W.	Sto	159.443

Returned medals:

Applegate, W.F.	Ord	192.848
Austin, W.G.	Cpl	Ch6.868
Beck, P.D.	Ord	192.668
Broadbridge, J.	Sto	282.872
Buttrey, H.W.	Pte	Ch5.338
Chapman, F.F.	Lieut	
Manning, T.	Arm/Crew	343.053

H.M.S. AURORA

H.M.S. Aurora was an Armoured Cruiser of 5,600 tons and 300 x 56 feet. Her armament consisted of 2 x 9.2 in and 10 x 6 in guns. The vessel was built in Pembroke Dock and launched on 28th October 1887. She was sold on 2nd October 1907 to Payton at Milford Haven.

Bars	*Total*	*Returned*	*Entitled*
TF & RP	*47*	*1*	*46*
TF	*11*	*1*	*10*
RP	*262*	*4*	*258*
None	*234*	*3*	*231*
	554	*9*	*545*

Notes:

K - Medal presented by H.M. The King on 8th March 1902.

Bars: TAKU FORTS, RELIEF OF PEKIN.

Baker, P.J.	Ord	192.538
Barnes, A.J.	Band	340.760
Bowden, R.P.	AB	142.827
Brady, J.	Sto	287.233
Briggs, A.E.	Ord	185.449
Burry, F.J.	Sto	287.144
Callaghan, H.T.	AB	191.762
Catlin, E.J.	Ord	197.796
Collins, A.	Sto	278.171
Cosway, W.	Ord	192.595
Crowley, F.	Sto	291.729
Crutchley, A.F.	Midn	
Discombe, F.	Ord	194.521
Edwards, C.	Sto	278.241
Finegan, J.	Sto	278.215
Foale, P.	Ord	192.594
Franks, A.A.	Band	340.446
German, H.	Ord	192.570
Gibson, H.	Arm/Crew	341.843
Ham, G.F.	Ord	185.610
Heard, A.	Ord	196.234
Helson, S.J.	Ord	192.587
Hoare, F.	AB	143.508
Hobbs, R.	Ord	185.202
Horsham, W.	PO1	90.659
Hurcom, H.	Ord	182.749
Keen, T.	Pte	Ply8.797
Kemp, T.W.	Act/Comdr	
Kennard, W.J.	Sto	287.194
King, F.	Blksmth/Mte	341.894
Lang, S.	AB	190.518
Martin, A.H.	Ord	192.240
Moss, C.R.	Ord	189.096
Parsons, C.W.	Band/Cpl	124.493
Paul, J.J.	Ch/Yeo/Sig	145.179
Richards, E.H.	Ord	190.147
Roderick, E.E.J.	L/Sig	180.697
Rowe, J.	Ord	193.276
Sharland, T.	Ord	191.790
Sharp, H.	Sto	287.154
Smyth, W.J.	AB	151.609
Spillane, J.	Sto	278.528
Sullivan, J.	PO1	111.305
Uren, G.	AB	179.183
Wells, W.	Band	129.198
Williams, H.E.	AB	109.114

Duplicate medals:

Brady, J.	Sto	287.233
Callaghan, H.T.	AB	191.762
Rowe, J.	Ord	193.276

Returned medal:

Badge, S.T.	Ord	187.907

Bar: TAKU FORTS.

Ahern, P.	Sto	282.834
Ainger, F.G.P.	Ord	192.243
Clarke, J.R.	Ord	191.483
Clemens, E.	Ord	197.545
Hodges, A.	L/Sto	132.260
Lamb, G.R.	Ord	183.684
McCabe, R.	Band	148.426
Philp, T.	L/Sto	160.728
Powell, G.J.	PO1	124.331
Urell, S.S.	Carp/Mte	110.207

Bar: TAKU FORTS *continued.*

Duplicate medals:

Ahern, P.	Sto	282.834	
Lamb, G.R.	Ord	183.684	*

* *Two duplicate medals issued.*

Returned medal:

Johnston, M.	Ord	189.038

Bar: RELIEF OF PEKIN.

Algar, S.G.	AB	155.018	
Armstrong, W.F.	L/Cpl	Ply6.282	
Arnold, W.	Pte	Po8.302	K
Ashley, C.R.	Pte	Ply8.820	
Ballard, C.F.	Lieut		
Barrett, F.	Blksmth/Mte	341.806	
Barrett, J.	Ord	193.915	
Bate, A.	AB	180.843	
Bates, R.	Ord	182.060	
Bawn, E.	Ord	188.482	
Bayly, E.H.	Capt		
Bell, J.	AB	177.886	
Berriball, W.A.	AB	185.119	
Berry, E.J.	Ord	191.622	
Blackmore, C.	Ord	185.210	
Blatchford, J.D.	AB	189.335	
Boland, A.	PO2	95.296	
Bosley, W.W.	Ord	189.145	
Bowden, W.	Cpl	Ply5.148	
Bowles, J.J.S.	Ord	191.083	
Brown, A.J.	Cpl	Ply6.094	
Bryant, A.	AB	180.256	
Burke, B.	AB	118.088	
Bury, C.W.	Pte	Ply8.670	
Carley, M.	AB	193.925	
Carroll, P.	PO2	118.063	
Chalet, E.F.	AB	181.450	
Clark-Hall, R.H.	Midn		
Cole, W.J.	Ord	187.550	
Collings, W.S.	PO1	138.720	
Collins, D.	PO1	127.983	
Collins, J.H.	AB	126.205	
Collins, W.J.	Pte	Ply7.129	
Connelly, T.	AB	193.917	
Connolly, M.	Ord	193.913	
Cook, A.J.	Arm/Crew	341.233	
Cook, W.J.	Bugler	Ply7.685	
Cooper, G.F.	Sergt	Ply4.978	K
Cooper, W.	Pte	Ply8.816	
Cossey, A.E.	Asst/Engr		
Cotter, P.	AB	184.275	
Cousins, A.	AB	179.796	
Cree, G.B. *alias* F. Kane.	Pte	Ply8.529	
Cudd, J.A.	AB	162.488	
Culverwell, H.	Pte	Ply8.826	
Currell, J.H.	AB	181.445	
Dale, S.G.	AB	194.516	
Davies, T.	Pte	Ply5.816	
Day, J.W.	ERA	268.434	
Deasey, J.	AB	193.912	
Dickson, C.B.	Midn		K
Docking, C.	Ord	190.093	
Donovan, D.	AB	183.764	
Dring, C.D.	Pte	Ply8.214	
Driscoll, M.	AB	180.334	
Drown, T.	AB	189.083	
Dunn, D.	AB	183.407	
Eddiford, H.	Pte	Ply4.814	
Eden, J.	Pte	Ply5.317	
Edwards, L.	AB	186.004	
Endacott, A.B.	AB	191.151	
Farrant, W.H.	Pte	Ply7.805	
Fforde, T.R.	Midn		
Fielding, J.	Cpl	Ply6.830	
Filewood, W.F.	Q/Sig	193.353	
Finn, P.	AB	185.951	
Finnemore, J.L.	Ord	194.492	
Fishlock, G.T.	Pte	Ply8.516	
Flood, J.	Ord	194.023	
Flynn, P.	AB	180.845	
Flynn, P.	Ord	183.776	
Fogden, T.	Pte	Ply4.292	
Frary, W.	L/Cpl	Ply5.125	
Freebury, E.	Ord	192.620	
Gagg, C.	AB	153.942	
Gates, W.J.	L/S	177.870	
Geogheon, W.	AB	193.908	
Gonterias, E.F.	AB	151.923	
Gorman, T.	Ord	183.400	
Gribble, E.J.	Sto	160.745	
Gunn, E.	ERA	268.356	
Halahan, H.C.	Midn		
Hall, H.F.	L/Sergt	Ply6.863	
Hambly, F.	AB	194.508	
Hann, W.F.	Ord	191.503	
Hanning, J.	L/Shpwrt	159.888	
Hanning-Lee, F.C.	Midn		
Hansell, A.E.	Pte	Ply4.266	
Hayes, J.	PO1	131.455	K
Haylock, W.	Pte	Ply8.450	
Heaston, A.E.	Ord	197.900	
Heath, B.W.	Pte	Ch9.064	
Helyar, J.	Pte	Ply8.828	
Hemans, C.R.	Midn		
Hickey, J.J.	2/Yeo/Sig	168.752	
Hill, A.	L/S	157.989	
Hill, C.	Ord	180.711	
Hill, G.M.	Midn		
Hingston, C.	AB	179.631	
Hodges, H.	PO1	152.164	
Honey, W.E.T.	AB	180.000	
Hooper, G.	AB	157.301	

Bar: RELIEF OF PEKIN *continued.*

Name	Rank	Number	
Horn, G.	Ord	192.545	
Hornibrook, J.	Ord	189.344	
Hughes, A.P.	Asst/Payr		
Humphrey, G.H.	L/Cpl	Ch11.032	
Hunt, G.S.	Pte	Ply8.831	
Hurford, A.	Act/Sergt	Ply5.935	
Hutton, R.J.	Pte	Ch10.298	
Huxham, R.J.	L/S	150.850	
Jackson, R.	L/S	119.472	
James, E.S.	AB	180.588	
Jarman, C.H.	Ord	194.497	K
Jarvis, J.H.	PO2	158.918	
Jenkins, H.	Pte	Ply8.602	
Johnson, P.	AB	173.966	
Johnson, W.	AB	182.081	
Jones, A.	AB	183.866	
Kelly, J.	Sto	135.139	
Keogh, P.J.	AB	181.253	
Kingcome, W.W.	AB	143.440	
Kingsley, J.	AB	156.151	K
Kinver, J.	AB	184.229	
Le Scelleur, G.H.	AB	156.802	
Lamerton, A.J.G.	Ord	195.722	
Lane, J.	AB	193.921	
Lang, W.J.	AB	179.593	
Lapidge, J.E.	Ord	189.075	
Lavers, G.	Ord	194.509	
Lee, W.J.	Sto	278.306	
Lewis, F.G.	AB	158.982	
Libby, T.	PO2	155.287	
Lloyd, H.T.R.	Capt(RMLI)		
Loughman, A.	AB	190.608	
Lunt, W.O.	Ch/PO	90.605	
Luxton, W.	L/S	165.524	
Luxton, W.J.	Pte	Ply5.436	
Lynch, T.	AB	193.934	
McAllister, E.	Sto	283.540	
McCabe, B.	Pte	Ply8.838	
McCarthy, J.	AB	193.910	
McCracken, J.T.	Ord	197.888	
McGee, G.T.	AB	169.473	
McGuigan, A.	Pte	Ply6.409	
Martin, W.T.	PO1	128.006	
Maunder, J.	L/S	127.173	
Mayle, W.	AB	192.195	
Mitchell, E.F.J.	Q/Sig	173.167	
Mitchell, F.G.	Pte	Ply8.817	
Mitchell, H.	Pte	Ply8.395	
Mitchell, J.E.	Ord	194.127	
Mitchelmore, A.T.	AB	189.067	
Mole, F.W.	AB	188.479	
Molesworth, F.G.	L/S	180.664	
Moo Ah.	Dom		
Moore, C.H.	PO1	123.729	
Morgan, J.	Sto	287.132	
Moynihan, J.	PO1	150.967	
Murch, A.E.	Ord	192.585	
Murphy, J.	AB	181.395	
Murphy, J.	AB	183.765	
Mutch, W.G.	Pte	Ply8.833	
Neil, E.	AB	184.887	
Nelmes, A.E.	AB	180.276	
Nelson, F.	Pte	Ply6.824	
Nolan, W.	AB	185.784	
Noonan, W.	AB	180.740	
Northcott, G.R.	AB	191.402	
O'Callaghan, J.	AB	158.359	
Oldrieve, L.	Ord	189.676	
Orley, G.C.	Ord	192.179	
Parsonage, W.	AB	185.723	K
Parsons, J.E.	Sto	288.568	
Perrin, W.J.	Sto	280.056	
Perring, W.	Ord	194.494	
Piggott, J.E.	AB	184.641	
Poi Ah.	Dom		
Ponsford, F.	Sto	276.189	
Powell, G.B.	Lieut		
Powell, J.	Pte	Ply8.818	
Power, E.F.	Surgn		
Power, W.	AB	193.923	
Prew, H.	AB	156.761	
Price, W.	Ord	188.251	
Prosser, A.	Pte	Ply5.059	
Prynn, T.	AB	178.330	
Quincey, W.	PO1	98.448	
Randall, H.G.	Pte	Ch9.042	
Rayner, G.H.	2/SBStd	163.967	
Rea, J.	PO2	166.592	
Rendle, J.R.	Ord	181.201	
Revatta, T.	AB	184.029	
Rew, A.H.	Ord	191.484	
Richards, W.J.	AB	184.496	
Robinson, C.M.N.	AB	183.136	
Rodda, S.A.	Sto	288.593	
Rooke, H.W.	Arm	141.518	
Roper, C.D.	Lieut		
Roskruge, S.	AB	194.507	
Russell, H.E.	AB	179.431	
Sam Ah.	Dom		
Sams, C.H.H.	Midn		
Sanders, R.	Ord	191.979	
Scoble, J.H.	Ord	192.238	
Scully, E.W.	Sto	288.590	
Seddon, J.W.	Pte	Ch8.945	
Sercombe, E.R.	Sto	288.579	
Shanahan, J.	Sto	283.293	
Sharp, E.	Pte	Ply7.704	
Shea, R.	AB	179.757	
Shepherd, J.	Pte	Ply8.814	K
Shore, W.R.E.	AB	126.994	
Skinner, R.	AB	157.855	
Skinner, W.C.	AB	179.656	
Sly, T.N.	PO1	120.900	
Smith, A.G.	Lieut		
Smith, L.	AB	183.864	
Spear, W.	PO2	132.146	

Bar: RELIEF OF PEKIN *continued.*

Spillane, J.	Ord	187.803	
Spry, A.N.	AB	176.092	
Squire, D.	Q/Sig	183.127	
Staughton, A.W.	Cpl	Ply8.216	K
Steer, C.E.S.	AB	159.703	
Stevens, A.C.	AB	181.219	
Stowell, A.	Pte	Ply7.652	
Strain, P.	Pte	Ply5.611	
Stribley, R.	AB	180.025	
Sumpter, T.E.	Pte	Ply7.390	
Syson, J.L.	Asst/Clerk		
Tancock, S.J.	AB	191.624	
Taylor, A.	Pte	Ply6.428	
Taylor, F.E.	Ord	193.355	
Taylor, T.H.	PO1	126.852	
Toohey, W.	Ord	193.930	
Townsend, A.	PO1	111.337	
Toyer, W.	Pte	Ply5.075	
Tredant, J.V.	Carp/Crew	342.322	
Wakeham, W.G.	PO2	165.566	
Wakem, J.	Act/Ch/Sto	153.231	
Ward, W.R.	AB	188.267	
Wardle, G.H.	AB	186.238	
Webb, F.I.	Ord	194.515	
Webb, G.T.R.	Pte	Po6.918	
Webber, H.H.	AB	194.520	
Wheeler, W.J.	Ord	192.502	
Wickham, H.	Pte	Ply7.538	
Williams, A.E.	PO1	144.659	
Williams, J.	Sto	159.535	
Williams, P.	AB	193.933	
Williamson, C.H.	AB	183.977	
Willmott, J.R.	Ord	191.135	
Wills, J.C.	AB	184.156	
Wills, W.	AB	192.579	
Wiseman, H.E.	Pte	Ply8.762	
Wright, R.W.	AB	147.419	
Wynn, W.J.	Pte	Ply8.839	
Yalland, J.P.	AB	147.090	
Young, A.	Pte	Ply2.515	

Duplicate medals:

Armstrong, W.F.	L/Cpl	Ply6.282	
Ballard, C.F.	Lieut		
Barrett, J.	Ord	193.915	
Chalet, E.F.	AB	181.450	
Filewood, W.F.	Q/Sig	193.353	
Freebury, E.	Ord	192.620	
Hall, H.F.	L/Sergt	Ply6.863	
Hambly, F.	AB	194.508	
Jenkins, H.	Pte	Ply8.602	
Johnson, P.	AB	173.966	*
Lane, J.	AB	193.921	
Lavers, G.	Ord	194.509	
Loughman, A.	AB	190.608	
Nolan, W.	AB	185.784	
Williamson, C.H.	AB	183.977	

* *Two duplicate medals issued.*

Returned medals:

Doran, O.	AB	188.588
Gigg, A.H.	Pte	Ply7.271
Himest, W.N.	L/Cpl	Ply8.841
Robertson, J.	Pte	Ply6.745

NO BAR MEDALS.

Acomb, J.	PO1	115.657
Babbage, G.	AB	179.376
Backman, C.	AB	186.824
Baker, J.	Sto	277.705
Bargewell, M.T.	PO1	120.611
Barker, S.H.	Band	357.305
Beesley, J.	Pte	Ply9.325
Beggs, W.	Sto	287.192
Bennett, E.R.	Ord	189.146
Benson, K.H.	Midn	
Bentley, G.	Ord	185.607
Bernays, L.A.	Midn	
Binmore, E.G.	Ord	192.264
Blaney, S.	Sto	292.705
Blunt, H.L.	Dom	355.488
Bodys, J.H.	Act/ERA	269.967
Bonney, W.	Sto	168.470
Brealey, W.J.	Sto	288.578
Brown, W.A.J.	Pte	Ply8.919
Bryden, R.	Pte	Ply9.664
Bull, H.	AB	170.542
Burt, C.R.	Sto	278.199
Cameron, J.	Sto	278.321
Carter, J.H.	Bugler	Ply9.281
Carter, W.T.	Sto	151.398
Chapman, F.W.	PO2	158.382
Chelton, E.C.	AB	176.029
Ching Ah.	Dom	
Chong Ah.	Carp	
Chong Ah	Dom	
Cock, G.E.	Gunr	
Coffey, R.	Sto	149.178
Coleman, W.	Carp/Mte	158.110
Collins, J.	ERA	268.655
Collins, T.P.	Sto	278.267
Cook, M.	Shpwrt	342.388
Cooper, W.	Band	340.988
Corley, W.	AB	180.910
Corridan, M.	Sto	276.303
Cottrell, W.J.	Sto	287.190
Cowl, G.	L/Sto	149.220
Cubbard, P.	Sto	292.134
Dailey, G.A.J.	Plmbr	340.160
Dampier, C.F.	Comdr	
Darke, W.C.	Sto	137.067

NO BAR MEDALS *continued.*

Davey, G.	Sto	278.232
Dilworth, D.	Sto	277.121
Drake, C.W.K.	Sh/Std/Asst	341.624
Dudley, C.H.	L/Sto	152.112
Duncan, J.	AB	196.883
Dyer, F.W.	Pntr	158.962
Eagle, H.J.	Act/ERA	269.693
Edwards, G.	Sto	288.591
Elliott, J.H.	Sto	145.772
Evans, E.	Pte	Ply4.497
Ferris, J.	Sto	353.383
Fettes, A.	Pte	Ply7.549
Finn, P.J.	Sto	283.046
Fitzpatrick, A.	Sto	292.220
Flowers, W.	Ch/Cook	98.359
Foo Ah.	Dom	
Foreman, E.E.P.	Asst/Clerk	
Foubister,	Pte	Ply8.693
Freer, A.P.	Pte	Ply7.554
Gagg, H.J.	Ord	192.265
Gatley, W.	Sto	288.587
George, T.	Pte	Ply9.697
Ghom, F.	AB	171.173
Gibson, A.	AB	179.798
Gillard, J.	Pte	Ply5.275
Golder, F.	AB	168.100
Goodridge, W.G.	Sto	283.067
Gray, C.	L/S	173.931
Grieves, J.	Pte	Ply9.672
Griffin, M.	Sto	286.285
Griffiths, A.	Sig	197.494
Griffiths, A.	L/Shpwrt	341.589
Groom, W.S.	AB	165.578
Hard, W.J.	Ord	194.499
Hardy, J.A.	L/Sto	162.165
Harfoot, H.	L/Sto	160.739
Harris, W.J.	Sto	288.603
Harvey, P.	AB	183.676
Hawken, E.	Sto	286.476
Hayes, J.	L/Sto	156.970
Hayes, J.	Sto	278.176
Healy, T.	L/Sto	154.176
Hembry, R.	AB	183.564
Henderson, A.	AB	191.234
Hexter, F.A.	L/Sto	161.184
Hing Ah.	Dom	
Hobbs, J.H.	Sto	285.175
Holt, H.	Sh/Std/Asst	340.838
Hong Ah.	Dom	
Hoo Ah.	Carp	
Hooper, E.C.	Gunr	
Hooper, T.	Arm	156.567
Hopla, J.	Sto	289.505
Huggett, E.	Sail	125.665
Hurrell, E.J.	Ch/Sto	130.025
Hutchings, S.	Sto	288.576
Ingham, J.	Ord	196.827
Jolley, J.H.	Ord	191.719
Jones, C.	Sto	163.098
Kearns, J.	Ch/Sto	104.939
Kelly, R.	PO1	168.607
Knight, H.E.	Ord	197.832
Lanclett, W.G.	Carp	
Lanham, C.	Band	340.834
Lardeaux, W.E.	L/Sig	182.445
Larkins, A.E.	AB	158.516
Lavender, G.	MAA	150.020
Lee, W.	AB	129.854
Letcher, J.H.	Ord	194.500
Lory, W.M.	Fl/Surgn	
Lown, R.J.	AB	181.039
Lynch, M.	Cooper/Crew	340.909
McCarthy, M.	Sto	139.631
McDermott, F.J.	Sto	278.317
McDonald, C.H.	AB	164.511
McDonald, F.A.	Pte	Ply9.456
McGregor, J.	AB	188.959
McQuade, A.	Sto	277.718
Mabb, W.J.	Fl/Engr	
Martin, E.H.	Midn	
Matthews, W.J.	Lieut	
Meade, J.	Sig	193.920
Metters, H.J.	PO1	120.588
Miller, H.	L/Sto	152.739
Moore, H.	Sto	154.943
Moore, W.	Pte	Ply6.020
Mordaunt, C.	Ord	196.886
Morley, W.	Ch/ERA	132.281
Morrell, A.W.	Payr	
Moyse, W.J.	Blksmth	151.870
Mundy, T.C.	2/Yeo/Sig	173.981
Nash, H.	AB	155.320
Nealis, T.	Sto	288.168
Newsted, E.J.	AB	184.135
Nicholas, R.C.	Ch/ERA	114.244
Nicholson, E.V.	Ord	191.400
Page, G.H.	Engr	
Parker, F.J.	Ord	192.531
Parker, G.	Ord	194.512
Parsons, S.J.	Sto	288.573
Patterson, E.	Bosn	
Perkins, H.	Ord	183.138
Perry, A.	Ord	185.112
Petherick, W.	Ch/Sto	129.375
Phillips, A.	Sto	294.145
Piggott, C.	L/S	163.891
Pomeroy, J.	Sh/Cpl	116.963 K
Pong Ah.	Dom	
Potter, V.R.	ERA	268.230
Powney, C.	Pte	Ply8.784
Price, Rev. A.R.	Chaplain & N. Instr	
Priscott, W.P.	2/Wrtr	144.658
Prowse, H.C.	ERA	268.898
Purse, I.	Ord	184.818
Pym, J.	Pte	Ply3.571

NO BAR MEDALS *continued.*

Quinn, T.	Sto	292.129
Rich, F.	Ch/Sto	138.089
Richards, R.H.	Sh/Cpl	140.728
Ritchie, T.	Sto	141.744
Rooney, G.C.	Lieut(RMLI)	
Rowett, F.J.	Ch/Sto	137.536
Ryan, P.	Sto	281.657
Sainsbury, J.	Cook/Mte	340.881
Sambells, W.H.	Ch/Sto	130.031
Sampson-Way, N.F.E.G.	Capt(RMLI)	
San Ah.	Dom	
Sargent, J.J.	Asst/Engr	
Saundby, G.T.S.	Midn	
Saunders, W.	Sto	289.874
Schofield, W.	Pte	Ply6.613
Scott, S.	Sto	289.353
Searle, C.	Ord	184.571
See Ling.	Carp	
Segu.	Carp	
Shea, J.	Sto	292.128
Sherridan, T.	Sto	148.856
Sibley, C.J.	AB	157.647
Smith, W.W.	Pte	Ply4.265
Snell, R.J.M.	PO1	152.166
Squire, F.	Pte	Ply2.237
Stacey, S.G.	Sto	129.370
Staddon, J.R.	AB	168.272
Stapleton, T.	Bosn	
Stark, J.	AB	179.598
Stewart, J.	Pte	Ply8.117
Swatman, W.H.	PO1	150.996
Sweeney, W.J.	L/Sto	152.197
Tang Ah.	Dom	
Taylor, J.A.	Band	164.619
Taylor, J.W.	L/S	114.308
Tellam, J.	Sto	278.266
Thomas, W.	Cooper	126.487
Thomas, W.G.	Sto	288.580
Thorn, R.W.	Sh/Std	124.966
Tie Ah.	Dom	
Tredrea, T.	Ord	184.574
Tremeer, F.	L/Sto	159.519
Trewhela, C.H.	PO1	107.497
Turpin, G.	Ch/Arm	127.883
Twigg, F.W.D.	Midn	
Vowles, F.E.	AB	185.353
Waits, W.J.	ERA	268.847
Walsh, D.	Sto	283.848
Walsh, W.	Pte	Ply5.164
Waters, W.W.	AB	171.570
Weakley, R.H.	Sh/Cpl	350.123
Wei Ah.	Dom	
West, H.	Ord	197.482
White, W.H.	PO2	164.403
Williams, H.J.	Sto	276.526
Williams, J.G.	Sto	130.765
Williams, R.H.	Sh/Std/Asst	343.023
Wills, C.S.	Lieut	
Wilton, A.E.	L/Sto	161.168
Winter, F.W.	Ord	192.523
Winter, W.	Band	100.787
Witt, E.F.	Pte	Ply8.840
Woodley, W.	Pte	Ply8.856
Woods, J.H.	Ord	191.382
Woolsey, F.A.	L/S	159.708
Worth, A.	SBStd	133.437
Yeandle, R.	Pte	Ply5.626
Yen Ah.	Dom	
Ying Ah.	Carp	
Yip Ah.	Dom	
You Ah.	Dom	

Duplicate medals:

Dampier, C.F.	Comdr	
Finn, P.J.	Sto	283.046
Groom, W.S.	AB	165.578
Harris, W.J.	Sto	288.603
Lardeaux, W.E.	L/Sig	182.445
Rowett, F.J.	Ch/Sto	137.536
Williams, R.H.	Sh/Std/Asst	343.023
Woodley, W.	Pte	Ply8.856

Returned medals:

Gaskin, P.	Pte	Ply8.560
Pyne, T.	Sto	139.192
Williams, N.	Sto	290.956

H.M.S. BARFLEUR.

H.M.S. Barfleur was a Battleship of 10,500 tons and 360 x 70 feet. Her armament consisted of 4 x 10 in, 10 x 4.7 in and 2 x 9 pdr guns. The vessel was built in Chatham Dock Yard and launched on 10th August 1892. She was sold on 12th July 1910 to C. Ewen at Glasgow.

Bars	*Total*	*Returned*	*Entitled*
TF & RP	*70*	*0*	*70*
TF	*23*	*1*	*22*
RP	*282*	*10*	*272*
None	*408*	*10*	*398*
	783	*21*	*762*

Notes:

K - Medal presented by H.M. The King on 8th March 1902.

1 - The duplicate medal was returned as the original medal was recovered.

Bars: TAKU FORTS, RELIEF OF PEKIN.

Name	Rank	Number	Note
Abel, H.F.	Sto	284.918	
Allen, H.C.	Midn		
Astell, H.T.	AB	193.435	
Bailey, A.E.	Pte	Ch7.352	
Ball, A.A.	AB	188.942	
Beckingham, V.J.	PO1	115.738	
Blackburn, F.	Ord	187.012	
Blackman, A.	Gunr	RMA4.206	
Blowers, J.G.	AB	178.526	
Brett, S.	PO1	121.532	
Brown, J.	AB	187.333	
Caley, H.E.	PO1	163.183	K
Carter, C.	Gunr	RMA6.509	
Carter, J.	AB	189.200	
Cassells, C.N.D.	Pte	Ch3.657	
Clancy, J.	Pte	Ch2.017	
Clippingdale, J.H.	AB	193.278	
Cobb, E.W.	Gunr	RMA4.961	K
Collier, R.K.	AB	183.066	
Cornabe, W.E.	Midn		
Cornish, H.J.	AB	188.389	
Crapnell, J.	Gunr	RMA4.859	
Dix, C.P.	Midn		
Downes, J.	AB	174.723	
Dumbrell, J.	Gunr	RMA3.938	
Farquharson, F.	AB	187.300	
Farthing, C.A.	L/Cpl	Ch8.813	
Field, G.H.	AB	149.938	
Green, A.E.	Pte	Ch8.793	
Grover, E.W.	Ord	188.808	
Harrington, H.	Pte	Ch6.142	
Harvey, F.J.	Sto	286.335	
Higgs, H.E.	L/S	174.152	
Huntley, A.	Pte	Ch7.464	
Hurdle, A.W.	AB	189.210	
Johnson, F.	AB	164.787	
Jupp, H.C.	AB	187.299	
Kesbey, J.E.	Pte	Ch9.179	
King, J.	AB	162.904	
Lanagan, D.	Pte	Ch5.823	
Leach, W.	Pte	Po8.521	
Lee, T.J.	Gunr	RMA4.851	
Maclaren, H.J.	AB	193.153	
Martin, W.J.	Gunr	RMA4.861	
Mayne, R.C.	Midn		K
Messenbird, G.H.	Act/QM/Sergt	RMA3.487	K
Packwood, E.	Pte	Ply7.513	
Pankhurst, W.	Pte	Ch5.667	
Parsons, E.J.	AB	181.553	
Potter, S.E.	AB	181.665	
Price, C.T.	AB	160.296	
Rubbins, T.	AB	187.276	
Ryman, C.W.	Bugler	Po8.261	
Shipley, E.	Pte	Ch8.760	
Shore, L.H.	Midn		
Strudwick, A.	Ord	187.215	
Surman, C.	Pte	Ch7.264	
Thake, J.W.	Ord	189.202	
Tichborne, Rev G.M.	Chaplain		K
Timmins, W.	AB	187.758	
Tristram, H.J.	Pte	Ch6.873	K
Walker, G.W.	L/S	160.237	
Walmsley, W.	AB	173.653	
Warren, C.	Pte	Ch8.772	

Bars: TAKU FORTS, RELIEF OF PEKIN *cont.*

West, C.H.	AB	171.011	
West, W.J.	Sto	280.915	
Winser, E.	PO2	173.149	
Wise, H.	AB	188.903	
Woodward, F.R.	PO1	113.195	
Wrottesley, F.R.	Flag/Lieut		K

Duplicate medals:

Caley, H.E.	PO1	163.183	
Harvey, F.J.	Sto	286.335	
Kesbey, J.E.	Pte	Ch9.179	
Timmins, W.	AB	187.758	
Winser, E.	PO2	173.149	*

* *Two duplicate medals issued.*

Bar: TAKU FORTS.

Aves, G.	Pte	Ch6.173
Barnett, F.C.	AB	192.299
Bowers, F.G.	Ord	188.072
Brackey, H.W.	AB	179.689
Brown, T.	Sto	280.317
Bing, W.J.	Ord	188.203
Coombes, F.J.	Ord	187.196
Cullingford, G.E.	2/Yeo/Sig	157.791
Davis, C.F.	AB	188.400
Holtley, J.H.	AB	197.636
L'Aime, W.J.	Ch/Sto	123.342
Long, W.T.	AB	185.323
Merchant, R.	AB	188.076
Midgley, H.W.	N. Instr	
Octgenn, J.R.	AB	186.907
Oliver, T.	PO1	153.195
Parks, A.E.	Ch/PO	125.081
Peart, R.	Ord	188.043
Wainwright, J.A.	Gunr	RMA4.809
Warner, A.	Sto	281.499
Watson, J.W.	PO2	144.693
Williams, R.S.	Lieut	

Returned medal:

Webb, T.J.	Ord	186.019

Bar: RELIEF OF PEKIN.

Adams, H.C.	AB	188.899	
Alexander, J.H.	Act/MAA	129.046	
Allen, J.C.	L/Sig	165.052	
Armstrong, H.G.B.	Capt(RMLI)		K
Ashby, A.W.	Pte	Po8.946	
Aylen, A.E.	Asst/Payr		
Bailey, G.W.	Gunr	RMA6.505	K
Beatty, D.	Comdr		K
Beck, T.C.	Gunr	RMA4.862	
Bedford, S.J.	L/S	172.520	
Bees, J.	Gunr	RMA4.785	
Bell, E.	Ord	188.109	
Bell, J.	Gunr	RMA4.853	
Bowden, J.J.	Pte	Ch5.943	
Bowerbank, H.L.	Gunr	RMA5.798	
Bowern, F.J.	Gunr	RMA5.291	
Bowman, J.B.	AB	188.074	
Brandon, S.J.	Gunr	RMA6.172	
Brewster, J.R.	Pte	Ply3.436	
Bromley, J.R.	AB	177.710	
Browne, G.L.	Midn		
Buddle, C.	Pte	Ch8.978	
Bunting, A.W.	Pte	Ch9.668	
Busley, S.	Gunr	RMA5.260	
Butler, E.	AB	188.464	
Butt, P.C.	Gunr	RMA4.756	
Buxey, W.H.	Sh/Std/Asst	341.129	
Caddy, A.	PO2	147.424	
Carmichael, H.C.	Midn		
Carpenter, G.E.	Ord	197.548	
Carter, J.	Gunr	RMA5.079	
Challess, C.J.	Sergt	Ch5.107	
Chandler, W.G.	Pte	Po8.840	
Chenery, A.G.	Sto	285.392	
Christmas, W.J.	PO2	163.312	K
Cloke, T.H.	PO2	160.456	
Cockram, J.R.	AB	187.298	
Coe, C.	AB	187.307	
Collett, J.E.	AB	188.370	
Collins, M.	PO1	138.152	
Conning, H.R.	L/Shpwrt	340.653	
Cooper, A.	AB	189.055	
Cox, W.R.	AB	182.282	
Cromie, F.N.A.	Midn		
Culmer, A.H.	AB	193.079	
Cummings, G.	AB	188.988	
Cummins, H.C.	AB	187.015	
Dale, W.T.	AB	187.093	
Daley, E.	L/S	156.453	
Davidson, J.	Ord	193.155	
Davidson, W.	AB	193.146	
Davies, E.	AB	187.700	
Dawes, W.S.	AB	166.044	
Day, H.	Gunr	RMA4.066	
Deasley, C.G.	L/S	173.419	
Dewse, R.J.	Pte	Ch8.108	
Divers, H.	Sto	276.104	
Donald, J.	AB	187.745	
Donaldson, A.P.	Midn		
Donovan, R.	Sto	291.404	K
Drew, J.W.	PO1	164.974	K
Duthie, J.R.	Sergt	Ch7.868	
Dyble, W.J.	L/S	165.782	
Dyke, G.W.	Arm	136.000	
Edwards, C.	Pte	Ch7.152	
Edworthy, J.E.	AB	193.265	K

Bar: RELIEF OF PEKIN *continued.*

Name	Rank	Number	
Egan, G.F.	Sto	282.752	
England, R.B.	Midn		
Englefield, A.	Pte	Po8.152	
Esdaile, F.S.D.	Midn		
Farmer, A.	AB	156.955	
Fazackarley, J.	Sto	290.674	
Fensom, G.	Sto	280.878	
Field, F.L.	Lieut		K
Field, V.E.	Ord	197.306	
Finch, A.E.	AB	193.350	K[1]
Finch, A.J.	ERA	268.150	
Foot, T.J.	AB	162.769	
Foreman, J.	AB	173.748	
Fountain, T.A.	Sergt	Ch2.821	
Frazer-Hurst, L.	Civ/Med/Pract		
Freeme, G.E.	PO1	151.097	
Gardner, T.	Act/SBStd	150.330	K
Garnett, J.	Gunr	RMA5.162	
Garrod, F.	Gunr	RMA4.835	
Gibbons, M.	Ord	193.874	
Gibbs, V.F.	Midn		K
Gilbert, H.W.	Pte	Ch8.113	
Gill, P.	Sto	277.639	
Girdlestone, W.	2/Yeo/Sig	179.071	
Glass, R.J.	Bugler	RMA6.287	
Golden, P.	AB	193.873	K
Gorman, P.	Gunr	RMA4.865	
Greaves, F.A.	Ord	187.078	
Green, G.H.	AB	187.014	
Grimwood, A.W.	AB	176.513	
Guy, B.J.D.	Midn		K
Hall, J.F.	St/Surgn		
Hallett, E.	Dom	357.504	
Hallett, R.	L/S	142.804	
Hardy, W.	Sto	149.714	
Harper, H.	PO1	148.460	
Harrison, A.	Ord	187.017	
Harvey, W.H.	AB	143.475	
Hawkes, W.	AB	185.260	
Heald, B.W.	PO1	127.109	
Heron, W.	Sto	285.537	
Hibberd, T.	Pte	Ch9.036	
Hibbs, F.A.	AB	194.012	
Higgs, W.	Carp/Crew	342.652	
Hogg, J.A.	Ord	189.293	
Hogger, A.W.	L/Sig	179.580	
Hollinsworth, C.J.	Ch/ERA	128.230	K
Holness, A.S.	AB	169.063	
Hopkins, W.	Ord	182.543	
Horne, W.J.	Gunr	RMA6.098	
Horton, A.	PO1	154.004	
Houchen, A.	AB	166.747	
Hows, H.W.	Ord	184.168	
Hughes, A.	PO2	169.471	
Hughes, F.	Gunr	RMA4.341	
Jago, A.	Sh/Cook	169.749	
James, W.W.	Q/Sig	160.578	
Janaway, J.	Sto	280.325	
Jarvis, H.	Pte	Ply8.585	
Jellicoe, E.H.	Lieut		K
Jennings, A.	AB	156.825	
Johnson, H.C.	Midn		
Johnson, H.E.	AB	193.862	
Johnson, W.E.	Pte	Ch7.238	
Keeley, F.	AB	188.725	
Kelly, P.	AB	193.888	
Kennedy, E.C.	Lieut		
Kenway, T.H.	Pte	Ply4.002	
Kerr, W.J.	Arm/Mte	340.463	
Kerwin, H.J.	AB	179.577	
Kidd, J.D.	Ord	190.407	
King, P.G.	AB	187.988	
King, W.E.	Col/Sergt	RMA2.872	K
Kiy, T.F.	AB	188.253	
Laird, D.J.	Ord	187.182	
Lamerton, J.H.	L/Shpwrt	161.191	
Leaney, T.	Sto	253.190	
Learmouth, B.L.L.	Civ/Med/Pract		
Lewis, J.	Pte	Ch7.208	
Lindsey, J.	Sto	285.918	
Long, A.E.	Gunr	RMA6.422	
Longhurst, G.F.	Midn		K
Lowe, P.G.	Sto	279.935	
Lowey, L.H.	AB	193.164	
Luard, H. du C.	Lieut		
Luke, E.V.	Major(RMLI)		K
Lynn, F.	Sto	277.973	
McCarthy, T.	AB	182.293	
McDonald, K.	2/Cooper	342.476	
McLeod, J.E.	AB	193.253	
McQuillan, A.	Ord	187.830	
Marett, P.C.J.	L/S	158.223	
Marriott, G.	Pte	Ch9.473	
Marshall, G.	PO2	178.141	
Martin, F.J.	AB	187.497	
Martin, W.H.	AB	187.098	
Maynard, J.E.	Pte	Po8.925	
Mears, W.J.	PO2	158.171	
Miller, A.	AB	141.212	
Miller, R.	AB	181.585	
Mills, W.	AB	186.948	
Moore, A.	L/S	144.186	
Morgan, T.R.	Gunr	RMA6.450	
Morley, C.R.	AB	187.331	
Morrison, W.	AB	193.028	
Moss, G.	L/Sto	160.073	
Munro, A.	AB	183.981	
Murray, A.C.	Q/Sig	180.726	
Murrell, J.E.	Ord	192.935	
Nelson, J.T.	AB	183.941	
Newcombe, W.E.	PO1	155.132	
Nicholas, J.	Carp/Mte	153.257	
Nicholson, J.M.	3/Wrtr	343.898	
Norton, A.E.	Ord	186.076	
Norton, H.	AB	188.075	
O'Brien, J.	Ord	187.456	

Bar: RELIEF OF PEKIN *continued.*

Name	Rate	No.	
Ott, G.	AB	185.259	
Outen, C.	AB	188.668	
Palmer, J.	AB	186.914	
Palmer, W.	L/Sto	159.445	
Pardon, G.H.	Ord	187.122	
Parker, T.F.	AB	184.185	
Parsons, T.E.	AB	194.020	
Patrick, F.	L/Sto	277.642	
Patterson, W.	Ord	189.050	
Peek, H.	Sto	280.340	
Phillimore, V.E.B.	Lieut		
Pierce, H.J.	Sto	279.509	
Piesse, F.A.	Pte	Ch5.253	
Piesse, H.	AB	177.377	
Pilkerton, H.	AB	171.622	
Pittock, W.C.	AB	183.712	
Plant, F.	Ch/PO	117.099	
Price, P.J.	Yeo/Sig	147.430	
Purchase, C.E.	AB	129.195	
Reynolds, W.M.	Pte	Ch8.928	
Rhodes, C.T.	AB	164.934	
Richards, W.B.	ERA	269.118	
Ridgley, E.R.	Gunr	RMA6.408	
Riseborough, J.	AB	180.352	
Rivers, J.H.	AB	193.082	
Roberts, R.R.	AB	183.419	
Robertson, J.E.	PO1	146.716	
Rogers, T.J.	Ord	187.096	
Rooke, J.	Sto	286.361	
Ross, H.	AB	188.093	
Ross, J.	Sto	279.535	
Salmond, J.S.C.	Midn		
Salter, E.C.	Ord	187.300	
Sanderson, R.	L/S	177.323	
Sang Foo.	Dom		
Saunders, H.S.	AB	161.556	
Sawyer, H.	AB	192.497	
Schiller, F.O.von	AB	187.161	
Sear, A.	AB	187.306	
Sendall, W.C.	Gunr	RMA6.233	
Sharp, H.J.	L/Sto	160.024	
Silsby, J.	AB	185.270	
Skinner, G.	L/Sto	125.242	
Smeed, H.T.	Gunr	RMA6.128	
Smith, C.	Sto	286.320	
Smith, E.C.	Asst/Engr		K
Smyth, E.C.	Civ/Med/Pract		
Spenceley, H.	AB	197.638	
Spencer, H.	Cpl	Ch6.219	
Spreadbury, G.H.	AB	124.362	
Starkie, J.	Sto	285.787	
Stimpson, H.	Dom	358.205	
Stirling, A.J.B.	Lieut		
Stoker, T.J.	Pte	Ch9.515	
Strachan, J.	Gunr	RMA2.021	
Streeter, H.M.	AB	188.228	
Stuart, F.	Sto	286.331	
Swallow, J.H.	Sto	286.323	
Taplin, W.	Sto	171.976	
Taylor, R.	AB	189.229	
Thom, A.	AB	186.919	
Thurger, C.J.	PO1	113.132	
Todd, F.W.	Sto	285.785	
Triance, S.C.	Gunr	RMA6.196	
Tubby, C.W.	Ord	188.805	
Tum Ah.	Dom		
Ventries, W.	AB	188.082	
Versey, J.	AB	185.307	
Wakefield, J.	Pte	Ch8.812	
Walsh, A.	Sto	287.217	
Ward, E.G.	AB	161.797	
Ward, W.J.	L/S	125.843	
Warren, J.T.	AB	187.936	
Watson, W.D.	Ord	189.693	
Webb, W.	Sto	282.357	
Whibley, E.E.	AB	188.715	K
White, F.J.	Ord	191.558	
White, J.W.	Arm/Crew	340.496	
White, W.W.	AB	187.009	
Whiteway, H.F.	PO2	167.737	
Williams, W.A.F.	AB	161.621	
Wilson, A.	AB	187.107	
Wilson, H.G.	Asst/Payr		
Winter, A.E.	AB	183.467	
Wrangles, G.	Gunr	RMA4.790	
Wrey, W.B.S.	Act/Comdr		
Wysard, A.T.	Surgn		
Yeo, E.	Pte	Ch8.728	
Yock Ah.	Dom		
Young, D.O.G.	AB	187.771	

Duplicate medals:

Name	Rate	No.	
Allen, J.C.	L/Sig	165.052	
Bell, J.	Gunr	RMA4.853	
Bromley, J.R.	AB	177.710	
Cummings, G.	AB	188.988	
Dale, W.T.	AB	187.093	
Dyble, W.J.	L/S	165.782	
Gibbons, M.	Ord	193.874	
Golden, P.	AB	193.873	
Heald, B.W.	PO1	127.109	
Hibberd, T.	Pte	Ch9.036	
Kerwin, H.J.	AB	179.577	
Morrison, W.	AB	193.028	
Munro, A.	AB	183.981	
Murrell, J.E.	Ord	192.935	
Robertson, J.E.	PO1	146.716	
Spreadbury, G.H.	AB	124.362	
Todd, F.W.	Sto	285.785	*

* *Two duplicate medals issued.*

Bar: RELIEF OF PEKIN *continued.*

Returned medals:

Barrett, J.W.	Cpl	RMA2.454
Buchan, M.	Gunr	RMA5.217
Buck, J.B.	AB	179.110
Copping, W.	AB	177.968
Durrant, H.	Sto	281.076
Shipton, W.	AB	183.938
Smith, E.	AB	193.258
Terry, W.J.	Sto	280.919
Wallace, F.	AB	188.772
Wells, E.L.	AB	187.145

NO BAR MEDALS.

Addy, E.	Ch/Arm	154.635	
Aitken, J.J.	Sto	286.312	
Allen, W.	SBStd	150.307	
Allwood, W.	Sto	279.021	
Anderson, W.	Boy	199.605	
Arnold, T.H.	PO1	123.225	
Arthur, E.J.	Ord	199.756	
Ashby, E.C.	Sig	197.871	
Askill, T.	Ch/Sto	131.152	
Austin, H.	Sig	202.342	
Bailey, A.G.	Sto	294.169	
Barclay, E.	AB	197.630	
Barnes, W.	Ord	200.952	
Barratt, W.H.	AB	171.806	
Barrett, J.H.	Ord	197.753	
Barrow, T.F.	Sto	289.362	
Bartlett, C.P.	Asst/Engr		
Baxter, G.L.	L/S	168.398	
Bayford, J.W.	L/Sto	162.730	
Beales, D.	Sto	279.082	
Beatty-Pownall, C.P.	Lieut		
Beckingham, A.	Sto	279.068	
Benzing, A.R.	Ch/Band	112.343	
Berry, C.J.	L/Shpwrt	341.648	
Betts, J.A.	Ord	183.940	
Bilefield, F.	Cooper	139.674	
Bird, J.	Ord	197.792	
Bishop, G.	Blksmth	142.055	
Blackmore, J.	Sto	291.951	
Blair, W.	AB	179.746	
Blair, W.	AB	189.978	
Bland, H.	Ord	176.208	
Blundell, G.A.	Ord	199.883	
Bowring, R.	Ord	197.870	
Brand, H.	Pte	Ch6.518	
Bray, A.C.	AB	146.216	
Brazier, A.	ERA	158.817	
Brickell, S.C.	Ord	197.282	
Brooks, L.	Sto	280.310	
Broomfield, G.J.	Gunr	RMA7.640	
Brown, J.C.	Sto	280.924	
Brown, W.	ERA	269.086	
Bruce, Sir J.A.T.	Rear Admiral		K
Buesden, W.R.	Sto	278.011	
Bugg, C.	AB	190.153	
Burford, F.	PO1	142.918	
Burgess, R.	Band/Cpl	85.309	
Burn, G.J.	ERA	268.389	
Cable, F.	L/Sto	279.505	
Callaghan, P.	Sto	279.072	
Cameron, W.	Ch/Sto	138.622	
Capell, F.	Sto	279.066	
Card, N.	Ord	197.752	
Carr, R.G.	Sto	285.525	
Carroll, W.H.	AB	156.667	
Catchpole, W.F.	Q/Sig	191.391	
Catling, W.E.	AB	169.926	
Cavanagh, M.	Sto	290.976	
Champion, W.H.J.C.	Bosn		
Chan Ah.	Carp/Crew		
Chan Su	Dom		
Chaplin, A.W.	Boy	200.066	
Chapman, J.	AB	172.492	
Chee Ah.	Carp/Crew		
Cholmley, G.F.	Midn		
Chong Ah.	Dom		
Chong Mok.	Dom		
Clarke, A.	Sto	280.897	
Clarke, J.C.	Sto	285.789	
Clarke, W.J.	Boy	203.477	
Cloke, J.R.	Ch/Sto	147.772	
Coggins, R.	Sto	286.595	K
Colbert, F.	AB	171.492	
Colton, A.	AB	158.418	
Colvin, E.S.	Carp/Crew	342.116	
Connolly, T.J.	Ord	184.952	
Corke, A.E.	Cook/Mte	340.872	
Cox, C.	Q/Sig	185.723	
Craven, F.J.	SB/Attn	350.444	
Creasey, G.	Sto	279.055	
Crook, G.B.	Sto	284.068	
Crozier, L.H.	Lieut		
Cummins, T.G.	Ch/Wrtr	120.299	
Currans, J.	Sto	285.898	
Curtice, W.	Sto	278.853	
Dadswell, E.	Sto	285.526	
Danby, W.H.	Gunr	RMA7.883	
Daniell, H.	Band	155.651	
Davies, E.J.	Sto	294.168	
Davies, J.	Sto	285.786	
Davies, J.C.	Sto	294.081	
Davis, W.D.	Ord	198.711	
Dawson, E.W.	Carp/Crew	342.115	
Dawson, F.	Ord	197.433	
Dempster, E.S.	PO1	137.892	
Dilworth, E.R.	Gunr	RMA7.917	
Dodd, G.N.	Act/ERA	269.935	
Donabie, J.H.	ERA	166.460	
Donnan, R.J.	Q/Sig	188.586	

NO BAR MEDALS *continued.*

Drew, W.	Boy	199.811
Dumble, E.G.W.	Sh/Std/Asst	176.920
Dunbar, C.A.R.F.	Fl/Payr	
Duplock, C.	Boy	202.345
Eames, G.E.	Pntr	133.628
Eddy, C.	Yeo/Sig	184.285
Edwards, D.	L/Sto	123.247
Edwards, R.B.	AB	185.261
Elliott, W.H.	Ord	191.571
Elton, J.W.	Sh/Std	95.443
Emberley, A.A.	Act/Ch/PO	118.725
England, E.H.	Sh/Std/Boy	342.222
Esau, T.	L/Carp/Crew	342.557 K
Eustace, J.B.	Comdr	
Evans, E.	L/Sto	153.893
Fairman, S.A.	Sto	277.376
Fick, W.J.	Band	341.491
Files, R.A.E.	Gunr	RMA7.793
Fitzpatrick, J.	Boy	202.948
Fleetwood, J.J.	Gunr	RMA6.784
Foo Ah.	Dom	
Foord, T.	Sto	281.056
Frost, R.J.	Ord	197.805
Frost, W.H.	AB	180.653
Fudgett, T.C.	Sig	197.424
Fung Len.	Dom	
Gabriel, C.H.	Cpl	Ch6.949
Galiani, A.	Band	354.559
Geach, C.	Sto	283.073
Gee, C.	Sto	276.450
Gifkins, W.F.	Sto	279.367
Gillard, F.S.	Shpwrt	166.662
Gilpin, A.J.	Sto	290.921
Goddard, G.W.	Plmbr/Mte	341.504
Grandfield, C.	L/Sto	155.595
Grant, C.	Ch/Cook	119.910
Grant, C.	Sail	190.873
Graves, G.R.	PO2	154.234
Gray, H.J.	Sto	286.482
Green, J.	PO1	115.869
Grimshaw, A.	Ord	201.870
Hambling, T.	AB	179.677
Hammond, J.	L/S	161.245
Hammond, J.R.	2/Yeo/Sig	158.869
Hands, J.J.	Yeo/Sig	145.316
Hardy, R.	Cpl	RMA3.363
Harod, A.J.	Gunr	
Harod, H.A.	AB	189.004
Harris, J.T.	AB	175.678
Harrison, T.F.	Fl/Payr	
Harwood, G.	L/Sto	152.628
Hayhow, H.	Sto	290.912
Head, J.	Ord	202.520
Head, R.	Ord	193.121
Henderson, H.	Pntr	117.105
Henderson, J.	Ord	187.764
Hewitt, A.E.	Sto	295.172
Hewlett, G.	Secretary	
Hickley, C.S.	Comdr	
Hill, G.W.	Pte	Po10.196
Hill, J.N.	Comdr	
Hillier, A.E.	AB	184.198
Hines, R.J.	Ord	200.061
Hing Ah.	Dom	
Hing Li.	Dom	
Hocking, J.	ERA	154.151
Hodges, A.	AB	148.458
Hoo Ah.	Dom	
Hopkins, S.	Midn	
Hopkyns, J.W.	Asst/Engr	
Horton, G.	Sto	277.903
Howard, C.	L/Sto	158.336
Huckstep, R.A.	Sto	278.572
Hunt, W.	Ord	187.138
Hunter, J.J.	Ch/Sto	126.084
Hurst, C.	Pilot	
Hustler, T.	Sto	286.329
Hutchinson, G.P.	Act/ERA	269.803
Innes, A.	Sto	176.824
Jackman, W.E.H.	Asst/Payr	
Jackson, J.	MAA	150.016
Jenkins, C.	PO2	155.982
Johns, E.E.	AB	144.626
Johnson, A.W.	Pte	Po10.257
Johnson, H.W.	Band	154.231
Johnston, A.	AB	165.550
Jones, A.	AB	184.755
Keith, A.	Sergt	RMA5.209
Kenny, J.W.	AB	187.005
Ketteringham, E.	PO1	121.423
Kiddle, E.B.	Lieut	
King, F.	Sto	280.893
Kingstone, W.G.	AB	187.147
Knapton, H.E.	Plmbr	341.268
Knight, H.	Ord	204.217
Knott, G.	PO1	127.068
Knowlden, J.	L/Sig	159.122
Kong Ah.	Dom	
Korriener, C.	Gunr	RMA6.932
Labdon, J.	Pte	Po10.255
Lam Ah.	Dom	
Landry, A.J.	Ord	194.288
Lee Ah.	Dom	
Legerton, H.	Band	340.739
Legge, E.	Ch/Sto	127.897
Lewis, E.	Ch/Sto	130.878
Licari, P.	Band	174.098
Linford, A.T.	ERA	268.508
Linnen, W.T.	AB	179.295
Lissenden, A.	L/Sto	160.511
Lyon, F.H.	Asst/Engr	
McBurney, S.	Sto	287.118
McCarthy, T.	PO1	144.320
McConnell, J.A.	Arm/Crew	285.313
McConnillis, J.	Ord	201.848
McDonald, H.J.	Sto	286.115

NO BAR MEDALS *continued.*

Name	Rank	Number
McEvoy, J.	AB	181.992
McGill, J.	AB	168.630
McLeod, J.	Carp	
Mackin, P.	Sto	288.444
Mardon, E.E.	AB	196.503
Marshall, R.F.	SBStd	150.352
Martin, A.	Sto	289.871 K
Martin, J.Mc.C.	St/Surgn	
Martin, J.R.	Arm	130.305
Martin, T.	Sto	286.322
Matthews, F.J.	PO2	134.796
Matthews, J.W.	Band	115.766
Mears, G.H.	Carp/Mte	168.217
Meredith, T.C.	Gunr	RMA6.900
Metherall, F.	AB	138.099
Miller, T.D.	2/SBStd	350.230
Mills, A.	Sto	279.516
Mills, A.J.	Yeo/Sig	147.738
Mills, J.	Sto	281.486
Moir, G.	Sh/Cpl	350.159
Moorey, E.E.	ERA	269.160
Morley, W.	AB	117.785
Morrish, W.D.	Asst/Clerk	
Moss, W.J.	Ord	187.514
Munro, T.	Sto	285.779
Murphy, B.	Sto	285.550
Mustoe, H.J.	Gunr	RMA6.052
Mutton, W.E.	L/Shpwrt	342.132
Nelson-Ward, P.	Comdr	
Nem Ah.	Dom	
Newing, W.	Sto	280.636
Newman, C.E.	Sto	280.916
Newton, A.G.	2/Wrtr	172.428
Newton, J.J.	Ord	197.802
Noble, F.B.	Lieut	
Noble, J.	PO1	164.670
Nolan, W.	AB	179.848
Noonan, J.F.	Sto	285.832
Norris, C.	Dom	357.760
Norris, G.H.	Boy	199.644
Norris, J.	Cooper/Crew	177.422
Norsworthy, J.	AB	168.104
Oldfield, G.T.	Pte	Ch7.473
Overbury, T.L.	AB	177.245
Packham, B.E.	Sto	280.882
Palmer, G.A.	Sto	283.677
Parr, A.W.	L/Sto	167.297
Parsons, G.	Fl/Engr	
Partridge, F.	L/S	169.596
Pashler, H.G.	Ord	193.237
Pateman, J.T.	Sto	280.195
Patterson, M.	Sto	291.492
Pavitt, F.A.	Sto	280.876
Payne, J.	Boy	199.643
Payne, J.W.	Sto	286.319
Pays, D.G.	PO2	140.739
Peain, J.	Bosn	
Pelham, H.T.	PO1	125.730
Pendreich, J.	Gunr	RMA5.525
Pentecost, W.H.	Pte	Ch10.806
Percival, G.E.	Ord	197.634
Perkins, A.J.	Pte	Ch10.244
Peters, F.	AB	161.471
Phair, D.R.	Bosn	
Phillips, C.	Ord	196.847
Phipps, T.	Sto	280.900
Pierce, H.E.	Boy	202.344
Pinkerton, A.	AB	172.199
Poole, W.	Band	340.388
Pottinger, J.	Sto	292.311
Povall, J.H.	PO2	155.841
Powell, H.	Sto	290.101
Powell, I.	Sto	278.431
Poy Ah (1).	Dom	
Poy Ah (2).	Dom	
Price, C.	Sto	280.618
Price, T.	Sh/Cpl	128.110
Prior, W.	Sto	278.654
Purkis, W.	Sto	280.303
Quick, J.H.	PO2	169.844
Raven, C.B.	Band	340.745
Ray, A.F.	Pte	Ch8.362
Ray, H.T.	Ord	197.281
Ray, J.	AB	187.120
Read, W.	AB	186.779
Redston, A.B.	Ord	188.854
Renouf, J.	Blksmth/Mte	175.832
Rice, W.H.	L/S	166.727
Ridd, A.J.	Gunr	RMA7.827
Roche, T.P.	PO1	165.533
Sadler, F.	AB	187.506
Salmon, S.	Ord	199.979
Scales, C.M.	Q/Sig	163.265
Scott, D.	Ord	180.133
Scott, J.	Carp/Mte	133.328
See Ah.	Dom	
Seldon, H.	L/Sto	149.759
Shaw, F.	AB	158.425
Shergold, E.	Ord	197.214
Shipway, B.	Band	146.515
Shreeve, T.A.	AB	174.739
Sibley, R.	PO1	130.134
Silk, A.W.	Band	169.733
Simmons, C.H.	PO2	136.127
Sims, W.H.	Sto	287.104 K
Sing Ah.	Dom	
Sladen, W.	Q/Sig	189.913
Slingo, T.	Act/Gunr	
Smissen, R.	L/Sto	158.009
Smith, G.	Sto	285.784
Smith, H.	Sto	278.447
Smith, J.H.	Ch/ERA	129.280
Smith, W.	AB	151.964
Snell, H.	L/S	129.851
Snell, S.F.	Band	135.682
Soo Wing Ah.	Dom	

NO BAR MEDALS *continued.*

Sowden, A.J.	Ch/PO	115.812
Sparks, E.	Sh/Cpl	163.599
Speed, A.	Sto	281.077
Squires, T.	Sto	292.297
Stampton, A.	L/Sto	147.485
Stigings, T.G.	AB	190.191
Stoner, W.H.	Sto	170.078
Stoupe, H.	Pntr	341.883
Strans, F.	Band	357.034
Tabrett, F.	Sto	280.168
Taylor, G.A.	Q/Sig	189.694
Taylor, H.	Sto	279.507
Taylor, W.	Boy	202.533
Telford, S.L.	ERA	268.520
Terry, C.A.	Boy	202.486
Ting Ah.	Dom	
Tinning, J.	AB	187.103
Tomkinson, C.	Pte	Ch2.507
Toy Ma Lai.	Dom	
Triggell, A.	Sto	355.752
Tunnicliffe, F.	Sto	152.454
Tyler, J.H.	AB	156.169
Vanstone, J.	Sto	294.180
Vasey, S.W.	Fl/Surgn	
Vulder, F.R. de	Ord	200.568
Waite, H.	L/Sto	156.496
Wall, H.	AB	178.837
Wallis, J.	Sh/Std/Asst	341.757
Walters, F.A.	Sto	281.063
Walters, H.J.	AB	181.047
Ward, E.	Boy	202.339
Ware, W.A.	Ord	205.931
Warrender, G.J.S.	Capt	
Waters, T.	Sto	279.001
Watson, A.	2/Yeo/Sig	178.811
Weaver, G.	ERA	268.219
Webb, H.	Ord	197.425
Weeks, J.	Blksmth/Mte	181.685
Weeks, W.M.	Act/Carp	
Welch, F.J.	AB	185.291
Westcott, R.G.	Sto	289.883
Whisker, E.	Sto	280.922
White, E.	Sto	280.315
White, F.J.	Sto	294.177
Whiting, J.	L/Sto	149.680
Wholley, W.	PO1	110.871
Wibrew, J.E.	Sto	280.917
Wilding, T.	Band	341.011
Wilkie, J.	Sto	290.875
Willcox, C.	Ord	197.831
Williams, E.	Act/Gunr	
Williams, H.	Yeo/Sig	147.425
Wilson, F.W.	Band	340.884
Wing Ah.	Dom	
Withers, J.	L/Sto	153.799
Wo Ah.	Dom	
Wood, D.	Sto	279.508
Wood, W.	Ord	192.670
Woods, C.H.	Sto	153.670
Wright, G.S.	Ord	192.903
Wright, W.	Engr	
Yeo, W.J.	L/Carp/Crew	340.213
You Ah.	Dom	
You Chin.	Dom	
Young, W.A.	Civ/Med/Pract	
Yuen Ma Dah.	Dom	
Yung Ah.	Dom	

Duplicate medals:

	Barratt, W.H.	AB	171.806
	Brickell, S.C.	Ord	197.282
	Brown, W.	ERA	269.086
	Chapman, J.	AB	172.492
	Davis, W.D.	Ord	198.711
	Donnan, R.J.	Q/Sig	188.586
	Drew, W.	Boy	199.811
	Grant, C.	Sail	190.873
	Hopkins, S.	Midn	
	Hunt, W.	Ord	187.138
	Jones, A.	AB	184.755
	Labdon, J.	Pte	Po10.255
	Mardon, E.E.	AB	196.503
	Miller, T.D.	2/SBStd	350.230
	Mills, A.	Sto	279.516
	Moss, W.J.	Ord	187.514
	Pinkerton, A.	AB	172.199
	Price, T.	Sh/Cpl	128.110
K	Ray, A.F.	Pte	Ch8.362
	Read, W.	AB	186.779
	Terry, C.A.	Boy	202.486
	Welch, F.J.	AB	185.291
	Wilson, F.W.	Band	340.884

Duplicate medal - without issue no. on roll:

Johnson, A.W.	Pte	Po10.257

Returned medals:

Allen, E.	Gunr	RMA7.803
Chitty, C.	Ord	197.824
Chivers, B.	Sto	295.022
Doughty, J.C.T.	Ord	197.283
Hamerton, G.E.	Sto	294.130
Pasmore, W.	Ord	193.759
Pike, W.	Ord	197.319
Pyne, M.J.	PO1	129.057
Small, W.	Boy	203.478
Waller, C.	Ord	197.633

H.M.S. BONAVENTURE.

H.M.S. Bonaventure was a 2nd class Cruiser of 4,360 tons and 320 x 49½ feet. Her armament consisted of 2 x 6 in, 8 x 4.7 in and 8 x 6 pdr guns. The vessel was built in Devonport Dock Yard and launched on 2nd December 1892. She became a Depot Ship in 1910 and was sold on 12th April 1920 to Forth S. Breaking Co.; she was finally broken up in October 1920.

Bars	*Total*	*Returned*	*Entitled*
None	*350*	*8*	*342*
	350	*8*	*342*

Notes:

K - Medal presented by H.M. The King on 8th March 1902.

NO BAR MEDALS.

Name	Rank	Number	
Aldridge, E.	Midn		
Allan, R.	Pte	Ply7.588	
Allen, H.C.	AB	179.275	
Anear, A.A.	L/S	157.298	
Ash, W.	Sto	286.166	K
Ashworth, J.H.	L/Sto	159.979	
Austin, F.M.	Act/Sub Lieut		
Axworthy, J.H.	Q/Sig	181.210	
Back, J.T.	AB	179.345	
Baker, J.	Sto	286.164	
Baker, W.	PO1	112.963	
Ballam, W.G.	PO1	142.368	
Barnett, W.T.	Sto	155.480	
Barrett, D.	Sto	127.881	K
Barry, M.	AB	128.727	
Bartlett, G.W.	Sto	174.349	
Bassett, J.R.	L/Sto	164.681	
Beavis, W.J.	Act/MAA	350.148	
Beer, A.W.	MAA	106.613	
Bell, A.L.	Midn		
Benn, E.P.St.J.	Engr		
Bentley, T.J.J.	AB	155.801	
Berry, T.	ERA	268.750	K
Best, G.	AB	188.900	
Bettinson, J.	Ch/Sto	132.808	K
Bickford, S.	L/Sto	126.491	K
Bigg, T.E.J.	Sub Lieut		
Bignell, W.J.	Sto	158.564	K
Blair, P.W.	PO1	124.056	
Blake, J.	AB	170.823	
Blake, W.H.	Ch/Cook	132.845	
Bond, W.G.	Sto	175.817	
Bow Ah.	Dom		
Bow, J.	AB	180.336	
Bowen, J.	PO2	159.675	
Bowles, H.	Pte	Ply5.252	
Bragg, S.J.	AB	159.121	K
Bright, F.G.	Pte	Ply8.364	
Brooke, B.V.	Lieut		K
Brooking, R.	Pte	Ply5.041	
Bryant, W.	Sto	151.393	
Buckingham, T.	Ch/Sto	133.784	K
Bull, E.C.	Sto	285.043	
Bull, H.	L/Cpl	Ply2.780	
Burgess, T.	Sto	285.612	
Burke, A.F.	AB	155.184	
Burleigh, W.	L/Sto	124.280	
Buscombe, S.	Sto	158.356	
Butland, O.H.M.	Act/2/Ck/Mte	353.099	
Butler, J.	AB	139.281	
Buzzo, A.E.	PO1	113.560	K
Byrne, J.	Sto	283.527	
Callaghan, O.	Sto	281.419	
Campbell, J.	Sto	283.541	
Carbis, W.H.	AB	179.644	
Casey, W.	SB/Attn	350.470	
Cavanagh, P.	Sto	165.703	
Chai Ah.	Dom		
Chalk, G.H.	L/Sto	113.960	
Challice, F.	L/Sto	158.833	
Chamberlain, J.	SB/Attn	177.463	
Clarke, R.W.	AB	146.267	
Clarke, W.	AB	138.659	
Clayton, A.	Pte	Ply7.933	
Cleave, B.	Sto	283.671	
Collin, J.T.	Carp/Crew	341.850	
Coombes, C.W.	2/Yeo/Sig	147.101	
Cooper, H.E.	Dom	357.359	
Cooper, S.M.	Sergt	Ply4.177	
Corkson, H.	Pte	Po7.643	
Cornall, A.T.	AB	147.612	
Costello, J.P.	AB	160.592	K
Couch, G.	Sh/Std	102.671	
Coulthread, E.	Pte	Ply5.367	
Coussins, R.J.	L/S	157.865	K
Creamer, J.	Sto	286.127	
Creber, J.	Gunr		
Crook, H.P.	Blksmth/Mte	155.597	
Crowley, T.	Sto	286.289	
Crowley, T.J.	St/Surgn		
Cruze, A.J.	AB	181.206	
Cumming, E.E.	AB	179.623	

NO BAR MEDALS *continued.*

Name	Rating	Number	
Curran, P.	AB	189.354	
Curtis, J.H.	Ch/ERA	127.869	
Davey, W.	Sto	280.396	
Dean, H.	AB	189.244	
Delbridge, J.	AB	177.259	
Derrick, H.J.	Sto	286.147	
Doney, J.	L/Sto	276.317	
Downey, W.J.	Sto	282.646	K
Driver, W.H.	AB	176.374	
Eales, J.W.	AB	177.872	
Edmunds, R.	Pte	Ch8.775	
Eley, W.	AB	188.481	
Ellis, W.F.	Pte	Ply6.446	
Ellison, W.	Pte	Ply8.374	
Endacott, W.	AB	180.864	
Fairbank, F.W.	Lieut		
Fat Ah.	Dom		
Fearne, C.	AB	188.437	
Finegan, D.	Sto	286.134	K
Fisher, J.R.	Q/Sig	155.908	
Fittall, S.G.	Pte	Ply7.697	
Fletcher, W.J.	Midn		
Fogarty, J.M.	AB	191.101	
Foster, A.J.	2/Wrtr	165.271	K
Foster, F.A.	Pte	Ply6.249	
Frankis, H.R.	ERA	268.627	
Freeney, T.P.	AB	176.998	
Galvin, J.	Ord	188.311	
Gater, W.	Sto	280.935	K
Geeleher, P.	Sto	280.577	
Gibbs, H.T.C.	Midn		
Gill, W.L.	St/Payr		
Golds, W.T.	AB	166.850	
Grant, J.T.	Ord	171.117	
Grassam, H.	AB	181.851	
Haine, H.	Sto	162.113	K
Hall, C.	PO1	117.736	K
Hall, G.	AB	188.445	
Halliday, G.H.	Act/Ch/Sto	149.170	
Hammacott, G.	AB	187.549	
Hammond, A.E.	Sto	286.601	
Hammond, M.	L/Sto	139.953	
Hansen, I.P.	AB	188.871	
Harford, W.	ERA	268.866	
Harman, D.	SBStd	139.984	
Harris, H.T.	AB	181.703	
Harris, J.	Shpwrt	341.422	
Harris, S.H.	Sto	165.376	K
Hatch, R.	Sto	285.892	
Hayhurst, R.	AB	120.937	
Hayward, G.H.	Sto	282.847	K
Healy, C.R.	PO1	155.613	K
Heaton, S.	Act/ERA	269.971	
Hendry, C.	L/Sergt	Ply5.067	
Henrick, W.	Sto	286.116	
Hexter, W.	L/S	159.153	K

Name	Rating	Number	
Hill, J.	PO2	160.288	K
Hing Ah.	Dom		
Hird, A.	AB	155.165	
Hitchcock, H.	Sto	155.418	
Hockley, F.	L/S	157.635	
Holland, A.J.	AB	188.820	
Holmes, C.A.	Sto	283.549	
Holmes, T.F.	AB	187.552	
Hose, W.	Lieut		
Hoy Ah.	Dom		
Hughes, H.	SB/Attn	350.454	
Hughes, J.	Pte	Ply6.431	
Hung Ah.	Dom		
Hutchings, A.	Sto	167.909	
Hutchison, J.	AB	180.315	
Isaac, E.J.	Sto	292.669	
Jackson, W.T.	Pte	Ply7.737	
James, R.	Sto	292.700	
Jay Ah.	Dom		
Jones, A.	Sto	175.830	K
Joyce, M.	Sto	286.505	
Kane, Rev. I.	Chaplain & N.Instr		
Kendall, W.H.	Carp/Mte	145.702	
Keogh, M.S.	Sto	286.276	
Keohane, D.	AB	182.658	K
Kerr, J.	Sto	283.339	
Kerswill, E.R.	AB	183.459	
Kidney, J.	Sto	280.572	
Kilgour, P.V.	Midn		
Kim Ah.	Dom		
Kimmings, C.	Bugler	Ply2.899	
King, F.J.	AB	185.249	
Kirby, W.H.	Ch/Sto	143.148	
Kitt, J.	L/Sto	151.861	
Kitt, J.J.	Arm/Mte	340.375	
Knott, A.	AB	161.791	K
Lambert, T.	Pte	Ply5.290	
Lamplough, S.	AB	189.043	
Langham, J.T.	AB	188.577	
Lawford, S.L.K.	Midn		
Lees, T.O.H.	Lieut(RMLI)		
Lemon, W.R.	Ch/ERA	145.822	
Lewin, W.H.	Sto	284.322	K
Lewis, J.	Ch/Sto	147.359	
Lillicrap, A.	Arm/Mte	340.234	
Ling Ah.	Dom		
Lloyd, J.H.	AB	184.685	
Lowe, J.	AB	179.563	K
Lucid, M.	Sto	286.129	K
Luff, L.W.	Q/Sig	160.942	
Lyons, P.	Sto	286.288	
McCarthy, J.	Sto	174.144	
McColl, T.	AB	189.990	
McCubbin, J.	Sto	286.372	
McGonigle, A.J.	Sh/Cpl	350.183	
McGuire, W.A.	AB	190.747	
McLeod, A.	Cooper	340.996	K

NO BAR MEDALS *continued.*

Name	Rank	Number	
McMahon, M.	Sh/Std/Asst	160.420	
McMillan, J.	Ord	198.022	
Ma Chang Lung.	Dom		
Mardon, H.	L/Shpwrt	341.461	
Marshall, S.	Sto	148.748	
Marshall, W.	Sto	286.162	K
Mason, T.W.	Pte	Ply6.070	
Matthews, P.	Ord	197.621	
Maunder, H.	PO1	130.263	
Maxted, F.E.	AB	188.894	
May, E.	AB	182.517	
Maynard, T.	Sto	282.941	
Miell, C.F.	AB	183.675	
Moon, F.J.	L/S	186.184	
Moore, J.S.	Cpl	Ply5.835	
Morris, G.W.	AB	189.180	
Morrison, A.	AB	178.986	
Neligan, J.G.	Midn		
Newcombe, R.	Sail/Mte	148.439	
Nind, F.D.	Clerk		
Noble, L.	Sto	286.278	
Norquay, W.	PO2	183.493	
Norton, J.E.	Plmbr	340.104	K
Nugent, R.A.	Lieut		
O'Halloran, E.	L/Sto	165.313	
Old, W.F.	Sto	280.412	
Owen, J.A.	Asst/Engr		
Palmer, J.W.	Pte	Ply7.692	
Parker, S.	PO1	118.412	
Parkman, W.	Pte	Ply2.862	
Partridge, W.H.	L/S	173.541	
Patey, J.	PO1	144.206	
Payne, W.	AB	126.642	
Pengelly, A.	PO2	170.557	
Perrin, W.	AB	184.786	
Peters, H.G.	Sto	174.367	K
Phillips, M.	Ord	201.878	
Phillips, W.F.	AB	178.009	
Phipps, W.D.	Midn		
Ping Ah.	Dom		
Pomeroy, W.J.	PO2	147.840	K
Porteous, G.	Ord	197.609	
Porton, C.	Pte	Ply5.785	
Potter, C.J.	Sto	286.168	K
Potter, P.G.	AB	180.273	
Reece, E.	AB	189.983	
Regan, D.	PO1	153.308	
Reid, W.	Yeo/Sig	142.072	
Reid, W.	AB	190.398	
Rendle, T.	AB	179.191	
Renny, T.J.	Ch/Arm	99.691	
Revell, C.	Sto	292.122	
Reynolds, C.H.	AB	169.492	
Richards, E.	AB	170.276	
Richards, E.	Ord	180.265	
Roberts, P.	Sto	174.339	K
Robinson, C.	AB	182.189	

Name	Rank	Number	
Robinson, R.	AB	172.600	
Rogers, E.	Sto	281.658	
Rowley, J.H.J.	Arm	129.213	
Russell, A.	AB	155.861	
Russell, T.W.	AB	184.154	
Ruther, F.H.	AB	155.944	
Satterly, H.	AB	155.035	
Sawle, C.J.G.	Capt		
Scamp, T.	ERA	268.621	
Schafer, J.S.	Act/Sub Lieut		
See Ah.	Dom		
Sheehan, J.	Sto	279.908	
Shobbrook, L.	AB	182.276	
Shobbrook, W.H.	Q/Sig	183.581	
Sloan, C.	AB	179.862	
Sluggett, A.	AB	178.312	
Smale, E.G.	L/Sto	158.834	
Smith, F.P.	St/Engr		
Smith, W.	Sto	285.178	
Smith, W.H.	Ch/ERA	129.287	
Soo Ah.	Dom		
Spittle, D.	AB	189.995	
Steed, H.	Sto	280.992	
Steel, J.	Gunr		
Steer, C.M.	PO1	147.870	
Stevens, W.T.	Sto	280.116	
Stewart, V.	Sto	277.132	
Stocker, S.	Sto	285.700	K
Street, H.	Sto	174.391	
Sullivan, J.	AB	145.255	
Sullivan, P.	AB	182.663	
Summer, J.D.	Act/Gunr		
Summerrill, A.	Sto	167.900	
Sutton, E.	Surgn		
Sutton, H.G.	Pilot		
Swann, T.H.	Sto	292.930	
Taion Ah.	Dom		
Taylor, A.	Asst/Payr		
Taylor, A.	AB	179.541	
Temple, C.T.	Pte	Po6.144	
Thacker, W.J.	Pilot		
Thomas, G.E.H.	Sto	281.239	
Thomas, M.J.	Pte	Po6.125	
Threlfell, G.	Lieut		
Tillard, A.T.	Midn		
Tiltman, J.T.	L/Sto	163.713	
Tom Ah.	Dom		
Tosh, J.T.	AB	190.408	
Towell, A.R.	L/Sto	156.143	
Treadaway, E.	Ord	197.872	
Treby, J.	AB	187.547	
Tregenza, W.H.	Shpwrt	121.516	
Trenaman, J.	Pntr	121.527	K
Trevethan, F.T.	PO1	145.154	
Turner, J.	Sto	282.625	
Urell, C.	AB	150.968	
Vaughan, H.M.	Pte	Ply8.419	
Veale, G.W.	ERA	268.577	
Violet, A.	Sto	355.474	

NO BAR MEDALS *continued.*

Vivian, E.	Carp/Crew	341.851
Wagstaff, C.	L/Sig	145.858
Walker, C.J.	AB	148.472
Wallace, M.	Sto	153.108
Walsh, J.	Pte	Ply8.704
Wannell, C.H.	Carp	
Ward, J.	AB	170.283
Ward, J.	Pte	Po3.484
Ward, T.A.	L/Sto	129.374
Waterhouse, A.E.	AB	190.382
Wealleans, G.	AB	170.763
Wheeler, A.	Ord	197.604
Wherley, R.	Ord	197.652
Whiskin, W.	AB	188.994
White, W.	Sto	280.998 K
Williams, F.J.	AB	183.961
Williams, H.	AB	176.765
Williams, J.	L/Carp/Crew	342.057
Williamson, T.	Sto	290.398
Willis, F.	AB	189.135
Wilmot, J.	Sto	276.213
Wilson, A.J.	SB/Attn	350.468
Wim Ah.	Dom	
Wingett, S.T.	Ch/Sto	130.775
Winn, W.	Pte	Ply7.747
Wood, H.	Ord	197.651
Woodley, A.	Sto	284.010
Wyles, W.	2/SBStd	152.544
Yew Ah.	Musn	

Duplicate medals:

Barnett, W.T.	Sto	155.480
Bright, F.G.	Pte	Ply8.364
Ellis, W.F.	Pte	Ply6.446
Fisher, J.R.	Q/Sig	155.908
Holmes, C.A.	Sto	283.549
Hutchings, A.	Sto	167.909
Kilgour, P.V.	Midn	
Lewin, W.H.	Sto	284.322
McCubbin, J.	Sto	286.372
Maxted, F.E.	AB	188.894
Phipps, W.D.	Midn	*
Reynolds, C.H.	AB	169.492
Russell, T.W.	AB	184.154
Summer, J.D.	Act/Gunr	
Taylor, A.	AB	179.541
Wherley, R.	Ord	197.652
Williams, J.	L/Carp/Crew	342.057

* *Two duplicate medals issued.*

Returned medals:

Brundell, W.	Pte	Ply4.915
Dineen, D.	Sto	281.459
Eagland, J.W.	L/Sto	170.501
Evans, J.	AB	186.533
Malone, A.	AB	186.859
Ryan, J.	AB	189.278
Thacker, A.E.	Pte	Ply8.008
Thornton, E.W.	Pte	Po3.891

H.M.S. CENTURION.

H.M.S. Centurion was a Battleship of 10,500 tons and 360 x 70 feet. Her armament consisted of 4 x 10 in, 10 x 4.7 in and 8 x 6 pdr guns. The vessel was built in Portsmouth Dock Yard and launched on 3rd August 1892. She was sold on 12th July 1910 to Ward at Morecambe.

Bars	*Total*	*Returned*	*Entitled*
TF & RP	*20*	*0*	*20*
TF	*8*	*0*	*8*
RP	*402*	*12*	*390*
None	*344*	*12*	*332*
	774	*24*	*750*

Notes:

Missing detail in the medal roll is indicated by the use of brackets; the spaces inside the brackets are not intended to indicate the exact amount of missing detail.

K - Medal presented by H.M. The King on 8th March 1902.

1 - Noted on roll as A.D.C. to Admiral.

2 - Noted on roll as Actg.Payr.in Daphne 10 June - 19 July '00.

3 - Roll states, "Run, Appn for restoration 1906, to wait 3 years."

4 - Clasp number (3) entered on roll, but roll also states, "clasp not sent."

5 - This man is also on the roll for H.M.S. Alacrity as entitled to a no bar medal.

6 - Roll states,"Deprived on authority of C.M. 1902."

Bars: TAKU FORTS, RELIEF OF PEKIN.

Brown, G.S.	Pntr	341.474	
Duckworth, F.	ERA	268.184	K
Evans, E.T.	Sto	281.432	
Fazey, C.	L/S	114.858	
Goodwin, S.J.	Pte	Ch6.151	
Hailwood, J.	L/S	135.000	
Highbee, E.W.	Act/ERA	269.531	
Hill, S.W.	PO1	165.126	K
Huffer, H.	AB	176.333	
Kilpatrick, R.	Asst/Engr		
Langmaid, W.	L/Shpwrt	163.678	
Lepla, L.	Pte	Po8.233	
Lynch, W.G.	AB	182.753	
Noble, A.	Cooper/Crew	278.052	
Parry, F.G.	Sh/Cpl	350.119	
Perkins, A.J.	AB	137.695	
Prickett, C.B.	Midn		
Tickell, J.C.	Ch/PO	81.108	
Walcott, C.C.	Act/Lieut		
Wilkins, C.	Sto	279.750	

Duplicate medals:

Fazey, C.	L/S	114.858
Walcott, C.C.	Act/Lieut	

Bar: TAKU FORTS.

Curtis, W.	Pte	Ply5.903
Lee, G.	Pte	Po8.246
McCardle, J.	Cpl	Ply5.167
O'Neale, E.	Pte	Po8.255
Smith, A.J.	Pte	Po8.277

Bar: TAKU FORTS *continued.*

Smith, C.H.	Pte	Po5.611	
Taylor, F.W.H.	Sig	185.837	
Wales, A.	Gunr	RMA5.752	

Bar: RELIEF OF PEKIN.

Adams, J.J.	L/S	148.437	
Alexander, G.B.	Midn		
Allott, J.	Sto	281.904	
Alton, F.C.	Secretary		K
Amos, W.	Pte	Ch8.242	
Armstrong, T.	Sto	281.871	
Ashby, H.	AB	190.246	
Atkinson, B.G.	AB	139.203	
Attrill, J.	Ch/Carp		K
Attwood, J.A.E.	AB	185.840	
Bailey, A.	Pte	Po8.241	
Bailey, S.R.	Midn		K
Baillie, W.K.	AB	183.251	
Bairne, J.	Gunr	RMA5.780	
Baker, G.W.	AB	193.635	K
Balcomb, G.	AB	179.328	
Bamber, W.L.	Lieut		
Bamford, J.G.	PO1	151.101	
Barker, B.	ERA	269.360	
Barnes, A.H.	L/S	179.316	
Bartle, H.	L/Sto	280.508	
Bartlett, F.A.	AB	176.279	
Bastable, F.	L/Sto	128.350	
Bastard, G.E.	AB	183.036	
Batchelor, W.	AB	184.682	
Baxter, W.	AB	186.409	
Beach, H.G.	L/S	176.923	
Beale, B.	Sto	282.127	
Beaumont, A.	Sto	149.838	
Benewith, A.	AB	184.597	
Bentley, W.D.B.	PO1	138.849	
Bevis, A.	AB	183.480	
Beyts, H.W.H.	Capt(RMA)		
Bigg, F.W.	AB	185.001	K
Bigham, C.C.	Lieut(Army)		1
Blackman, F.L.	Sto	280.742	
Bolton, H.S.	Ord	183.671	
Bone, E.R.	AB	184.684	
Bone, S.H.	AB	158.529	
Borrett, G.H.	Lieut		
Bowman, J.	Sergt	Ply2.762	
Boyes, H.	Midn		
Bradley, J.W.	PO2	154.373	
Breeds, F.	AB	191.559	
Brett, B.	AB	183.246	
Bridges, G.	Blksmth/Mte	340.374	
Brien, J.	Sto	286.629	K
Bromley, C.W.	Q/Sig	181.778	
Bromley, J.	AB	191.847	
Brooks, H.	Gunr	RMA5.657	
Brown, A.E.	AB	191.593	
Brown, F.	Sto	281.985	
Brown, W.G.	AB	157.615	
Bruce, G.H.	Cpl	Ch5.442	
Bryson, J.	Ord	198.639	
Bubb, J.	Gunr	RMA4.819	
Bull, T.	Gunr	RMA5.735	
Bundy, A.C.	AB	197.207	
Burford, A.A.	AB	151.601	
Burke, C.D.	Midn		
Burnett, A.	Act/Arm	128.533	
Burns, R.	Pte	Po8.292	
Burton, G.R.J.	AB	143.494	
Butler, F.	L/Sto	175.921	
Butler, W.R.	L/Sig	160.779	
Button, H.	Ord	193.432	K
Callaway, H.C.B.	Gunr	RMA5.705	K
Caller, H.J.	L/Sto	154.257	
Castle, E.W.	AB	156.093	
Catt, J.	Sto	281.184	
Caven, W.	Sto	282.957	
Chapman, W.C.	PO1	124.133	
Clapson, G.H.	Gunr	RMA5.734	
Clark, G.	AB	103.747	
Clayton, J.	Sto	280.520	
Clayton, W.	AB	121.994	
Clifford, P.	AB	166.230	
Cochrane, M.E.	Sub Lieut		
Cockerill, H.B.	AB	186.252	
Cockey, G.H.	Engr		K
Coldwell, W.C.	AB	147.340	
Coleman, W.	AB	196.191	
Compton, A.	AB	183.242	
Cook, W.S.	AB	178.643	
Coombes, J.R.	L/S	138.490	
Cooper, R.E.	PO2	152.899	
Cooper, W.	AB	185.827	
Corbett, G.C.	Sto	282.964	
Cornwell, J.	AB	161.530	
Cottam, S.	AB	192.392	K
Coulstock, F.	AB	186.961	
Cresdee, W.J.	Sto	281.304	
Crosse, W.H.	PO1	127.826	
Cruickshank, J.	Sto	281.886	
Cufley, J.	AB	184.373	
Currie, S.	L/Sto	277.206	K
Curtis, J.W.	Arm	143.242	
Davey, J.E.	AB	184.706	
Davidge, C.	Act/Gunr		
Davies, J.	AB	110.673	
Davies, W.H.	Sergt	RMA3.498	K
Davis, J.C.	Midn		K
Davis, J.C.	2/Yeo/Sig	171.600	
Davison, W.J.	AB	162.423	
Derkin, J.H.	PO2	150.763	
Devine, T.	Q/Sig	185.736	
Dinwoodie, J.	Sto	282.143	K
Douglas, P.W.	Midn		
Duly, W.K.	Gunr	RMA5.769	

Bar: RELIEF OF PEKIN *continued.*

Name	Rank	Number	
Durrant, C.	Pte	Po6.212	
Eccleston, T.	Sig	185.512	
Edbury, C.	Sto	281.914	
Edney, H.C.	AB	192.009	
Edwards, J.L.	Bugler	Ch8.151	K
Edwards, W.	Sto	282.137	
Eley, W.	AB	185.496	
Ellis, A.E.	Pte	Po8.634	
Ellis, G.	Bosn		K
Emery, E.W.	AB	186.974	
Emery, H.	L/Sig	157.115	
Engholm, F.W.	Ord	196.970	
Erskine, T.	Plmbr/Mte	341.290	
Evans, T.A.	Sto	281.659	
Fair, G.M.K.	Lieut		
Farie, J.U.	Lieut		
Fat Ah (2).	Dom		
Felton, I.	Pte	Po8.250	
Few, E.	Cook/Mte	340.877	
Fifield, W.E.	Carp/Crew	343.707	
Finch, T.	Sto	292.475	
Floyd, S.	Sto	281.436	K
Ford, F.	Pte	Po5.715	
Ford, F.A.	AB	137.944	
Foreman, A.G.	PO1	169.195	K
French, H.	L/Sto	149.450	
Frisby, E.	Pte	Po3.599	
Frost, E.	Sto	192.128	
Fryer, G.T.	AB	125.018	
Gage, W.	Pte	Po8.243	
Gainsley, J.H.	Act/Bombdr	RMA3.257	
Gale, C.G.	Sto	282.044	
Gambling, J.	AB	186.978	
Gardener, W.J.	AB	184.686	
Gardner, D.C.	AB	188.610	
Garnett, W.	AB	183.963	
Gathercole, E.	AB	183.696	
Gay, G.	AB	162.918	
Goldfinch, A.	Dom	128.492	
Goldstein, L.	Gunr	RMA5.730	
Goodban, J.	L/S	184.996	K
Gosford, H.	AB	185.812	
Gosling, C.	L/Sto	152.679	
Goulding, J.	AB	150.929	
Granville, C.D.	Capt		K
Greasley, G.W.	L/Sto	280.845	K
Greavett, F.W.W.	AB	177.218	
Green, G.A.	AB	191.544	
Greening, R.	AB	151.106	
Griffiths, W.E.	AB	183.248	
Gunn, S.	Sergt	Ply5.107	K
Guy, A.	Pte	Po8.245	
Hagger, E.C.	AB	184.736	
Hamer, A.V.	Sto	281.186	
Hamilton, G.C.	AB	184.696	
Hanmore, C.W.	AB	149.661	
Harcourt, T.	AB	179.696	
Harris, C.H.	Sto	280.714	
Hart, W.H.	AB	184.998	K
Hawes, G.H.	Pte	Po8.906	
Hayhow, R.J.	AB	152.212	
Hellyer, A.J.	Carp/Mte	158.057	K
Henderson, J.	Sto	283.730	
Herring, E.	L/Shpwrt	164.080	
Hewitt, G.E.	Gunr	RMA5.448	
Hewitt, R.W.	Sto	281.586	
Hickling, J.S.	Gunr	RMA5.293	
Hipple, H.	AB	148.724	
Hobbs, W.	Pte	Po8.240	
Hood, C.T.	AB	180.094	
Horgan, F.	Sto	280.093	
Hornigold, H.	AB	186.982	
Horscroft, C.B.	AB	184.732	
Hosier, T.W.	AB	150.891	
House, W.H.	ERA	268.402	
Hucker, A.E.B.	AB	102.268	
Hung Ah.	Dom		
Hussey, A.B.	Pte	Po8.964	
Ingroville, T.P.	AB	170.306	
Ivery, G.	Pte	Po8.878	K
Ivory, J.O'D.	Sto	286.376	
Jackson, H.L.	AB	190.268	
Jago, F.	2/Yeo/Sig	182.802	K
James, G.D.	Gunr	RMA5.930	
Jeffery, F.G.	Sto	282.128	
Jellicoe, J.R.	Capt		K
Jermain, R.L.	Midn		
Jing Tu.	Dom		
Johnson, H.R.	Gunr	RMA5.999	
Johnson, T.A.	AB	166.373	
Johnson, W.	AB	176.171	
Johnstone, J.R.	Major(RMLI)		K
Jones, W.B.C.	Midn		
Jordan, J.J.	AB	173.932	
Jordan, P.J.M.	AB	160.124	
Joyce, W.E.	PO2	169.533	
Jupp, W.H.	Gunr	RMA5.665	K
Keegan, A.J.	AB	149.668	
Kemp, G.	Gunr	RMA4.562	
Kimber, J.H.N.	AB	188.336	
King, A.	Gunr	RMA3.687	
King, F.	AB	186.346	
Kippen, C.	Pte	Po6.974	
Knowles, C.	Pte	Ply9.126	
Lambert, C.	Pte	Po7.799	
Lawrence, H.J.	Sergt	Po1.494	
Lawson, L.A.	Pte	Po8.247	
Legg, W.	PO1	129.130	
Lepine, R.J.	Pte	Po3.846	K
Lewis, A.M.	AB	157.596	
Littlejohns, W.G.	Asst/Payr		K
Livermore, A.G.N.	L/S	183.633	K
Lloyd, W.T.	Ord	190.614	
Lockyer, W.J.	AB	182.455	
Long, E.J.	AB	140.074	
Louch, H.W.	Pte	Po7.272	

Bar: RELIEF OF PEKIN *continued.*

Name	Rank	Number	
Lowther-Crofton, E.G.	Lieut		
Loy Ah.	Dom		
Luttrell, J.L.F.	Lieut		K
McAulay, W.	Sto	286.375	
McBride, J.	AB	186.415	
McElligott, M.	PO1	151.904	K
McGeorge, J.W.	L/Shpwrt	341.351	K
McKee, G.	AB	186.414	
McKenzie, J.	Pte	Po9.034	K
McLean, W.G.	Sh/Std/Asst	350.336	K
Madge, L.J.H.	PO1	142.846	K
Manisty, H.W.E.	Asst/Payr		
Marden, W.	Gunr	RMA5.239	
Martin, H.	Gunr	RMA5.718	
Maze, D.E.	Ch/ERA	131.777	
Melbourne, H.	Ord	196.369	
Mercer, E.	Ord	197.902	
Metcalf, C.H.	L/Cpl	Po6.163	K
Miller, H.C.	L/Sergt	RMA3.413	K
Mills, J.C.	Sto	282.122	K
Mintram, A.S.	AB	186.700	K
Moore, W.	L/S	157.414	K
Morgan, H.	AB	166.381	
Morgan, W.	AB	182.941	
Moull, W.D.	2/SBStd	350.416	K
Mulcahy, E.	Sto	286.732	K
Neale, H.J.	AB	192.921	
Negus, C.H.	AB	187.722	
Neil, W.	AB	189.313	
Neilson, J.	Gunr	RMA5.754	
Newman, A.J.	Sto	281.536	
Newman, S.G.	AB	185.348	
Newton, J.	Sto	282.147	
Nichols, S.	Sto	171.194	
Nicholson, W.A.	Pte	Po8.036	
Osborne, E.O.B.S.	Midn		
Outram, C.	AB	185.897	
Parsons, A.	Sto	170.229	
Paskins, T.F.	Ord	189.165	
Pay, J.R.	AB	193.464	
Pearman, H.E.	Pte	Ply8.603	
Pearton, W.J.	AB	180.912	
Penn, W.	AB	149.951	
Phillips, W.	Sto	281.631	
Pickthorn, E.B.	St/Surgn		K
Pitman, A.E.	AB	109.455	
Pond, C.H.	PO1	112.574	
Pook, E.R.	Gunr	RMA6.774	
Poulter, E.R.	Sto	120.468	
Povey, G.	AB	186.391	
Powlett, F.A.	Flag Lieut		
Prior, G.W.C.	Sto	286.362	
Priscott, A.	Bugler	Po6.711	
Purnell, E.O.	AB	183.754	
Rann, W.H.	Gunr	RMA4.240	
Read, J.	AB	118.704	

Name	Rank	Number
Read, T.B.	L/Cpl	Po3.695
Reed, F.	AB	185.669
Reeve, A.D.	AB	179.283
Reeves, G.J.	AB	188.625
Reeves, J.	AB	184.708
Regis, H.W.	Yeo/Sig	123.562
Restall, T.J.	L/S	151.659
Richards, R.C.	AB	118.046
Richardson, G.P.	AB	185.810
Richardson, J.	L/S	170.038
Riley, E.W.	Asst/Engr	
Roberts, A.E.	AB	173.913
Robinson, A.E.	Blksmth/Mte	341.124
Rodden, C.	AB	160.642
Rogers, W.H.	PO2	157.415
Rotter, C.J.E.	Payr	
Russell, F.	Bombdr	RMA6.409
Sammels, F.E.	Act/Gunr	
Samphier, H.	PO2	137.166
Sanderson, J.E.	AB	182.968
Sasse, A.J.	AB	184.348
Sawkins, E.J.	AB	190.281
Searle, J.	Pte	Ch8.612
Seymour, Sir. E.H.	Vice Admiral	
Shailer, T.P.	Sto	111.634
Sharpe, F.	AB	188.893
Shephard, H.L.	Midn	
Shepherd, W.J.	AB	184.293
Shilston, A.E.	PO1	121.405
Sibbald, T.M.	Fl/Surgn	
Silvester, J.	PO2	150.755
Simpson, E.J.	Pte	Po6.748
Sinclair, C.H.	Lieut	
Sippets, G.	AB	185.799
Skipsey, R.	AB	143.729
Small, A.	L/S	148.266
Smith, Rev.E.F.H.	Chaplain & N. Instr	
Smith, F.	Pte	Ply4.983
Smith, G.	Sto	292.073
Smith, J.A.	Ord	191.864
Smith, M.	Arm	129.367
Smith, W.J.	Gunr	RMA4.466
Smyth, D.W.	PO1	171.503
Solen, J.T.	Pte	Po4.379
Spencer, A.	AB	121.844
Spiller, G.	PO1	124.233
Spratley, A.	AB	184.008
St. John, St.A.O.	Midn	
Stainfield, A.F.J.	Pte	Po8.252
Stanberg, E.	Cook/Mte	340.949
Starr, G.H.	Asst/Engr	
Stevens, R.	Gunr	RMA5.851
Stimpson, H.	Gunr	RMA4.294
Sullivan, J.	PO2	152.858
Summerton, H.	Pte	Po5.040
Swiggs, A.E.	AB	189.160
Tabuteau, A.E.	Clerk	
Tagg, G.W.	AB	123.861

Bar: RELIEF OF PEKIN *continued.*

Tai Ah.	Dom		
Tanner, J.F.	Gunr	RMA5.771	
Taylor, F.	AB	185.898	
Temple, G.H.	AB	179.709	
Thompson, A.C.	Sto	176.043	
Thompson, W.	ERA	268.357	
Toal, J.	Sto	282.730	
Tooze, S.J.S.	PO1	156.075	
Torrington, B.	L/Sto	149.558	K
Towner, F.H.W.	Sto	280.718	
Townsend, J.T.	Sto	280.748	
Townsend, T.	AB	174.826	
Tripp, R.	PO2	151.105	
Trodd, H.M.	L/Sergt	Po7.625	
Tulett, J.	AB	157.604	
Turner, E.	PO1	179.102	
Vine, W.G.	PO2	165.150	K
Venton, L.	Sto	286.596	K
Waghorn, B.B.	Sto	286.521	
Wah Ah.	Dom		
Walker, E.	Sto	280.253	
Walker, J.	AB	188.619	
Walker, W.G.	Gunr	RMA6.102	
Wan Ah.	Dom		
Wardner, E.C.	AB	165.392	
Waters, J.	Sto	286.052	K
Webber, E.	PO1	128.620	
Webber, F.A.	Dom	123.957	K
Welch, G.W.	AB	186.305	
West, F.	Pte	Ch8.975	
Weston, E.	Gunr	RMA5.415	
Whaley, W.	PO1	102.529	
Whatley, F.	AB	183.479	
Whitecross, P.A.	AB	137.409	K
Whyte, C.L.C.B.	PO2	147.436	
Wildbore, R.F.	AB	159.070	
Wilkinson, F.W.	Sto	282.983	
Wilkinson, W.	AB	186.986	
Willcox, O.H.	Gunr	RMA4.267	K
Williams, G.	AB	183.260	K
Willis, J.C.	L/S	160.836	
Wilson, F.O'B.	Midn		
Wilson, W.	L/S	139.993	
Wilson, W.	AB	183.912	
Wing Ching.	Dom		
Woodriffe, S.C.	PO1	146.145	
Wright, T.	L/S	161.349	
Wyatt, E.S.	Ch/PO	104.052	
Yates, J.T.	Gunr	RMA5.890	
Ying Ah.	Dom		
Young, M.	Sto	286.622	K

Duplicate medals:

Bull, T.	Gunr	RMA5.735	
Caller, H.J.	L/Sto	154.257	
Cockerill, H.B.	AB	186.252	
Douglas, P.W.	Midn		
Edwards, J.L.	Bugler	Ch8.151	
Engholm, F.W.	Ord	196.970	
Ford, F.	Pte	Po5.715	
Hart, W.H.	AB	184.998	
Hayhow, R.J.	AB	152.212	
Ivory, J.O'D.	Sto	286.376	
McBride, J.	AB	186.415	
Morgan, W.	AB	182.941	
Neale, H.J.	AB	192.921	
Priscott, A.	Bugler	Po6.711	
Robinson, A.E.	Blksmth/Mte	341.124	
Shephard, H.L.	Midn		*
Smith, J.A.	Ord	191.864	
Waghorn, B.B.	Sto	286.521	
Waters, J.	Sto	286.052	

* *Three duplicate medals issued.*

Returned medals:

Anwyle, F.	Sto	283.173
Briggs, F.W.	Pte	Po8.239
Durkan, J.	Sto	280.853
Foster, F.H.	Pte	Ply8.594
Higlett, F.W.	AB	184.804
Holloway, J.	Gunr	RMA5.772
Hurman, H.O.	Q/Sig	184.793
Jennings, A.G.	Sto	286.340
Lock, T.F.	AB	185.834
Lunn, E.	Gunr	RMA5.767
Mitchell, W.	Sto	165.215
Parsons, R.	AB	184.683

NO BAR MEDALS.

Adams, T.R.	Sail	158.182
Adcock, C.H.	Ord	196.905
Anderson, E.C.	Sig	191.161
An( ), R.	Ord	190.410
Appleton, E.J.	AB	185.802
Arrowsmith, E.	Band	174.197
Arthur, J.	Ord	188.175
Ashton, W.	AB	185.372
Bailey, C.W.	Ch/ERA	149.446
Bainbridge, W.J.	Pte	Ch7.842
Bannister, C.	AB	182.971
Barfoot, W.	Sh/Cpl	133.754
Barrett, A.A.	Band	152.275
Barter, H.R.	Ord	197.746
Batty, J.J.	Pte	Ply8.292
Baystrong, A.W.	Cpl	RMA5.673
Belben, C.S.	Ch/SBStd	119.810
Bell, T.H.	Ord	197.549
Benson, W.H.	Band	153.924
Betsworth, F.W.	Ord	198.313
Betts, J.	AB	184.717
Bignell, D.E.	AB	160.799

NO BAR MEDALS *continued.*

Name	Rating	Number
Bignell, L.D'O.	Midn	
Binning, A.J.H.	ERA	268.006
Blake, W.A.	Gunr	
Bone, G.	Gunr	RMA3.698
Bosley, J.W.	L/Sto	172.243
Bower, W.H.	Ord	197.444
Bratt, A.	Ord	179.012
Bray, A.G.	Ord	184.728
Brice, W.G.	Ch/Cook	101.313
Bridges, C.H.	Sto	281.205
Brooks, J.	Gunr	RMA6.082
Brown, B.F.	Sto	281.585
Bruce, R.	Ord	203.114
Brumham, W.	Sh/Std	107.858
Buckley, R.E.	Ord	189.737
Bull, W.J.	Asst/Payr	
Bundy, A.E.	Ord	188.193
Caffery, W.H.	Sto	283.835
Campbell, J.	Pte	Ply9.132
Campbell, J.G.	PO1	126.727
Campbell, J.G.	Sto	281.290
Carnie, G.R.	AB	186.996
Carr, A.	Ord	197.624
Carroll, D.	L/Sto	95.285
Carroll, J.	L/S	153.998
Chambers, J.	AB	184.788
Charman, E.G.	AB	185.814
Chin Ah.	Dom	
Chong Ah.	Dom	
Chow Kai.	Dom	
Chow Yung.	Dom	
Clarke, W.	AB	140.712
Cloke, F.W.	AB	185.806
Coates, G.	Sto	286.360
Cobb, S.H.	AB	189.073
Coe, C.A.	PO1	144.656
Coe, F.E.	Sto	280.733
Cole, H.	Q/Sig	186.663
Colesby, L.V.	AB	183.487
Collis, J.	AB	183.367
Colquhoun, J.	Sto	283.250
Connor, J.	Sto	281.956
Cook, A.G.	AB	179.712
Cookson, R.	PO1	128.769
Coomber, W.H.	Clerk	
Coombes, T.	Sto	108.885
Cornwall, R.	Pte	Po10.201
Cousens, A.T.	Sto	281.183
Cox, H.	Sto	155.252
Cox, R.H.	Sto	290.643
Crack, J.V.	PO1	101.191
Craven, W.H.	PO1	127.688
Cripps, J.J.	Ch/Sto	133.709
Croucher, C.	L/Sto	151.436
Cubitt, A.E.	St/Payr	
Cunningham, H.F.W.	PO2	143.046
Dabner, A.W.	Ch/Sto	129.406

Name	Rating	Number
Danks, C.	Act/ERA	269.617
Dealey, P.E.	PO1	128.969
Dewing, C.	Act/Sergt	Ply6.481
Ditch, W.G.	Act/Ch/Sto	149.805
Dodd, G.W.	L/Sto	280.806
Dorey, F.W.	L/Sto	146.791
Doud, T.	Cooper	164.270
Doyne, H.W.G.	St/Surgn	
Driscoll, M.	Sto	278.683
Duggan, R.	Ch/PO	53.908
Dunn, C.	Sto	281.907
Eaves, H.R.	Band	155.583
Ebel, B.	Sto	283.906
Erridge, C.B.	SBStd	138.162
Evans, H.	Band	177.894
Fairfax, W.	Gunr	RMA6.846
Farrant, C.R.	Pte	Po8.234
2 Farrow, B.R.	Ord	197.608
Fat Ah (1).	Dom	
Faulkner, A.E.	Band	173.303
Ferguson, T.	Q/Sig	150.862
Festing, M.C.	Lieut(RMLI)	
Field, C.J.	Sto	277.897
Finch, S.G.	L/Sto	280.524
Fitzpatrick, W.	AB	174.638
Fon Ah.	Dom	
Fong Ah.	Dom	
Foo Ah.	Dom	
Forbes-Sempill, Hon. L.	Lieut	
Ford, F.	Fl/Engr	
Forward, B.	Ord	197.826
Freshwater, C.H.	AB	178.826
Fry, J.	Pte	Po10.198
Fryer, J.	Pte	Ply8.583
3 Gitsham, W.	AB	184.698
Goddard, C.	L/Cpl	Po7.801
Goodison, A.	Sto	286.358
Gosling, A.O'B.	L/S	157.595
Gotts, R.	Sto	281.525
Gouldthorpe, G.F.	Ord	196.843
Gower, R.A.	Ord	198.312
Grant, F.	Ch/PO	123.553
Green, R.W.	Q/Sig	183.793
Gregory, J.J.	PO1	128.096 K
Haimes, W.	Sto	285.035
Hale, H.	Sto	278.066
Hammond, F.C.	SBStd	129.673
Hannah, T.	AB	151.983
Hardiman, E.W.	Pte	Po5.673
Harris, E.A.	AB	186.371
Harrison, F.	Act/Gunr	
Headland, A.A.	Ch/Sto	146.614
Hearn, T.J.	Sig	191.649
Hele, R.	PO1	108.337
Hing Ah.	Dom	
Hiscock, R.J.	Arm/Crew	340.380
Hjul, C.E.	AB	181.078
Hockin, C.J.	Ord	197.772

NO BAR MEDALS *continued.*

Name	Rating	Number	
Hodges, W.C.	2/SBStd	340.958	
Horton, W.H.	Ch/Arm	116.538	
Hounsome, C.	PO1	119.426	
Howard, J.W.	Sto	280.720	
Hussey, F.	PO1	137.999	
Ixer, S.	Sto	280.726	
James, H.	Yeo/Sig	140.468	
Jasper, E.H.A.	AB	184.531	
Jeff, W.H.	AB	186.807	
Jeffrey, H.	AB	115.834	
Jenkins, W.H.	Sto	292.323	
Johnson, C.S.	Asst/Clerk		
Joiner, J.	AB	184.134	
Jones, E.J.	AB	162.332	
Killick, M.J.	PO2	157.171	
Kington, W.	AB	118.308	
Kirkbright, J.	Sto	289.912	
Kirby, F.H.	AB	183.466	
Kwung Ah	Dom		
Laidler, C.R.	Arm/Crew	340.381	
Lambert, A.	PO1	118.862	
Lamport, R.	Sto	282.005	
Landeryon, W.	Ord	195.872	
Lawrence, F.	Ch/Sto	113.274	
Leahy, T.B.A.	Lieut(RMA)		
Leal, H.	Act/2/Sh/Ck	170.579	
Lee, F.	Sto	281.902	
Lee, H.	Ord	197.748	
Lewis, W.H.	Pte	Ply8.757	
Limpkin, C.	Shpwrt	341.692	
Livingstone, R.	Boy	199.879	
Lockhart, C.	Yeo/Sig	135.868	
Long, E.	Sto	281.858	
Lord, G.	Ord	184.692	
Loy Ah.	Dom		
McAvoy, P.	Gunr	RMA6.758	
McCaul, P.	Act/ERA	269.758	
McCoy, C.	Gunr		
McGinnity, S.	Gunr	RMA5.648	
McVea, H.	Sto	281.442	
Macey, A.S.	AB	184.716	
Mahoney, M.	Sto	287.236	K
Malyon, W.J.	Ch/ERA	114.922	
Mant, E.	Sto	281.913	
Marsh, G.J.	AB	183.125	
Masters, H.S.	Ord	197.968	
Matthews, A.A.	Band	167.053	
Matthews, H.H.	Band	173.305	
Matthews, S.	Ch/Carp/Mte	145.321	
May, G.	Sto	284.486	
Meldrum, E.J.	Ord	198.330	
Meloy, A.R.	Ch/ERA	128.536	
Miller, A.	AB	178.003	
Miller, J.	AB	158.583	
Mitchell, A.	PO2	158.851	
Moore, A.	Gunr	RMA5.776	
Moore, H.	Band	97.935	

Name	Rating	Number	
Morgan, L.W.	PO1	133.240	
Morrison, D.	ERA	269.756	
Mosby, F.	Sto	284.464	
Moy Ah.	Dom		4
Muddiman, A.	Act/ERA	269.575	
Newbury, S.H.	Ord	194.037	
Newman, T.	Pte	Po10.229	
Newman, W.S.	Sto	281.910	
Newton, E.	L/S	155.179	
Nicholson, R.	AB	165.666	
O'Neill, P.J.	Sto	281.648	
Oram, J.	Ord	197.828	
Organ, P.C.	AB	195.625	
Owen, W.	Cpl	Po8.738	
Painter, H.A.	Ord	197.817	
Palmer, G.	Ord	197.816	
Pardon, H.J.	Sh/Cpl	350.073	
Passell, G.T.	Shpwrt	95.616	
Patten, C.	Sig	183.905	
Patterson, R.	Sh/Std	88.475	
Pearce, J.J.	Plmbr	341.293	
Pears, J.	Sto	281.920	
Pemble, E.H.	Ch/PO	128.587	K5
Pepper, F.G.	L/Shpwrt	149.493	
Phillips, E.W.	Ord	197.502	
Pickard, H.	Sto	282.418	
Pike, G.W.	Band	173.725	
Pitcher, E.W.	Pte	Ply8.851	
Powell, J.E.	Surgn		
Pugh, A.H.	AB	164.825	
Quance, E.	2/SBStd	350.377	
Qui Ah.	Dom		
Qui Pin.	Dom		
Ranscombe, G.	Band	340.923	
Ransom, W.	Sto	280.484	
Raymond, J.	Band	132.750	
Raymond, W.J.	Sto	290.823	
Rees, F.	Ch/Sto	129.521	
Reid, W.S.	Asst/Engr		
Reynolds, J.	Pte	Po10.249	
Richards, J.	L/Shpwrt	158.736	
Richardson, W.L.	AB	191.586	
Riley, J.J.	Sto	286.356	
Risdon, J.	Pte	Po10.208	
Rivers, A.S.	Sh/Std/Asst	341.955	
Roberts, C.	L/Sto	127.607	
Roberts, T.	Pte	Po10.237	
Robertson, R.	Ord	193.827	
Robinson, C.	Pte	Ply8.849	
Rowe, J.W.	Sto	151.460	
Runnalls, W.J.	Cook/Mte	166.120	
Russell, J.R.	Sto	353.528	
Russell, S.P.B.	Midn		
Sambells, J.C.	AB	195.871	
San Ah.	Dom		
Scrimshaw, F.A.R.	L/Sto	280.826	
Seabrook, G.	Pte	Po10.199	
Sein Oski.	Carp/Crew		
Selden, W.	Act/Ch/Sto	152.707	

NO BAR MEDALS *continued.*

Shan Foon.	Dom	
Sharman, W.H.	Shpwrt	340.818
Sharp, J.T.	Ord	198.138
Sheehan, T.	PO1	118.087
Sherbrooke, H.G.	Lieut	
Shipperley, G.	Ord	197.508
Sing Ah.	Dom	
Sing Ah.	Pntr	
Sing Yung.	Dom	
Skinner, J.H.	2/SBStd	350.356
Sky, A.	L/Sto	123.920
Smith, D.E.	Clerk	
Smith, R.H.	Ord	197.750
Snell, A.J.M.	Pntr	166.934
Snook, H.	Pte	Po10.233
Soo Ah.	Dom	
Sou Ah.	Dom	
Sowter, J.A.	PO1	130.118
Sponder, F.H.	ERA	153.620
Stay, A.H.	Sto	152.580
Stephens, G.M.	Sh/Cpl	154.744
Stevenson, T.S.	Blksmth	132.452
Stockley, W.	Sto	281.300
Stoney, R.	Sto	282.145
Street, A.F.	L/Sto	175.952
Street, G.	Bosn	
Street, J.T.	Pte	Ply8.854
Studham, W.	AB	152.822
Sumby, G.W.	Sto	276.390
Swan, W.W.	AB	184.993
Symonds, F.W.	AB	159.690
Taylor, F.W.	L/Sig	161.133
Thomas, G.W.	Ord	206.668
Thompson, A.S.	Ord	191.869
Thompson, H.	Ch/Wrtr	136.115
Thorpe, H.B.	Gunr	RMA3.503
Ting Sui.	Dom	
Tripp, A.G.	L/Carp/Crew	116.938
Trout, F.C.	Sh/Std/Asst	341.754
Tuck, E.S.	Surgn	
Tucker, J.	Ord	191.576
Tucker, W.G.	Ord	198.315
Tugwood, J.	Band	173.242
Tuke, J.A.	Comdr	
Twine, W.H.	PO1	123.193
Underhill, F.	Q/Sig	191.443
Upton, W.T.	Sto	286.559
Vine, G.T.	AB	175.307
Wa Kim.	Dom	
Wake, St.A.B.	Midn	
Walker, W.R.	Sto	280.754
Waterman, F.C.	Ord	198.320
Watson, G.F.	Pte	Po8.628
Way Ah.	Dom	
Weaver, G.W.	Pte	Po10.223
Webb, F.	Ord	184.330
Webb, J.W.	Sto	278.607
Wellington, A.	PO1	155.329
Welsh, J.G.	Ch/Band	124.260
Wensley, E.J.	2/SBStd	166.985
West, C.W.	Gunr	RMA7.723
West, E.	Band	148.490
White, E.C.	AB	149.939
White, W.B.	Ord	197.806
Wilkins, G.L.	Gunr	RMA7.905
Wilks, A.	AB	169.891
Williams, P.	Gunr	RMA7.893
Willis, R.J.	Boy	197.504
Wilmer, H.	Band/Cpl	155.650
Wilson, C.E.	MAA	121.044
Wilson, F.	AB	185.929
Wilson, W.W.J.	Arm	168.569
Wise, J.G.E.	L/S	183.472
Wooster, J.T.	Sto	289.657
Wright, C.	Sto	281.891
Wright, W.	Band	340.057
Wright, W.D.	Ord	198.740
Young, W.	Ord	197.517
Yung Ah.	Dom	

Duplicate medals:

Caffery, W.H.	Sto	283.835
Gitsham, W.	AB	184.698
Green, R.W.	Q/Sig	183.793
Hockin, C.J.	Ord	197.772
Killick, M.J.	PO2	157.171
Kwung Ah.	Dom	
Lord, G.	Ord	184.692
Masters, H.S.	Ord	197.968
Richards, J.	L/Shpwrt	158.736
Richardson, W.L.	AB	191.586
Riley, J.J.	Sto	286.356
Street, A.F.	L/Sto	175.952
Street, J.T.	Pte	Ply8.854
Tucker, W.G.	Ord	198.315
Webb, F.	Ord	184.330 *
Webb, J.W.	Sto	278.607
White, W.B.	Ord	197.806
Wilson, F.	AB	185.929

* *Four duplicate medals issued.*

Duplicate medals - without issue no. on roll.

Arthur, J.	Ord	188.175
Bower, W.H.	Ord	197.444
Cox, R.H.	Sto	290.643
Driscoll, M.	Sto	278.683
Freshwater, C.H.	AB	178.826
Gouldthorpe, G.F.	Ord	196.843
Hjul, C.E.	AB	181.078
Jeff, W.H.	AB	186.807
Livingstone, R.	Boy	199.879
Miller, A.	AB	178.003
Newbury, S.H.	Ord	194.037
Raymond, W.J.	Sto	290.823

NO BAR MEDALS *continued.*

Duplicate medals - without issue no. on roll continued:

Robertson, R.	Ord	193.827
Runnalls, W.J.	Cook/Mte	166.120
Shipperley, G.	Ord	197.508
Studham, W.	AB	152.822
Thomas, G.W.	Ord	206.668
Watson, G.F.	Pte	Po8.628
Willis, R.J.	Boy	197.504

Returned medals:

Ahern, M.	Sto	289.833
Barker, W.T.	AB	186.701
Beck, J.F.	Ord	184.710
Bogle, R.	Sto	286.611
Brown, W.	Gunr	RMA6.484
Dufner, F.	Sto	291.746
Lawson, G.E.	Gunr	RMA7.263
Millington, H.E.	Ord	181.989
Neave, J.C.	AB	181.799
Owen, W.	Sto	280.541
Stevens, W.H.	PO2	147.400
Williamson, J.C.	AB	186.413 [6]

H.M.S. DAPHNE.

H.M.S. Daphne was a Sloop of 1,140 tons and 195 x 28 feet. Her armament consisted of 8 x 5 in guns. The vessel was built in Sheerness Dock Yard and launched on 29th May 1888. She was sold in February 1904.

Bars	*Total*	*Returned*	*Entitled*
None	*141*	*5*	*136*
	141	*5*	*136*

NO BAR MEDALS.

Name	Rank	Number
Adams, A.H.	Pte	Ch8.052
Agnew, D.	Lieut	
Allen, A.E.	Ch/Sto	143.297
Attrill, E.A.	Pte	Po8.958
Bacon, F.	AB	145.010
Bacon, W.T.	Ch/Carp/Mte	169.203
Bailey, A.R.	AB	198.829
Ball, F.J.	Sh/Cpl	120.901
Barron, H.C.	Arm/Mte	340.317
Battye, T.	ERA	268.688
Bennett, W.	2/SBStd	150.451
Bicker, W.J.	Sto	155.769
Bird, W.A.	AB	191.608
Blake, A.	PO1	153.991
Bontoft, J.F.	Ord	193.398
Borrow, J.J.	AB	155.675
Botten, T.	2/Yeo/Sig	169.118
Bourne, B.G.	Arm/Crew	341.763
Bowes, J.	AB	178.362
Boyle, W.H.	Lieut	
Bunce, B.R.	Ord	198.617
Choy Kong.	Dom	
Chup Ah.	Dom	
Clarkson, S.J.	AB	195.250
Clay, H.P.	Pte	Ch9.030
Codd, T.W.	Act/ERA	269.908
Coe, A.G.	AB	180.967
Cook, W.J.	L/S	168.159
Coysh, C.W.	AB	192.622
Crees, F.	L/Sto	152.727
Davis, W.J.	Ch/Sto	137.778
Denmark, J.	Sto	279.069
Dobson, C.	Sto	276.458
Donaldson, T.	Ord	191.925
Doy, W.A.	Pte	Ch4.221
Earnest, W.C.	3/Wrtr	341.314
Ellis, C.	AB	198.640
Ellison, A.E.	AB	180.205
Elmes, F.H.	Pte	Ply8.672
Ferris, R.	Sail/Mte	173.430
Fitzgerald, W.	L/S	126.678
Foster, R.	L/Sto	130.099
Foy, W.	Sergt	Ply4.141
Furnandez, T.	Sto	286.648
Gains, G.R.	AB	187.519
Gale, W.	AB	183.196
Gander, E.A.	AB	198.304
George, S.E.	Sto	285.646
Gin Ah.	Dom	
Ginnare, M.	Pte	Ch9.120
Godfrey, H.R.	Lieut	
Godwin, B.	PO2	162.537
Gooch, S.	Sto	286.650
Goulding, G.	Sto	153.465
Griffiths, P.J.	Asst/Engr	
Hall, E.	AB	198.624
Halsey, H.	AB	168.295
Hambrook, A.J.	Ord	193.856
Harding, J.J.	AB	181.661
Harris, G.	PO2	126.714
Harrison, A.J.	AB	191.642
Harrison, H.	AB	174.177
Harwood, W.	Sto	278.581
Hatch, F.J.	L/Sig	156.834
Hawton, A.	L/Shpwrt	341.529
Hayward, G.T.	Sto	162.038
Head, E.A.W.	Ch/Engr	
Hellings, T.	L/Sto	153.092
Hooper, I.	Sto	278.005
Horrigan, M.	Gunr	
Howe, J.D.J.	PO1	163.145
Inman, J.	Pte	Ch9.053
Jenner, A.E.	AB	179.976
Johns, S.	Shpwrt	343.051
Johnson, A.	Ord	197.644
Johnston, T.	AB	179.953
Keene, G.A.	AB	170.655
Knee, H.	AB	177.250
Kow Ah.	Dom	
Lawson, W.	Sig	193.406
Leyland, J.	PO1	161.368
Locock, J.	AB	190.250
McDonald, G.	AB	184.059
McKie, H.	AB	107.334

NO BAR MEDALS *continued.*

Maddock, J.T.	AB	160.249
Maloney, M.	Pte	Ch8.984
Mann, H.	AB	177.698
Markey, J.	Sto	286.481
Matthews, H.	AB	198.298
Miller, A.E.	Sto	286.730
Moss, W.	Sto	277.977
Mulley, R.J.	Pilot	
Neal, F.	PO2	158.866
Neilson, J.	L/Sto	276.011
Neve, G.H.	AB	191.207
Nevin, P.	Sto	174.331
O'Riordan, J.	AB	155.056
Ommanney, H.N.	Act/Payr	
Ospreay, P.G.	AB	198.306
Outred, W.W.	AB	198.643
Parfitt, G.	Pte	Ch6.448
Partridge, T.	Q/Sig	189.739
Paul, G.	Blksmth	340.369
Renyard, E.	AB	185.712
Richardson, M.	AB	173.025
Richardson, T.	Pntr	188.256
Riches, R.J.	L/S	173.426
Roberts, F.H.J.	Sh/Std	164.121
Rushforth, J.C.	AB	180.440
Seal, W.	AB	184.381
Shield, F.	Carp/Crew	342.267
Sibbald, W.	Sto	277.920
Smith, O.	Sto	290.949
Starkey, J.	AB	178.551
Stokes, C.E.	Ch/Sto	132.341
Taylor, G.	Pte	Ch8.990
Triggs, W.G.	PO1	163.287
Trythall, W.R.	Surgn	
Venn, J.H.	Ch/PO	111.817
Wallis, G.M.	ERA	268.433
Walton, W.	Pte	Ch1.763
Warburton, J.	ERA	268.167
Ward, G.W.	AB	179.873
Ware, E.A.	Pte	Ch7.904
Waugh Ah.	Dom	
West, R.	Sto	286.675
Westley, F.	AB	162.956
Whittaker, J.	Ord	197.553
White, S.J.	Sto	286.664
Willcox, H.J.L.W.H.	Lieut	
Winnington-Ingram, C.W.	Comdr	
Winyard, J.W.	PO1	161.420
Woodward, A.J.	L/S	139.730
Yoners, G.	Pte	Ch2.219
Young, C.E.	2/Sh/Cook	163.685
Yow Ah.	Dom	

Duplicate medals:

Blake, A.	PO1	153.991
Harding, J.J.	AB	181.661
Jenner, A.E.	AB	179.976 *
McDonald, G.	AB	184.059
Maloney, M.	Pte	Ch8.984
Partridge, T.	Q/Sig	189.739
Paul, G.	Blksmth	340.369
Ward, G.W.	AB	179.873
White, S.J.	Sto	286.664

* *Two duplicate medals issued.*

Returned medals:

Jackson, H.P.	AB	179.783
Phillips, W.	Pte	Po10.252
Somerville, H.C.	Lieut	
Vincent, D.	Pte	Ch6.042
Wilkins, H.C.	Sto	277.905

H.M.S. DIDO.

H.M.S. Dido was a 2nd class Cruiser of 5,600 tons and 350 x 54 feet. Her armament consisted of 5 x 6 in, 6 x 4.7 in and 9 x 12 pdr guns. The vessel was built by The London & Glasgow Co. and launched on 20th March 1896. She became a Depot ship in 1913 and was sold on 16th December 1926 to May & Butcher at Maldon.

Bars	*Total*	*Returned*	*Entitled*
None	*466*	*6*	*460*
	466	*6*	*460*

Notes:

Missing detail in the medal roll is indicated by the use of brackets; the spaces inside the brackets are not intended to indicate the exact amount of missing detail.

K - Medal presented by H.M. The King on 8th March 1902.

1 - Roll states, "Personal Appn. for dup 28/8/12. Original pawned."

NO BAR MEDALS.

Name	Rank	Number	
Aglionby, C.E.	Midn		
Allen, G.W.	Ord	196.567	
Allen, J.	Pte	(Ch .)	
Anderson, C.	Pntr	163.585	
Anderson, H.	Ord	206.999	
Apsey, J.C.	L/S	176.290	
Archer, W.E.	Ord	196.968	
Arding, T.	AB	188.145	
Arthur, J.	Sto	286.653	K
Atkins, W.J.	L/Shpwrt	165.182	
Atkinson, T.	Ch/Sto	113.126	
Attridge, F.	Ord	185.872	
Ault, J.	AB	191.919	
Ayres, W.F.	PO1	131.382	
Bain, W.	Sto	287.412	
Banks, W.G.	Ord	195.883	
Barham, E.A.	L/Sto	276.074	
Barker, A.	ERA	268.696	
Barker, W.	Pte	Ch6.281	
Barlow, W.L.	AB	187.724	
Barrow, B.W.	Sub Lieut		
Barry, T.F.	Act/Carp		
Bassindale, A.	Sto	286.643	
Bastock, C.	Sto	287.626	
Bate, H.	Pte	Ch6.850	
Bates, E.	AB	179.109	
Bayford, W.F.	Sto	276.072	
Beadell, A.E.	Ord	195.820	
Beck, W.J.	AB	182.939	
Beckett, T.B.	AB	190.170	
Bell, C.F.	Pte	Ch6.521	
Bennett, A.W.	Ord	196.566	
Birch, E.J.	Midn		
Bird, C.J.	Pte	Ch8.675	
Birt, F.J.	Sto	278.646	
Blackburn, F.B.	Sto	286.066	
Blackburn, F.W.	Pte	Ch1.907	
Blatherwick, G.	Midn		
Bloomfield, H.	L/Sto	277.094	
Boon, W.	Pte	Ch9.334	
Bostock, F.H.	Midn		
Bowden, W.	Sto	287.628	
Brabazon, M.	Sto	285.967	
Bray, E.E.	St/Surgn		
Brett, J.W.	AB	189.984	
Bristow, G.A.	Ord	197.622	
Bristow, J.	Pte	Ch10.483	
Brock, A.E.R.	Gunr		
Brogan, J. *alias* D. Breslin.	Sto	287.038	
Brooker, F.	Ord	202.769	
Brown, J.E.	Ord	190.626	
Brown, R.	AB	163.142	
Bryant, A.A.	AB	196.260	
Buchanan, W.J.	Pte	Ch2.694	
Buckley, W.	Sto	289.905	
Burden, H.W.	Boy	199.511	
Burgess, R.E.	L/Sto	276.465	
Burr, G.F.W.	Ord	192.730	
Busby, W.J.	AB	142.099	

NO BAR MEDALS *continued.*

Busuttil, L.	Cooper	141.789
Butcher, W.	L/Sto	147.724
Callen, P.W.O.	Ord	195.557
Cameron, R.C.	AB	191.903
Cameron, W.	Ord	191.929
Candy, E.W.	AB	196.254
Cannon, E.	Ord	196.579
Carter, W.	Ord	196.194
Caseley, A.	Ord	207.354
Castle, F.C.	Ord	197.070
Chamberlain, T.E.	Pte	Ch9.367
Chang Ah.	Dom	
Chapman, J.H.	Gunr	
Chee Teck.	Dom	
Chi Hon.	Dom	
Chivers, W.S.B.	Ord	207.414
Chong Lee.	Dom	
Christie, A.	L/Sto	137.422
Clack, W.	Q/Sig	188.368
Clackett, W.B.	Sto	175.961
Clarke, P.T.	Ord	190.440
Clarke, W.H.	Pte	Ch5.979
Cleveland, M.W.	AB	197.155
Clift, T.	Pte	Ch7.538
Clinch, E.H.	Sh/Std	123.659
Cloves, W.T.	L/S	173.990
Cobble, W.E.	L/Sto	172.262
Coll, E.	Ord	207.000
Collings, A.J.	Sto	280.156
Collingwood, C.C.	PO1	147.379
Colquhoun, W.G.	Asst/Engr	
Connell, R.	Sto	282.810
Connelly, F.	AB	191.912
Consall, F.	Ord	193.772
Conway, J.R.	Pte	Ch9.177
Cook, E.	Pte	Ch9.323
Cook, G.	L/Sto	123.327
Cookson, E.C.	Midn	
Corksley, H.G.	Arm/Crew	163.462
Cornwall, S.	AB	195.961
Cowan, R.	Sto	285.962
Cowan, W.	Ord	200.326
Cowin, W.	AB	197.125
Cowley, J.	AB	190.567
Cowper, J.F.	Sto	286.056
Creagh-Osborne, F.O.	Lieut	
Crosbie, F.	Ord	197.050
Cundall, J.L.	Ord	196.469
Curteis, W.J.	PO1	160.810
Daly, J.F.	PO2	153.360
Dann, W.	AB	148.106
Davie, A.T.	AB	194.555
Davies, S.M.	PO1	119.460
Davis, F.	AB	189.453
Day, J.H.J.	AB	171.506
Deackes, G.S.	Dom	356.001

Deasy, D.	Sto	285.323
Desmond, D.	PO2	102.736
Devlin, J.T.	AB	196.278
Devoil, S.E.	Pte	Ch3.719
Dicks, F.	Sto	291.339
Dickson, R.	Ord	191.922
Ditchman, A.E.	Ord	195.831
Donoghue, G.	Ord	196.235
Donovan, T.	Sh/Cpl	141.964
Dooling, J.	AB	165.154
Dorman, J.	ERA	268.459
Drane, A.J.	AB	195.549
Drury, F.	Pte	Ch8.346
Dudley, W.J.	Sto	292.283
Duffell, A.E.	PO2	162.256
Duffield, A.B.	AB	192.101
Dunn, W.J.	Pte	Ch8.703
Eaman, A.E.	Ord	192.106
Earle, T.H.	Midn	
Edwards, A.F.	Ord	196.249
Elliott, P.	AB	186.911
England, G.	Sto	287.645
English, T.	Ord	191.500
Epworth, H.J.	AB	192.107
Erskine, S.E.	Comdr	
Fabian, S.P.	AB	162.838
Farrow, M.	Sto	282.073
Featherstone, J.	Pte	Ch3.363
Ferguson, A.	Sto	279.531
Ferrer, P.H.	Ord	201.902
Fey, J.	Ord	207.018
Fill, G.	Sto	152.422
Fletcher, J.	AB	194.004
Forster, F.J.	L/S	182.600
Fowler, H.	Ord	199.508
Fowler, M.T.B.	Asst/Payr	
Fowler, S.	Sto	286.059
Francis, R.R.	AB	196.427
Friend, W.J.	AB	166.871
Frost, H.A.	AB	180.604
Fulton, D.H.	Ord	191.923
Fun Ah.	Dom	
Gall, C.	Ord	193.756
Gallon, W.	PO2	182.146
Gant, W.J.	AB	164.312
Gardener, G.	Sto	149.213
Gaskin, P.G.	L/S	166.544
Geary, M.	Pte	Ch5.400
Gibson, F.J.B.	Midn	
Gillon, J.	Ord	195.508
Giltrap, W.G.	AB	181.595
Ginn, W.	Q/Sig	192.117
Glanville, S.	PO1	144.214
Glenister, E.	Ord	197.147
Goddard, C.J.	PO2	174.695
Goggin, M.	Ord	189.557
Gommer, D.	Ch/ERA	122.209
Goodard, L.G.	Ord	207.418
Goodchild, G.F.	Sto	277.937

NO BAR MEDALS *continued.*

Gordon, T.	AB	196.482
Gorey, W.J.	Sto	293.337
Govier, R.C.	PO1	134.194
Gow, H.J.	Act/ERA	269.026
Graley, T.J.	AB	195.715
Gran, J.C.	Ord	195.520
Gravelling, A.	AB	174.732
Green, S.J.	Sto	292.356
Greening, D.C.	L/Sergt	Po6.722
Gregory, C.E.	Pte	Ch6.447
Gregory, F.	ERA	268.377
Gregory, H.	AB	181.624
Griffen, E.	Ord	195.874
Griffiths, G.	Ord	196.212
Gruitt, J.	Ch/Sto	139.686
Guy, K.A.F.	Midn	
Guymer, D.H.	Pte	Ch9.791
Hales, A.	L/Sto	279.016
Hall, W.A.	Ord	207.425
Hammond, G.H.	L/Sto	170.062
Harden, F.B.	AB	180.754
Harding, F.C.	AB	195.515
Harley, A.	AB	184.176
Hartley, J.	Sto	286.367
Harvey, J.	Sto	160.678
Harvey, W.	AB	193.783
Haselton, G.J.	Ch/Sto	146.862
Havard, T.	Pte	Ch5.879
Haynes, W.J.	Sto	292.349
Henderson, A.	Arm	154.163
Hicks, J.	SBStd	133.062
Higham, W.	Ord	196.248
Hignett, T.J.	Sto	286.075
Hill, S.A.G.	Midn	
Hills, H.J.	AB	174.180
Hitchen, W.	AB	192.115
Hobbs, A.H.	Ord	197.144
Hodges, N.D.	Lieut	
Holland, F.	AB	199.214
Holland, W.	Sto	289.891
Holmes, A.	AB	192.105
Holmes, J.W.	Pte	Ch9.273
Hooker, R.W.	Pte	Ch8.959
Hooper, W.	AB	163.264
Horner, W.H.	Ord	191.524
Horton, A.E.	Pte	Ch8.837
Houghton, T.	Yeo/Sig	143.071
Howard, W.E.	Sto	171.074
Hoy, C.W.	Sto	286.083
Hughes, H.J.	AB	171.044
Hughes, W.	ERA	164.216
Humby, W.P.	Ord	192.003
Hume, I.W.	Ch/Sto	141.118
Hunt, H.	Ord	197.934
Huntley, E.W.	Ord	195.556
Hurren, J.	AB	187.010
Hurst, J.E.	AB	190.974
Hurt, G.W.	AB	196.582
Inman, E.T.	Lieut	
Iredale, C.	AB	158.615
Jackson, A.	Pte	Ch8.481
Jackson, F.	Arm	340.667
Jackson, Rev. F.H.	Chaplain & N. Instr	
James, F.	Pte	Ch7.651
James, H.H.	Sto	279.151
Jay, A.E.	3/Wrtr	340.475
Jeffrey, H.J.	Sto	286.062
Jeffreys, L.	Pte	Ch8.702
Jenkins, E.	AB	194.609
Jennings, A.W.	AB	165.648
Johnson, C.	Sto	286.074
Jury, F.T.	AB	195.481
Keeyung Ah.	Dom	
Kendrick, E.	Ord	196.220
Kent, F.H.	Sh/Std/Asst	340.542
Kincaid, R.	Sto	285.966
King, R.S.	ERA	158.012
Kirby, W.J.	Sail/Mte	107.791
Knight, A.P.	Pte	Ch6.013
Knights, J.	AB	196.253
Knott, H.	AB	180.727
Lambert, C.P.	L/Sto	163.530
Lambert, T.G.	Sto	285.963
Lambert, W.W.	Ord	190.154
Langham, W.	AB	170.682
Langley, T.E.	Ch/Sto	127.888
Lawton, E.	Sto	291.610
Leaney, G.	Pte	Ch9.329
Leary, P.	Sto	293.649
Ledwith, M.	Sto	293.700
Leeson, W.G.	Sergt	Ch3.292
Legate, J.	Engr	
Legg, H.	Sto	286.081 K
Leishman, J.	Sto	286.077
Leong Ah.	Dom	
Lewis, H.T.	Pte	Ch8.680
Lindsay, F.W.	Sto	152.715
Linton, R.J.	Sto	286.068
Lloyd, W.	Boy	199.965
Long, G.A.	Ch/Sto	126.380
Lord, T.H.	Ch/PO	118.779
Lowry, W.	PO1	158.610
Luk Ah.	Dom	
Lumbard, J.	Pte	Ch7.282
McEwen, J.	Ord	191.910
McGuinness, W.	Boy	200.043
McIntosh, W.	Ord	196.197
MacKay, A.	L/Cpl	Ch5.448
McKay, D.	AB	196.426
McKinnon, J.M.	Sto	284.965
MacKinnon, L.D.I.	Midn	
McLean, G.	L/S	169.856
McLean, J.	Sto	285.134
McMullin, C.H.	Lieut	
McNile, H.C.	Act/ERA	269.836

NO BAR MEDALS *continued.*

Name	Rating	Number
McPhee, J.R.	AB	191.909
Magee, C.F.N.	AB	158.334
Mahon, J.	Ord	193.785
Mahoney, C.	Sto	163.575
Manley, G.E.D.	Lieut(RMLI)	
Mansell, G.	Cook/Mte	354.737
Martin, E.A.	PO2	164.702
Mason, J.E.	Sto	282.786
Matthews, A.	AB	105.849
Matthews, A.	Sto	293.672
Matthews, E.H.	AB	179.224
Matthews, T.J.	Ord	194.164
Maxted, G.F.	AB	188.343
May, A.F.	PO1	156.791
May, G.	PO2	150.795
Miller, S.	Ord	192.123
Miller, W.J.	Ord	194.572
Mills, J.H.	PO1	123.716
Milton, H.C.	Arm/Crew	341.454
Mitchell, A.E.	Sto	289.904
Mitchell, T.	AB	148.371
Morgan, E.K.	Ord	197.117
Morgans, A.J.	2/SBStd	350.376
Morris, R.A.	L/S	148.109
Mott, T.J.	AB	196.430
Mulcahy, B.	Ord	197.309
Mullins, C.J.	Pte	Ch10.185
Nash, H.	Act/Ch/Sto	154.256
Newman, W.	AB	189.538
Nicholls, C.W.H.	L/Sig	159.163
Norman, A.H.	Midn	
Norris, H.H.	Pte	Ch8.694
Norris, J.	L/Sto	276.094
Norster, J.G.	Ch/PO	87.720
Northcote, E.A.	Ch/Sto	100.224
Nudd, C.	Ord	201.621
O'Malley, E.D.J.	Surgn	
Oakes, W.B.	AB	193.090
Orchard, J.	Sto	170.472
Osborne, J.W.	Ord	195.478
Oseman, W.E.	L/Sto	172.879
Palfrey, W.H.	Carp/Mte	113.586
Palmer, W.H.	Pte	Po9.091
Parsons, W.G.	AB	193.740
Patterson, A.W.	PO1	140.338
Paveley, J.H.	Ord	195.532
Pay, J.N.	PO1	140.702
Peacock, J.R.	AB	192.111
Pennington, F.	Ord	190.929
Pert, A.	Sto	285.964
Phillips, E.	Dom	92.940
Phillips, G.T.	Carp	
Ping Ah (1).	Dom	
Ping Ah (11).	Dom	
Pooley, E.	Ord	194.557
Poulson, T.	AB	195.460
Pratt, A.	Ord	193.496
Preston, H.	Ord	194.560
Priddice, W.W.	Sto	294.171
Pullen, U.	PO1	135.079
Quirk, D.H.	Sto	(.)
Rawlingson, F.E.	Ord	207.002
Rayner, A.A.	Ord	196.193
Reid, W.	AB	181.028
Reynolds, H.	Pte	Po8.128
Richardson, T.	AB	191.918
Rimer, A.J.	Ord	196.956
Ring, J.	Ord	188.307
Roberts, H.	Pte	Ch5.187
Roberts, W.J.	Ord	195.394
Robertson, A.	Musn	355.152
Rogers, E.	Boy	199.507
Rogers, S.P.	Sto	285.835
Rooke, W.G.	Ord	199.648
Rose, W.	L/S	178.322
Rowe, C.	Sergt	Ch1.837
Russell, W.F.	AB	166.302 1
Salmon, J.	AB	156.087
Sanderson, W.	Sto	286.057
Sanson, F.	Sto	293.540
Saul, G.W.	Dom	358.071
Saunders, A.	Pte	Ch9.139
Saville, C.T.	Cpl	Ch9.885
Savin, W.	PO1	151.971
Sawyer, A.E.	Boy	199.492
Scott, W.H.	Pte	Ch3.809
Scott, W.R.	Gunr	
Seaman, T.	Payr	
Setterfield, F.W.	Sto	286.055
Shadwell, H.	Ord	193.763
Sharp, T.	Shpwrt	163.647
Sharp, W.H.	Boy	199.566
Shea, D.	Sto	285.339 K
Shead, T.H.	Boy	199.473
Sheard, R.	AB	195.569
Shelvey, H.J.	AB	149.408
Shoesmith, W.	AB	179.080
Short, W.E.	Ch/PO	135.776
Simmonds, H.	L/Sto	276.070
Simmonds, H.W.	Carp/Crew	342.063
Simons, W.	AB	169.825
Skinkfield, C.W.	Carp/Mte	170.072
Smallwood, D.J.	Boy	199.858
Smith, F.H.	Sto	276.882
Smith, G.A.	AB	192.591
Smith, G.A.	Act/ERA	269.558
Somerville, J.	Sto	281.081
Spillett, G.	AB	158.579
Spry, F.M.D.	Ch/Engr	
Stanley, R.L.	Dom	356.784
Stapleton, J.W.	Sto	286.061
Stevens, P.R.	Midn	
Stewart, A.	AB	191.916
Stone, W.	Carp/Crew	342.059
Stoneman, H.C.	Carp/Mte	145.536
Stubbs, A.J.	2/Yeo/Sig	164.840

NO BAR MEDALS *continued.*

Sturvey, F.	Pte	Ch8.686
Sudbury, G.	AB	138.202
Summers, H.	Carp/Crew	340.061
Summers, J.D.	AB	195.513
Surridge, A.J.	AB	156.276
Sutherland, H.	AB	164.546
Symonds, G.L.	L/Sig	148.224
Tappenden, E.H.	Sto	167.264
Thrower, W.	Sto	285.958
Tillard, P.F.	Capt	
Tindall, S.G.	Bugler	Ch8.912
Tinnock, E.	AB	192.110
Tinsley, T.E.	Pte	Ch8.570
Tristram, H.B.	AB	161.104
Turner, E.H.	Ord	195.847
Turner, H.	Sto	293.608
Turner, P.	Shpwrt	342.478
Venables, C.A.	AB	142.823
Vercoe, W.G.	Dom	353.432
Walker, A.G.	L/S	166.124
Walker, P.L.	Q/Sig	192.511
Walsh, W.H.	MAA	124.616
Warburton, T.	Ord	198.134
Ward, F.	Sto	293.699
Ward, G.A.C.	Lieut	
Waterman, A.	Sto	281.948
Watson, W.	Sto	286.084
Watts, G.	Sto	293.595
Webling, G.	Pte	Ch9.348
Weir, W.	AB	179.445
West, G.	Sto	147.152
West, J.	AB	196.279
White, J.	PO1	135.686
White, J.A.	AB	196.281
Whitfield, H.G.	Sto	293.607
Wicks, F.C.	Ord	194.554
Wild, W.F.	Pte	Ch6.581
Wilkinson, J.	Ord	192.120
Willcock, W.R.	Cpl	Po8.585
Williams, J.J.	Sto	292.284
Williamson, C.H.	Sto	286.856
Willis, T.	AB	160.183
Wilson, C.H.	Sh/Cpl	350.017
Wilson, G.T.	Sto	285.965
Wilson, J.	L/S	124.866
Winter, S.	L/S	156.296
Wood, G.	Pte	Ch8.563
Wrigglesworth, T.J.	AB	196.256
Wright, G.C.	Ord	196.241
Wright, G.F.	PO2	180.113
Wright, H.	Ord	199.499
Young, G.R.	Ord	195.943
Young, J.	AB	195.526
Yu Ching.	Dom	
Yuen Lum.	Dom	

Duplicate medals:

Allen, G.W.	Ord	196.567
Barker, A.	ERA	268.696
Barrow, B.W.	Sub Lieut	
Birch, E.J.	Midn	
Birt, F.J.	Sto	278.646
Bloomfield, H.	L/Sto	277.094
Brooker, F.	Ord	202.769
Burden, H.W.	Boy	199.511 *
Clack, W.	Q/Sig	188.368
Corksley, H.G.	Arm/Crew	163.462
Cowley, J.	AB	190.567
Dickson, R.	Ord	191.922
Dooling, J.	AB	165.154
Eaman, A.E.	Ord	192.106
English, T.	Ord	191.500
Farrow, M.	Sto	282.073
Gillon, J.	Ord	195.508
Gruitt, J.	Ch/Sto	139.686
Hammond, G.H.	L/Sto	170.062
Iredale, C.	AB	158.615
Kincaid, R.	Sto	285.966
MacKinnon, L.D.I.	Midn	
McLean, G.	L/S	169.856
Matthews, A.	Sto	293.672
May, G.	PO2	150.795
Summers, J.D.	AB	195.513
Watson, W.	Sto	286.084
Williams, J.J.	Sto	292.284

* *Two duplicate medals issued*

Returned medals:

Braybrook, A.	AB	195.530
Clarke, I.A.	Blksmth	340.089
Friday, F.F.	Plmbr/Mte	341.771
Gray, C.	Ord	191.243
Weatherley, E.J.	PO1	112.676
West, T.	Pte	Ch5.562

H.M.S. ENDYMION.

H.M.S. Endymion was a 1st class Cruiser of 7,350 tons and 360 x 60 feet. Her armament consisted of 2 x 9.2 in, 10 x 6 in and 12 x 6 pdr guns. The vessel was built by Earl and launched on 22nd July 1891. She was sold on 16th March 1920 to Evans at Cardiff.

Bars	*Total*	*Returned*	*Entitled*
TF & RP	*25*	*0*	*25*
TF	*10*	*0*	*10*
RP	*291*	*11*	*280*
None	*296*	*8*	*288*
	622	*19*	*603*

Notes:

Missing detail in the medal roll is indicated by the use of brackets; the spaces inside the brackets are not intended to indicate the exact amount of missing detail.

K - Medal presented by H.M. The King on 8th March 1902.

1 - Roll states, "Medal on stock 5/10/45, 'found'."

2 - Roll states, "Run - Restored under AMA691/15. Sent to party, 01/16."

3 - Roll states, "Not entitled to clasp 3, detached."

Bars: TAKU FORTS, RELIEF OF PEKIN.

	Baines, W.R.	Sto	289.650
	Brett, I.J.	PO1	167.834
	Christie, J.	Sto	287.577
	Collins, W.	PO2	139.352
	Crossland, E.	AB	162.268
	Dennett, J.W.	PO1	158.466
	Dering, N.R.	AB	145.549
	Filmore, J.	AB	171.121
	Fletcher, F.C.	Sto	286.119
	Hart, M.S.	AB	177.709
	Hayes, T.	PO1	95.266
	Heritage, H.	Ch/Sto	129.029
	Hudson, J.W.	Sto	289.637
	Hulbert, A.R.	Lieut	
	Jacka, W.E.	Sto	289.466
	Jackson, W.A.	Sto	169.252
	Jacob, F.W.	AB	187.481
	Jeffery, R.	PO1	110.627
	Miller, F.D.	L/S	158.209
	Mills, W.	PO2	166.138
	Ransom, J.G.	PO1	155.151
	Savage, G.J.	AB	144.231
	Slater, J.	AB	108.429
	Swanston, J.	3/Wrtr	343.356
	Wiltshire, W.J.W.	Sh/Cpl	149.337

Duplicate medals:

Hudson, J.W.	Sto	289.637
Miller, F.D.	L/S	158.209

Bar: TAKU FORTS.

	Bartlett, E.C.	AB	163.394
	Briggs, H.G.	Midn	
	Cain, B.	PO2	160.265
	Chadwick, F.	AB	165.757
K	Evans, J.	Sto	281.591
	Green, W.C.	L/S	160.933
	Meerin, W.	AB	160.692
	Rose, C.	PO2	160.886
	Wiley, R.C.	2/Yeo/Sig	124.719
	Wyatt, E.J.	AB	171.606

H.M.S. ENDYMION.

Bar: RELIEF OF PEKIN.

Name	Rating	Number	
Adams, D.	Sto	289.648	
Adkins, C.A.	AB	194.098	
Akehurst, E.J.	PO1	123.194	
Arnold, A.W.	Pte	Po9.560	
Ash, F.T.	Pte	Po8.530	
Austin, J.T.	Pte	Po8.718	
Avent, W.S.	AB	197.136	
Bailey, J.	PO1	149.657	
Baker, C.W.G.	Cpl	Po7.718	
Baldock, W.	AB	156.091	
Banfield, A.	L/S	160.890	
Barlow, A.W.	AB	184.170	
Barnard, G.	Sto	284.789	
Barrett, F.	Ord	190.190	
Bartlett, T.C.	Pte	Po7.101	
Barton, R.	Pte	Po9.573	
Batchelder, J.S.	Sto	135.609	
Bell, J.G.	Sergt	Po6.091	
Billett, J.W.	AB	148.885	
Bleach, R.H.	Ord	200.787	
Boothby, W.O.	Comdr		
Bowhey, A.H.	Ord	192.846	
Boxwell, F.G.	AB	188.877	
Bradley, J.L.	L/Cpl	Po8.943	
Braithwaite, L.W.	Sub Lieut		
Brander, J.A.	Ord	192.870	
Briard, F.W.	AB	184.604	
Bristow, J.A.	Pte	Po9.571	
Brooker, H.	Ord	194.393	
Brownrigg, H.J.S.	Midn		
Buck, P.	Sto	276.722	
Buckley, J.	AB	189.357	
Burgess, F.	Ord	197.093	
Burrows, W.J.	Ord	194.983	
Butt, J.	Ord	192.173	
Buttonshaw, H.F.	SBStd	140.886	
Buzzacott, R.W.	AB	157.937	
Callaghan, G.A.	Capt		
Carr, R.	AB	162.953	
Carraher, M.	AB	192.135	
Carter, A.J.	PO2	167.872	
Cartwright, W.A.	Pte	Po8.806	
Catchpole, J.	AB	188.962	
Cater, H.	AB	168.391	
Cavan, T.	AB	193.209	
Chandler, W.	Pte	Ch9.131	
Chapman, F.J.	Pte	Po9.563	
Charles, G.W.	PO1	129.795	
Charlo, H.	PO1	152.172	
Cheeseman, A.	L/Sto	169.050	
Chesnutt, T.	Ord	196.447	
Clancy, M.	AB	144.284	
Clark, W.	Sto	280.189	
Clarke, J.C.	AB	175.327	
Cole, G.	Ord	190.138	
Coleman, W.	Sto	287.549	
Colomb, H.W.	Lieut		
Combs, J.	2/Yeo/Sig	155.628	
Connolly, A.	AB	144.161	
Constable, J.W.D.	Bugler	Po8.688	
Conway, C.E.	Ch/PO	112.358	
Cowell, R.A.	PO2	151.057	
Cox, W.H.	Sto	289.667	
Craggs, E.E.	Arm/Crew	117.789	
Crow, A.G.	AB	171.119	
Curtis, J.E.	Ord	191.750	
Davey, A.C.	PO1	164.380	
Day, G.	Pte	Po8.760	
Day, J.	Sto	280.338	
Denyer, R.	Sto	287.519	1
Dickinson, J.H.	PO2	165.054	
Doig, R.O.M.	Capt(RMLI)		
Dryman, A.	Pte	Po9.572	
Duff, W.	Sto	281.606	
Dummer, S.	AB	164.345	
Ealey, J.	Ord	183.655	
Eastman, G.	Pte	Po8.976	
Edgington, C.	Ord	195.230	
Edwards, G.J.E.	Pte	Po8.145	
Ewens, S.	Pte	Po9.068	
Facey, A.J.	Sto	158.342	
Flack, H.H.	Ord	195.635	
Flory, W.	AB	147.621	
Fluellen, H.W.	Ord	192.781	
Ford, H.	PO1	118.530	
Ford, W.J.	Ord	197.743	
Francis, A.G.	AB	185.677	
Frith, E.O.	PO1	166.037	
Galliford, J.T.	L/Sergt	Ch6.793	K
Gaskin, R.H.	Yeo/Sig	151.559	
Gill, R.P.J.	Ord	190.184	
Gill, S.	Pte	Po9.554	
Golding, W.H.	AB	178.736	
Goodman, F.	Carp/Mte	163.611	
Goubert, E.J.	L/S	162.824	
Gould, J.	Sto	175.972	
Govin, J.	Pte	Po2.311	
Grapham, W.A.	Ord	195.637	
Graves, W.J.H.	Sto	283.017	
Gray, A.	L/Sto	276.140	
Green, A.	Sto	167.191	
Griffiths, H.G.	Ord	190.613	
Grose, I.W.	Arm	124.049	
Guerin, P.	AB	178.500	
Gun Ah.	Dom		
Gussin, G.H.	Ord	195.380	
Hall, G.	Sto	286.725	
Hallett, W.P.	Ord	191.456	
Hamilton, F.	Sto	289.656	
Hann, F.	Pte	Po4.539	
Hanna, J.	Ord	197.016	
Hardy, J.H.	AB	143.045	
Hargadon, J.	AB	191.375	
Hartnett, E.	Ord	194.177	
Harvey, G.F.	Plmbr	340.670	
Hatton, J.D.	Ord	192.282	

H.M.S. ENDYMION.

Bar: RELIEF OF PEKIN *continued.*

Name	Rank	Number
Hayes, S.J.	Pte	Po9.553
Hayward, G.	Pte	Po2.375
Hazelhurst, J.	Sto	288.686
Henry, W.S.	Ord	195.376
Herrick, H.	Pte	Po6.445
Hewitt, B.L.	Midn	
Hodgers, M.	Ord	197.843
Hodgers, N.	AB	197.857
Hodges, T.	AB	156.375
Holder, S.E.	Midn	
Holland, H.A.	SB/Attn	350.425
Holmes, J.	Ord	198.108
Homan, E.A.	Midn	
Howse, C.A.	Pte	Po9.579
Hurrell, H.G.	Ord	197.054
Hurren, J.	Ord	197.813
Hutchins, W.G.	Pte	Po8.771
Hutchinson, D.	Cpl	Po9.323
Isaac, J.H.	PO1	148.091
James, T.	Ord	193.016
Jones, A.	Pte	Po8.209
Jones, E.	L/S	169.432
Jones, J.	Ord	192.606
Jones, P.S.	AB	139.105
Jones, W.	Pte	Po8.740
Joyce, T.	Sto	289.233
Kelsey, G.W.	Arm	135.259
Kinch, G.H.	Ord	196.771
King, W.J.	Pte	Po9.566
Kirkham, W.C.	L/S	175.557
Kite, H.	Sto	169.059
Knight, G.H.	AB	163.023
Lawrence, H.A.	L/Sig	171.390
Legg, G.	L/Shpwrt	163.613
Leggett, A.S.	AB	158.149
Leishman, Rev.J.C.	Chaplain	
Lewis, W.	AB	182.693
Liddell, H.	Cook/Mte	340.880
Lock, C.J.	Pte	Po9.390
Logan, W.	Pte	Po9.558
Louge, W.A.	Pte	Po8.823
Lowen, H.	Pte	Po9.567
Luck, G.E.R.	Arm/Crew	341.362
Luker, W.	PO1	151.798
McClure, H.R.	Midn	
McDermott, J.	AB	195.236
McGachen, F.S.	Midn	
McIntosh, D.	Sto	285.206
Macnamara, E.D.	Surgn	
Mann, G.	Ord	192.926
Mansbridge, J.	AB	193.936
Marchant, W.	Pte	Po9.575
Martin, A.E.	Ord	192.445
Martin, J.C.	L/S	171.157
Merritt, C.W.	Q/Sig	191.274
Mesov, C.	Sto	285.199
Mills, G.R.	Ord	195.634
Mitchell, G.J.	AB	170.362
Montgomery, J.W.	Shpwrt	342.702
Moore, G.F.	Cpl	Po5.936
Moore, M.	AB	173.166
Morris, M.	Ord	196.477
Murphy, D.	L/S	143.856
Murphy, R.	Ord	197.844
Neighbour, A.E.	Pte	Po8.952
Nethercott, C.	Ord	193.431
Newlove, G.	Sto	280.877
Newman, H.C.	PO1	139.206
Northover, F.	Sto	289.225
Oake, A.A.J.R.	Pte	Po9.564
Oakley, J.	L/Cpl	Ch7.612
Osborne, F.	Ord	192.599
Owen, A.	Pte	Ch11.613
Parker, C.W.	Bugler	Po8.441
Parker, J.J.	Pte	Po9.565
Parsons, G.	Ord	195.630
Pask, W.	AB	124.694
Pearson, J.	Ord	194.972
Perrin, R.H.	AB	159.665
Phillips, A.F.	AB	125.051
Phillips, J.W.	Pte	Po8.321
Philpot, W.	Pte	Po8.820
Pink, J.	Pte	Po8.729
Popplestone, E.D.	Ord	196.804
Powell, F.	Lieut	
Price, A.	Pte	Po9.574
Price, W.	Ord	190.070
Pym, F.E.	AB	197.183
Quaife, A.	Pte	Po7.958
Randells, C.	Ord	196.445
Ravenall, W.G.	Pte	Po9.556
Read, W.J.	Ord	192.064
Reddan, P.	AB	195.969
Redwood, A.	Ord	192.516
Rennell, W.J.	Ord	192.893
Reynolds, E.G.	Pte	Po5.117
Rhimes, R.	Sto	281.707 2
Richards, F.G.	L/S	162.216
Richards, W.	Pte	Po8.766
Rimmer, C.	Q/Sig	174.567
Rixon, F.	AB	183.837
Robinson, E.G.	Midn	
Rogers, A.J.	Cpl	Po6.819
Roskelly, J.A.	Ord	193.310
Ross, A.	Ord	192.647
Rowsell, D.W.	AB	140.249
Russell, F.R.	Ord	187.069
Sanctuary, G.W.	Pte	Po9.578
Saunders, A.E.	Ord	194.569
Scanlan, E.E.	Ord	195.642
Seager, J.	Sto	146.126
Semple, A.	Pte	Po9.438
Shanahan, F.	PO2	156.111
Silk, E.S.	Engr	

H.M.S. ENDYMION.

Bar: RELIEF OF PEKIN *continued.*

Simpson, T.	Ord	196.481
Smale, R.G.A.	Ord	192.842
Smart, J.	Pte	Po8.813
Smith, J.	2/Wrtr	166.261
Smith, J.	Sto	287.054
Smith, W.	Ord	191.049
Smith, W.	Pte	Po9.447
Soper, J.	AB	112.182
Speight, B.	Ord	195.354
Stanford, W.	Pte	Ply7.749
Start, G.	AB	192.300
Strachan, A.	Pte	Po8.743
Sweet, G.E.	AB	161.508
Symes, F.	L/S	165.132
Taylor, W.	ERA	269.208
Templeman, E.J.	Sig	194.786
Thomas, J.L.	Fl/Surgn	
Thompson, A.	PO1	121.592
Thornton, J.H.	Pte	Po9.370
Thurstan, N.M.C.	Midn	
Tier, L.E.	Asst/Payr	
Tonkin, W.E.	PO2	167.843
Towton, T.F.	AB	177.024
Tucker, E.C.	Ord	195.629
Tyrell, W.	Ord	196.493
Usmar, B.	AB	188.181
Vince, J.J.	Pte	Po9.581
Vinicombe, G.W.	AB	188.689
Walker, G.	AB	147.313
Walker, P.	Ord	195.201
Walsh, T.	Ord	194.545
Watson, D.	Ord	192.403
Weller, J.H.	Ord	194.916
Widdicombe, W.H.	Sh/Cpl	139.826
Wilcox, W.	AB	190.756
Wilkins, R.J.	L/S	176.487
Williams, E.	AB	144.632
Williams, T.	Pte	Po9.550
Windsor, A.H.	Pte	Po9.551
Woo Ah.	Dom	
Woodward, W.T.	Sto	289.658
Woolacott, H.J.	Ord	195.623
Wooldridge, S.E.	PO1	139.778
Wooledge, W.C.	Ord	194.761
Wooley, T.	L/Sto	279.557
Wright, J.B.	Pte	Po5.481
Wright, R.	AB	167.503
Wyer, J.	Ord	190.155
Yates, B.C.	Ord	192.941
Yates, J.	Sto	289.623

Duplicate medals:

Barlow, A.W.	AB	184.170
Barrett, F.	Ord	190.190
Burrows, W.J.	Ord	194.983
Cartwright, W.A.	Pte	Po8.806
Cater, H.	AB	168.391
Denyer, R.	Sto	287.519 *
Eastman, G.	Pte	Po8.976
Gray, A.	L/Sto	276.140
Green, A.	Sto	167.191
Guerin, P.	AB	178.500
Gussin, G.H.	Ord	195.380
Hartnett, E.	Ord	194.177
Hatton, J.D.	Ord	192.282
Hazlehurst, J.	Sto	288.686
Hodgers, M.	Ord	197.843
Hutchins, W.G.	Pte.	Po8.771
Jones, W.	Pte	Po8.740
McDermott, J.	AB	195.236
Marchant, W.	Pte	Po9.575
Moore, M.	AB	173.166
Read, W.J.	Ord	192.064
Reddan, P.	AB	195.969
Rimmer, C.	Q/Sig	174.567
Semple, A.	Pte	Po9.438
Tier, L.E.	Asst/Payr	
Williams, T.	Pte	Po9.550

Returned medals:

Bryan, H.W.	Pte	Po9.576
Davis, P.	AB	159.245
Gordon, F.	PO1	101.621
Haines, J.	Pte	Po8.757
Hoggarth, J.B.	Sto	286.668
Ingram, C.H.	L/S	176.856
Nash, W.P.	Ord	200.780
Simmons, J.W.	AB	190.465
Sinclair, G.	Ord	182.321
Smith, W. *alias* Semple, W.	L/S	158.855
Stevens, W.	Sto	280.873

NO BAR MEDALS.

Ashton, J.	Pte	Po6.466
Ashwell, W.	Ord	197.908
Ayre, W.R.	PO2	171.045
Baker, W.	AB	197.072
Balls, T.H.	AB	166.532
Barnes, G.F.	Sto	277.363
Barnfield, T.	Band	164.405
Barrow, A.A.	AB	191.378
Bassett, F.H.	Pte	Ch7.283
Bayliss, C.N.	Ord	191.475
Bayly, R.W.U.	Midn	
Beaney, W.T.	Sto	289.193
Beavan, H.J.	L/S	170.396
Beck, T.N.	AB	184.605
Benstead, W.N.	Sto	289.620
Besant, T.F.	Midn	
Betty, W.H.	AB	143.739
Blair, A.	Sto	290.513
Blake, A.	Shpwrt	342.333

NO BAR MEDALS *continued.*

Blanchflower, E.C.	Clerk		
Blewett, C.	Pte	Ch6.721	
Bloomfield, W.	Band	340.750	
Blyth, W.H.	Sto	289.632	
Bond, J.	Pte	Ch6.145	
Bowers, F.	Pte	Ch7.306	
Boyland, A.	ERA	162.067	
Boyse, C.R.	AB	168.031	
Brazier, W.D.	Carp/Mte	154.343	
Brindle, A.	Pte	Po10.202	
Brown, G.E.	Sergt	Ch2.244	
Brown, T.A.	Pte	Ply6.376	
Bryce, W.J.	Sto	284.011	
Bull, A.	(L/)	342.225	
Bulman, J.	ERA	268.720	
Burrows, C.	Sto	281.696	
Burt, J.S.	PO2	149.367	
Butchers, A.	Sto	281.564	
Butt, F.T.	Pte	Ch10.175	
Byrne, H.H.	AB	184.370	
Callaway, A.B.	Sh/Std/Boy	341.828	
Carter, E.	AB	186.980	
Cartledge, J.	Sto	290.417	
Castle, A.	Sto	282.614	
Chang Ah.	Dom		
Chee Ah.	Dom		
Cheel, J.T.	Sto	287.017	
Cheong Ah.	Dom		
Chong Ah.	Dom		
Chun Ah.	Dom		
Coleman, J.	L/Sto	138.043	
Colyer, A.	Ch/Sto	138.167	
Connor, J.	Pte	Ch6.686	
Cook, S.	PO1	86.211	
Corry, W.C.	Sto	289.897	
Cox, A.	Ch/PO	129.397	
Crichton, C.L.M.	Midn		
Cross, E.	L/Sto	122.753	
Crosswell, C.	Sto	281.685	
Crowley, J.	Sto	288.688	
Curling, G.	AB	183.018	
Davey, R.	Sto	287.503	
De Satgé, F.G.	Midn		
Dennis, G.	AB	165.784	
Denton, W.	L/Sto	161.955	
Devereux, G.	Band	340.759	
Dexter, G.	Col/Sergt	Ch2.208	
Divers, E.S.	L/Sto	163.542	
Dodd, W.R.	MAA	117.806	
Dover, W.	Ord	197.597	
Dundas, W.	Pte	Po7.400	
Durrant, W.	Ch/Cook	132.820	
Earl, S.	Ord	201.346	
Earle, G.D.	Boy	201.551	
Easter, A.S.	Ord	191.824	
Edmonds, E.	Pte	Po10.230	
Edmonds, F.H.	Pte	Ch7.029	
Edwards, S.	Pte	Po10.247	
Ellis, A.J.	L/Sto	167.299	
Elton, W.G.R.	L/Sto	166.498	
Epsley, W.M.	PO1	96.688	
Evans, H.A.	AB	180.063	
Evans, H.G.	Ord	195.633	
Facey, W.G.E.	Ord	195.442	
Fanshawe, G.D.	Midn		K
Farrow, W.C.	AB	175.326	
Faulkner, I.	AB	159.848	
Fisher, J.S.	Ord	185.731	
Foreman, S.	Sto	281.710	
Fow Ah.	Dom		
Franklin, C.S.P.	N. Instr		
Fraser, W.St.J.	Midn		
Furlong, R.E.	Cook/Mte	340.939	3
Gann, H.	Ord	191.026	
Gatehouse, J.R.	AB	176.280	
George, F.W.	Sig	194.398	
German, E.	Pte	Ch8.026	
Gibbons, W.	Ord	195.016	
Gibney, E.	Pte	Ch6.629	
Gillingham, E.	Blksmth/Mte	287.931	
Golding, C.R.	Ch/Sto	132.307	
Goldsworthy, S.	Ord	195.857	
Goodger, L.	Ch/Sto	129.524	
Grossmith, A.	Ord	198.322	
Haines, J.	Pte	Po8.610	
Hale, E.F.	L/Sig	146.682	
Hambley, J.	Ord	192.609	
Hampton, F.J.	Ch/Sto	119.497	
Harding, A.E.	AB	192.642	
Harding, L.G.	Ord	196.221	
Hare, C.	AB	176.719	
Harland, H.	PO1	132.101	
Hart, H.W.	AB	192.350	
Hayler, J.	AB	184.475	
Haynes, W.T.	Ord	197.585	
Hearnden, A.	Sto	288.070	
Hedges, H.	AB	187.238	
Hibburt, W.E.	Ord	195.208	
Hill, A.B.	Sto	284.890	
Hillsden, J.W.	AB	137.687	
Hingston, G.	AB	150.849	
Hinks, T.W.	Sh/Std/Asst	341.581	
Hobden, G.	Sto	281.687	
Holmes, E.	Sto	289.223	
Holmes, F.	Sto	153.692	
Hoole, J.	Ch/ERA	141.015	
Horam, E.	Ord	192.469	
Hornsby, C.	Sto	287.058	
Hughes, T.	AB	120.052	
Hume, J.	Cooper	340.118	
Huntley, T.	L/Sto	154.765	
Ireland, A.T.	Pte	Ch6.295	
James, A.W.	AB	189.451	
James, G.	Carp/Mte	157.069	
Jary, E.J.	L/Sto	158.812	
Jayes, G.W.	Ord	191.019	

NO BAR MEDALS *continued.*

Name	Rank	Number
Jeal, A.F.	Sto	281.463
Johnson, T.	PO1	124.034
Johnstone, S.	Sto	282.822
Jones, J.H.	AB	196.911
Kellaway, F.B.	Ord	195.636
Kersley, J.	Band	164.627
Kilby, R.	Pte	Ch6.378
Kirby, R.	Gunr	
Knight, T.	AB	179.331
Knowlson, C.	Act/Ch/PO	112.334
Knox, T.	AB	178.133
Kun Ah.	Dom	
Lawson, J.F.	AB	142.535
Lee, W.J.	AB	155.042
Leong Ah.	Dom	
Lewis, W.J.	Ord	198.348
Littlewood, L.	Sto	276.078
Long, J.	Ord	191.961
Lowe, B.	L/Sto	120.427
Luxford, T.W.	Sto	283.521
McCarthy, T.	Pte	Ch6.467
McCaskil, M.	Pte	Po10.244
McColl, A.	Ch/Arm	90.038
McConnell, T.	AB	161.750
McGuire, W.	Ord	195.970
McGuire, W.	Pte	Ch7.315
McLeod, J.J.	ERA	160.101
Manley, J.	AB	111.315
Mannara, F.L.	Band	357.595
Marsh, W.	Sto	281.603
Marshall, F.	Sto	288.064
Marshall, J.W.	Pte	Ch6.018
Martin, W.	Sto	282.611
Massey, J.S.	Asst/Engr	
Matthews, J.	Sto	289.641
Messervy, C.deF.	Asst/Engr	
Meyer, E.	Band	82.871
Mill, G.R.	AB	181.011
Millington, T.J.	Sto	149.200
Minns, A.	Pntr	158.335
Moon Lem.	Dom	
Moore, A.U.	Lieut	
Moore, R.L.	Ord	191.585
Morgan, C.C.	Cpl	Ch5.097
Muir, J.	ERA	159.461
Naylor, J.W.	Sto	289.932
Neat, E.H.	Payr	
Nelson, M.H.H.	Lieut	
Nethercoat, E.	Ord	197.579
Newall, E.H.	Sto	292.025
Nocentini, W.A.	Band/Mstr	357.455
Norsworthy, A.E.	Sto	283.030
Oliver, R.	Bosn	
Orton, J.H.	Lieut	
Osband, J.E.	Boy	201.746
Osborne, G.J.	Sto	288.405
Owen, F.	Pte	Ch6.440

Name	Rank	Number
Pallella, F.	Band	163.947
Palmer, A.R.	Lieut	
Parsons, C.McN.	Capt(RMLI)	
Pascoe, R.	PO1	145.219
Pattenden, R.	L/Shpwrt	121.350
Pearce, G.	Ord	197.111
Phillips, W.E.	AB	180.125
Pitt, D.	Sto	167.142
Pittock, E.J.	Sto	281.705
Portlett, A.H.	Sh/Std	141.685
Price, C.R.	Pte	Ch6.634
Price, H.	Band	340.807
Rawson, J.	Sto	282.772
Reaston, J.	Sto	160.523
Renshaw, H.J.	Carp	
Richards, J.E.	Act/Ch/Sto	141.641
Roberts, A.	L/S	151.824
Rogers, T.	Band	340.960
Russell, P.	Sto	282.616
Ryan, P.E.	Sto	166.405
Sabey, W.	L/S	151.590
Sam Ah.	Dom	
Sharp, C.	AB	192.050
Shepherd, E.	Dom	91.204
Short, W.J.	Sto	289.642
Simpson, W.	Blksmth/Mte	341.725
Sing Ah (1).	Dom	
Sing Ah (2).	Dom	
Sing Cum.	Dom	
Slack, H.	AB	178.348
Smellie, R.G.P.	Q/Sig	184.487
Smith, A.	Sto	287.492
Smith, H.	Sto	135.480
Smith, H.	L/Sto	169.753
Smith, J.F.	ERA	268.527
Solfleet, G.	Asst/Payr	
Southron, G.	Act/ERA	269.818
Speight, S.S.	Ord	195.294
Spicer, J.	AB	193.035
Spillane, C.W.	Pte	Ch7.281
Stevens, W.H.	AB	170.704
Stickings, W.	Sto	283.028
Stroud, E.J.	Capt(RMLI)	
Stuart, J.J.	Fl/Engr	
Sullivan, F.	Bosn	
Summerfield, W.H.	Boy	201.712
Sutton, G.	Pte	Ch7.953
Taggart, J.	Ord	192.790
Te Ah.	Dom	
Teasdale, T.H.	Sto	289.192
Terry, C.	L/Sto	159.032
Thickett, T.	Boy	197.650
Thompson, C.J.	Ord	191.651
Thompson, E.	Sto	291.620
Titheridge, W.	Pte	Po10.232
Tonkins, B.G.	Pte	Ch10.268
Topple, G.F.	Sto	290.370
Totham, H.	Sto	288.418
Trevithick, R.J.	PO1	155.971

NO BAR MEDALS *continued.*

Tucker, C.	L/Sto	139.896
Tuk Chug.	Dom	
Underdown, W.	Ch/Sto	134.458
Vidler, A.E.	Boy	201.944
Walker, J.	Pte	Ch5.693
Walker, P.	Sto	282.354
Walker, R.L.	AB	185.750
Walling, W.G.	AB	168.293
Walter, E.F.	Sto	282.791
Wand, T.E.	Pte	Ch8.521
Warren, J.G.	Cooper	341.101
Washburn, G.F.	Act/Sh/Cpl	350.166
Waters, J.	ERA	269.571
Watson, J.A.	Sto	282.375
Watson, T.	AB	160.905
Wells, J.D.	Sto	286.985
Welsh, J.A.	Ord	192.389
Wheaton, J.D.	Sto	282.806
Whittle, F.	Ord	195.393
Wilkins, W.	Sail	87.686
Williams, J.G.	Pte	Ch9.978
Williamson, J.	ERA	159.603
Wilson, H.B.	Lieut	
Wiltshire, A.	Pte	Po10.194
Windsor, A.W.	Blksmth	165.179
Witt, E.C.	Ord	195.220
Wood, E.C.	Sto	289.649
Wood, F.J.	Ord	196.246
Wood, W.J.	Sto	289.639
Woodmore, F.	PO2	143.602
Woodriffe, J.	PO1	120.169
Woods, H.	AB	185.466
Wright, J.	Band	340.810
Wyld, E.A.	Bugler	Ch9.903
Yardley, J.	Sto	285.189
Young Ah.	Dom	
Youngman, J.	Ord	195.075

Duplicate medals:

Ashwell, W.	Ord	197.908
Brazier, W.D.	Carp/Mte	154.343
Callaway, A.B.	Sh/Std/Boy	341.828
Cheel, J.T.	Sto	287.017
German, E.	Pte	Ch8.026
Hobden, G.	Sto	281.687 *
Holmes, E.	Sto	289.223
Johnstone, S.	Sto	282.822
Matthews, J.	Sto	289.641
Morgan, C.C.	Cpl	Ch5.097
Wells, J.D.	Sto	286.985
Woodriffe, J.	PO1	120.169

* *Two duplicate medals issued.*

Duplicate medals - without issue no. on roll:

Meyer, E.	Band	82.871

Returned medals:

Fisher, H.	AB	192.911
Fleming, W.	Ord	192.130
Gardner, W.	Ord	201.069
Griffiths, T.	Ord	192.508
Griggs, J.	Pte	Ch8.776
Jones, F.	Sto	167.169
Maddison, A.	L/Sto	162.077
Whitty, E.E.	Pte	Po6.645

H.M.S. ESK.

H.M.S. Esk was an Iron Screw Gunboat of 363 tons and 110 x 34 feet. Her armament consisted of 3 x 64 pdr guns. The vessel was built by Palmer and launched on 28th April 1877. She was sold in May 1903 at Hong Kong.

Bars	*Total*	*Returned*	*Entitled*
None	*100*	*5*	*95*
	100	*5*	*95*

NO BAR MEDALS.

Abbott, J.R.	AB	174.259
Baker, F.W.	Ch/ERA	148.815
Bale, W.	Sto	153.900
Barnfield, W.J.	Cpl	Ply6.242
Blunt, W.F.	Lieut Comdr	
Bryan, E.	L/Sto	169.611
Burniston, H.S.	Surgn	
Butler, C.	L/Sto	153.694
Butler, W.	Pte	Ply8.735
Cartwright, J.	PO1	104.526
Chadwick, C.	Lieut Comdr	
Chang Ah.	Dom	
Chee Ah.	Dom	
Coaker, J.	AB	118.321
Cole, A.	Sto	284.761
Connolly, D.	AB	130.400
Couch, T.W.	Act/ERA	269.159
Creak, H.A.	Pte	Ply8.881
Cross, A.	AB	182.239
Davis, S.J.	AB	146.285
Denton, E.	Sh/Std	172.322
Donald, T.	AB	181.446
Dyer, H.	Sto	130.045
Fah Ah.	Dom	
Fitzpatrick, J.	AB	191.244
Frost, G.W.	AB	130.411
Fuge, F.	AB	172.503
Gale, R.	PO1	121.091
Garry, C.	Ch/ERA	145.814
Gasson, H.	L/Sig	151.058
Giles, G.	Carp/Mte	113.628
Goolden, A.C.	Lieut	
Hall, F.	AB	183.792
Hall, R.C.	PO1	136.491
Haynes, W.	AB	173.075
Herd, D.	ERA	269.549
Horne, A.D.	Q/Sig	173.699
Isaacs, F.C.	L/Sto	153.690
Johnson, W.J.	Gunr	
Joyes, G.T.	Arm/Mte	341.906
Kam Ah.	Dom	
Lloyd, J.	Sto	278.182
McCallig, P.	Sto	283.045
McCalman, D.	Sto	277.583
McDonald, G.	L/Sto	154.538
McKay, J.	PO1	121.381
Maddox, T.	AB	160.154
Mahoney, J.	PO1	102.927
Major, R.	Pte	Po8.555
Marner, R.	Sh/Cook	168.247
Marsh, W.	AB	189.838
Martin, R.	PO1	122.306
May, W.J.C.	Sh/Std	145.181
Morgan, C.A.	Pte	Ply8.793
Morton, C.A.	PO1	83.281
Neal, S.J.	L/S	154.386
Neale, J.H.	Pte	Po5.857
Neve, W.C.	AB	184.688
Nevin, J.	Sto	283.571
Newton, A.V.	Arm/Mte	340.046
Nurney, F.	AB	165.738
Page, W.Le.	AB	182.864
Palmer, J.P.	L/Sig	163.878
Parr, J.W.	Sto	175.879
Pepperell, J.	Sto	171.289
Perry, C.	AB	179.227
Poulter, W.E.	Pte	Po8.365
Power, M.	L/S	137.482
Puttick, F.F.	AB	174.746
Quick, P.E.	ERA	268.483
Rackham, W.	Cpl	Ch8.856
Rawlings, E.	Pte	Po7.274
Redman, J.	Sh/Cook	153.470
Russell, C.	Sto	170.236
Ryder, W.R.	Carp/Mte	140.958
Sargeant, R.	ERA	165.903
Searle, F.	AB	189.722
See Tsai Lo.	Pilot	
Simmons, E.	AB	182.027
Steirn, B.	Sto	278.071
Sum Ah.	Dom	
Swann, G.	Sto	153.770
Teed, A.	PO1	132.954
Thomas, A.	AB	138.201
Tindale, H.E.	Q/Sig	189.728
Venters, J.	AB	179.088
Wafer, G.	Sto	171.366
Watt, J.G.	Surgn	

NO BAR MEDALS *continued.*

Webster, F.C.	Pte	Ply8.913
Wells, H.J.	Sto	282.126
Weston, S.	L/Sto	154.966
Williams, A.	Ord	196.907
Wilson, R.	ERA	148.607
Wong Ah.	Pilot	
Woods, F.	Sto	282.130

Duplicate medals:

Neve, W.C.	AB	184.688 *
Pepperell, J.	Sto	171.289
Puttick, F.F.	AB	174.746
Russell, C.	Sto	170.236
Searle, F.	AB	189.722

* *Two duplicate medals issued.*

Returned medals:

Arlington, L.	Pte	Ply5.685
Hardy, J.	AB	115.819
Maxwell, J.	Pte	Po2.548
Murrin, J.	L/S	188.318
White, J.	Sto	281.692

H.M.S. FAME.

H.M.S. Fame was a Destroyer of 340 tons and $210\frac{1}{2}$ x $19\frac{1}{2}$ feet. Her armament consisted of 1 x 12 pdr, 5 x 6 pdr and 2 torpedo tubes. The vessel was built by Thornycroft at Chiswick and launched on 15th April 1896. She was sold on 31st August 1921 at Hong Kong.

Bars	*Total*	*Returned*	*Entitled*
TF & RP	*3*	*0*	*3*
TF	*60*	*2*	*58*
RP	*1*	*0*	*1*
None	*3*	*0*	*3*
	67	*2*	*65*

Notes:

K - Medal presented by H.M. The King on 8th March 1902.

Bars: TAKU FORTS, RELIEF OF PEKIN.

Name	Rating	Number
Brady, H.W.	AB	188.620
Keyes, R.J.B.	Lieut Comdr	
Tomkinson, W.	Lieut	

Bar: TAKU FORTS.

	Name	Rating	Number
	Aldworth, J.	Sto	285.245
	Bannister, A.	Q/Sig	188.455
	Bartlett, G.	L/Sto	125.845
	Bickham, W.	Sto	292.693
	Burton, W.	Sto	167.786
	Carroll, G.	PO1	135.737
	Cassells, F.	Ch/Sto	140.413
	Chapman, F.	Sto	283.131
	Conlon, M.	Sto	283.530
	Cook, T.J.	Sto	284.950
	Copplestone, W.J.	Act/ERA	269.212
	Devlin, H.	Sto	289.832
	Dunstel, W.	Sto	279.555
	Edge, F.P.	PO2	153.932
	Faulkner, E.	AB	187.226
	Fawcett, J.	Sto	288.142
	Fitch, F.	Sto	283.626
	Fitzpatrick, W.	Sto	292.137
	Furzland, F.J.	Sto	292.305
	Goodwin, E.	Ch/Sto	130.321
	Hallifax, C.	L/Sto	164.151
	Hannagan, J.	AB	186.213
	Howard, S.	Sto	282.594
	Jackson, G.	PO2	132.608
	Jeffs, J.	Sto	174.385
	King, H.	Sto	282.609
	Knight, G.G.	Ch/Engr	
	Lillie, F.H.	Sto	284.925
K	Lockett, T.W.	AB	177.224
	McKenzie, J.	L/Sig	171.543
	Mace, R.J.	AB	187.477
	Marshall, J.Y.	Sto	154.723
	Mascull, G.	Gunr	
	Nye, H.W.	AB	187.378
	Orsborn, H.	Sto	281.589
	Pamely, A.	ERA	268.601
	Parrott, W.	AB	189.405
	Partridge, A.T.	AB	138.418
	Pearson, W.	Sto	283.498
	Pidgeon, A.J.	Ch/ERA	134.471
	Riddle, E.C.	Sto	283.609
	Royce, W.C.	AB	185.498
	Scott, G.L.	Act/ERA	269.310
	Sears, G.T.	Sto	283.496
	Shapter, J.W.	L/Sto	161.183
	Shaw, H.J.	L/Sto	152.238
	Simmonds, W.A.	Cook/Mte	341.108
	Tack Ah.	Dom	
	Taylor, F.	Sto	284.896
	Thomas, W.	AB	186.900
	Tuttle, G.H.	AB	185.988
	Wanstall, T.W.	AB	181.893
	Whitehead, H.	Sto	283.499
	Wicks, W.G.	Ch/Sto	118.656
	Willey, W.H.	Sto	282.805
	Witty, J.T.	Sto	280.355
	Worthington, J.G.	AB	187.788
	Young, W.J.	PO1	147.673

H.M.S. FAME.

Bar: TAKU FORTS *continued.*

Duplicate medals:

Bartlett, G.	L/Sto	125.845 *
Devlin, H.	Sto	289.832

* *Two duplicate medals issued.*

Returned medals:

Lawson, R.	Sto	151.884
Putt, J.	Sto	279.734

Bar: RELIEF OF PEKIN.

Campbell, K.R.	Capt	

NO BAR MEDALS.

Blackwood, A.T.	Sub Lieut	
Edwards, E.	Engr	
Richards, H.C.	Ch/Sto	129.277

H.M.S. GOLIATH.

H.M.S. Goliath was a Battleship of 12,950 tons and 390 x 74 feet. Her armament consisted of 4 x 12 in, 12 x 6 in and 12 x 12 pdr guns. The vessel was built in Chatham Dock Yard and launched on 23rd March 1898. She was sunk on 13th May 1915 by the Turkish Torpedo Boat Muavenet off Cape Helles.

Bars	*Total*	*Returned*	*Entitled*
TF & RP	*1*	*0*	*1*
RP	*1*	*0*	*1*
None	*791*	*31*	*760*
	793	*31*	*762*

Notes:

1 - A note on the roll states, " Clasp 3 to be attached."

2 - Roll states, "Run 2 July 07. Medal reissued 20/2/18."

3 - Roll states, "Lost in transit, replaced."

4 - Roll states, "Run 10.11.00. Application for medal refused."

5 - Roll states, "Man states he had medal in Haslar Hospital."

Bars: TAKU FORTS, RELIEF OF PEKIN.

Shaw, C.B.	Midn	

Duplicate medal:

Shaw, C.B.	Midn	

Bar: RELIEF OF PEKIN.

White, N.	Gunr	RMA5.901 [1]

NO BAR MEDALS.

Abrahams, J.R.	PO2	115.652
Aldridge, S.G.	Boy	201.489
Alexander, F.H.	Ord	202.152
Allison, F.G.B.	Arm	340.699
Ambler, R.C.	AB	171.660
Anderton, A.	L/S	166.285
Appleton, H.	L/Carp/Crew	343.172
Argent, R.	Sto	285.221
Arnold, H.P.	Gunr	RMA7.457
Assiter, A.	2/Yeo/Sig	168.358
Atherden, G.H.	ERA	268.912
Atkins, S.	AB	154.226
Aurey, F.W.J.	St/Payr	
Austin, F.K.	Pte	Ch6.547
Austwick, J.T.	Carp/Mte	128.059
Ayres, H.H.	Band	340.991
Bailey, F.	AB	172.740
Bailey, J.	Sto	292.035
Bailey, J.J.	Pte	Ch5.628
Baker, A.B.A.	Midn	
Baker, F.	Ord	198.031
Baker, G.F.	Boy	201.475
Baker, P.	Boy	201.170
Baker, R.F.	Midn	
Ball, S.	Bosn	
Balmforth, J.	AB	170.670
Banyard, F.E.	Pte	Ch10.609
Barrett, E.	Sto	292.858
Barringer, T.	Pte	Ch2.272
Bartlett, A.H.	AB	169.104
Bartlett, A.J.	PO1	129.906
Battig, A.	Band	146.519
Battison, W.	Q/Sig	194.108
Bayford, A.	Ord	198.359
Bean, J.F.	L/Sto	141.610
Beavis, R.J.	Ord	181.069
Beck, A.J.	Sto	290.428
Bedford, E.A.	Sto	291.931
Bee, J.	Ord	201.210
Belcher, H.	Boy	201.382
Bell, W.C.	Boy	202.076
Bendall, C.	L/S	155.719

H.M.S. GOLIATH.

NO BAR MEDALS *continued.*

Name	Rank	Number
Bennett, A.W.	Boy	201.392
Bennett, B.	Ord	201.272
Bennett, E.H.	Ord	193.860
Berry, S.	Gunr	RMA5.273
Biles, F.C.	Pte	Ch9.853
Bird, A.H.	Band	340.985
Bird, F.R.	Pte	Ch10.658
Black, D.J.	Sto	291.892
Blackburn, J.H.	Ord	194.326
Blogg, C.	Band	155.096
Blow, C.E.H.	Plmbr/Mte	292.372
Blowman, J.	Gunr	RMA7.599
Blyther, H.J.H.	PO2	172.723
Bodger, F.A.	Cpl	RMA5.201
Bodmore, J.	AB	185.517
Boltwood, T.G.	Ord	184.018
Bombroffe, J.H.C.	AB	164.907
Boorman, W.G.	Ord	201.651
Borland, J.McI.	Act/Lieut	
Boughton, T.W.	Ch/PO	120.946
Boulter, J.R.	Gunr	RMA7.579
Bowering, G.H.	Sto	294.157
Bowles, A.	Boy	201.238
Bowness, W.N.	Ord	191.435
Boyce, J.	Sto	293.068
Bradshaw, R.A.	Sto	291.910
Bradshaw, W.	Sto	291.856
Brattle, H.	Sto	383.135
Breakell, C.V.	Sto	292.083
Breeds, R.W.	AB	164.387
Brewster, J.	Sto	282.785
Briggs, J.	Ord	198.636
Bright, T.E.	Ord	202.980
Brock, N.B.C.	Midn	
Brockway, A.H.	AB	163.407
Brodie, J.B.	AB	156.290
Brooke, F.J.	PO1	128.011
Brown, A.A.	Boy	200.583
Brown, C.A.M.	Shpwrt	343.092
Brown, H.	Bugler	RMA5.582
Brown, H.L.A.	Boy	202.085
Brown, J.	Ch/Sto	138.170
Brunsdon, R.	Ch/Cook	135.203
Buckley, M.J.	Ord	199.430
Buike, W.J.	Boy	201.948
Bull, J.	Ord	193.415
Burden, E.J.	Sto	285.430
Burden, F.G.	Ord	198.156
Burke, H.E.	AB	186.638
Burr, E.H.	Sto	280.431
Burrett, W.H.	Pte	Ch7.400
Burridge, A.E.	Boy	201.463
Burroughs, W.F.	Boy	201.952
Bush, E.	Boy	201.384
Bush, J.T.	AB	164.810
Butler, E.R.	Boy	201.373
Buttonshaw, W.J.	Cook/Mte	354.629
Caesar, H.S.	L/Shpwrt	158.078
Calver, R.	Ord	197.943
Canham, R.C.	Ord	201.929
Cansdale, A.	AB	178.470
Carey, T.H.	Sto	290.878
Cargill, D.V.	Ord	189.843
Carlton, R.W.	Pte	Ch8.137
Carpenter, H.	Ord	201.208
Carter, R.	Ord	195.017
Carvell, A.	Gunr	RMA2.354
Casson, J.M.	Ord	195.791
Castle, J.H.	PO2	175.076
Challinor, F.W.	AB	134.996
Chapman, C.	Sto	135.482
Chilcott, F.W.	L/S	151.828
Chilvers, J.W.	L/Sto	158.019
Chittock, G.	Ord	202.984
Cholerton, T.E.	Q/Sig	187.853
Chow Ah.	Dom	
Christie, A.G.	ERA	269.271
Churchill, C.C.	Ord	201.543
Clacy, F.A.R.	Ord	195.177
Clark, A.	PO1	134.337
Clarke, A.F.	Boy	201.389
Clarke, F.W.	Boy	201.471
Clay, T.	Ord	195.058
Clements, S.T.	Boy	201.240
Clements, T.W.	AB	159.671
Cleveland, G.C.	PO1	166.144
Clifford, S.G.	Pte	Po10.236
Cochrane, G.J.	AB	147.696
Coe, W.E.	Ord	191.978
Cogger, F.	Boy	201.391
Cok Ah.	Dom	
Cole, C.J.	Ord	198.963
Coleridge, G.L.	Midn	
Collins, G.H.	Shpwrt	140.153
Collyer, F.	Pte	Ch8.175
Combstock, T.H.	PO2	159.206
Constable, W.H.	AB	191.229
Copeland, G.	Band	157.153
Cook, W.J.	AB	172.366
Corcoran, P.	Ord	199.061
Cornwell, G.J.	Boy	201.477
Cottingham, A.	AB	168.105
Cottrell, A.	Sto	294.161
Couch, F.G.	Arm/Mte	341.091
Coulter, C.	L/Sto	166.626
Cow Ah.	Dom	
Cox, J.G.	Ord	201.498
Craig, E.	PO1	129.979
Crane, J.B.	Pte	Ch5.405
Crawley, W.	Ord	198.565
Creese, F.W.	Ord	201.706
Crocker, J.H.	Ord	203.409
Crowne, C.H.	Boy	201.545
Crowson, G.	Boy	200.965
Cubitt, R.F.	Act/Ch/ Yeo/Sig	157.867

NO BAR MEDALS *continued.*

Cullen, W.O.D.	Q/Sig	191.300
Cullis, H.	Boy	201.215
Curtis, E.	Ord	200.460
Dale, A.W.V.	L/S	154.223
Dalling, E.C.	Ord	202.979
Daly, P.	Ord	194.868
Darville, F.D.	Sto	284.856
Dathan, Rev.J.D.	Chaplain	
Davey, E.C.	Ord	201.257
Davies, H.	Pte	Po10.214
Davies, I.	ERA	269.034
Davies, L.H.	Boy	201.479
Davies, R.	Ord	201.370
Davies, W.	Gunr	RMA7.695
Davis, C.	Gunr	RMA8.035
Daviss, T.H.	Gunr	RMA7.362
Dawson, A.B.F.	Lieut	
Dawson, B.	Sto	287.493
Day, H.	L/Sto	144.143
Day, R.C.	AB	169.121
Deacon, P.W.	AB	171.051
Debenham, W.C.	Ord	200.795
Deeble, J.A.	AB	202.991
Dellar, W.J.	Ch/PO	120.094
Denial, J.A.	Pte	Ch10.601
Dilley, F.	PO2	164.427
Dingley, A.T.	PO1	169.259
Dixon, P.	Sto	285.203
Dodd, H.A.	Ord	201.887
Dore, F.G.	AB	156.912
Douglas, J.	Gunr	RMA7.598
Dovley, W.	Gunr	RMA7.530
Doyland, P.J.	Ord	183.441
Doyle, T.W.	Sto	284.799
Druce, A.J.	Ord	202.969
Duhig, M.	Ord	198.055
Dunn, G.	Boy	201.014
Durkin, F.P.	Boy	201.822
Durling, A.H.	Pte	Ch10.607
Durrant, A.W.	PO2	170.706
Eagle, A.T.	Sto	292.672
Earl, P.A.	Boy	201.388
Earle, F.W.	Pntr	142.818
Easey, G.	Sto	289.588
Eastcott, R.T.	Ch/ERA	140.985
Eastman, J.F.	Gunr	RMA5.284
Echlin, G.C.	Lieut	
Edgill, T.	Sto	276.665
Edmonds, A.F.	Pte	Ch10.576
Edward-Collins, G.F.B.	Midn	
Edwards, J.	Pte	Po8.465
Egan, W.E.C.	Boy	201.472
Eldridge, J.S.	Boy	201.527
Elliott, G.H.	Boy	201.488
Ellis, W.	L/Sto	175.392
Elliston, A.E.	Boy	201.530

Evans, W.	Carp/Mte	163.677
Evans, W.	Pte	Ch10.660
Everett, C.G.	Ord	195.228
Ewens, A.	AB	174.032
Fackrell, A.B.J.	PO2	175.033
Farmer, A.H.	Sto	290.486
Farr, W.	Boy	201.221
Farwell, W.D.	Boy	201.205
Fawcett, W.J.	Dom	354.873
Fehilly, W.	Ord	199.058
Felgate, J.	PO1	158.383
Fender, S.A.	Boy	201.521
Ferris, W.C.	Boy	198.684
Field, W.	Boy	201.699
Filby, W.	Sto	285.403
Finch, L.J.	Pte	Ch10.574
Fishenden, W.	Cook/Mte	354.872
Fisher, A.E.	Ord	205.321
Fisher, J.J.	Ch/Sto	134.469
Fitzgerald, J.	Sto	291.106
Fitzpatrick, T.	Ord	199.436
Ford, F.W.	Ord	200.247
Ford, F.W.	Sh/Cpl	350.065
Foster, E.G.S.	PO1	141.197
Foster, J.	Band	148.487
Francis, J.E.	Ord	199.629
Fraser, J.D.	Sto	293.895
Fraser, W.	Sto	290.699
Fraser, W.	Plmbr	341.465
Freds, J.	Pte	Ch6.822
Freebourne, J.R.	Ord	195.011
French, G.	AB	168.030
Friend, F.	Ord	194.435
Frost, J.C.	ERA	269.121
Gale, J.	AB	180.402
Garrett, G.	Sto	145.462
Gasser, F.J.	L/Shpwrt	115.432
Gay, W.G.	Sto	292.739
Geary, J.	Ord	199.433
Gedge, R.	Sto	291.375
Gee, S.J.	Ord	194.421
Gellatly, J.	Pte	Ch5.973
George, R.E.	Ord	201.882
George, S.H.C.	AB	177.156
Gibson, C.	Ord	198.943
Giddy, R.C.	PO1	147.046
Gilbert, A.	Ord	199.261
Gilchrist, J.	Sto	284.928
Giles, D.A.	Boy	201.670
Gledhill, R.A.	Gunr	RMA7.323
Glover, T.	Boy	201.984
Godfrey, H.J.	Sto	285.545
Golley, R.L.	AB	171.742
Good, J.	PO1	141.503
Goodchild, F.	AB	175.132
Goose, W.	Gunr	RMA3.904
Gordon, D.R.	PO1	149.134
Graham, F.	Asst/Engr	
Grater, J.	L/Sto	160.722

NO BAR MEDALS *continued.*

Gregg, J.H.	Ord	192.431
Griswood, T.	Pte	Ch10.618
Gwynn, A.	AB	143.072
Gwyther, J.H.	AB	164.931
Haken, W.H.E.	AB	172.436
Hale, W.	AB	154.347
Hales, D.	Gunr	RMA8.028
Hall, J.	Act/Band/Cpl	112.945
Hamilton, G.W.	AB	175.490
Hammond, F.R.	Ord	199.262
Hammond, H.D.	Sh/Cpl	132.220
Hammond, T.	Sto	285.266
Hang Tuck.	Dom	
Hannaford, S.	Ord	199.233
Harbour, G.	Boy	201.169
Harley, J.	Cpl	Ch10.384
Harper, A.F.	St/Surgn	
Harper, R.J.	AB	156.352
Harris, H.G.	Sto	289.168
Harris, T.A.	Q/Sig	192.121
Harrison, H.	Act/ERA	269.895
Harvey, W.	Sto	285.546
Hastie, R.	Sto	291.633
Haves, T.	Asst/Payr	
Hawkes, C.	Boy	201.693
Hawkins, G.	Gunr	RMA8.029
Hawkins, J.	AB	134.156
Haydon, J.	Gunr	RMA5.694
Hayler, G.F.	Sto	171.103
Haylett, F.J.	Boy	201.397
Haynes, R.	Ord	202.965
Hayward, E.C.	Gunr	RMA4.829
Hazzard, F.C.	Ord	190.211
Head, C.H.	Midn	
Hearn, R.	PO1	136.827
Heath, A.F.J.	Q/Sig	189.520
Heather, P.	Asst/Clerk	
Heaver, S.	Ord	201.227
Hellings, J.P.	L/S	167.553
Henstridge, S.	Pte	Po10.240
Hewitt, D.W.	Surgn	
Hewitt, F.W.	Ord	201.193
Hewitt, J.	PO1	114.009
Heycock, C.C.	Midn	
Higham, H.A.	Gunr	RMA7.686
Highfield, J.	ERA	165.413
Hinds, C.	L/Sto	155.196
Hitt, W.	Ord	185.855
Hobbs, W.R.	Ord	193.260
Hobday, H.	PO1	115.838
Hock Ah.	Dom	
Holliday, S.A.	Sergt	RMA3.722
Hollywood, W.J.	Sh/Cpl	144.747
Holmes, J.W.F.	Boy	201.147
Holt, C.E.	AB	163.768
Hood, F.G.	ERA	269.083
Hood, J.L.C.	Midn	

Hopkins, J.W.	PO2	124.264
Hopwood, R.	Lieut	
Howard, J.W.	Midn	
Howell, F.	Ord	203.406
Howes, F.G.	Boy	201.482
Howlett, E.	Ord	201.015
Hudson, T.	AB	179.557
Hulbert, W.G.	Ord	192.612
Hultum, T.	Sto	280.612
Hung Ah.	Dom	
Hurst, S.	Gunr	RMA7.616
Hutchings, C.R.	PO1	158.320
Ingham, J.G.P.	Sub Lieut	
Inns, W.A.	Pte	Ch7.493
Inward, F.	PO1	123.602
Irons, W.F.	AB	164.339
Irvine, J.	AB	168.794
Isaac, T.J.	PO1	148.959
Jackman, A.E.	Blksmth/Mte	341.931
James, C.W.	Ord	202.123
James, G.E.	Ch/PO	125.738
Jane, A.	Sto	293.015
Jarvey, J.E.	Ord	201.509
Jeffery, G.	AB	117.316
Jenkins, W.	Ord	200.972
Jenkinson, W.	Cook/Mte	353.718
Jenner, W.E.	AB	184.836
Jew Ah.	Dom	
Jim Ah.	Dom	
Johnson, E.V.	Ord	201.294
Johnson, J.J.	Pte	Ch7.411
Johnston, W.H.	Boy	200.712
Jones, C.B.	Boy	201.220
Jones, C.R.	AB	176.438
Jones, S.H.	Ord	191.491
Jones, W.D.	PO1	149.606
Judge, H.H.	Sergt	Ch5.598
Kay Ah.	Dom	
Kehoe, J.J.	Boy	201.369
Kemp, T.	Pte	Po8.513
Kennard, E.	AB	166.365
Kennedy, C.P.	Sto	291.441
Kennish, W.	PO2	162.909
Kimber, J.W.	PO1	161.884
Kin Ah.	Dom	
King, G.H.	Sto	291.820
King, H.J.	Sto	285.159
Kissel, W.H.	AB	194.490
Kitchener, H.F.C.	Lieut	
Knapp, J.	Sto	285.888
Knight, P.	Sto	291.431
Knight, W.	Sto	290.496
Knowles, J.	Ord	202.998
Lack, R.	Sto	285.227
Ladbury, H.	Pte	Po5.790
Lamb, A.	Yeo/Sig	162.596
Lambert, A.P.	PO1	145.878
Lambert, H.	Pte	Ch4.058
Lambert, W.	Sto	177.409

NO BAR MEDALS *continued.*

Name	Rank	Number
Laming, T.F.	Gunr	RMA7.693
Lander, W.H.	L/Sto	138.044
Lane, T.	Boy	201.191
Langridge, F.	Ord	195.078
Langridge, W.	Ch/Sto	123.642
Lawrie, E.McC.W.	Midn	
Lee, W.J.	PO2	164.932
Lethebe, R.	Gunr	RMA5.950
Light, J.	AB	169.962
Lindsey, C.	Ord	191.386
Lister, E.H.	PO1	155.060
Little, J.	AB	168.020
Llewellyn, J.H.C.	AB	158.214
Lloyd, H.N.	2/SBStd	142.497
Lockyer, F.E.	Boy	201.487
Long, W.D.	3/Wrtr	340.409
Lord, W.	Gunr	RMA5.118
Loveridge, H.J.	Engr	
Loynes, T.W.	Ord	191.043
Ludby, W.E.	AB	166.082
Lum Ah.	Dom	
Lumb, A.	AB	170.447
Lung Ah.	Dom	
Lutz, S.G.	Boy	201.233
Lyons, J.W.	Act/Ch/Sto	143.954
McClinchey, J.	Sto	284.792
McDowall, J.	Pte	Ch8.085
McEwan, W.	Sto	292.891
McFarlane, D.	Sto	292.877
McGinty, J.	AB	191.316
McIntosh, D.	L/S	136.696
Mackenzie, D.	Cooper/Crew	343.117
McKinlay, A.W.	Asst/Engr	
McKissack, W.	Gunr	RMA7.472
McLellan, A.	AB	158.024
Macleod, D.	Ord	199.403
McMullen, W.	AB	182.886
McWhinnie, A.	Carp/Crew	343.180
Maher, O.P.	Sto	288.081
Mahon, P.L.	Pte	Ch10.412
Mansell, E.W.	Gunr	RMA7.704
Manton, R.	Act/ERA	269.968
Marhoff, J.B.E.	PO1	171.550
Markland, J.	PO2	166.273
Marriott, J.P.C.	Sh/Std/Boy	342.120
Marshall, H.G.	AB	187.265
Marshall, R.W.	Sergt	Ch10.725
Marshall, W.	Boy	201.949
Martin, A.E.	AB	166.092
Martin, J.H.	Ord	191.497
Mason, G.	Sto	284.823
Matthews, E.F.	Gunr	RMA7.744
Matthews, J.	Boy	201.155
May, A.	AB	189.738
Mesley, W.C.	Pte	Ch9.924
Mewett, J.G.	PO1	118.871
Middleton, A.M.	Pte	Ch10.538
Miles, G.T.	AB	164.845
Miles, W.	Band	341.010
Milford, J.	Ch/Arm	136.532
Milsom, J.	Sto	291.243
Mitchell, J.	Boy	199.060
Mocock, A.E.	AB	172.612
Montague, J.	L/S	155.147
Moon Yee.	Dom	
Moore, H.	Ord	182.667
Moore, T.J.H.	Boy	201.196
Morgan, W.	Ord	201.476
Morris, A.E.	SB/Attn	350.466
Morris, E.E.	AB	168.438
Morris, E.R.	ERA	268.807
Morris, J.	Gunr	RMA1.818
Morris, J.E.	Pte	Ch10.648
Morrison, A.	Cooper	161.077
Morton, H.C.	Lieut(RMLI)	
Munro, D.	Gunr	RMA5.412
Nagle, R.P.	Ord	201.524
Neech, A.J.	Ord	200.389
Neill-James, C.H.	Midn	
Newboult, C.H.	Sto	285.386
Newell, H.T.	Sig	196.301
Newton, I.	Arm/Crew	342.179
Nicholls, J.W.E.	Boy	201.195
Nicklin, G.	Blksmth	342.117
Nock, H.	Sto	282.951
Nolan, J.J.	Boy	199.466
Northrop, H.M.	Shpwrt	343.331
O'Brien, T.C.	Ord	201.504
O'Connor, E.	Sto	283.014
O'Connor, P.	Sto	293.959
O'Dogherty, F.B.	Asst/Engr	
O'Farrell, L.R.	Sto	291.890
O'Neil, J.	PO2	154.331
Oakley, H.A.	Pte	Ch10.595
Old, H.	Pte	Po10.209
Oram, F.	Ord	198.211
Otley, A.E.	AB	176.434
Ouslem, R.	Sto	292.394
Outram, H.G.	PO1	150.780
Pacey, W.F.	Ord	201.247
Palmer, H.	Ord	188.917
Palmer, J.	AB	181.625
Palmer, J.H.	Ord	204.388
Palmer, P.	Boy	198.753
Pardey, H.L.	Boy	201.385
Parsons, F.	Boy	198.219
Payne, W.J.	Sto	290.866
Peacock, F.	Ord	192.644
Pearce, T.	L/Sto	129.382
Pearcey, W.	AB	179.629
Peek, F.	Ord	183.264
Peel, W.	Ord	201.363
Pennell, H.L.	Midn	
Pennie, G.R.	Sto	291.119
Perkins, H.	L/Sto	130.752
Phillimore, R.F.	Comdr	

NO BAR MEDALS *continued.*

Pickard, A.H.	Sto	284.800
Pilford, W.J.	Boy	201.951
Ping Ah.	Dom	
Ping Tong.	Dom	
Pinneck, F.	Sto	285.482
Pitcher, L.	Ord	202.968
Plested, F.	Ord	201.538
Pocock, T.C.	Sto	294.151
Poffley, H.J.	Gunr	RMA5.272
Ponder, G.H.A.	AB	157.376
Poole, W.	Pte	Ch7.218
Porritt, T.E.	Sig	198.027
Potter, C.	PO2	155.278
Potter, G.	Sto	285.431
Pratley, J.	Sto	292.399
Pratt, J.E.	MAA	136.517
Pratten, H.	Sto	284.931
Preece, A.	Ord	201.483
Preston, A.	AB	159.650
Priston, R.B.	Fl/Engr	
Pritchard, E.	Ord	192.950
Prynn, S.J.	Ord	199.231
Pugh, L.G.	Sto	290.482
Purser, W.F.	Ord	201.380
Pym, H.R.	Act/ERA	269.938
Quantick, W.R.	AB	138.654
Querotret, J.	AB	183.184
Quested, T.	Sto	285.483
Quick, H.	Boy	201.462
Quigley, J.	Sto	294.588
Radcliff, E.S.	L/Sto	122.221
Radford, G.	PO1	125.717
Raffin, G.	AB	135.611
Ralph, D.	Boy	201.643
Ravenscroft, J.	Sto	284.807
Rawlings, H.O.	Midn	
Reader, M.J.	AB	172.665
Redgrove, H.	Sto	285.508
Reger, D.C.	Boy	201.168
Reid, J.H.	Sto	291.647
Reilly, M.	Sto	286.661
Revell, S.H.	Boy	201.407
Reynolds, J.A.	Boy	201.470
Reynolds, W.F.	AB	183.261
Richardson, A.E.	Sto	286.919
Richardson, A.W.	Gunr	RMA5.501
Richardson, W.	AB	166.714
Ricketts, R.R.	AB	181.006
Ridge, F.	Pte	Ch9.426
Ridgeon, M.	L/Sto	171.234
Ridout, B.	Ord	200.222
Riley, F.	Sto	291.827
Riley, W.	Boy	202.938
Robbins, G.	Ord	205.416
Robbins, W.F.	Gunr	RMA8.032
Roberts, F.	L/S	159.069
Robinson, E.J.	Boy	201.466
Robinson, H.	Arm/Crew	342.257
Robinson, S.	Pte	Ch10.110
Robinson, W.	Pte	Ch9.195
Rone, J.H.	AB	178.753
Rosser, F.	Sergt	Ch7.482
Rouse, H.	L/S	163.220
Rowbotham, W.	Gunr	RMA7.750
Rowe, S.	AB	152.143
Rowe, W.H.	Gunr	
Roy, N.F.	Asst/Payr	
Russell, G.H.	Gunr	RMA5.186
Rutherford, A.B.	PO2	160.672
Rutledge, J.G.	Act/ERA	269.962
Ryan, C.	L/S	177.312
Ryan, H.	L/Sto	279.197
Salisbury, J.H.	Ord	201.219
Salmon, G.J.	Boy	201.537
Samuel, W.	L/S	167.482
Saunders, J.R.	PO2	177.462
Savidge, W.H.R.	L/S	166.178
Scott, W.	Sto	285.801
Scowen, W.	Ord	198.373
Scroxton, J.H.	Pntr	342.806
Seabrook, H.	Carp/Crew	343.175
Seal, G.	Sto	283.399
Searls, L.	Ord	199.885
Shapland, C.J.	Band	341.270
Sharp, O.G.	Ord	197.243
Sharplin, W.P.	Ord	201.251
Shaw, E.	Act/Ch/PO	114.729
Shaw, J.D.H.	Lieut(RMA)	
Sheppard, C.	Gunr	RMA7.670
Sherred, W.T.	3/Wrtr	340.478
Sheryed, H.R.S.	Ord	201.266
Short, W.G.	Sto	284.233
Shorter, T.E.	Boy	198.953
Shropshire, A.G.	Ord	198.447
Shutler, G.S.	AB	158.587
Sie Ah.	Dom	
Silverton, J.R.	L/S	169.131
Simmons, F.	Act/Bombdr	RMA4.221
Simmons, F.G.	AB	156.649
Simon, I.	Ord	198.725
Simpson, R.	Pte	Ch6.580
Sinton, J.	Sto	292.517
Skinner, A.	Arm	151.131
Slater, F.	L/Sto	131.653
Slee, C.	L/S	158.932
Slocombe, F.E.G.	Bosn	
Sluce, S.	Boy	201.497
Smith, A.	Gunr	RMA6.220
Smith, A.C.B.	Ord	193.743
Smith, A.J.	Pte	Ch9.954
Smith, G.	Ch/Sto	121.267
Smith, H.N.	AB	191.489
Smith, J.A.	Sto	285.434
Smith, R.	Sh/Cpl	188.568
Smith, R.	Sto	291.847
Smith, T.H.	Ord	201.474

NO BAR MEDALS *continued.*

Name	Rank	Number
Snare, A.E.	Boy	201.230
Snellgrove, C.	Ord	201.386
Solomon, J.S.V.	AB	173.053
Soper, J.	Gunr	RMA7.711
Sparrow, A.W.	Ord	200.716
Spindler, D.	Sto	289.816
Spooner, J.H.	AB	165.580
Stamp, T.	Pte	Ch10.624
Stannard, A.E.	ERA	171.057
Stannard, R.	Sto	286.731
Stanynought, H.P.	Boy	201.484
Staples, A.G.	Boy	201.393
Stears, F.	Carp	
Steel, C.F.	Gunr	RMA7.140
Stephens, C.A.	Boy	202.111
Stevens, H.W.	Band	179.158
Stevens, S.	PO1	121.891
Stinchcombe, A.	AB	156.810
Stolliday, G.	L/Sto	160.072
Stone, F.	Sto	285.751
Storey, W.E.	AB	164.494
Streek, F.	Boy	201.523
Stringer, J.E.	AB	177.948
Strong, A.	Sto	285.484
Strong, F.E.K.	Sub Lieut	
Stuart, W.	PO1	133.947
Sturdy, G.	Sto	285.547
Sui Ah.	Dom	
Sullivan, E.T.	Sto	158.783
Sullivan, F.G.	Sto	294.136
Sullivan, M.	Ord	195.881
Sum Ah.	Dom	
Summerford, H.G.	Engr	
Surrey, C.T.	Band	341.014
Sutherland, D.	Sto	290.185
Swain, F.F.	2/Yeo/Sig	167.387
Sweeney, M.	Sto	290.711
Sweetland, G.H.	PO1	164.913
Swift, J.	Sto	292.070
Syson, I.	Sto	285.497
Talbot, A.	Ord	199.195
Tanner, O.F.	Pte	Po10.219
Taylor, D.J.	Boy	201.149
Taylor, H.P.	AB	165.309
Taylor, N.H.	Boy	201.486
Taylor, R.J.	Pte	Ch10.696
Taylor, W.H.	Ord	201.153
Thacker, A.P.	Pte	Ch10.559
Thomas, C.	AB	167.865
Thomas, C.H.	L/S	147.592
Thornton, G.S.	Boy	201.222
Thurgar, A.	Sto	291.897
Tilling, J.	Ord	202.969
Toms, L.	Ord	185.550
Tong, T.W.	Sto	284.141
Treadgold, W.G.	Ord	190.220
Treby, J.	Ord	199.232
Triggs, F.W.	Lieut	
Tuck, O.T.	N. Instr	
Tuck, S.	Boy	202.973
Tuck, W.J.	Sto	151.442
Turnbull, R.	Ord	193.829
Turner, A.	Ord	195.009
Turner, A.E.	Sto	277.059
Turner, E.	Sto	293.092
Turner, T.	Ch/Sto	142.268
Upton, P.J.	Ord	195.910
Vail, S.	Pte	Po10.205
Vaughan, A.	Sto	291.857 2
Venables, W.J.	Boy	201.529
Vennall, W.H.	AB	194.495
Vergette, J.J.	Pte	Ch10.535
Viney, R.	Midn	
Vinnicombe, F.W.	Ord	198.783
Virgo, A.E.	Ord	190.120
Wadley, W.J.	Bugler	Ch9.754
Wagstaff, T.H.	SBStd	150.408
Waldron, F.	L/Sergt	RMA4.071
Wall, F.	Sto	148.913
Walsh, L.	Ord	196.677
Warburton, F.M.	Ord	192.973
Ward, E.	L/Carp/Crew	342.326
Ware, W.	Sto	279.368
Warman, J.A.	Boy	201.457
Warren, J.	PO2	166.912
Washington, G.	Boy	201.381
Watson, A.	Ord	203.593
Watson, R.J.N.	Lieut	
Webb, W.C.	SB/Attn	150.484
Webster, R.	Ord	201.362
Wells, A.	AB	172.003
Wells, T.	Pte	Ch10.650
Welton, W.J.	Sto	283.951
West, F.C.	AB	164.400
West, S.	Ord	198.171
Weyman, H.	Ord	202.992
Whaley, W.	AB	158.863
Whayman, R.G.	Sto	283.029
Whelton, A.W.	Ord	203.932
White, G.	Sail	132.981
White, H.	Gunr	RMA7.816
White, W.J.	Ord	198.970
Whitewood, W.C.	SB/Attn	350.496
Wiffen, H.A.	Pte	Ch10.457
Wigginton, H.G.	Boy	201.535
Wild, A.H.	Sto	285.572
Wilks, A.	Boy	201.986
Williams, A.F.	AB	133.598
Williams, C.	Pte	Ch10.476
Williams, E.	Gunr	RMA6.207
Williams, E.H.B.	Midn	
Williams, J.	Sto	277.600
Williams, T.	Boy	202.108
Williams, T.C.	Ch/ERA	162.005
Willis, B.H.W.	Sto	152.409
Willis, T.	Sto	290.181

NO BAR MEDALS *continued.*

Willmott, C.	Pte	Ch6.840
Wilson, J.H.S.	Sto	291.642
Winthrop, E.	Lieut	
Wintz, L.E.	Capt	
Witthames, T.L.	L/S	174.501
Wood, A.H.	Sh/Std/Asst	341.502
Woods, F.	Ord	181.855
Woodward, E.A.	L/Sto	129.030
Woollcombe, C.G.L.	Midn	
Woolven, F.S.	Ord	184.100
Worledge, A.C.M.	Sh/Std	119.484
Worthington, H.	Capt(RMA)	
Wortley, J.W.	Pte	Ch8.645
Wray, A.	Ord	202.954
Wray, C.C.	Pte	Ch6.678
Wren, C.W.	Sto	279.691
Wyeth, C.E.	Gunr	RMA7.653
Yallop, F.T.	AB	165.564
Yapp, E.T.	Sto	291.626
Yeomans, H.G.	Ord	202.994
You Ah.	Dom	
You Law.	Dom	
Young Ah.	Dom	
Young, J.A.	Ord	201.924 [3]

Duplicate medals:

Balmforth, J.	AB	170.670
Bowering, G.H.	Sto	294.157
Bowness, W.N.	Ord	191.435
Briggs, J.	Ord	198.636
Burridge, A.E.	Boy	201.463
Clarke, A.F.	Boy	201.389
Combstock, T.H.	PO2	159.206
Coulter, C.	L/Sto	166.626
Cox, J.G.	Ord	201.498
Cullis, H.	Boy	201.215
Davey, E.C.	Ord	201.257
Dawson, A.B.F.	Lieut	
Dovley, W.	Gunr	RMA7.530
Fitzpatrick, T.	Ord	199.436
Gilbert, A.	Ord	199.261
Golley, R.L.	AB	171.742
Hales, D.	Gunr	RMA8.028
Harris, H.G.	Sto	289.168 *
Harvey, W.	Sto	285.546
Irvine, J.	AB	168.794
Jones, C.R.	AB	176.438
Kissel, W.H.	AB	194.490
McFarlane, D.	Sto	292.877 *
McWhinnie, A.	Carp/Crew	343.180
Morris, A.E.	SB/Attn	350.466
Morton, H.C.	Lieut(RMLI)	
Nagle, R.P.	Ord	201.524 *
Neill-James, C.H.	Midn	
Nicklin, G.	Blksmth	342.117
Nolan, J.J.	Boy	199.466
Oram, F.	Ord	198.211
Revell, S.H.	Boy	201.407
Reynolds, W.F.	AB	183.261
Ricketts, R.R.	AB	181.006
Rouse, H.	L/S	163.220
Salisbury, J.H.	Ord	201.219
Soper, J.	Gunr	RMA7.711
Stone, F.	Sto	285.751
Thomas, C.H.	L/S	147.592
Thornton, G.S.	Boy	201.222
Toms, L.	Ord	185.550
Webb, W.C.	SB/Attn	150.484
Wild, A.H.	Sto	285.572
Young, J.A.	Ord	201.924

* *Two duplicate medals issued.*

Duplicate medals - without issue no. on roll.

Briggs, J.	Ord	198.636
Griffiths, W.J.	Blksmth/Mte	286.584
Howell, F.	Ord	203.406
Kennard, E.	AB	166.365
Palmer, H.	Ord	188.917
Strong, F.E.K.	Sub Lieut	

Returned medals:

Antrobus, H.	Gunr	RMA6.664 [4]
Chapman, W.R.H.	Midn	
Clarke, H.E.	Gunr	RMA6.258
Cook, E.E.	Ord	199.221
Crawford, T.	Sto	293.907
Cunningham, A.	Gunr	RMA7.615
Easton, H.	Ord	187.944
Egan, T.	Sto	292.917
Elliott, C.	Pte	Ch10.616
Green, H.B.	Sto	288.776
Griffiths, W.J.	Blksmth/Mte	286.584
Hales, A.	Ord	184.530
Hawkins, J.H.	AB	118.122
Hunter, A.	Sto	285.269
Hurst, J.	Pte	Ch10.583
Jack, J.H.	Carp/Crew	343.058
Johnson, A.H.	Boy	201.481
Martin, H.J.	Act/ERA	269.991
Martin, W.	Pte	Po5.405 [5]
Murray, N.	Ord	197.848
Parker, J.A.	Pte	Ch10.556
Pope, F.P.	Bandmaster	169.047
Pull, E.	Ord	201.819
Rayner, J.	AB	164.340
Rogers, T.	Sto	292.315
Spence, H.	Sto	280.927
Thorne, G.W.T.	AB	175.252
Warren, H.	Gunr	RMA7.973
Whitmore, J.	AB	185.506
Wilson, F.W.	Ord	197.881
Wilson, S.A.	ERA	269.489

H.M.S. HART.

H.M.S. Hart was a Destroyer of 295 tons and 185 x 19 feet. Her armament consisted of 1 x 12 pdr, 5 x 6 pdr and 2 torpedo tubes. The vessel was built by Fairfield and launched on 27th March 1895. She was sold in 1912 at Hong Kong.

Bars	*Total*	*Returned*	*Entitled*
None	*57*	*1*	*56*
	57	*1*	*56*

Notes:

K - Medal presented by H.M. The King on 8th March 1902.

NO BAR MEDALS.

Andrews, J.W.	Ch/ERA	165.097	
Armstrong, J.G.	Lieut Comdr		
Baker, E.	Sto	284.924	
Baker, J.	Sto	286.450	
Beer, F.	L/Sto	125.288	
Bingham, J.E.	AB	164.801	
Binney, W.	Sto	286.767	
Brister, J.E.	Gunr		
Brown, C.	AB	169.914	
Bucknell, J.P.	Act/ERA	269.487	
Burke, J.	Sto	163.101	
Clarke, W.	Sto	291.885	
Deakins, G.	AB	159.293	
Dobbs, H.	Ch/Sto	128.355	
Driscoll, C.	L/Sto	159.919	
Elliott, C.H.	Sto	280.940	
Fenner, G.	AB	171.633	
Foster, J.	AB	171.580	
Freeman, G.	Cook/Mte	354.145	
Gledhill, P.	ERA	268.463	
Guttridge, W.	Sto	288.842	
Healey, T.	Ch/PO	86.386	
Hockings, S.J.	AB	183.288	
Hughes, J.	Sto	288.139	
Hunter, E.	Sto	160.014	
Hurst, H.E.	Gunr		
Johnson, A.E.	AB	176.421	
Jones, H.	L/S	194.025	
Key, R.W.	AB	178.805	
Killick, A.H.	ERA	154.516	
Lai Ah.	Dom		
Lewis, T.	Sto	98.565	
Luxton, H.W.	AB	181.202	
Perring, G.	PO2	151.067	
Perry, A.A.	L/Sto	152.354	
Power, J.	Sto	291.567	
Rashley, J.	Sto	287.962	
Regan, R.	Sto	287.254	
Rippin, W.	PO1	122.254	
Sala, A.	Sto	286.351	
Shaughnessy, P.	L/Sto	153.148	
Smith, F.	Sto	288.240	
Snell, W.H.	Arm	121.390	
Somers, L.J.	Sto	288.138	
Suttling, J.	Sto	287.357	K
Sutton, A.W.	Engr		
Thomas, W.G.	Sto	291.933	
Tom Ah.	Dom		
Tucker, G.H.	AB	189.587	
Turner, W.	Sto	281.579	
Wheeler, A.T.	AB	176.461	
Whittaker, F.	Sto	289.355	
Wicks, P.	2/Yeo/Sig	178.367	
Woodley, J.	L/Sto	153.138	
Woolgar, W.C.	AB	160.936	
Wright, R.B.	AB	157.348	

Duplicate medals:

Johnson, A.E.	AB	176.421
Wicks, P.	2/Yeo/Sig	178.367
Woolgar, W.C.	AB	160.936

Returned medal:

Gardner, T.	Q/Sig	144.618

H.M.S. HERMIONE.

H.M.S. Hermione was a 2nd class Cruiser of 4,360 tons and 320 x 49½ feet. Her armament consisted of 2 x 6 in, 8 x 4 in and 8 x 6 pdr guns. The vessel was built in Devonport Dock Yard and launched on 7th November 1893. She was sold on 25th October 1921 to Multilocular Ship Breaking Co. She was resold on 18th December 1922, was renamed Warspite and became a Training Ship. She was eventually sold in September 1940 to Ward.

Bars	*Total*	*Returned*	*Entitled*
TF & RP	*1*	*0*	*1*
None	*338*	*6*	*332*
	339	*6*	*333*

Notes:

K - Medal presented by H.M. The King on 8th March 1902.

1 - Roll states, "Man issued with medal on H.M.S. Fame."

Bars: TAKU FORTS, RELIEF OF PEKIN.

MacDonald, W.	Pte	Ply6.401	

NO BAR MEDALS.

Adams, R.J.	ERA	268.853	
Addy, J.P.	PO1	121.535	
Allen, C.H.	Ord	188.796	
Allen, E.A.	AB	121.815	
Armitage, A.F.St.C.	Lieut		
Ashton, J.W.	AB	177.706	
Babbage, S.J.	Bosn		
Babbage, W.H.	PO1	138.972	K
Baker, J.	Sto	155.876	K
Ballard, G.N.	Lieut		
Balls, G.	AB	179.400	
Banks, J.	Sto	153.895	
Barriball, T.	Q/Sig	192.879	
Baskerville, H.	L/Sig	138.976	
Bassett, E.W.T.	L/Sto	153.345	K
Battieshill, J.	PO2	160.573	
Beach, J.H.	Pilot		
Beer. S.	Sto	355.228	
Behenna, S.	Sh/Cook	141.755	K
Bennett, A.	Arm	130.949	
Bennett, W.H.	Blksmth	163.071	K
Bennington, J.W.	Fl/Engr		
Bett, W.	St/Surgn		
Bevis, W.C.	2/SBStd	164.103	
Bickell, R.	Ch/Sto	140.185	
Bickford, C.	AB	182.691	
Binstead, W.P.	PO2	136.502	
Blackmore, F.	AB	178.038	
Blades, T.J.	Sto	279.318	K
Bodkin, M.J.	AB	182.174	
Bowyer, R.W.	AB	129.219	
Boxall, M.	L/Sig	157.358	
Boyce, J.	L/Sto	147.501	
Bridges, F.J.	AB	180.720	
Browne, W.E.	ERA	268.255	K
Bryan, G.H.	Sto	286.165	
Bull, W.R.	L/Cpl	Ply8.276	
Bunbury, A.	Asst/Payr		
Burke, W.	Sto	289.428	
Burnett, J.	AB	189.061	
Burr, J.M.S.	Pilot		
Burt, E.H.	2/Wrtr	340.592	K
Cantrill, R.H.	Pte	Ply6.749	
Cape, F.G.	Sto	280.972	
Carnie, W.	Sto	281.014	
Carter, W.G.	Pte	Ply6.979	
Cathie, J.R.	PO1	117.032	
Cawse, J.	Pte	Ply8.389	
Chaffe, H.	Ch/ERA	164.691	
Chee Ah.	Dom		
Cheong Sing.	Dom		
Chop Ah.	Dom		
Chow Ah.	Dom		
Chung Yung.	Dom		
Coish, T.	Sto	282.065	
Coleman, T.	AB	178.948	K
Coles, A.T.	Bugler	Ply7.741	
Collin, F.	Sto	286.609	
Collins, W.J.	Sto	279.281	K

NO BAR MEDALS *continued.*

Cong Ah.	Dom		
Cook, T.R.	AB	189.610	
Cooke, J.	Pte	Ply4.254	
Cooke, R.R.	Midn		
Cooler, G.	Sto	286.148	
Courtis, T.E.	Gunr		
Cowler, W.J.	Sto	286.043	
Cree, J.A.	PO1	147.646	
Creech, F.A.	Q/Sig	159.319	
Crennell, J.	AB	155.793	K
Crimp, W.H.	AB	183.452	
Crockett, T.G.	Pte	Ply8.390	
Cruze, H.	Sto	176.683	
Cuming, A.	PO1	102.082	
Cumming, R.S.D.	Capt		
Curran, M.	Sto	282.633	
Curtis, W.	Carp/Crew	342.140	
Cutland, J.W.A.	Sto	277.111	
Daley, P.	Sto	281.030	
Daly, E.	AB	183.502	
Dalzell, Rev.H.	Chaplain & N. Instr		
Dash, J.	AB	179.647	
Davidson, E.G.W.	Lieut		
Davis, G.	AB	186.547	
Davis, J.P.	L/S	159.152	
Davis, J.T.	Sto	282.496	
De Thoren, O.E.A. de S.	Midn		
Dean, W.J.	L/S	135.720	
Dickerson, A.R.	AB	190.074	
Dilley, H.	Ord	197.797	
Dip Ah.	Dom		
Dixon, J.J.	AB	149.264	
Donaldson, D.	AB	189.952	
Dong Ah.	Dom		
Donnelly, H.	AB	177.795	
Doran, J.A.	PO2	156.458	
Dunn, E.	ERA	268.732	
Dunstan, T.J.	Ch/Arm	130.951	
Dymond, F.	Sto	285.660	
Ede, W.C.	Ch/Yeo/Sig	122.739	
Efford, E.A.	AB	186.113	K
England, F.G.	Sto	291.538	
Evans, G.	Pte	Ply7.484	
Farndell, A.	Pte	Po8.849	
Fat Ah.	Dom		
Fearby, T.A.	Pte	Ply6.434	
Fee, J.	Pte	Ply8.408	
Finch, A.	Sto	292.712	
Finch, F.E.	L/Sto	161.182	
Fisher, T.	Midn		
Fitzgerald, T.	AB	181.993	K
Flaherty, B.	Sto	286.503	
Flahive, J.	Sto	286.160	K
Flynn, J.	L/Sto	161.414	
Frawley, J.	AB	186.507	
Fry, A.S.	Pte	Po7.374	

Gallop, J.	AB	174.697	K
Gardner, A.	AB	155.025	
Gardner, A.	AB	189.690	
Gee Dee.	Dom		
George, H.J.	AB	188.866	
Gibson, J.W.	PO1	159.874	
Giljoy, W.R.	AB	178.355	
Gill, J.R.	ERA	115.787	
Gillingham, R.H.	Carp/Crew	341.726	
Goard, H.W.	Sto	276.924	K
Goggin, J.	PO1	110.319	
Gomm, A.E.	AB	183.300	K
Goodenough, W.E.	Lieut		
Grant, F.J.	Ord	193.240	
Grose, J.R.	Sto	286.157	
Grottick, E.	2/Yeo/Sig	161.625	
Ham, H.	Shpwrt	341.802	
Ham, W.H.	Sto	286.169	
Hamilton-Gordon, H.	Midn		
Hammond, C.C.J.	Engr		
Hannaford, W.	Sto	276.532	
Harding, W.G.	PO2	156.777	K
Hartnell, G.A.	Sto	281.671	
Harvey, C.J.	Ord	197.874	
Hawke, R.H.	L/Sto	147.498	
Hawkes, H.G.	AB	120.873	
Hawkins, G.	AB	145.873	
Hay, H.	Sto	145.505	
Hayes, J.	Sto	279.120	
Healy, G.F.	AB	165.721	
Hearn, E.	Shpwrt	340.721	
Hemmings, A.	Sto	278.869	
Hender, C.C.	L/Sto	163.691	
Henderson, R.G.H.	Act/Sub Lieut		
Hickey, H.	PO2	141.480	K
Hickley, S.A.	Lieut		
Hockings, R.	AB	179.181	
Hodder, S.	Plmbr	172.354	
Holder, J.	Pte	Ply5.301	
Holding, A.	Pte	Ply5.999	
Hopkins, E.N.	Asst/Payr		
Hopkins, L.P.	Sto	292.709	
Horton, J.W.	AB	189.445	
Horton, W.H.	PO1	111.474	
Howell, E.A.	L/S	145.546	K
Hughes, T.	Ord	197.546	
Hung Ah.	Dom		
Hunt, A.H.	Arm/Mte	177.028	
Hurrell, S.R.	AB	180.030	
Hutchings, F.J.	AB	178.112	
Hutton, J.A.S.	Midn		
Hyland, H.	AB	176.975	
Ingleton, A.	AB	123.063	
Ireland, A.	Sto	281.424	
Jackson, T.F.	AB	189.953	
James, W.J.	Sto	286.632	
Jarvis, G.E.L.	AB	179.562	
Jerrett, A.E.	Pte	Ply8.406	
Johns, W.	Sto	281.415	K

NO BAR MEDALS *continued.*

Name	Rank	Number	
Jones, G.F.	PO1	127.120	
Jones, J.	Sub Lieut		
Jordan, C.T.	AB	189.576	
Kee Ah.	Dom		
Keefe, R.	PO1	115.911	
Kellow, W.	Ch/Sto	135.965	
Kennedy, T.	AB	189.499	
Kirby, J.	PO2	163.999	
Kitt, J.A.	Ch/SBStd	133.436	
Kong Ah.	Dom		
Knapman, F.	Sto	281.357	
Knox, T.	Cooper	341.033	
Lamacraft, W.	Sto	285.589	
Latcham, I.	Pte	Ply8.410	
Le Mottée, J.B.	Midn		
Lewis, W.	Musn	103.429	
Liggett, T.	Pte	Ply7.901	
Little, C.J.C.	Midn		
Lloyd, H.	AB	185.616	
Loo Ah.	Dom		
Love, A.G.	AB	193.273	
McCandless, R.	AB	185.008	
McGann, J.	Sto	286.146	
McKenzie, R.L.H.	AB	170.403	
McKew, T.E.	AB	180.059	
McNaughton, A.	AB	186.593	
Makins, O.M.	Lieut		
Maloney, T.	L/Sto	149.871	
Manning, J.	Sto	176.994	
Mansell, J.	AB	120.964	
Maple, J.H.	Ord	196.901	
Margrie, W.H.	Ch/Sto	126.482	
Marshall, H.H.	AB	189.961	
Martin, G.P.	Pte	Ply8.355	
Martin, S.M.	AB	180.144	
Matthews, F.J.	AB	174.950	
Mepstead, W.J.	Cook/Mte	353.486	
Mildren, G.	L/Sto	153.032	
Miles, F.A.	PO2	151.759	
Miller, L.W.	Capt(RMLI)		
Mills, F.C.	L/Sto	131.655	
Milne, R.S.	AB	174.522	
Mooring, C.	Sto	281.547	
Morrell, C.H.	Carp/Mte	147.493	
Munelly, M.	Sto	177.092	
Murch, S.	AB	189.748	
Murphy, J.	Sto	277.648	
Murphy, S.	PO1	107.655	
Nash, J.J.	AB	191.080	
Naven, J.	Ord	197.642	
Neild, J.H.	Midn		
Nicholl, J.M.	AB	143.536	
Nunn, G.F.	AB	155.064	
O'Callaghan, J.	Sto	290.981	
O'Connor, M.	PO1	149.113	
Orr, J.	Sto	286.496	
Osborne, H.	Pte	Ply7.123	
Ough, T.	AB	185.998	
Owen, G.W.	AB	178.448	
Owen, I.P.	Sto	278.216	
Packer, V.	Sh/Std	159.597	
Paris, J.	Pte	Ply8.106	
Parker, A.C.	ERA	268.331	
Parker, W.	Act/Lieut(RMA)		
Pascoe, C.H.	AB	129.300	
Paul, C.	Sto	281.023	K
Pedrick, J.G.	L/Sto	146.221	
Pembroke, W.J.	AB	189.776	
Perry, S.	AB	189.956	
Pinn, J.	Sto	292.721	
Pitts, E.S.	Sto	282.101	
Pocock, C.G.	AB	184.753	
Pope, W.E.	Midn		
Porter, H.G.	Pte	Ply7.702	
Prout, W.H.	L/S	152.897	
Prynne, W.T.J.	Q/Sig	186.244	
Purse, J.W.	L/Sto	155.459	
Putt, A.W.	AB	153.941	
Quan Ah.	Dom		
Rayner, A.E.	AB	189.211	
Read, J.	PO1	128.152	K
Redmond, J.	AB	181.712	
Reed, A.E.	AB	145.313	
Regan, W.	L/Sto	133.811	
Rendle, W.	Ch/Sto	112.225	
Richards, J.	Sto	290.407	
Ridgway, C.T.	Carp		
Roberts, F.J.	L/Sergt	Ply5.029	
Robins, S.	Sto	286.155	K
Robins, S.	Pte	Ply8.407	
Rostins, F.C.	Sto	158.820	
Satchwill, S.	ERA	268.489	
Scott, F.	AB	180.764	
Scott, W.	Act/Sub Lieut		
Selley, J.	AB	177.248	
Sellick, C.R.	Sto	281.664	
Sharman, J.A.	AB	183.234	
Shaxton, T.	AB	177.315	
Simmons, W.G.	MAA	114.332	
Sims, W.A.	AB	167.995	
Sing Ah.	Dom		
Sisk, W.P.	Sto	171.340	
Smith, G.R.	ERA	268.981	
Smyth, A.P.	AB	179.554	K
Snow, D.	Sto	286.634	
Southard, J.H.	L/S	158.424	
Southcott, W.G.	Sto	289.866	
Spence, J.	AB	189.962	
Squires, F.J.	AB	183.297	K
Stannistreet, R.W.	Surgn		
Stattersfield, R.	Pte	Ply7.595	
Steed, W.G.	Sto	286.488	K
Stevenson, G.A.	AB	171.707	
Stokes, F.	L/S	163.247	
Stone, J.	Sto	281.414	
Sui Ah.	Dom		

NO BAR MEDALS *continued.*

Sutherly, F.J.	Sto	286.170	
Sweeney, J.	Sto	279.379	
Tempest, G.H.	AB	190.539	
Terry, A.	Pte	Ply8.093	
Thomas, A.E.	AB	176.278	
Thomas, F.H.	AB	176.277	
Thompson, G.	Ch/Sto	140.297	
Thompson, H.E.	AB	189.777	
Thompson, J.W.	Ord	189.958	
Thomson, E.M.R.	Gunr		
Thorn, H.	Pte	Ply8.421	
Thornbury, G.W.	L/Carp/Crew	341.937	
Tibbs, F.	AB	180.837	
Tickner, F.	Sto	277.125	
Tod, T.A.	AB	156.851	K
Toms, J.H.	Sh/Cpl	130.386	K
Tooley, T.	L/Sto	153.198	
Travis, F.	AB	180.353	
Turner, C.	Pte	Ply6.230	
Upham, J.	L/Shpwrt	341.671	
Vosper, W.T.	L/S	155.887	K
Waight, G.	Pte	Ply8.655	
Walters, F.J.	AB	180.937	
Warley, J.F.	AB	183.302	
Waterman, J.J.	Arm/Mte	340.376	K
Watson, R.	AB	184.749	
Webb, T.E.	AB	149.238	
Webber, J.S.N.	Asst/Payr		
Welham, H.	AB	164.507	
West, C.H.	Sh/Std/Asst	340.735	
White, A.	Ch/ERA	124.897	
White, J.	Sto	286.623	
Whitefield, W.	Sto	287.120	
Williams, R.H.	L/Sto	167.035	
Willis, A.	Sail/Mte	161.605	
Wilmot, J.R.	Sto	281.406	
Wilmot, R.	Ch/Sto	131.947	
Wilson, A.	Payr		
Wilson, T.	Ord	197.898	
Wood, H.	Pntr	341.797	K
Woodman, A.	AB	189.781	
Yeo, F.F.	Sto	279.625	

Duplicate medals:

Allen, C.H.	Ord	188.796	
Allen, E.A.	AB	121.815	
Beer, S.	Sto	355.228	
Bryan, G.H.	Sto	286.165	
Cathie, J.R.	PO1	117.032	
Coleman, T.	AB	178.948	
Cree, J.A.	PO1	147.646	
Marshall, H.H.	AB	189.961	*
Paris, J.	Pte	Ply8.106	
Shaxton, T.	AB	177.315	
Southard, J.H.	L/S	158.424	
Thompson, J.W.	Ord	189.958	
Thorn, H.	Pte	Ply8.421	
Tibbs, F.	AB	180.837	
Travis, F.	AB	180.353	
Watson, R.	AB	184.749	
Webb, T.E.	AB	149.238	
White, A.	Ch/ERA	124.897	

* *Two duplicate medals issued.*

Duplicate medal - without issue no. on roll:

Cree, J.A.	PO1	147.646

Returned medals:

Devlin, H.	Sto	289.832	1
Flooks, P.C.R.	AB	181.368	
Francis, A.	Sto	285.605	
McDonough, T.	Pte	Ply7.974	
Murray, J.	Sto	286.292	
Regan, J.	AB	126.025	

H.M.S. HUMBER.

H.M.S. Humber was a Destroyer of 295 tons and 194 x 19 feet. Her armament consisted of 1 x 12 pdr, 5 x 6 pdr guns and two torpedo tubes. The vessel was built by Fairfield and launched on 28th December 1895. She was sold on 10th April 1912 to Ward at Briton Ferry.

Bars	*Total*	*Returned*	*Entitled*
None	*105*	*2*	*103*
	105	*2*	*103*

Notes:

1 - Roll states, "D. after C.M.".

NO BAR MEDALS.

Name	Rank	Number
Ahern, D.	PO2	134.963
Andreole, M.	Pte	Ply8.376
Armour, J.	L/S	176.811
Barnett, H.	AB	118.296
Bawden, S.	L/Sto	129.263
Beer, G.A.	2/SbStd	150.371
Bennett, R.	Sto	292.296
Blades, E.H.	Pte	Ply8.369
Bradbury, G.W.	AB	169.803
Bunstone, J.	ERA	268.822
Burns, F.	Sh/Std	158.386
Callaway, H.H.E.	AB	185.599
Callaway, W.G.	AB	185.682
Castle, T.E.	AB	115.587
Chow Ah.	Dom	
Christie, J.	Sto	278.575
Clark, W.M.	L/Sto	171.066
Coaker, W.	AB	182.669
Collard, A.	L/Carp/Crew	164.138
Connett, J.J.	Pte	Ply8.371
Cook, F.	Sto	154.865
Cooper, T.	PO2	166.855
Couchman, S.	L/S	173.988
Cox, O.C.	Q/Sig	169.907
Craik, P.	Ch/ERA	162.008
Davies, G.E.	AB	187.499
Davison, H.J.	Comdr	
Dilloway, J.	Sto	283.318
Duffy, W.	AB	161.391
Duke, F.	AB	164.533
Dunn, R.W.	AB	187.689
Elliott, H.M.C.	Asst/Payr	
Finbow, E.	Dom	354.760
Foo Ah (1).	Dom	
Foo Ah (2).	Dom	
Forrester, J.	Sto	278.245
Foster, J.S.	AB	187.394
Fuller, J.	AB	179.513
Griffin, M.	Sto	292.136
Haines, E.	Surgn	
Hamilton, A.G.	Lieut	
Harpum, W.	Sto	279.071
Harvey, A.A.	Sto	287.091
Hebb, W.	Ch/Cook	119.934
Henderson, J.	Cooper	340.068
Hillier, W.H.	Pte	Ply8.033
Hurden, A.G.	AB	149.369
Irvine, R.	Act/Carp	
Jack, T.S.	Pte	Ply9.317
Janes, E.	Pte	Ply8.388
Janes, J.	Pte	Ply8.387
Jenkins, G.	PO1	111.302
Johnson, A.E.	Bosn	
Johnson, J.H.	Sh/Std/Asst	174.479
Keeler, T.W.	Sto	277.978
Kraatskow, E.	Sail/Mte	154.247
Leighton, D.	Ch/PO	124.328
Leighton, J.	Sto	292.167
Levinge, R.T.A.	St/Surgn	
Lock Ling.	Dom	
McGill, D.	Bosn	
McKnight, S.	Sto	292.135
Maders, F.	L/Sto	276.382
Malone, W.	Sh/Cpl	121.999
Matthews, S.W.	AB	177.747
Matthews, W.	Sto	294.184
Mayne, A.	Pte	Ply8.378
Merrall, F.	AB	174.932
Mounch, T.C.	L/S	175.485
Muir, T.	L/Sto	285.387
Murray, T.	AB	158.619
Norris, A.C.	PO1	118.461
Palmer, J.	L/S	151.039
Parnell, R.	Bosn	
Rendle, W.H.	PO2	145.082
Rex, G.	L/S	163.503

NO BAR MEDALS *continued.*

Riley, T.W.	AB	182.374
Rivett, J.	ERA	268.808
Roye, J.A.	Engr	
Russell, C.	Ch/PO	107.169
Sheldrick, E.W.	2/Wrtr	173.794
Shephard, W.	PO1	112.108
Shoo Ah.	Dom	
Sing Ah.	Dom	
Smith, J.	PO1	136.765
Sowden, G.	AB	149.372
Squires, R.	Sto	279.035
Thomas, J.	AB	156.596
Thompson, G.	AB	185.145
Thompson, J.	Sto	278.497
Tobin, E.	Ch/PO	99.429
Trow, E.	Pte	Po8.897
Tucker, E.	Sto	292.168
Tucker, E.A.	2/Wrtr	167.639
Tuffley, H.J.	PO1	113.692
Vigus, C.	AB	168.396
Walker, J.	L/Sto	155.251
Watts, J.	Cpl	Ply7.995
West, C.E.	AB	172.010
Whitnall, G.	L/Sto	165.405
Whittard, C.	Sto	160.499
Williams, J.	ERA	268.165
Wyatt, T.	Sto	152.582

Duplicate medals:

Blades, E.H.	Pte	Ply8.369
Bradbury, G.W.	AB	169.803
Cooper, T.	PO2	166.855
Dunn, R.W.	AB	187.689

Returned medals:

Humphries, C.	Ord	191.385 [1]
Moore, E.	AB	168.077

H.M.S. ISIS.

H.M.S. Isis was a 2nd class Cruiser of 5,600 tons and 350 x 54 feet. Her armament consisted of 5 x 6 in and 6 x 4.7 in guns (11 x 6 in from 1904). The vessel was built by London & Glasgow Co. and launched on 27th June 1896. She was sold on 26th February 1920 to Granton Ship Braeking Co.

Bars	*Total*	*Returned*	*Entitled*
	446	*14*	*432*
	446	*14*	*432*

Notes:

K - Medal presented by H.M. The King on 8th March 1902.

1 - Roll states, "Duplicate returned from Cambridge and taken on stock 8 March 1905. Returned to Mint Feb 1922."

2 - Roll states, "Run. Medal returned 11/1/08."

3 - Roll states, "Medal returned to office (run drawer) 18/4/02. Man deserted."

NO BAR MEDALS:

Aimes, J.	AB	142.330
Alexander, W.R.	Sub Lieut	
Ames, L.	Arm/Crew	284.898
Amis, R.	AB	177.207
Anderson, H.	Pte	Ch5.250
Andrews, R.	Blksmth	341.286
Aplin, W.	AB	184.542
Ashdowne, H.E.	AB	175.263
Ashley, C.	AB	190.579
Aspinall, J.W.	AB	185.919
Attridge, A.J.	Sto	285.900
Atwell, W.	Sto	285.938
Baggott, E.	Pte	Ch8.567
Baker, W.	Sto	283.152
Balcomb, S.A.	Pte	Ch9.415
Baldry, F.A.	Pte	Ch4.120
Ballard, G.A.	Comdr	
Bancroft, H.	Ord	200.233
Baney, A.L.	Sto	285.951
Barker, T.G.	AB	172.727
Bather, R.H.	Lieut	
Batten, S.	AB	182.264
Bayley, C.A.	Q/Sig	194.574
Bell, J.W.	L/S	180.743
Bellamy, W.H.	Ord	197.466
Bench, W.J.	AB	192.728
Bennett, W.J.	AB	170.922
Bigrig, G.H.	L/S	148.473
Bird, T.	AB	173.193
Black, J.	Sto	286.708
Blackmore, F.W.	Sto	293.281
Blaise, E.	Pte	Ch8.746
Bluett, B.W.	Midn	
Bond, A.E.	AB	179.904
Booker, T.	Dom	356.504
Borras, W.	AB	193.703
Bowdige, J.	Sto	284.690
Boyce, H.J.	Pte	Ch8.991
Boyd, H.A.	Sh/Std	165.910
Brattle, W.W.	AB	178.771
Bravery, H.S.	Ch/PO	128.177
Bright, G.W.	AB	193.232
Brightmer, G.	AB	188.067
Briglin, G.	Carp/Crew	341.535
Brinkley, W.J.	AB	194.549
Brooke, B.R.	Midn	
Brooks, A.	AB	192.568
Brooks, A.H.	Sto	284.941
Broon, G.W.	Sto	286.710
Brown, G.W.L.	AB	180.040
Brown, I.	Ord	194.582
Brown, R.	Pte	Ch9.360
Brown, W.	Pte	Ch9.363
Bruce, W.G.S.	AB	190.397
Bryant, G.	Sto	284.958
Bullbrook, E.	AB	144.309
Bulless, A.	AB	189.375
Burden, A.	Sh/Cpl	138.717
Burke, J.J.	Sto	162.699

NO BAR MEDALS *continued.*

Buzzacott, T.W.	L/Sto	168.410
Calrow, A.	Sto	285.945
Cameron, R.J.	AB	190.413
Camilleri, G.	Dom	356.874
Campbell, J.	AB	190.387
Candy, G.C.	Midn	
Carder, E.G.	Shpwrt	342.136
Carey, E.	Sto	287.764
Carpenter, A.F.B.	Midn	
Carr, E.	PO2	179.743
Cawsey, N.	L/Sig	155.346
Chapman, E.	Sto	285.926
Chase, W.	Sto	293.321
Chesworth, J.	Pte	Ch9.039
Chick, T.G.	Pte	Ch7.950
Choy Ah.	Dom	
Chung Ah.	Dom	
Chung Wah.	Dom	
Cilibertie, J.	Musn	356.986
Clark, A.G.	Pte	Ch8.872
Clark, W.T.	AB	177.654
Clarke, F.	L/Sto	149.444
Clarke, H.	AB	192.487
Cleary, T.	Sto	290.348
Coley, E.F.	Pte	Ch8.711
Conway, F.	AB	174.888
Cook, F.	AB	193.942
Cook, J.	Sto	284.936
Cook, J.C.	Sergt	Ch5.543
Cornford, S.	AB	190.197
Cornish, W.	L/Sto	167.797
Corser, A.	AB	161.951
Coutts, J.	Ch/ERA	160.010
Cowling, J.W.	AB	189.433
Cox, F.	Sto	285.899
Cox, H.I.	Sto	155.203
Cracknell, A.	AB	175.069
Craig, W.A.	AB	174.642
Crane, W.	Sto	285.929
Craxton, H.	AB	193.105
Crook, E.C.	Pte	Ch8.835
Crowle, R.	Sto	293.327
Cunningham, A.	Pntr	341.185
Curran, C.	AB	195.261
D'Oyly, H.R.N.	Lieut(RMLI)	
Davies, F.	Pte	Ch6.494
Davies, T.	Shpwrt	341.926
Davis, A.J.	AB	195.828
Dawson, P.	Sto	288.323
Delury, T.	AB	193.858
Demuth, R.W.	AB	190.180
Dennington, F.	AB	166.583
Dolphin, D.F.	Midn	
Donelly, J.	AB	194.021
Donker, A.	Bugler	Ch7.884
Donovan, A.F.	Gunr	
Dowdell, P.	Ord	197.514

Driver, W.J.	AB	192.178	
Dyer, F.W.	2/Wrtr	353.084	
Ede, W.H.	Sto	293.334	
Edwards, F.J.	AB	189.642	
Elgie, H.	Sto	293.330	
Ellson, T.	PO1	161.098	
Entwistle, R.	Sto	276.669	
Fairbrother, B.	PO2	167.943	
Farnsworth, R.H.	Sto	279.004	
Farrier, F.	AB	194.556	
Faunt, W.N.	AB	181.072	
Felton, W.	Sto	280.171	
Finch, H.	Pte	Ch4.740	
Findlay, P.	Ord	191.411	
Finnimore, J.G.	Sto	285.842	K
Fitzgerald, T.G.	Sto	288.337	
Flewers, J.S.	Pte	Ch5.189	
Fook Jang.	Dom		
Foote, H.	AB	191.932	
Ford, H.J.	PO1	155.181	
Foreman, J.	Ch/Sto	129.536	
Forster, G.	Sto	285.902	
Forster, S.A.	AB	136.603	
Foster, R.	Arm	146.368	
Fox, H.J.	AB	180.927	
Francis, T.	AB	190.950	
Freeman, F.	AB	188.843	
Freeman, R.	L/Sto	152.433	
Frith, C.E.	Pte	Ch8.577	
Gamble, W.H.	AB	191.016	
Giddings, W.H.J.	AB	189.688	
Gilham, A.	PO1	145.162	
Gillies, J.	AB	189.992	
Gittins, C.W.V.	PO1	161.571	
Glasspole, W.H.	Engr		
Goffer, W.J.	AB	182.010	
Gold, G.	AB	189.991	
Goodman, A.A.	AB	186.784	
Gorrie, W.	Pte	Ch8.031	
Grady, W.H.	PO1	113.138	
Grant, A.D.	Midn		
Gray, F.	AB	190.321	
Green, A.J.	AB	191.439	
Gregory, J.G.	L/S	181.007	
Griffiths, A.J.	Sail/Mte	118.480	
Grogan, E.H.J.	Lieut		
Gumbrell, A.	Ord	199.821	
Hammond, L.H.P.	Asst/Engr		
Handcock, G.S.	AB	187.578	
Handsley, A.E.	Sto	286.707	
Hardy, E.R.	Sto	284.955	
Hardy, W.	AB	159.068	
Harman, J.E.	PO2	161.586	
Harrington, H.C.	AB	194.590	
Harris, A.	Cook/Mte	341.544	
Harrison, T.	Sto	282.369	
Harvey, A.E.	Sto	176.634	
Harvey, F.A.	Sto	289.898	
Harvey, T.	Sto	285.950	

NO BAR MEDALS *continued.*

Name	Rank	Number
Hatton, W.J.	AB	193.100
Hayter, W.	L/S	166.328
Hayward, J.	AB	190.604
Hayward, T.Z.	Carp/Crew	342.199
Head, W.	AB	194.027
Henderson, G.M.	Capt	
Heriot, T.	AB	181.968
Hersey, C.W.	L/Sig	157.431
Hewett, H.G.	Midn	
Hewland, W.J.	Pte	Ch9.106
Hill, A.E.	AB	184.305
Hing Ah.	Dom	
Hinton, R.F.	AB	187.305
Holloway, W.	Sto	286.092
Holmes, W.J.	PO1	149.330 K[1]
Homewood, J.	Sto	155.600
Hooker, G.	AB	165.635
Horley, A.F.	Plmbr/Mte	341.533
Horwill, W.H.	AB	189.628
Houseman, E.S.	Lieut	
Howell, F.C.	AB	190.603
Howes, W.	ERA	268.156
Hull, W.	L/Cpl	Ch2.759
Humphrey, G.L.P.	Ord	200.088
Humphries, F.	AB	193.727
Hung Ah.	Dom	
Hurst, R.G.	Midn	
Husk, H.J.	Ord	200.266
Innes, J.G.	Ord	199.178
Jackson, H.	Sto	286.667
Jarman, A.	AB	184.970
Jennings, C.	AB	190.601
Johnson, J.H.	L/Sto	154.260
Johnstone, J.	Ord	200.342
Jones, Rev.P.H.	Chaplain & N. Instr	
Kai Ah.	Dom	
Kan Ah.	Dom	
Kennard, D.A.	Pte	Ch8.804
Kent, A.	AB	189.712
Kerslake, I.C.	Boy	199.864
Kidd, A.	St/Surgn	
Kirby, G.T.	L/S	170.264
Kite, H.	Sto	277.987
Knight, B.	AB	189.734
Knight, C.W.	Act/ERA	269.740
Kum Ah.	Dom	
Lane, J.A.	Lieut	
Langabeer, J.E.	Ch/Arm	149.126
Langston, E.W.	AB	167.523
Lau Ah.	Dom	
Laundon, H.	AB	188.585
Lawrence, J.G.	PO1	119.162
Legg, M.	PO1	155.168
Leggett, R.J.	L/Sto	172.239
Lewis, G.R.	Sto	282.355
Lewis, H.	AB	191.554

Name	Rank	Number
Linnell, G.H.	L/S	168.324
Lister, W.	AB	190.879
Lloyd, R.	Act/Ch/PO	124.305
Lowe, A.J.	Pte	Ch9.784
McBean, J.	Ord	181.377
McCann, W.J.	Arm/Crew	341.467
McConnell, W.F.	MAA	124.446
McDonald, D.	Ord	192.426
McDonald, D.G.	Carp	
McInnes, D.	AB	181.013
McKay, J.K.	AB	195.819
McKellar, J.	Ord	193.836
Mackenow, E.F.	AB	188.013
Mackie, R.W.	2/SBStd	350.412
McLachlan, J.	Sto	166.431
McQueen, R.	AB	185.515
McShea, J.P.	L/S	187.784
Main, D.A.	AB	195.832
Margesson, W.H.D.	Lieut	
Marsh, W.E.	PO2	168.169
Marsh, W.G.	Ord	193.269
Martin, H.J.	Pte	Ch8.979
Martin, J.	AB	197.114
Martin, J.G.	Ch/Sto	142.034
Maslin, A.	Pte	Ch9.152
Masterson, P.	Sto	283.354
Mathias, A.L.	ERA	172.250
Matthews, G.H.	Ord	196.788
Mattocks, J.W.	Sto	174.421
May, R.C.	AB	168.374
Mead, A.	Pte	Po8.619
Mercer, R.	AB	180.793
Merriott, T.	Pte	Ch10.149
Meyers, J.H.	Sto	285.405
Miller, J.H.	Carp/Mte	133.087
Miller, J.R.	PO1	149.357
Millward, A.	Ch/ERA	151.133
Milton, D.P.	AB	197.139
Mitchell, A.E.	AB	192.550
Moat, J.	Yeo/Sig	155.021
Molyneux, T.	AB	163.769
Money, J.	Sto	287.052
Monteith, J.	Sto	286.949
Montgomery, A.	Pte	Ch2.318
Moorshead, T.	Shpwrt	111.382
Morris, J.P.	AB	169.570
Mosley, W.	Ch/Cook	116.107
Moss, F.W.	Sergt	Ch3.215
Mount, F.J.	AB	193.179
Muirhead, J.	Pte	Ch8.707
Murray, H.J.	L/S	146.712
Naper, G.W.E.	Midn	
Napier, J.R.	AB	195.459
New, H.	Act/Ch/Sto	149.439
Newill, J.	Midn	
Nicholls, J.	AB	193.937
Nixon, C.	Ch/Sto	109.383
Norman, H.G.	Q/Sig	190.322
Norman, W.D.	AB	181.101

NO BAR MEDALS *continued.*

Northcott, J.H.	PO2	157.195
O'Brien, C.	Sto	288.364
O'Connell, J.	Sto	289.444
O'Connor, C.	Sto	286.662
O'Connor, G.	AB	193.279
Oliver, S.H.	AB	196.272
Osenton, H.P.	Sto	281.500
Over, M.	Boy	199.866
Overton, G.	Sto	283.636
Owen, F.	Sto	293.326
Page, J.	AB	194.013
Paice, J.	Pte	Ch9.365
Pape, A.	AB	195.479
Parsons, W.H.	Pte	Ch9.351
Pass, A.	Carp/Mte	145.725
Patheyjohns, C.	PO1	136.112
Patterson, A.	Arm	341.067
Patterson, J.	AB	193.399
Payne, H.R.	L/Sto	154.809
Peddie, J.W.	AB	177,126
Perkins, F.G.	L/Sto	164.217
Phillips, J.W.	Sto	279.951
Pickett, T.J.	Pte	Ch8.688
Pitcher, A.J.	2/Cooper	279.089
Pitkin, H.	L/Sto	149.839
Plunkett, B.	AB	172.203
Pollard, A.J.	Pte	Ch4.171
Porteous, C.	ERA	269.909
Potter, W.J.	Pte	Ch6.519
Prescott, A.	AB	169.912
Proctor, T.A.	AB	189.942
Pyman, B.	AB	190.207
Pyne, F.	L/Sto	160.500
Pysden, T.D.	AB	189.577
Redman, F.	PO1	151.519
Rees, J.D.	St/Engr	
Reeve, A.E.	AB	171.765
Reynolds, A.J.	Sto	289.227
Rice, C.	AB	194.563
Richardson, C.	AB	191.389
Richardson, W.G.	Sto	285.930
Ripley, A.W.	L/Sergt	Ch7.111
Roberts, A.C.	Q/Sig	180.324
Roberts, F.G.	Sto	293.325
Roberts, J.E.	ERA	268.780
Roberts, W.	AB	166.851
Rolfe, W.A.	PO2	161.151
Rose, F.	Sto	283.696
Rose, S.	PO1	167.548
Rudkin, G.H.	Pte	Ch8.733
Russell, E.J.	ERA	268.222
Ryan, T.	AB	171.028
Ryan, T.	AB	194.015
Sams, E.C.B.	AB	190.669
Schmonsees, W.J.	AB	193.573
Scott, F.S.	Gunr	
Scott, J.W.	Midn	

Searle, C.	AB	193.730	
Searle, T.C.	AB	196.793	
Sedgwick, F.	Sto	289.224	
Sharp, S.R.	Ch/Sto	152.406	
Shaughnessy, J.	L/Carp/Crew	342.009	K
Shaw, R.	AB	195.476	
Sheaff, A.E.	PO2	170.869	
Sheals, J.J.	AB	161.948	
Sheard, J.W.	Pte	Ch5.700	
Shepherd, G.	AB	185.192	
Shepley, A.	AB	166.795	
Shin Ah.	Dom		
Shoebridge, H.F.	ERA	269.037	
Simmons, W.R.	AB	192.833	
Simpson, W.	AB	196.457	
Sing Ah.	Dom		
Skeer, H.J.	AB	190.905	
Slater, C.	AB	197.047	
Sleeman, E.	AB	197.122	
Sloper, H.	Pte	Ch9.725	
Smith, J.	AB	197.031	
Smith, W.E.	Ord	197.830	
Southwell, W.H.	Ch/ERA	160.545	
Stafford, A.J.	Ch/Sto	128.653	
Standish, E.P.	AB	174.808	
Staple, W.	PO2	142.861	
Stapleton, T.	Pte	Ch7.325	
Stephens, W.K.	Asst/Payr		
Straw, F.S.	PO2	170.755	
Sturman, T.E.	AB	167.969	
Styles, A.	AB	174.840	
Styles, C.	L/Sto	161.033	
Suffolk, C.J.	Pte	Ch8.753	
Sullivan, F.	AB	197.860	
Sullivan, M.	AB	161.154	
Sutherland, W.H.	Sh/Cpl	120.671	
Symes, H.J.	Ch/PO	121.067	
Tandy, F.T.	Pte	Po9.759	
Tatham, H.H.	Midn		
Taylor, A.	L/S	181.660	
Taylor, B.F.	AB	197.140	
Taylor, C.J.	L/Sto	148.324	
Taylor, T.	SBStd	121.820	
Terry, E.W.J.	Sto	280.352	
Terry, W.	Pte	Ch10.214	
Thaxter, A.J.	Sto	286.093	
Thomas, G.C.	Sto	285.910	
Thomas, S.C.	AB	171.599	
Threadgould, E.W.	Ord	200.334	
Tonge, H.	Sto	284.827	
Toye, T.A.	AB	195.824	
Treagus, J.F.	Sto	293.328	
Trotman, E.E.	PO1	147.033	
Tucker, W.H.	AB	135.822	
Turner, E.	Sto	293.331	
Turner, G.	AB	168.789	
Turner, J.	Pte	Ch10.221	
Twitchett, E.G.	Sto	165.899	
Walker, A.	AB	191.525	

NO BAR MEDALS *continued.*

Walker, W.C.	AB	165.038
Wall, H.	AB	179.255
Walley, W.J.	Cpl	Po4.391
Watt, C.	Pte	Ch9.352
Webber, W.E.	Sto	285.952
Weedon, G.C.	AB	190.063
Wellard, W.A.	AB	181.113
Weller, H.J.	2/Yeo/Sig	159.630
Welsh, T.	AB	184.945
Wheeler, W.T.J.	AB	190.066
White, F.	AB	193.729
Whitehead, C.	Sto	286.090
Wiggins, T.	Pte	Po8.393
Wilde, H.J.	AB	190.441
Wilson, A.F.	AB	192.820
Wilson, R.B.	AB	177.791
Wing Ah.	Dom	
Winter, A.E.	Ch/ERA	153.141
Wise, A.	Sto	277.911
Wood, C.A.	Pte	Ch6.412
Wood, J.A.	Fl/Payr	
Wright, J.	L/S	170.534
Wynter, G.C.	Midn	
Yeoman, C.R.	AB	195.839
Youngman, C.T.	AB	191.498
Yow Ah.	Dom	

Duplicate medals:

Bancroft, H.	Ord	200.233
Boyd, H.A.	Sh/Std	165.910
Brooks, A.	AB	192.568
Brown, F.	Ord	193.735
Brown, W.	Pte	Ch9.363
Cilibertie, J.	Musn	356.986
Clark, A.G.	Pte	Ch8.872
Clarke, H.	AB	192.487
Craxton, H.	AB	193.105
Curran, C.	AB	195.261
Day, H.	AB	166.715
Demuth, R.W.	AB	190.180
Entwistle, R.	Sto	276.669
Fox, H.J.	AB	180.927
Gittings, C.W.V.	PO1	161.571 *
Gray, F.	AB	190.321
Griffiths, A.J.	Sail/Mte	118.480
Harman, J.E.	PO2	161.586
Lewis, G.R.	Sto	282.355
McKellar, J.	Ord	193.836
McQueen, R.	AB	185.515 *
McShea, J.P.	L/S	187.784
Oliver, S.H.	AB	196.272
Over, M.	Boy	199.866
Roberts, W.	AB	166.851
Rose, F.	Sto	283.696
Scott, J.W.	Midn	
Shaw, R.	AB	195.476
Simmons, W.R.	AB	192.833
Thomas, S.C.	AB	171.599
Wilson, A.F.	AB	192.820
Yeoman, C.R.	AB	195.839

* *Two duplicate medals issued.*

Returned medals:

Boddy, J.T.	Sto	280.268
Breen, C.G.	Sh/Std/Asst	341.753
Brown, F.	Ord	193.735
Cann, G.	Sto	293.746
Clarke, H.P.	Pte	Ch8.815
Day, H.	AB	166.715 [2]
Fulcher, H.	Sto	279.033
Hackshaw, H.	AB	188.496
Lavin, M.	Ord	194.591
Moss, J.	Ord	191.526
Naughton, D.	Sto	289.258
Pritchard, H.	Ord	193.733 [3]
Roddy, J.	AB	180.966
Tinsley, J.H.	AB	193.574

H.M.S LINNET.

H.M.S. Linnet was a Composite Screw Gunvessel of 756 tons and 165 x 29 feet. Her armament consisted of 2 x 7 in and 3 x 20 pdr guns. The vessel was built by Thames Iron Works and launched on 30th January 1880. She was sold on 27th April 1904 as salvage vessel Linnet.

Bars	*Total*	*Returned*	*Entitled*
None	*98*	*3*	*95*
	98	*3*	*95*

Notes:

1 - This man's service number is incomplete on the roll.

NO BAR MEDALS.

Name	Rank	Number
Abbott, H.	Sto	177.419
Ames, J.	AB	181.534
Amsdell, C.R.	AB	179.030
Anderson, J.	Sto	276.082
Bailey, G.J.	L/Sto	278.077
Bastin, A.A.	Pte	Po7.955
Black, G.A.	AB	137.996
Blowers, H.E.	Sail/Mte	165.613
Bridgman, J.	Pte	Ch3.154
Brown, A.E.	Q/Sig	179.565
Brown, J.H.	ERA	269.265
Butterworth, J.C.	ERA	99.489
Callan, J.	Sh/Std	159.852
Calnan, T.J.	AB	140.767
Chin Ah.	Dom	
Clark, A.	Cpl	Ch7.341
Clarke, G.	AB	144.105
Cockburn, R.	PO2	177.471
Coleman, M.	Pte	Ch3.878
Connor, F.	Arm/Mte	340.138
Crow, J.	AB	182.618
Dark, H.C.	Sto	278.615
Davey, W.J.	AB	193.429
Denton, A.	Ord	189.599
Dowson, H.	AB	178.717
Edwards, J.H.	AB	176.764
Evans, E.J.	Ch/Carp/Mte	149.490
Foo Ah.	Sto	
Foody, J.	AB	184.064
Gearing, A.T.	AB	185.816
Gilbert, A.	Pte	Ch7.451
Gillett, W.S.	Lieut	
Graham, T.J.	Sto	162.747
Gray, A.	AB	277.614
Gudridge, W.L.	AB	187.328
Hall, W.	PO1	169.646
Higgins, J.	Pte	Ch8.272
Hills, T.W.	ERA	145.537
Hoe Ah.	Dom	
Hooper, E.	AB	151.605
Houghton, G.	Pte	Ch8.227
Hung Ah.	Dom	
Jones, A.	L/Sto	133.708
Jones, W.	Sto	154.066
Karby, R.C.	Pte	Ch8.355
King, A.E.	Sto	276.453
Liddell, J.	AB	188.254
Ling Po.	Dom	
Logan, W.A.	AB	180.486
McCartney, A.C.	AB	180.621
Mack, T.	Ord	183.928
Marston, F.C.	Gunr	
Massey, A.	AB	159.586
Masters, A.	Sto	278.580
Meikle, T.C.	Surgn	
Morgan, F.D.	Art/Engr	
Morris, A.J.	Q/Sig	159.265
Ngoo.	Dom	
Nodder, R.H.	AB	161.001
Odell, S.	AB	180.615
Oxbrow, J.W.L.	L/Shpwrt	117.226
Ozenbrook, H.	AB	186.772
Peacock, J.W.	AB	178.585
Phillips, F.H.	Shpwrt	341.567
Piper, F.	AB	183.863
Pleace, W.G.	Pte	Ply8.843
Rice, W.L.	AB	182.53 [1]
Richards, G.R.	AB	185.344
Roome, P.W.	Asst/Payr	
Saunders, T.W.	L/Sto	170.862
Sears, A.T.	2/SBStd	350.339
Sharp, H.E.	Lieut	
Sim, J.G.	L/S	172.194
Skinner, W.F.	PO1	128.054
Smith, W.F.	PO1	114.213
Smythe, W.W.	Comdr	

NO BAR MEDALS *continued.*

Sow Ah.	Sto	
Stroud, W.J.	Ch/PO	144.276
Stuart, E.C.H.	Lieut	
Sullivan, H.	Sto	277.603
Tai Ah.	Dom	
Taylor, G.W.	AB	171.726
Thrower, J.H.	2/Yeo/Sig	145.172
Tinkler, J.	Sh/Cook	148.000
Trivett, H.K.	AB	185.604
Walden, H.J.	AB	193.165
Walke, A.A.	Act/Carp	
West, W.P.	Sto	293.025
Whytock, M.	AB	184.984
Williams, T.	PO1	168.142
Windebank, R.	Pte	Po8.544
Witter, T.	Sto	286.745
Woolnough, G.	L/Sto	155.604
Yohe Ah.	Sto	
Yut Ah.	Dom	

Duplicate medals:

Bailey, G.J.	L/Sto	278.077
Blowers, H.E.	Sail/Mte	165.613
Callan, J.	Sh/Std	159.852
Edwards, J.H.	AB	176.764
Gudridge, W.L.	AB	187.328
Karby, R.C.	Pte	Ch8.355
McCartney, A.C.	AB	180.621

Returned medals:

Kitto, G.E.	Pte	Ch7.265
Marley, J.	Sto	285.145
Molloy, J.	Sto	281.155

H.M.S. MARATHON.

H.M.S. Marathon was a 2nd class Cruiser of 2,950 tons and 265 x 42 feet. Her armament consisted of 6 x 6 in and 9 x 6 pdr guns. The vessel was built by Fairfield and launched on 23rd August 1888. She was sold on 11th August 1905 to Ward at Preston.

Bars	*Total*	*Returned*	*Entitled*
None	*235*	*9*	*226*
	235	*9*	*226*

Notes:

1 - Roll marked "Run". Medal restored and issued 1935.

2 - Roll shows medal returned from Sutlej and placed in run draw. There is no note that the medal was reissued.

3 - Roll states, " D after C.M.

NO BAR MEDALS.

Ainsworth, F.S.	Asst/Engr	
Almond, J.	Sto	284.998
Ambrose, J.	Sto	148.661
Amos, A.	PO2	134.342
Andrews, A.J.	AB	196.263
Andrews, W.	Sto	293.418
Angel, G.	Ord	201.128
Arnold, B.B.	Pntr	341.812
Atterbury, S.T.	Sto	278.681
Barsby, T.	Pte	Po8.311
Bassett, A.	AB	179.147
Beer, P.	AB	173.325
Bell, H.	Pte	Po6.112
Bennett, H.	Ch/PO	85.870
Blackford, M.	Ord	201.163
Body, G.W.	Ch/Sto	135.436
Bourton, H.T.	Pte	Po6.433
Bowbrick, H.	Sto	283.384
Boyer, G.C.A.	Payr	
Brandon, F.J.	Pte	Po5.722
Braxtone, G.	PO1	119.075
Bridger, A.	AB	191.325
Browning, C.	Sto	285.874
Buckley, A.E.	Ord	189.069
Burden, B.F.	Ch/Wrtr	133.076
Burt, W.J.	AB	169.421
Butler, P.	Sto	291.496
Campbell, D.	AB	168.766
Candy, C.E.	AB	201.323
Cann, J.A.	AB	167.435
Carter, T.	Sto	282.707
Charlo, S.A.H.	Sig	194.358
Clasper, H.	AB	162.821
Cole, A.E.	AB	145.887
Colman, G.J.	AB	161.448
Cording, T.	AB	118.299
Corker, R.	ERA	269.156
Cotton, C.	AB	193.259
Cox, G.W.	Sto	291.583
Cundle, A.H.	AB	178.070
D'Souza, M.A.	Dom	353.039
Dale, W.H.	Ord	201.067
Davies, J.	Sto	277.859
Day, C.	L/Sto	279.483
Dennett, J.W.	Sto	279.481
Dewar, K.G.B.	Lieut	
Diaz, S.	Dom	122.518
Dore, C.W.	L/Sig	183.222
Douglas, J.G.	Pte	Po8.869
Dray, G.A.	Sto	190.709
Dunkason, C.G.	AB	191.301
Eagle, W.	L/Sto	176.596
Edwards, B.	Sto	278.534
Eley, L.W.	AB	157.408
Ellen, F.	Sto	286.247
Ellsmore, H.	Sto	291.959
English, O.McD.	Lieut	
Faint, W.H.	Pte	Po8.098
Farquett, C.	Gunr	
Fernandes, P.F.	Dom	357.307
Fernandez, J.	Seedie	356.700
Field, J.G.M.	Capt	
Finch, N.	Pte	Po8.836
Fisher, E.	L/Sto	171.204
Fisher, W.	Sto	288.274
Fowles, A.S.	Sto	286.233

NO BAR MEDALS *continued.*

Name	Rating	Number
Fox, T.G.	2/SBStd	350.257
Freckelton, J.	AB	120.307
Freeman, H.W.	Cpl	Po6.921
Frost, A.	Ord	201.096
Fryer, G.H.	Engr	
Galton, A.	Sto	284.977
Gates, G.	PO2	167.236
Gates, W.G.	Ord	201.075
Gaymer, T.	AB	155.733
Gee, A.	Sto	279.971
Gladwell, T.C.	Sto	291.692
Goldhawk, A.T.	AB	166.179
Goodman, F.B.	ERA	269.331
Gordon, J.	Pte	Po8.799
Gould, C.	Ord	200.392
Grayston, J.	L/S	126.928
Hammond, H.	Ord	201.072
Hargreaves, A.	Sto	279.342
Haydon, T.	Sto	290.262
Hazel, P.J.	Clerk	
Heath, S.	Sto	279.977
Hinde, W.C.	Sto	276.981
Hockless, L.H.	AB	191.335
Hodge, W.G.	Act/Ch/Sto	146.842
Hookey, E.	Sto	285.859
Humby, C.H.	Sto	291.965
Hunt, A.H.	Sto	291.807
Hurley, P.	Sto	292.038
Husband, A.	Sto	355.986
Ide, A.J.	PO1	119.323
Ilsley, E.H.	ERA	268.299
Jeffery, J.	AB	167.727
Jerrard, R.W.	AB	183.496
Johnston, A.A.	Sto	149.836
Jones, E.J.	AB	194.534
Jones, R.W.	St/Engr	
Joynes, W.H.	Pte	Po8.305
Keates, C.	Sh/Cook	137.019
Keene, W.	Pte	Po8.835
Kennett, M.F.	Boy	201.076
Kent, W.	AB	170.023
King, J.F.	Arm/Crew	175.343
King, W.F.	AB	182.003
Kingswell, C.W.	L/Sto	161.659
Kirby, C.	Pte	Po8.832
Knowles, A.H.	Ord	191.384
Lang, W.B.	Pte	Po4.353
Lansdown, W.	AB	142.372
Leary, T.	Sto	162.142
Lee, A.J.	L/Sto	130.692
Lee, E.J.	Sto	286.536
Legge, A.J.	Sh/Cpl	132.350
Lewendon, W.G.	AB	166.338
Long, S.	Sto	286.246
McCarthy, J.	PO1	89.568
McCormack, J.	Sto	290.678
McDougall, E.	L/Sto	161.283
McKendrick, J.	Arm/Mte	152.073
McLeod, J.	AB	162.317
McMullen, W.	Sto	285.846
Machado, J.S.	Dom	357.805
Mahagan, S.H.	Boy	201.491
Maidment, H.J.	AB	180.381
Mansell, C.	AB	160.647
Martin, A.R.	PO2	149.375
Mascall, V.G.	Sto	291.693
Matthews, G.H.	Ch/ERA	122.694
Maxwell, H.	Sergt	Po2.565
Maynard, W.H.	Sto	286.237
Messenger, W.	AB	189.019
Mihlenstedt, F.	PO1	124.573
Miles, G.J. *alias* Elliott.	L/Sto	153.627
Mills, E.E.	L/Cpl	Po3.682
Morey, W.J.	AB	169.387
Munro, C.L.	AB	193.939
Nash, C.G.	Sto	291.682
Newton, A.	Ch/Arm	114.286
Newton, W.A.	Act/ERA	160.011
Nightingale, G.H.	AB	172.470
Noy, E.	Sto	288.293
Nutbeam, H.	Sto	290.067
Oliver, H.	Sto	291.801
Page, J.	L/S	162.518
Palmer, E.T.	Sh/Std/Asst	341.401
Palmer, R.	2/Yeo/Sig	170.573
Palmer, S.H.	Ch/Carp/Mte	118.506
Parkes, A.J.	L/Sto	157.076
Parks, G.H.	AB	171.545
Parslow, C.H.	AB	187.164
Pavely, H.G.	L/S	172.507
Peck, W.	Carp/Mte	341.862
Percival, J.E.	AB	181.359
Pereira, D.P.	Dom	358.363
Pink, H.J.	AB	169.995
Pollard, W.	Sto	278.150
Porter, F.	L/Sto	278.355
Pote-Hunt, R.	Admlty Pilot	
Powell, E.F.	AB	155.290
Prestridge, A.G.C.	Plmbr/Mte	341.654
Pringle, T.	Sto	278.047
Rainey, J.	AB	152.001
Redfern, A.	AB	184.102
Rees, S.H.	AB	184.319
Remedio, A.J.	Dom	139.077
Remedios, S.	Dom	355.197
Roberts, A.	PO2	168.043
Roberts, J.	Sto	285.464 [1]
Robins, A.	Sto	293.184
Robinson, E.A.	L/Sto	276.033
Rodrigues, P.P.	Dom	356.701
Rogers, W.	Ch/Sto	143.708
Rose, F.W.	AB	147.381
Rowan, J.	Sto	291.799
St. John, F.G.	Lieut	
Sandsford, F.J.	Sto	291.726

NO BAR MEDALS *continued.*

Name	Rank	Number
Saunders, G.E.	Sto	286.211
Saunders, G.H. *alias* Withers.	PO1	119.084
Sewell, C.	AB	169.043
Sharrott, W.	L/Sig	136.176
Sheppard, C.E.	Pte	Po8.703
Silvester, H.	L/Carp/Crew	342.215
Smith, J.B.	Blksmth	167.648
Stephens, E.S.	Sh/Std	140.846
Stephenson, E.	Sto	278.148
Stone, F.	Pte	Po8.746
Stott, W.G.	St/Surgn	
Stretch, H.	L/Sto	278.358
Strong, W.	Act/Ch/Sto	136.028
Stuart, T.	Act/ERA	269.187
Sullivan, J.	Sto	282.929
Sullivan, W.	Pte	Po8.532
Swampilee, P.	Carp/Crew	342.766
Sweeney, J.	AB	179.864
Taylor, J.A.	AB	157.815
Thake, A.E.	Yeo/Sig	184.884
Thornley, G.S.	Sub Lieut	
Tiller, T.	AB	194.528
Tippett, A.R.	ERA	161.078
Tomlinson, R.W.	Pte	Po8.753
Triggs, W.	Ch/Sto	129.625
Tucker, T.G.	Sto	160.381
Tull, E.	AB	176.985
Tungate, W.	L/Sto	278.374
Vaughan, C.F.	AB	193.868
Vine, F.H.	Ch/Sto	150.703
Viney, W.H.	AB	189.015
Wainscott, G.	ERA	269.287
Walsh, W.P.	AB	184.617
Warner, W.T.	Cooper	134.449
Warren, J.M.D.E.	Lieut	
Watson, H.	Sto	284.973
Watson, W.J.	Sto	287.652
Weeden, A.C.	AB	166.888
Wescomb, E.	PO1	130.505
Whitmore, S.	Sto	286.590
Whittle, A.	ERA	268.040
Wilkinson, C.B.B.	Q/Sig	170.916
Williams, J.A.	ERA	148.617
Williams, W.	L/Shpwrt	341.541
Wood, J.	Sto	276.673

Duplicate medals:

Name	Rank	Number
Cosh, S.	AB	184.828
Dunkason, C.G.	AB	191.301
Eagle, W.	L/Sto	176.596
Fowles, A.S.	Sto	286.233
Galton, A.	Sto	284.977
Gladwell, T.C.	Sto	291.692
Gould, C.	Ord	200.392
Hinde, W.C.	Sto	276.981
Lewendon, W.G.	AB	166.338
Nash, C.G.	Sto	291.682
Noy, E.	Sto	288.293
Oliver, H.	Sto	291.801
Robins, A.	Sto	293.184
Viney, W.H.	AB	189.015
Warren, J.M.D.E.	Lieut	

Returned medals:

Name	Rank	Number	
Baldock, J.W.	AB	172.708	
Canty, F.D.	AB	186.151	
Cosh, S.	AB	184.828	
Ellard, A.	Sto	291.254	
Flynn, R.M.	Sto	290.216	2
Gardiner, G.J.	Sto	290.677	3
Harris, W.G.	Sto	290.259	
Pomphret, A.G.	Sto	291.719	
Tippett, F.H.H.	Sto	285.641	

H.M.S. ORLANDO.

H.M.S. Orlando was an Armoured Cruiser of 5,600 tons and 300 x 56 feet. Her armament consisted of 2 x 9.2 in, 10 x 6 in and 10 x 3 pdr guns. She was built by Palmer and launched on 3rd August 1886. She was sold on 11th July 1905 to Ward at Morecambe.

Bars	*Total*	*Returned*	*Entitled*
TF & RP	*82*	*1*	*81*
TF	*37*	*2*	*35*
RP	*199*	*5*	*194*
None	*223*	*3*	*220*
	541	*11*	*530*

Notes:

K - Medal presented by H.M. The King on 8th March 1902.

1 - Roll indicates that clasp 3 was originally sent to recipient then later clasps 2 & 3 were sent with a request for the original clasp 3 to be returned.

2 - This recipient is noted as "Run 17/9/02"; but a further note says that recipient was allowed to keep the medal.

3 - A duplicate medal was issued 11.9.15 but returned 2.2.16.

4 - This man received medal with bar for Legation Guard.

Bars: TAKU FORTS, RELIEF OF PEKIN.

Name	Rank	Number	Note
Andrews, J.	AB	128.827	
Arnold, P.	Arm/Mte	353.478	
Batten, W.	AB	190.943	
Beard, E.E.	AB	193.704	
Bennett, E.H.	AB	187.880	
Bliss, E.E.V.	Pte	Po9.127	
Bonner, W.G.	AB	190.471	
Brown, A.J.	L/S	151.913	
Campbell, H.	AB	193.990	
Coles, H.	AB	187.899	
Crockford, A.J.	Sto	288.538	
Daglish, T.R.	AB	192.439	
Davey, F.	AB	190.379	
Davidson, W.	Sto	288.743	
Davis, E.D.	Sto	144.785	
Davis, E.R.W.	Sto	287.755	
Doidge, H.	Q/Sig	160.680	
Dommett, E.G.	AB	173.850	
Dowling, H.C.	Dom	151.003	
Drury, H.T.G.	AB	191.802	
Dunn, W.	AB	187.391	
Eggleston, G.T.	Sto	282.213	
Elphick, S.	AB	194.355	
Evans, R.	Sto	279.349	
Ferris, E.	Ord	189.622	
Fletcher, C.	AB	187.913	
Fox, A.	Sig	194.656	
Green, S.J.	AB	154.036	
Grice, E.	AB	191.522	
Hall, J.H.	AB	192.113	
Hansler, G.A.	AB	179.720	
Harris, W.J.	Ord	188.009	
Herbert, D.deC.A.	Midn		
Hicks, H.R.	PO2	149.616	1
Holmes, J.N.	AB	197.100	
Howard, J.W.	Ord	194.657	
Joel, W.	Sto	166.056	
Johnson, J.W.	L/S	156.990	
Jones, W.T.	AB	161.921	
Kimplin, J.J.	Sto	283.206	
King, G.	Sto	162.648	
Kipling, J.	PO2	126.447	
Knights, G.	Pte	Po5.991	
Lockyer, R.L.	AB	179.947	
McDonnell, J.	Sto	283.456	
Mann, G.F.	Sto	284.980	
Martin, W.T.	L/S	151.373	
Massey, F.T.	AB	184.357	

H.M.S. ORLANDO.

Bars: TAKU FORTS, RELIEF OF PEKIN *cont.*

Matthews, G.	AB	191.817
May, E.H.	Pte	Po5.211
Murray, J.	Pte	Po4.622
Murray, N.	AB	194.551
Mustion, H.T.	Pte	Po9.345
Nobbs, W.H.	AB	186.703
Olding, P.H.	PO2	151.644
Oliver, H.H.	AB	192.171
Perfect, H.M.	Lieut	
Phillips, H.	Bosn	
Pigott, A.L.	AB	192.956
Planten, T.G.	Ord	194.687
Prows, J.	Pte	Po3.354
Pulford, H.R.	Pte	Po7.911
Robinson, E.P.	Pte	Po9.237
Robinson, W.	Sto	293.293
Roche, J.	Sto	292.331
Rogers, J.E.	AB	185.718
Sidsaff, W.	Ord	194.654
Stagg, E.F.	AB	174.174
Stripp, A.E.H.	PO2	147.392
Thompson, W.	AB	169.625
Thornton, J.	Pte	Ply5.951
Toogood, A.	AB	191.822
Turner, A.	AB	193.552
Welch, A.	Pte	Po2.943
Welch, J.	Sto	287.754
Whatley, G.	AB	191.842
White, J.	AB	166.197
Wighton, M.	Ord	197.635
Wilkinson, H.	L/S	139.718
Wood, J.	Ord	197.564
Wood, S.	AB	178.503

Duplicate medals:

Andrews, J.	AB	128.827
Murray, J.	Pte	Po4.622
Roche, J.	Sto	292.331
Turner, A.	AB	193.552

Returned medal:

Walker, W.	Sto	288.149

Bar: TAKU FORTS.

Ashley, F.	AB	191.839
Baker, J.H.	Ord	198.657
Barnes, A.	Ord	199.040
Burgess, S.	PO1	138.734
Cuddon, E.G.	Ord	194.136
Cutler, F.H.	Ord	193.365
Dale, R.R.	AB	181.804
Edmonds, W.	Sto	287.761
England, F.J.	AB	191.352
French, R.	AB	191.413
Green, B.	Ch/Sto	138.133
Grier, W.J.	Ord	193.402
Halloran, T.	PO1	117.007
Hamilton, T.E.	Ch/Sto	139.866
Harms, C.	PO1	138.929
Higgins, C.	Gunr	
Hughes, J.E.	AB	186.123
Hyde, R.	Lieut	
Lee, J.	PO1	150.890
McDonnell, W.H.	Sto	286.281
Osborne, S.	AB	184.090
Painter, E.	Sh/Cpl	350.150
Partington, T.W.E.	Midn	
Perkins, D.G.	Ord	197.231
Peterson, A.	Ord	197.645
Sewell, F.A.	AB	197.821
Spink, F.	Sto	282.996
Steel, A.	L/Sto	158.727
Vick, H.J.	Sto	292.322
Watson, G.W.	Ord	194.444
Westbrook, E.E.	AB	187.935
White, E.	Ord	194.341
Whittaker, W.H.	AB	192.849
Wood, W.	PO1	132.982
Wortt, A.J.	AB	190.904

Duplicate medals:

Hughes, J.E.	AB	186.123
Steel, A.	L/Sto	158.727
Wortt, A.J.	AB	190.904

Returned medals:

Lillie, J.E.	Ord	193.964
Proctor, F.E.	Ord	196.114

Bar: RELIEF OF PEKIN.

	Allen, G.W.	Band/Cpl	158.970
	Allen, W.B.	Sto	288.978
	Aymer, F.	AB	161.550
	Bailey, G.F.	PO2	140.038
	Barge, L.	AB	185.726
	Barnes, W.	L/S	161.247
	Bennett, J.W.	Sto	151.534
	Berrecloth, W.J.	Ord	194.694
	Berry, H.	Ord	197.904
2	Betts, W.	Shpwrt	340.888
	Bicknell, D.	AB	147.106
	Bingham, W.	AB	170.653
	Bisson, P.E.	AB	177.875
	Blyth, R.	Band	340.634
	Bocock, F.T.	AB	185.707
	Brogan, E.A.	AB	184.599
	Burke, J.H.T.	Capt	
	Burnicle, R.	AB	177.041

Bar: RELIEF OF PEKIN *continued.*

Name	Rank	Number	
Buttrick, W.	PO1	147.456	
Campion, H.C.T.	AB	180.148	
Carpenter, R.J.	Sergt	Po5.593	
Carter, R.H.	Asst/Clerk		
Catton, W.H.	ERA	268.296	
Chapman, A.W.	Band	340.579	
Chapman, J.H.	PO2	147.000	
Clark, A.V.	AB	190.788	
Clarke, A.E.	Sto	288.963	
Cole, E.	AB	171.400	
Collett, J.A.	Midn		
Cook, F.W.	Pte	Po9.114	
Cook, J.F.	AB	182.153	
Cooper, A.	PO2	152.818	
Cox, C.R.	PO1	129.796	
Craddock, E.H.	Ord	193.819	
Cranston, A.G.	AB	183.203	
Crout, J.	Band	357.147	
Cummings, B.J.	L/S	143.745	
Cunningham, C.	L/S	172.363	
Cunningham, J.E.	AB	186.540	
Curchod, C.S.	AB	194.251	
Curd, B.	Band	340.737	
Daily, J.	AB	180.161	
Davidson, T.H.	AB	171.583	
Dines, J.	AB	193.525	
Donovan, T.	AB	170.316	
Drake, A.	AB	160.129	
Drew, C.H.	AB	173.468	
Duke, F.G.	AB	177.955	
Dumaresq, C.P.	Midn		
Dunleavy, J.	AB	188.878	
Durham, J.	AB	191.840	
Easman, F.G.	AB	171.613	
Edwards, J.W.	Sto	279.781	
Edwards, J.W.	Shpwrt	342.457	
Elliott, W.	Sto	279.794	
Ellis, J.H.	PO1	139.733	
Ettie, O.R.B.	Bugler	Po8.657	K
Eyles, H.	PO1	157.785	
Fisher, F.C.	Lieut		
Fitz, H.P.	AB	171.632	
Foot, R.G.	AB	183.531	
Gaion, S.	L/Sig	184.704	
Gamblen, H.V.	PO2	161.502	
Garforth, F.E.M.	Lieut		
Gaskin, W.R.	Sto	280.017	
Gates, C.	Sto	285.276	
George, H.E.	L/S	162.772	K
Giles, H.	PO1	87.954	
Gingell, W.	Sergt	Ply3.769	
Gipps, G.	Midn		K
Glew, J.	AB	194.653	
Goble, A.T.	AB	175.495	
Godfrey, W.J.	Sto	276.417	
Griffin, P.	Sto	290.942	
Grigg, C.	AB	187.895	
Hanson, L.	AB	192.751	
Hawkins, B.R.	Ord	195.558	
Hewitt, J.	Pte	Po9.254	
Hibberd, A.E.	AB	186.657	
Hicks, T.G.	L/Sergt	Po5.588	
Higgins, T.E.	AB	169.386	
Hinton, F.	L/S	147.697	
Hoddell, W.	AB	179.715	
Hodgkins, J.H.	Pte	Po9.246	
Hood, A.	AB	189.191	
Hood, F.G.K.	AB	158.460	
Howard, T.	Sto	288.981	
Hunt, F.F.	PO1	129.175	
Hussey, F.J.	AB	178.735	
Hutton, A.F.	Sto	283.691	
Irish, H.	Ch/Sto	162.097	
Jefferson, H.	Lieut		
Johnson, F.A.	Pte	Po9.249	
Johnson, J.	Sto	354.902	
Jones, F.T.	L/Cpl	Po9.276	
Keeling, J.E.	Ord	194.111	
Kelling, W.C.	AB	183.532	
King, C.E.	Pte	Po9.242	
Lee, J.R.	Sto	278.544	
Lewis, A.	Pte	Po9.343	
Littledale, H.F.	Midn		K
Lye, A.H.T.	Cpl	Po5.395	
McCarthy, M.	AB	193.256	
McDonald, J.	Sto	288.492	
McGuire, P.	Gunr		
McIlhone, C.	Sto	288.516	
Marr, J.E.	Pte	Po6.918	
Marwood, F.G.	AB	191.041	
Mason, E.J.	AB	188.006	
Meade, W.E.	Sh/Std/Asst	341.020	
Mills, H.T.	AB	179.839	
Mills, W.	AB	176.241	
Milroy, W.G.	Sto	282.207	
Molyneux, J.	Sto	279.762	
Moore, J.	Carp/Mte	131.768	
Morley, W.	Pte	Po9.250	
Mosley, R.G.	AB	184.324	
Mowatt, W.H.	L/S	160.158	
Mulford, B.	L/Sto	158.581	
Murray, E.F.	Asst/Payr		
Murrell, W.	Sto	281.335	
New, C.H.	L/S	142.224	
Newcombe, H.J.	Pte	Po9.240	
Norman, W.C.	AB	169.038	
North, G.	AB	191.343	
Oats, W.J.	Ord	191.136	
Padbury, W.F.	PO1	86.245	
Page, J.	Pte	Po7.459	
Palmer, F.A.	AB	190.000	
Parker, W.J.	Sto	288.962	
Parr, W.	AB	193.207	
Parsons, J.H.	Sto	288.549	
Parsons, L.V.	Ord	191.341	
Payne, T.C.	AB	147.713	

Bar: RELIEF OF PEKIN *continued.*

Penney, G.E.	AB	152.284
Perry, W.H.	AB	194.109
Phillips, P.	Band	340.806
Picot, G.P.	AB	153.356
Plant, W.J.	Sto	288.272
Polhill, T.	PO1	113.832
Pope, W.J.	AB	194.337
Purchess, J.	AB	179.091
Ransom, T.	Pte	Po9.142
Rees, J.H.	AB	185.409
Reynolds, G.L.	Band	340.910
Robbins, A.H.	L/Shpwrt	340.333
Roberts, F.W.	PO1	109.054
Robinson, C.V.	Midn	
Robinson, E.J.	Pte	Po9.292
Robinson, G.	AB	191.851
Robinson, H.	Pte	Po8.934
Samways, G.	AB	153.532
Searls, P.	Sto	291.789
Shea, J.	Ord	195.886
Smith, R.	AB	196.208
Snelgrove, W.	AB	184.269
Spencer, F.	Ord	192.826
Stanley, E.A.B.	Midn	
Staples, E.C.	Sig	185.724
Stillwell, H.G.	Pte	Po8.874
Sturgess, H.	AB	184.327
Symes, T.	AB	173.324
Taplin, W.	AB	177.774
Taylor, A.	Pte	Po9.241
Taylor, G.W.	Midn	
Taylor, W.J.	L/S	128.091
Thomas, H.	PO1	126.498
Thomson, D.E.	Cooper/Crew	340.069
Tubb, J.V.	AB	179.987
Tuck, T.	AB	184.815
Tyler, A.J.G.	AB	165.167
Wadham, A.J.	Pte	Po9.291
Walker, J.E.	AB	162.456
Webster, A.	Sto	289.433
Wedge, A.G.	AB	179.036
Weippert, A.E.	AB	176.425
Wellard, H.R.	AB	117.015
West, G.H.	AB	192.030
Wheeler, R.G.	AB	188.651
Whettingsteel, G.	L/Shpwrt	138.139
White, W.F.	PO1	107.642
Whiteing, C.A.	PO1	125.874
Whitmore, A.	AB	162.314
Willcox, T.	AB	182.758
Wills, T.W.	Ord	184.785
Wilson, W.	Ord	192.617
Winter, H.M.	Pte	Po9.229
Woolfries, H.W.	AB	170.663
Wright, P.N.	Comdr	
Wright, W.	Sto	279.480
Yeatman, S.A.	Sto	278.671
Young, F.	Pte	Po9.347
Young, G.T.	Sto	288.537
Young, J.H.	Midn	

Duplicate medals:

Cummings, B.J.	L/S	143.745
Dines, J.	AB	193.525
Donovan, T.	AB	170.316
Edwards, J.W.	Sto	279.781
Fitz, H.P.	AB	171.632
Gipps, G.	Midn	3
Marr, J.E.	Pte	Po6.918
Molyneux, J.	Sto	279.762
Newcombe, H.J.	Pte	Po9.240
Oats, W.J.	Ord	191.136
Plant, W.J.	Sto	288.272
Robinson, G.	AB	191.851

Returned medals:

Billingsley, F.	Pte	Po7.586
McJurey, W.J.	AB	191.906
Mason, J.W.	AB	184.515
Rowney, J.H.	Sto	283.792
Sullivan, J.	AB	118.089

NO BAR MEDALS.

Anderson, W.J.	AB	179.791
Arnold, H.G.	Ch/PO	96.554
Ashdown, G.	Ord	197.559
Attwood, E.A.	Q/Sig	192.912
Austen, G.	Ch/Cook	73.374
Baker, A.W.	Pte	Po9.218
Bawden, W.C.	Sto	284.333
Bayley, S.	Boy	201.176
Biden, E.J.	St/Surgn	
Biggen, A.	Pte	Po10.218
Birt, G.E.	AB	188.021
Black, D.	Asst/Engr	
Blackford, M.J.B.	ERA	268.307
Blackman, G.D.	Ord	194.340
Blackman, H.W.	Sto	174.578
Bond, J.	Ord	193.345
Boulton, A.	AB	183.143
Boys, E.	Cook/Mte	176.578
Bradbury, W.	Boy	199.926
Braddock, J.	AB	194.952
Bradley, D.	Pte	Po3.232
Brewer, C.E.	AB	176.483
Broad, H.F.W.	L/Cpl	Po7.609
Brock, A.A.	Ord	198.324
Brooker, E.	Blksmth	340.627
Bunker, A.	Ord	188.770
Butt, J.W.	Ord	200.351
Cant, H.	Sto	277.194
Carter, H.	Pte	Po7.054

NO BAR MEDALS *continued.*

Name	Rank	Number
Cartwright, F.	SB/Attn	350.405
Chambers, A.	Ord	200.833
Chambers, J.E.	Blksmth/Mte	180.441
Charlton, E.F.B.	Comdr	
Cheen Ah.	Dom	
Cheesman, H.	L/Sto	141.268
Ching Ah.	Dom	
Chisham, J.A.	Ch/ERA	159.399
Churchill, J.	AB	179.015
Clark, J.	Sh/Cpl	106.932
Clemits, F.	SB/Attn	350.445
Clout, J.	Sto	288.834
Collins, D.	Ord	194.188
Collins, H.W.	Pte	Po7.283
Collins, T.	Pte	Po7.120
Congdon, R.	Ord	201.152
Connor, P.	Sto	284.420
Cooke, A.J.	Q/Sig	190.214
Cooper, S.	Blksmth/Mte	341.540
Corcoran, T.	AB	191.948
Cordery, E.	AB	175.016
Coward, F.C.	Ord	194.479
Crabbe, A.E.M.	PO1	120.526
Cronin, D.	Sail	119.365
Crossman, R.F.	Midn	
Daglish, R.	Arm	97.021
Dare, G.R.	Sto	281.515
Davenport, P.	SB/Std	140.882
Davis, E.	L/Sto	140.475
Dean, C.A.	Sto	283.360
Dennitts, J.S.	Ord	196.498
Dent, W.	Ord	196.708
Do Ah.	Dom	
Dobbin, A.T.	Sto	280.836
Dodd, C.R.	Sh/Std/Boy	341.830
Donovan, M.	Ord	194.170
Dore, G.W.	PO1	121.031
Dudman, A.E.	Ord	191.014
Dunford, J.	Pte	Po3.645
Dunnaway, W.	L/Sto	145.396
Edson, W.	Sto	286.892
Enticknapp, G.	L/Sto	153.804
Fayrer, E.J.	Sh/Std	109.626
Fie Ah.	Dom	
Fisk, F.	Cpl	Po9.421
Fleming, L.	Ord	201.305
Foo Ah (I).	Dom	
Foo Ah (II).	Dom	
Fox, A.	PO2	157.611
Frampton, E.	Sto	286.890
Fraser, J.	Ord	197.563
Freegard, A.	Pte	Po10.235
Freeman, A.	MAA	150.056
Freeman, G.	Pte	Po6.730
Gander, C.W.	ERA	268.291
Godber, J.R.	Ord	199.015
Gore, J.	Boy	198.954

Name	Rank	Number
Graham, B.J.	Pte	Po9.287
Graham, W.S.	Ord	194.338
Grainger, H.	L/Sto	156.690
Green, W.	Sto	277.847
Griffin, E.A.	AB	156.118
Hammond, H.	Sto	356.048
Harman, J.	Sto	161.655
Harris, G.	Ord	191.738
Hart, W.	Sto	147.790
Harvey, W.E.	Pntr	133.043
Hawkins, H.G.	Act/ERA	269.987
Hawkins, W.G.	Sto	278.697
Hill, H.	Sto	292.309
Hinselwood, G.	Boy	198.586
Hobbs, J.	PO1	112.043
Hodge, G.	Ch/Arm	105.511
Hooker, W.	Pte	Po4.593
Horlock, F.A.	Ord	194.040
Hoy, A.	Pte	Po9.235
Hoy (I) Ah.	Dom	
Hoy (II) Ah.	Dom	
Hussey, H.	Ord	197.818
Jenson, F.E.	Ord	199.997
Johnson, A.J.	Ord	182.972
Jones, J.H.	Cooper	124.821
Lake, H.J.	Ord	190.428
Lewis, F.	Arm/Crew	341.758
Lock, W.	2/Yeo/Sig	174.839
Lomax, F.	AB	190.468
Loy Ah (I).	Dom	
Loy Ah (II).	Dom	
McGeoghan, J.	AB	191.221
McGrath, P.	Band	125.398
McKenzie, R.	PO2	146.656
Maeer, A.W.	Boy	199.969
Manning, J.J.	AB	122.278
Marks, T.	Bosn	
Matthews, E.C.	Sto	278.364
Maunder, J.	Sto	277.784
Meeres, B.H.	Chaplain	
Middleton, W.E.	Sub Lieut	
Miller, D.McR.	Sto	288.303
Mitchell, C.	Carp/Mte	111.757
Mitchell, E.	AB	134.822
Mitchell, H.	Sto	282.676
Mon Ah.	Dom	
Monk, E.J.	Shpwrt	340.994
Monkcom, G.W.L.	2/Wrtr	165.960
Morrey, G.	Ord	195.823
Morris, C.	L/Sto	118.967
Mundy, J.	Sto	282.013
Murray, J.	Ord	197.905
Myles, T.	ERA	269.438
Nettle, A.H.	Ord	194.690
O'Sullivan, H.D.E.	Capt(RMLI)	
Palmer, A.	Ord	194.940
Paton, F.C.R.	Asst/Engr	
Peters, T.	Sto	276.472
Pilcher, J.	Ch/ERA	116.531

NO BAR MEDALS *continued.*

Pople, J.	Pte	Po9.145
Pratt, T.	Ch/Sto	127.491
Pratt, T.W.	L/Sto	129.562
Pronger, W.	Yeo/Sig	132.062
Rawlings, J.	Pte	Po7.305
Reid, E.S.	Surgn	
Render, G.	Ord	197.640
Rogers, B.	Ord	185.115
Rose, W.H.	Sergt	Po4.404
Ryan, K.C.	Midn	
Ryder, W.	Ord	186.032
Saunders, A.	Ord	193.360
Saunders, G.	Sto	288.262
Saunders, S.	Dom	355.628
Schofield, W.	Pte	Po10.231
Scofield, W.	Ch/Sto	123.463
Seymour, R.	L/Carp/Crew	340.108
Shawyer, W.J.	Pte	Po10.242
Silk, E.E.	Payr	
Simmons, J.	ERA	269.269
Sing Ah.	Dom	
Skinner, G.M.	Midn	
Slade, W.T.R.	AB	190.942
Smith, H.P.M.	Pte	Po10.127
Smith, R.	Ord	197.903
Spires, R.	Sto	279.471
Spraggett, W.S.	Ord	199.935
Stevens, W.H.	Ord	194.235
Stitson, L.W.	Boy	199.934
Stone, F.	L/Sto	160.412
Street, M.R.	Ch/ERA	126.973
Sweetingham, C.	PO1	123.198
Symes, J.	AB	187.932
Tai Ah.	Dom	
Taylor, G.R.	St/Engr	
Taylor, W.	Sto	162.625
Tee, P.	Sto	163.635
Thornton, G.E.	Sto	146.884
Ti Ho.	Dom	
Tiller, W.	Ord	192.779
Ting Fung.	Dom	
Todd, S.W.J.	Carp	
Townsend, E.	L/Sto	163.729
Tremayne, A.H.	Lieut	
Turner, W.	Sto	291.157
Turrell, J.	Ord	194.346
Vassallo. E.	Bandmaster	357.254
Vear, G.E.	Sto	279.474
Wadge, A.	AB	184.663
Walker, F.	Ord	194.161
Walker, W.C.	Ord	199.998
Wallace, W.	Ch/Sto	139.858
Walters, A.	ERA	269.290
Want, A.	Ord	193.753
Ware, C.	Sto	152.608
Ware, J.H.	SBStd	112.896
Watch, H.V.H.	Asst/Engr	
Waters, A.E.	Sto	279.765
Waters, E.	AB	158.665
Waters, R.	L/Sto	174.580
Waterson, H.	Pte	Po4.997
Way Ah.	Dom	
Webster, J.R.	Ord	199.538
White, J.	N. Instr	
White, W.	Plmbr	151.444
Why Ah.	Dom	
Williamson, R.	Sto	276.414
Wilson, A.	AB	205.966
Windsor, C.	Ch/Sto	116.791
Wing Ah.	Dom	
Woodard, G.	Pte	Po10.112
Ying Ah.	Dom	
Yok Ah.	Dom	
You Ah.	Dom	
Youngs, W.G.	Sh/Cpl	150.749

Duplicate medals:

Black, D.	Asst/Engr	
Bradbury, W.	Boy	199.926
Butt, J.W.	Ord	200.351
Connor, P.	Sto	284.420
Crossman, R.F.	Midn	
Dennitts, J.S.	Ord	196.498 *
Freegard, A.	Pte	Po10.235
Middleton, W.E.	Sub Lieut	
Slade, W.T.R.	AB	190.942

* *Two duplicate medals issued.*

Duplicate medal - without issue no. on roll:

Spires, R.	Sto	279.471

Returned medals:

Antonio, D.B.	Band	358.727
Fagg, A.	AB	175.979
Ormiston, J.	Pte	Po9.546 [4]

H.M.S. PEACOCK.

H.M.S. Peacock was a Composite Screw Gunboat of 755 tons and 165 x 30 feet. Her armament consisted of 6 x 4 in guns. The vessel was built in Pembroke Dock and launched on 22nd June 1888. She was sold on 15th May 1906 to Ellis at Chepstow.

Bars	*Total*	*Returned*	*Entitled*
TF & RP	*1*	*0*	*1*
None	*83*	*2*	*81*
	84	*2*	*82*

Notes:

K - Medal presented by H.M. The King on 8th March 1902.

1 - Roll states,"Ret 20/3/12 found in 'Defence' (in broken state). Dup 1119. New medal sent to Attentive."

2 - Roll states, " Retd. dismissed Service 4.9.02. Medal in run drawer."

Bars: TAKU FORTS, RELIEF OF PEKIN.

Veasey, W.	Pte	Ply7.981	

NO BAR MEDALS.

Adams, H.	L/S	147.035	
Avery, W.	AB	176.090	
Baker, W.J.	Ch/Sto	130.728	
Barnes, P.J.	AB	153.997	
Battersby, G.H.	L/Sig	155.312	
Bazley, W.	Q/Sig	191.787	
Beauchamp, G.	Act/Ch/Sto	112.823	
Bills, W.W.	Engr		
Boundy, W.	Pte	Ply4.465	
Breen, J.	Sto	285.044	
Brooking, W.J.	AB	120.543	
Bryson, J.T.	Sto	289.361	
Buckler, R.F.	AB	159.064	
Burt, G.H.	ERA	268.495	K
Buse, C.E.	Pte	Po10.253	
Canley, A.R.	PO1	124.333	K
Carroll, D.	AB	184.271	
Cawse, J.	AB	159.134	
Clare, W.W.	PO1	90.330	
Coode, C.P.R.	Lieut		
Cook, A.J.	Pte	Ply5.052	
Cove, J.P.	ERA	268.543	
Davis, W.	AB	161.582	
Dawe, W.	Gunr		
Denman, T.	Sergt	Po3.160	
Donegan, W.	Sto	285.590	1
Down, A.E.	PO1	131.148	
Elliott, J.T.	L/Sto	131.437	
Flower, W.J.	2/Sh/Cook		
Harding, H.	AB	176.375	
Harris, W.T.	Sto	284.078	
Hartin, J.	PO1	139.905	
Horswell, J.	ERA	148.841	K
Howard, R.J.	Lieut		
Jarvis, G.	AB	179.278	
Jarvis, T.T.	AB	184.759	
Jeffery, W.H.	L/Sto	149.342	
Kefo.	Dom		
Kin Ah.	Dom		
King, C.W.	AB	184.404	
Ladlow, J.R.	Pte	Ply8.025	K
Lester, F.	Pte	Ply8.070	
MacKay, R.H.R.	Lieut		
McNeilly, T.	AB	185.530	
Mann, E.	Carp/Mte	161.737	
Marsh, W.	L/S	181.807	
Mathew, W.E.	Surgn		
Matthews, G.	PO1	136.224	K
Medlock, E.	AB	157.351	
Millen, H.	AB	174.471	
Ming Ah.	Dom		
Moist, R.E.	PO2	148.246	
Payne, A.E.	Sto	286.617	K
Penter, L.	L/Carp/Crew	341.594	
Peters, J.B.	Arm	147.267	
Ping Ah (I).	Dom		
Ping Ah (II).	Dom		
Pollard, J.	AB	140.067	
Rafferty, J.	Pte	Ply7.550	

NO BAR MEDALS *continued.*

Reed, W.A.	AB	163.325
Rees, A.G.	Ch/Wrtr	127.791
Roberts, J.D.	AB	147.492
Rolls, J.J.	Sh/Std	158.891
Rouse, A.	AB	149.259
Shepherd, R.G.	Pte	Po10.261
Short, T.	AB	118.596
Smith, J.C.	AB	159.101
Smyth, W.	AB	184.644
Staples, J.	AB	155.921
Sutton, W.	AB	170.413
Taylor, A.	Ch/Sto	146.302
Taylor, P.	L/Sto	279.257
Thomas, G.	Sto	286.177
Thorne, A.	Pte	Ply4.219
Udy, R.T.	AB	184.608
Webb, W.	Sto	281.397
Webber, J.	Sto	285.064
Welch, H.	Boy	197.575
White, J.	PO2	153.976
Winter, J.H.	AB	154.372
Wright, R.N.	PO2	156.815

Duplicate medals:

Bryson, J.T.	Sto	289.361
Buckler, R.F.	AB	159.064
Buse, C.E.	Pte	Po10.253
Donegan, W.	Sto	285.590
Webb, W.	Sto	281.397
Welch, H.	Boy	197.575

Returned medals:

Bowden, W.R.	L/S	139.037
Butson, J.	2/SBStd	350.247

H.M.S PHOENIX.

H.M.S. Phoenix was a Sloop of 1,050 tons and 185 x 32½ feet. Her armament consisted of 6 x 4 in guns. The vessel was built in Devonport Dock Yard and launched on 25th April 1895. She capsized on 18th September 1906 in a typhoon at Hong Kong; she was raised and sold on 7th January 1907.

Bars	*Total*	*Returned*	*Entitled*
RP	*13*	*0*	*13*
None	*108*	*6*	*102*
	121	*6*	*115*

Notes:

K - Medal presented by H.M. The King on 8th March 1902.

Bar: RELIEF OF PEKIN.

Alston, A.G.	Lieut	
Baker, C.	Arm/Mte	156.618
Barnett, A.	Sail/Mte	160.742
Benoke, A.S.	Pntr	341.927
Collings, W.H.	AB	164.776
Cremin, M.	Ch/PO	117.291
Dupen, A.P.L.	Engr	
Fraser, R.G.	Capt	
Jope, J.	PO1	130.179
Kennedy, J.	AB	172.952
Lewis, G.	Dom	355.697
Reynolds, J.J.	Gunr	
Weaver, W.	AB	151.984

NO BAR MEDALS.

Almon, E.	Ord	203.938	
Annesley, J.S.	Asst/Payr		
Argeat, F.H.	AB	165.558	
Avent, F.J.	AB	183.092	
Barrett, F.G.	ERA	268.676	
Bassett, J.H.	Ch/ERA	133.114	
Beard, T.J.	Q/Sig	162.886	
Beer, E.A.	Sto	279.632	
Blake, A.J.	AB	162.509	
Bolt, W.H.	Sto	291.741	
Bradley, F.R.	L/S	175.027	
Brinton, H.J.	Pte	Ply9.445	
Button, T.H.	L/Shpwrt	161.723	
Cardiff, J.	Pte	Ply9.446	
Chin Ah.	Dom		
Chu Ah.	Dom		
Collins, W.	PO2	120.656	
Connor, T.J.	Pilot		
Coughlan, D.	Sto	280.578	
Cow Ah.	Dom		
Cross, J.T.	AB	133.816	
Cross, W.E.	Ord	203.629	
Cudlip, F.J.	PO2	154.388	
Cutcliffe, E.G.	PO1	160.353	K
Davey, W.H.	L/Cpl	Ply7.368	
Dillon, G.J.	AB	195.870	
Duck Ah.	Dom		
Elliott, A.J.	AB	162.774	
Elliott, L.	Act/ERA	269.364	
Ellis, W.	Sto	176.701	
Flynn, J.	Sto	291.728	
Frost, R.	Sto	280.114	
Gardner, G.	Sto	280.136	
Gellibrand, H.B.	Lieut		
Gillard, A.J.	Sto	175.823	
Green, A.E.	PO1	125.999	
Greenough, H.J.	Pte	Ply6.816	
Griffiths, D.	Sto	291.740	
Gunn, D.	Pte	Ply9.447	
Hagan, W.	AB	162.442	
Hallett, T.J.	Lieut		
Heal, W.N.	Ord	187.108	
Hernon, M.	AB	152.198	
Howe, R.	Sto	294.178	
Hunter, F.	Q/Sig	117.328	
Jackson, C.H.	2/SBStd	350.395	
Jeffery, T.W.	Sh/Std	169.311	
Jenkins, J.	PO1	141.872	
Jeremy, A.H.	Surgn		
Jope, J.	Ord	203.628	
Keating, T.	AB	192.618	
Knight, F.	Sto	291.744	
Knowles, A.	AB	164.448	
Laing, W.G.	L/Sto	169.286	
Langmead, F.	Carp/Crew	341.804	
Lavers, J.	Ch/Sto	123.241	
Lear, J.H.	Ch/Sto	129.249	

NO BAR MEDALS *continued.*

Lear, T.	Ord	203.599
Leary, T.	Sto	280.117
Lehane, E.	AB	164.279
Locke, H.J.	Pte	Ply9.449
Lum Ah.	Dom	
McLean, A.	Sh/Cpl	150.036
Meadus, W.J.	Sto	291.745
Medder, S.	L/Sto	132.271
Miller, W.E.	AB	146.338
Mills, H.	PO1	165.730
Mitchell, J.	Pte	Ply3.617
Moist, S.	AB	118.255
Murray, J.	Pte	Ply2.859
Newton, E.C.	AB	171.674
Nong Ku.	Dom	
Nunan, J.	AB	192.354
Owen, W.	Sergt	Ply3.659
Paley, T.H.	AB	156.871
Palmer, E.J.	AB	193.347
Passey, J.	Q/Sig	194.198
Patterson, C.J.	ERA	268.567
Payne, F.J.	Sto	279.574
Pike, F.	AB	171.519
Raby, H.	L/Sto	161.285
Rogers, E.C.	AB	154.389
Rowe, W.J.	Ord	203.613
Scott, W.	AB	164.615
Searle, W.J.R.	Ord	205.402
Shea, J.	AB	199.804
Sow Ah.	Dom	
Stickland, W.J.	2/Sh/Cook	163.683
Sung Ah.	Dom	
Taylor, W.	AB	197.469
Thomas, J.J.	Act/Ch/Carp/Mte	149.485
Thorn, H.J.	2/Yeo/Sig	172.505
Townsend, W.	Sto	280.111
Trout, R.H.	L/S	154.033
Veale, W.	Shpwrt	342.918
Vickers, H.	AB	157.216
Vigurs, J.	L/Sto	121.119
Walsh, P.	AB	182.287
Ward, W.H.	AB	170.748
Warren, E.H.	Pte	Ply5.351
Webber, W.H.	Sto	280.676
Windeatt, A.J.	Ch/Sto	120.130

Duplicate medals:

Avent, F.J.	AB	183.092
Beer, E.A.	Sto	279.632
Gillard, A.J.	Sto	175.823
Knight, F.	Sto	291.744
Searle, W.J.R.	Ord	205.402
Trout, R.H.	L/S	154.033

Duplicate medals - without issue no. on roll:

Elliott, L.	Act/ERA	269.364

Returned medals:

Brien, J.	AB	190.058
Dutton, J.H.	Ord	197.912
Glover, J.	Pte	Ply9.448
Gregory, J.	AB	183.685
Hyde, B.	Pte	Ply7.506
Wynn, T.	Pte	Ply4.644

H.M.S. PIGMY.

H.M.S. Pigmy was a Composite Screw Gunboat of 755 tons and 165 x 30 feet. Her armament consisted of 6 x 4 in guns. The vessel was built in Sheerness Dock Yard and launched on 27th July 1888. She was sold on 4th April 1905 to Cox at Falmouth.

Bars	*Total*	*Returned*	*Entitled*
None	*80*	*6*	*74*
	80	*6*	*74*

NO BAR MEDALS.

Alford, F.	Sto	286.602
Annison, F.	AB	180.801
Bannister, F.A.	Ord	193.282
Bigsworth, W.A.	PO1	168.316
Boorman, W.W.	L/Sto	172.273
Borchard, W.A.	AB	171.156
Briggs, H.D.	Lieut	
Broomfield, H.H.	Pte	Ch9.158
Bunyan, F.	AB	170.817
Buxton, P.	Sto	286.690
Chittenden, F.	AB	186.140
Clarke, R.H.	Ord	197.909
Cooper, W.E.	AB	164.979
Cornwell, J.W.	AB	187.472
Crocker, J.R.	Sh/Cook	153.469
Culham, W.E.	Ch/ERA	136.710
Cum Ah.	Dom	
Curtain, W.J.	Gunr	
Ellis, A.	PO1	142.094
Farquhar, D.	ERA	268.366
Fixter, G.G.	L/Sto	153.645
Flowerdew, A.H.	L/Carp/Crew	340.637
Frewen, E.L.	Lieut	
Galloway, A.H.	AB	179.468
Gibb, H.	AB	165.134
Gibbs, W.E.	L/Sig	152.833
Gibson, W.	Pte	Ch3.197
Giggins, W.	Pte	Ch7.363
Green, J.F.E.	Lieut	
Gwillam, C.F.	AB	184.175
Hall, A.E.	Pte	Ch9.724
Harflett, S.J.	AB	183.250
Harling, C.	L/S	140.606
Harris, F.	Ch/Wrtr	133.200
Harrison, R.S.	Pte	Ch7.421
Harvey, J.	PO2	167.766
Hazel, T.	2/SBStd	350.359
Hill, C.W.	Pte	Ch9.050
Hobart, G.W.	Ch/Sto	130.311
Holding, G.C.	Carp/Mte	128.237
Howell, T.W.	Q/Sig	189.168
Hunt, G.T.	L/Sto	175.356
Hurley, W.	Sto	286.626
Ketley, F.J.	PO2	172.642
Lucas, G.E.	L/Sto	155.225
Lucie, J.	Boy	200.044
Luxton, J.W.	PO2	176.369
McNeill, W.	Ord	197.600
Minney, R.	Ord	200.045
Moore, T.	Sto	286.646
Ney, O.H.	Pilot	
Nimmo, F.H.	Surgn	
O'Brien, J.	Ord	198.704
Pearce, H.C.	L/S	170.747
Pickup, G.	AB	171.901
Press, J.H.	AB	193.313
Pullman, S.F.	PO1	164.754
Searle, H.W.	Pte	Ch9.001
Selden, J.	Sto	165.990
Shaw, W.	Arm/Mte	278.613
Sherrell, F.W.	ERA	268.562
Silvertop, A.E.	Lieut	
Spackman, H.J.	Ch/Sto	151.684
Sutherland, W.	AB	190.883
Tatum, A.A.	Ord	200.057
Taylor, W.M.C.	PO1	150.852
Tein Ah.	Dom	
Townsend, W.E.	Engr	
Vercoe, W.H.	Sto	293.051
Wackett, E.W.	Act/Sh/Std	140.924
Weekes, J.	Sto	174.462
West, P.	AB	168.127
Westbury, H.R.	L/Sergt	Ch6.914
Wickes, W.J.	AB	125.713

Duplicate medal:

Frewen, E.L.	Lieut	

Returned medals:

Fai Ta.	Dom	
Holloway, A.E.	Ord	193.283
Jim Ah.	Dom	
Tung Ta.	Dom	
Woodhams, C.	AB	193.303
You Ah.	Dom	

H.M.S. PIQUE.

H.M.S. Pique was a 2nd class Cruiser of 3,600 tons and 300 x 43½ feet. Her armament consisted of 2 x 6 in, 6 x 4.7 in and 8 x 6 pdr guns. The vessel was built by Palmer and launched on 13th December 1890. She was sold on 9th May 1911 to Rudge.

Bars	*Total*	*Returned*	*Entitled*
None	*294*	*5*	*289*
	294	*5*	*289*

Notes:

1 - Medal noted on roll as returned for correction.

NO BAR MEDALS.

Name	Rank	Number
Ahern J.	Ord	197.711
Allchin, G.H.	Pte	Po10.207
Angel, D.	Arm/Crew	283.052
Arthur, J.	Pilot	
Astbury, H.J.	Pte	Ply8.778
Avery, W.	Carp/Crew	340.032
Babb, W.	AB	157.863
Back, H.J.W.	Sh/Std/Asst	149.124
Baker, L.	AB	172.728
Bale, G.W.	PO2	162.587
Bannister, W.J.	Boy	201.714
Bartlett, J.S.	Sto	280.115
Bates, A.	AB	172.035
Batten, G.	L/Sto	112.269
Batten, W.	Sto	280.673
Beamer, A.	Pte	Ply7.831
Bennett, C.S.	Ord	193.339
Bennett, F.C.	AB	197.450
Berrie, D.	Lieut	
Best, W.	PO1	118.600
Billing, A.	Sto	280.099
Bishop, H.W.	Ord	197.353
Bissett, A.H.	L/Sto	139.184
Bissett, W.	Ch/Sto	125.219
Bomyer, T.J.	L/Sto	130.094
Bond, E.J.	Sto	127.629
Bone, T.	Sail/Mte	154.963
Boo Ah.	Dom	
Booth, B.T.H.	Ord	196.973
Boss, A.	ERA	268.537
Brandon, C.G.R.	Lieut	
Branton, F.C.	PO1	149.310
Brassington, J.H.	Sto	290.408
Breadon, G.C.	PO2	144.267
Brooke, J.	Sto	290.853
Brown, F.W.	Ord	197.362
Brown, W.H.	PO2	144.228
Browne, A.	Bugler	Ply9.104
Browning, R.J.	Sto	175.431
Buckingham, S.H.	L/Sto	157.553
Bulley, F.W.	3/Wrtr	340.150
Burley, W.	Sto	145.519
Burroughs, A.G.	AB	190.692
Burrows, E.	AB	185.213
Byrne, J.	Sto	276.258
Cahill, J.	Sto	283.838
Campbell, E.	Boy	201.175
Campbell, G.	Sto	279.246
Carr, J.	Ord	197.708
Carrick, J.J.	Sto	290.885
Carter, G.	Pte	Po10.204
Chadburn, J.	Pte	Ply8.500
Chandler, J.A.	L/Cpl	Ply5.655
Charleston, J.G.	ERA	165.691
Chilcott, R.E.	Lieut	
Coakley, S.	Boy	197.703
Coleman, A.G.	ERA	268.747
Collings, A.	AB	169.820
Collins, J.	Sto	291.900
Condon, J.	Ch/Sto	117.972
Cooksley, E.	L/Sto	141.085
Coombstock, J.	Sto	289.846
Cooper, J.	AB	177.302
Corcoran, J.	AB	165.752
Cornish, S.H.	Boy	201.211
Cosway, W.	AB	168.011
County, P.	L/Sto	139.619
Courtney, H.	Blksmth	342.552
Cowie, J.G.	AB	163.241
Crabb, F.	L/S	159.133
Crafts, A.E.	Pte	Ply8.538
Crimes, T.F.	Sto	173.588
Crotty, J.	Sto	283.839
Croxford, O.E.	Boy	201.109
Cusack, J.	Sto	166.612
Daley, M.	Ord	196.163

NO BAR MEDALS *continued.*

Name	Rating	Number
Daniel, N.	Sto	281.009
Demellweek, W.	AB	171.809
Dempsey, W.	Sto	291.559
Donoghue, J.	Pte	Ply7.213
Donovan, P.	Sto	283.118
Downs, H.	Sto	276.590
Driscoll. J.	Sto	118.248
Duck, W.	Sto	170.517
Duffy, J.	Sto	279.254
Dugdale, W.	Pte	Ply9.292
Durden, G.R.	Boy	201.172
Dusting, T.E.	Sh/Std/Asst	341.550
Dwyer, T.	Sto	284.106
Dyer, G.	AB	160.564
Dyer, J.M.	Ord	185.611
Easton, J.E.	AB	178.764
Edmonds, C.P.	Pte	Ply7.231
Elliott, W.	L/S	166.868
Ellis, J.J.	Pte	Ply8.752
Enright, F.	Yeo/Sig	102.192
Fairthlough, M.	AB	188.414
Far Lee Koi.	Dom	
Farley, H.J.	Sto	289.872
Fedvick, J.	Ord	193.152
Fennesy, R.	Pte	Ply9.201
Flynn, J.	Ord	199.688
Foo Ah.	Dom	
Fook Ah.	Dom	
Fou Ah.	Dom	
Fourte, E.C.	AB	164.778
Frost, G.	Sto	290.121
Garde, P.	AB	173.361
Garland, J.S.	Pte	Ply7.566
Garton, G.	Sto	292.115
Gartrell, J.	Ch/Sto	130.111
Gearing, E.H.	Act/Bosn	
Gerry, G.	L/Sto	123.414
Gidley, W.	L/Sto	118.662
Gillespie, R.	Sto	289.248
Good, W.	Sto	290.107
Graham, E.R.	Asst/Payr	
Grant, E.N.	Boy	201.106
Grant, W.C.	Asst/Engr	
Gray, J.	Pte	Ply8.488
Greenan, A.	AB	168.356
Greens, G.W.	PO1	134.856
Griffen, J.	Sto	291.493
Grubb, A.E.	Sh/Cpl	350.063
Grundy, W.	Ch/Arm	145.545
Gwyer, C.	Sto	280.390
Hackett, W.	Surgn	
Hall, W.	PO1	117.771
Halley, J.	Sto	284.288
Hannon, P.	L/Sto	154.929
Harding, F.	AB	165.303
Hardy, S.G.R.	Boy	199.528
Harrett, L.	Ord	193.567
Harris, H.	Q/Sig	193.423
Harvey, W.J.	Sto	153.041
Hattrick, G.	L/Sig	181.079
Hayes, D.	Ord	192.390
Hayman, G.A.	Sto	279.850
Heskins, A.E.	Sto	155.442
Hickey, P.	Ord	195.893
Hillman, T.W.	Pntr	341.917
Hitchcock, W.M.	Dom	358.016
Hope, G.	Pte	Ply9.131
Horne, W.G.	Pte	Po10.225
Horton, H.	Ord	198.649
Hughes, H.	Act/Engr	
Humphries, A.W.	Ord	198.522
Ingham, A.	Ord	196.286
Ingham, F.J.	Boy	199.530
Jankinson, B.	Pte	Ply8.646
Jerman, H.	Sto	163.065
John, R.	Pte	Ply9.276
Jones, E.C.	MAA	115.006
Jude, P.	Sto	153.078
Jureyeff, F.	PO1	109.765
Knight, C.A.	Ch/Sto	119.369
Lacey, A.	Sto	290.924
Laity, W.H.	Ord	193.134
Lavington, W.	L/Sto	120.761
Lenden, G.H.	Sto	162.163
Leonard, F.C.	Payr	
Lloyd, T.J.	AB	167.072
Lock, A.T.	L/S	112.523
Lock, H.A.	Dom	146.761
Lock, S.N.	AB	149.265
Lomax, A.E.	Sto	290.123
Long, M.	AB	157.530
Lovelock, F.	PO1	114.898
Lynch, P.	AB	185.787
McDonald, A.	Q/Sig	188.517
McDonald, C.A.	AB	160.270
Macdonald, W.B.	Lieut	
McGinty, J.	Ord	193.831
Maclean, C.L.	Lieut	
McLean, J.	AB	179.160
McNamara, J.J.	AB	167.227
McQuillan, P.	Ord	192.138
Mace, J.	ERA	268.607
Maddick, G.H.	L/Sto	141.031
Mairs, E.H.	Sto	177.297
Martin, R.J.	Boy	199.529
Matthias, H.J.	Sto	290.926
Maunder, A.	Carp/Mte	143.619
Mead, J.H.	AB	129.491
Metcalfe, R.	AB	159.487
Milsted, W.J.	Cpl	Ply4.919
Morrell, S.G.S.	Carp	[1]
Morris, J.	Pte	Ply9.420
Munday, J.	Sto	290.822
Murphy, J.	Sto	284.112
Murphy, M.W.	Ord	198.713
Murray, J.	AB	172.205

NO BAR MEDALS *continued.*

Name	Rank	Number
Murray, W.	2/Cooper	342.411
Nelson, A.	Pilot	
Nicholson, J.	Pte	Ply9.116
Nip Ah.	Dom	
Nolan, G.	Pte	Ply6.728
North, G.H.	2/SBStd	175.577
Northcott, F.	Sto	289.510
Nurse, C.J.	Pte	Ply7.647
O'Byrne, J.K.	Ord	192.400
O'Driscoll, B.	Sto	281.723
O'Leary, D.	Arm/Crew	342.562
Oxford, C.	Art/Engr	
Page, J.S.	Cook/Mte	341.319
Parsons, F.	Sto	161.732
Paul, G.R.	Dom	358.015
Pearce, F.B.	Ord	193.326
Pearce, S.G.	L/S	149.233
Peay, W.R.	Pte	Ply6.986
Peever, G.C.	Ord	201.162
Pethick, F.	Sto	292.157
Phillips, F.	Sto	168.713
Pomeroy, A.	AB	163.965
Poo Ah.	Dom	
Potter, J.A.S.	Gunr	
Potter, W.	Sto	290.675
Power, E.	Sto	277.656
Pritchard, F.	Ord	197.454
Punshon, A.E.	Yeo/Sig	177.629
Quick, T.	AB	163.335
Redmond, P.	AB	136.512
Rendell, W.	PO1	111.622
Reynolds, H.C.	Capt	
Richards, E.G.	Sto	290.811
Ridley, H.J.	L/Sig	187.669
Roberts, T.	AB	166.282
Roberts, W.	PO1	115.038
Robinson, C.	Boy	201.113
Rockey, J.T.	Sto	286.167
Rogers, G.H.	Sto	290.389
Rookes, W.	Pte	Ply8.857
Roy Ah.	Dom	
Ryder, E.C.	Ord	198.515
Ryder, G.H.	AB	155.863
Ryder, N.J.	Ch/Sto	139.612
Sambells, B.	ERA	269.327
Sampson, W.	Sto	131.721
Sampson, W.	Ord	198.147
Savage, H.	Boy	201.158
See Ah.	Dom	
Sellick, H.A.	Sto	291.750
Sellick, S.	Sto	162.170
Shea, M.	Ord	198.708
Sheenan, J.	Sto	283.861
Shell, J.J.	Sh/Cook	141.866
Simmonds, V.	Ord	197.251
Simpson, D.	ERA	269.227
Sleep, W.	Arm/Mte	158.882
Slocombe, R.	L/S	141.167
Smith, C.	L/Shpwrt	131.208
Soo Ah.	Dom	
Staddon, N.O.	Shpwrt	342.838
Stansbury, W.	ERA	268.110
Stoat, W.	Sto	159.548
Sullivan, P.	Ord	198.705
Tabb, A.	Sto	282.746
Tallamy, J.H.	L/Carp/Crew	342.632
Taylor, C.	Sto	290.397
Taylor, E.N.	AB	168.021
Thomas, J.N.	Plmbr/Mte	342.679
Thompson, B.	AB	151.047
Thomson, W.H.	Sub Lieut	
Thorn, W.	Sto	276.157
Toms, E.C.	AB	143.999
Train, S.	PO1	134.784
Truscott, J.	Gunr	
Vanstone, W.H.	Sto	290.640
Vercoe, C.	PO2	154.375
Vidler, W.T.	Q/Sig	179.343
Voaden, H.	Ch/ERA	154.956
Wakeham, W.G.	AB	149.299
Walsh, W.R.	AB	156.429
Walters, E.	AB	171.664
Ward, F.J.	Ord	181.956
Ward, G.	L/S	178.055
Ward, J.	L/Sto	145.939
Watson, D.J.	Pte	Po10.206
Webb, A.T.	Ch/Engr	
Webber, H.F.	Sergt	Ply3.713
Webber, W.T.	PO1	148.233
Weedon, T.	Pte	Ply9.209
Wells, J.W.	Boy	201.256
Wheatcroft, O.	Ord	189.786
Williams, J.T.	Act/Bosn	
Wood, W.T.	Pte	Ply2.853
Wooldridge, R.	Ch/Sto	142.243
Wreford, A.W.	AB	164.758
Yeats, A.A.	Ord	198.523

Duplicate medals:

Name	Rank	Number
Bannister, W.J.	Boy	201.714 *
Batten, W.	Sto	280.673
County, P.	L/Sto	139.619
Cusack, J.	Sto	166.612
Dempsey, W.	Sto	291.559
Donovan, P.	Sto	283.118
Driscoll, J.	Sto	118.248
Elliott, W.	L/S	166.868
Garde, P.	AB	173.361
Ingham, A.	Ord	196.286
Lacey, A.	Sto	290.924
Tabb, A.	Sto	282.746
Tallamy, J.H.	L/Carp/Crew	342.632
Taylor, C.	Sto	290.397
Wells, J.W.	Boy	201.256

* *Two duplicate medals issued.*

NO BAR MEDALS *continued.*

Duplicate medal - without issue no on roll:

Knight, C.A.	Ch/Sto	119.369

Returned medals:

Bloomer, J.	Sto	291.575
Holmwood, S.	Sto	289.924
Shea, J.	Sto	154.183
Veasey, J.	Sto	164.696
Wai Ah.	Dom	

H.M.S. PLOVER.

H.M.S. Plover was a Composite Screw Gunboat of 755 tons and 165 x 30 feet. Her armament consisted of 6 x 4 in guns. The vessel was built in Pembroke Dock Yard and launched on 18th October 1888. She was sold on 27th April 1927 at Gibraltar.

Bars	*Total*	*Returned*	*Entitled*
None	*82*	*8*	*74*
	82	*8*	*74*

Notes:

K - Medal presented by H.M. The King on 8th March 1902.

NO BAR MEDALS.

Name	Rank	Number	Note
Abbott, W.	AB	179.744	
Ambrose, J.	AB	180.451	
Askew, W.J.	Pte	Ply8.572	
Baldwin, W.E.	AB	178.332	
Bell, D. *alias* Tweedie.	Pte	Ply8.596	
Bickford, G.F.	AB	178.126	
Blyth, A.	Pte	Ply5.289	
Bryant, J.H.	AB	183.879	K
Budden, H.	2/Sh/Cook	173.821	
Cahill, J.	PO2	178.661	
Chisman, E.	Engr		
Chowen, W.J.	Ch/Sto	129.267	
Coe, G.	Sto	280.426	
Cottrell, J.W.	Gunr		
Cowper, C.V.deM.	Lieut		
Creighton, J.W.	Sto	284.500	
Cummings, J.	AB	176.309	
Dale, S.	Pte	Po6.835	
Driscoll, J.	AB	181.382	
Emmett, J.H.	AB	118.499	
Flack, C.	ERA	269.041	
Ghey, H.W.	ERA	269.314	
Gorey, R.H.	2/SBStd	350.372	
Harris, J.	L/Carp/Crew	341.046	
Heath, W.J.	AB	190.560	
Heyburn, H.	AB	181.082	
Hill, H.	Ch/Sto	122.743	
Holladay, F.H.	L/Sig	184.676	
Horne, F.	AB	190.205	
Horton, J.H.	Pte	Ply2.524	
Jackson, W.	Surgn		
James, F.G.	L/S	154.396	
Kearns, T.	L/S	179.769	
Kidney, A.	AB	182.632	
Knapman, E.	Sto	278.603	
Lain Ah.	Dom		
Lane, M.	L/Sto	139.625	
Lillis, H.F.G.	L/Sto	147.011	
Litton, A.J.	Sh/Std	158.887	
Loy Ah.	Dom		
McCarthy, J.	AB	182.637	
McCubbin, M.	Cpl	Ply5.220	
Marks, C.	AB	190.192	
Matthews, A.	Carp/Mte	157.470	
Menzies, L.	Lieut		
Miners, W.H.	Sto	287.285	
Montgomery, J.	AB	174.650	
Owens, J.M.	Ch/ERA	132.252	
Parkhouse, E.	Ch/Sto	123.937	
Payton, J.H.	PO2	174.878	K
Pollard, D.B.	AB	151.585	
Porter, W.A.	PO1	147.096	
Press, W.B.	AB	185.823	
Ratty, W.	Arm/Mte	152.999	
Regan, T.O.	AB	181.706	
Reid, M.	PO1	130.355	
Reinold, H.O.	Lieut		
Richards, S.J.	Ch/Wrtr	109.625	
Riddells, S.	L/Sto	120.370	
Sangwell, H.S.	AB	190.193	
Sleeman, W.	AB	181.233	
Sowersby, J.F.	Pte	Ply3.151	
Stannaway, D.	PO1	129.841	
Sullivan, W.	Sto	154.570	
Thompson, A.	Pte	Ply4.646	
Tippar, J.	Sto	126.418	
Vaisey, H.J.	Q/Sig	182.417	
Webber, W.	AB	182.811	
Westgate, R.	L/Sto	148.791	
Weston, W.G.	AB	170.024	
White, P.H.	Sub Lieut		
Willey, F.H.	Pte	Ply8.806	
Winsor, W.H.	AB	193.243	
Withycombe, J.H.	PO1	145.265	

H.M.S. PLOVER.

NO BAR MEDALS *continued.*

Duplicate medal:

Vaisey, H.J.	Q/Sig	182.417

Duplicate medal - without issue no on roll:

McOnnell, W.J.	Pte	Ch6.177

Returned medals:

Aitken, A.	ERA	268.634
Ching Ah.	Dom	
Fong Ah.	Dom	
Hain Ah.	Dom	
Ling Ah.	Dom	
McOnnell, W.J.	Pte	Ch6.177
Shaw, W.	Sto	284.604
Young Ah.	Dom	

H.M.S. REDPOLE.

H.M.S. Redpole was a Composite Screw Gunboat of 805 tons and 165 x 31 feet. Her armament consisted of 6 x 4 in guns. The vessel was built in Pembroke Dock Yard and was launched on 13th June 1889. She was sold on 15th May 1906 to Cox at Falmouth.

Bars	*Total*	*Returned*	*Entitled*
None	*79*	*7*	*72*
	79	*7*	*72*

NO BAR MEDALS.

Abrahams, E.	AB	180.863
Attwater, H.	PO2	160.199
Bacon, R.L.K.	Ch/Wrtr	131.909
Brown, J.	Sto	289.551
Buckley, D.	L/Sto	176.745
Butcher, J.	AB	169.548
Cadman, W.	Sub Lieut	
Child, C.H.	Sto	283.196
Corbett, C.F.	Lieut	
Cousins, H.G.	Ord	198.021
Creagh, A.L.A.	AB	183.993
Crowley, T.	AB	188.913
Daly, W.A.	AB	178.939
Dell, H.	L/Sig	167.696
Doyle, R.C.	Ch/Sto	119.827
Driskell, W.J.G.	Sto	292.727
Dunn, C.F.	Engr	
Evans, W.	PO1	139.434
Fairclough, J.	AB	163.784
Ferris, R.O.	PO1	123.190
Field, H.	AB	180.640
Garratt, J.F.	Q/Sig	186.880
Goodman, R.J.	2/SBStd	350.313
Gouge, T.H.	ERA	269.184
Gwyer, G.	AB	183.984
Hamilton, E.	PO1	111.688
Hamilton, J.	Pte	Ply7.369
Hannaford, E.G.	AB	178.743
Harger, A.J.	Pilot	
Haskins, R.	Sto	354.560
Hawkings, S.	L/Sto	158.493
Hine, F.A.	Pte	Ply5.443
Hopkins, T.E.	Sh/Cook	165.965
Hurd, S.	Sto	283.218
Johnson, C.E.	AB	188.547
Johnson, J.	AB	139.404
Law, G.W.	AB	174.510
Lewington, W.	Pte	Ply4.917
Long, E.	Act/PO2	174.138
Makin, J.F.	Pte	Ply9.682
Morton, W.	AB	173.885
Moyle, S.P.	L/Sto	153.338
Oliver, J.	Sto	283.184
Passmore, E.C.	L/Carp/Crew	340.030
Reeby, A.J.C.	Ch/Sto	139.613
Roberts, F.P.	PO1	146.113
Rowe, A.C.	Pte	Ply2.746
Rowe, W.S.	Sto	148.783
Scriven, J.	AB	180.767
Sheward, C.R.	Surgn	
Smabridge, H.	AB	182.684
Smith, F.	Pte	Ply4.017
Stevens, H.	Ord	177.844
Stone, G.B.	Pte	Ply8.953
Storey, T.	Pte	Ply8.582
Symons, J.F.	AB	192.369
Thorne, J.J.	Sto	283.215
Tinney, C.	Carp/Mte	163.070
Tippett, J.G.	Arm/Mte	155.771
Toyne, D.	Cpl	Ply7.097
Tremeer, T.W.	ERA	140.978
Trevethan, C.E.	Sh/Std	168.536
Tunstall, P.A.	L/S	155.824
Warrey, G.J.	AB	182.766
Weaver, S.	AB	183.892
Webley, W.T.	Gunr	
Weekes, A.A.	ERA	268.622
White, C.	Lieut	
Willey, A.T.	L/S	145.155
Williams, S.	Ch/Sto	126.390
Wrixon, E.	Ord	190.989
Yue Ah.	Dom	

Duplicate medals:

Haskins, R.	Sto	354.560
Hine, F.A.	Pte	Ply5.443
Symons, J.F.	AB	192.369
Tunstall, P.A.	L/S	155.824
Weaver, S.	AB	183.892

Returned medals:

Harvey, F.C.	Sub Lieut	
Ming Ah.	Dom	
Moore, J.	Ord	198.051

H.M.S. REDPOLE.

NO BAR MEDALS *continued.*

Returned medals continued:

Po Ching.	Dom	
Sing Ah.	Dom	
Wright, F.A.	AB	181.183
Yuen Ah.	Dom	

H.M.S ROSARIO.

H.M.S. Rosario was a Sloop of 980 tons and 180 x 33 feet. Her armament consisted of 6 x 4 in guns. The vessel was built in Sheerness Dock Yard and was launched on 17th December 1898. She became a Depot ship in 1910 and was sold on 11th November 1921 at Hong Kong.

Bars	*Total*	*Returned*	*Entitled*
None	*110*	*1*	*109*
	110	*1*	*109*

Notes:

1 - This man is noted on the roll as 'Run' and his medal was returned to the Mint in Feb 1922. However, the roll is further endorsed with, " Run removed. New medal engraved."

NO BAR MEDALS.

Bailey, J.E.	Sto	284.867
Baker, H.E.	AB	172.539
Bale, C.	AB	160.638
Ball, W.	Sto	291.815
Bangert, H.S.	Ord	201.092
Barrett, A.E.	AB	180.808
Bavin, F.W.	AB	162.341
Beakes, T.H.S.	AB	182.929
Bettinson, H.	Ch/Sto	127.873
Blackmore, A.	Sto	288.835
Bolster, F.	Surgn	
Botting, A.	ERA	268.766
Brash, P.S.	L/S	180.365
Bray, W.	Sto	285.161
Campbell, D.	Lieut	
Charleson, A.	AB	173.112
Chew, A.	AB	162.789
Chin Ah.	Dom	
Curtis, F.J.	ERA	268.796
Danaher, W.E.	Sh/Std	152.180
Dennison, A.N.	L/Sto	143.094
Down, W.	AB	126.632
Espley, H.P.	Boy	200.398
Farrant, A.J.	AB	172.648
Fernley, C.H.	Boy	201.360
Foley, D.P.	Q/Sig	191.303
Freathy, S.J.	AB	116.967
French, H.E.	AB	166.043
Full, J.	AB	166.081
Gander, G.A.	Ord	191.637
Gill, A.	Sto	291.089
Green, A.G.	AB	185.591
Greenwood, A.	Sto	286.187
Gunn, W.J.	Sto	277.875
Hamilton, C.A.W.	Comdr	
Harod, W.	PO1	99.148
Hartley, J.H.	Arm/Mte	340.824
Hawkins, E.R.	Pte	Po10.250
He Ah.	Dom	
Hedderly, J.	Sig	189.124
Hogben, J.	Sto	291.225
Hopper, A.E.	Sto	276.773
Howse, S.	Art/Engr	
Hughes, R.J.	ERA	141.801
Humphries, F.	2/Yeo/Sig	184.697
Impey, A.	AB	168.008
Inman, E.J.	PO1	163.177
Jacobs, A.	L/Carp/Crew	163.672
James, C.F.	Pte	Ch10.069
Keddie, C.	Boy	201.437
Kirkealdy, D.D.	Ord	197.542
Legge, F.G.	PO2	173.027
McConnell, J.	Ord	200.880
Millhouse, H.	L/Sto	162.066
Mills, D.	Ch/Carp/Mte	123.109
Mitchell, J.E.	ERA	269.122
Mogridge, G.	2/Sh/Cook	146.278
Noake, B.S.	Lieut	
Osborne, A.	Ch/Sto	143.525
Pang Ah.	Dom	
Parker, W.G.	AB	175.082
Pearce, R.W.	L/S	171.564
Peek, J.A.	Sail/Mte	139.828
Pender, C.A.	PO1	149.633
Pile, J.	L/Shpwrt	174.397
Ping Ah.	Dom	
Poisden, E.G.	Sto	284.829
Press, A.G.	2/SBStd	350.401
Preston, L.G.	Lieut	
Puckey, J.	Gunr	
Pugh, W.	PO1	135.876
Ransom, A.C.	Asst/Payr	

NO BAR MEDALS *continued.*

Redhouse, C.	Ch/PO	121.732
Reed, H.G.	L/Sto	157.014
Rhoades, A.	AB	180.375
Richards, E.	AB	166.217
Rosevear, R.J.	AB	173.169
Routhan, A.	Ord	191.562
Salisbury, J.H.	Ord	185.737
Sallows, W.	Pte	Ch6.884
Samuels, A.G.	Pte	Ch8.020
Sandford, W.H.	Pte	Ch9.575
Scott, J.T.	L/Cpl	Ch8.382
Sheehan, P.	Sto	265.322
Sheppard, H.	Pte	Ch10.589
Shotten, R.	Ord	200.245
Sinclair, J.E.	Musn	358.089
Skinner, E.A.	Sto	291.228
Strassen, H.J.	Sto	285.153
Sweeney, A.J.	AB	168.089
Swinton, J.	Ord	200.882
Thomas, C.B.	Sto	285.441
Tombs, F.W.	Pte	Ch10.329
Triscott, F.	AB	183.281
Turner, H.W.	Pte	Ch5.120
Walters, G.M.	Sto	172.259 [1]
Ward, W.T.	Carp/Crew	343.169
Warman, A.	Pte	Ch10.647
Watkins, G.	PO2	157.193
White, C.	Sergt	Ch6.558
White, G.	Sh/Cpl	140.683
Whiteoak, J.E.	Sto	285.144
Williams, H.S.	Sto	291.202
Williams, J.	Ch/Sto	141.132
Wilmott, G.	Pte	Ch7.173
Wilson, A.	L/Sto	132.375
Wilson, A.S.	Pilot	
Wilson, P.	AB	165.046
Ying Ah.	Dom	

Duplicate medals:

Baker, H.E.	AB	172.539
Blackmore, A.	Sto	288.835
Hopper, A.E.	Sto	276.773
Impey, A.	AB	168.008
Inman, E.J.	PO1	163.177
James, C.F.	Pte	Ch10.069
Richards, E.	AB	166.217
Whiteoak, J.E.	Sto	285.144

Duplicate medal - without issue no on roll:

Pugh, W.	PO1	135.876

Returned medal:

Davis, G.T.	Dom	358.088

H.M.S. SNIPE.

H.M.S. Snipe was a River Gunboat of 85 tons and 108 x 20 feet. Her armament consisted of 2 x 6 pdr guns. The vessel was built by Yarrow and launched at Poplar in 1898. She was reported as sold on 2oth November 1919 at Hong Kong, but was listed in 1921.

Bars	*Total*	*Returned*	*Entitled*
None	*28*	*8*	*20*
	28	*8*	*20*

Note:

K - Medal presented by H.M. The King on 8th March 1902.

NO BAR MEDALS.

Bath, A.	L/Sto	162.126
Bevan, W.	Sto	286.161
Doyle, J.E.	Sto	287.359
Fitzgerald, W.	Carp/Mte	154.663
Freemantle, S.J.	AB	180.935
Hawton, R.	Ch/ERA	142.162
Hull, W.	ERA	269.345
Humby, G.	Arm/Crew	187.781
Oldham, A.H.	Lieut	
Parrott, H.C.	AB	180.948
Perry, J.	Ch/PO	92.582
Robinson, F.G.	Sh/Std/Asst	340.532
Rockett, A.W.J.	AB	156.790
Schooling, A.F.	PO1	143.937
Tait, J.B.C.	AB	177.793
Temple, E.C.	AB	176.204
Underhill, C.	PO1	130.609 K
Williams, W.J.H.	PO1	135.983
Woods, J.	AB	181.042
Woolcombe, A.	Surgn	

Returned medals:

Fat Ah.	Dom	
Moa Ah.	Sto	
On Wo.	Sto	
Rowlands, J.D.	L/Sto	147.940
Sam Ah.	Sampan Man	
Sen Ah.	Sampan Man	
Sing Ah.	Dom	
Yen Wing.	Dom	

H.M.S. TERRIBLE.

H.M.S. Terrible was a 1st class Cruiser of 14,200 tons and 500 x 71 feet. Her armament consisted of 2 x 9.2 in, 12 x 6 in and 16 x 12 pdr guns. The vessel was built by Thomson and launched on 27th May 1895. She became a Training Ship in August 1920 and was renamed FISGUARD III. She was sold in July 1932 to Cashmore.

Bars	*Total*	*Returned*	*Entitled*
RP	*268*	*5*	*263*
None	*732*	*26*	*706*
	1000	*31*	*969*

Notes:

K - Medal presented by H.M. The King on 8th March 1902.

1 - Medal roll states, "Medals found and returned from Jupiter 21.10.05. Papers under Dup 671." Roll is also endorsed, "RET'D TO Mint Feb 22."

2 - These recipients were awarded the medal by the Army; see the roll for Naval Depot - Wei-hai-wei.

Bar: RELIEF OF PEKIN.

Abraham, F.J.	Pte	Po8.708
Ackland, A.C.	Midn	
Allen, F.	PO1	128.140
Andrews, A.G.	St/Surgn	
Annetts, J.	Pte	Po8.750
Ashley, W.	Pte	Po8.785
Ashton, F.	AB	161.127
Aylesbury, E.	Ord	185.628
Baldwin, A.	Sto	287.642
Balls, J.S.	AB	176.243
Barnard, F.R.	L/Cpl	Po8.007
Barrett, J.	PO2	144.271
Barritt, R.S.	Pte	Po7.048
Beard, T.B.	PO1	116.400
Bell, J.	Sto	283.394
Benn, J.	AB	190.096
Bennett, T.R.	Sto	284.703
Bird, C.E.	AB	189.960
Blackwell, J.	Sto	276.677
Blake, F.	AB	180.224
Blake, J.	Pte	Po2.015
Bland, A.	Ord	190.112
Bobbett, J.J.	AB	183.495
Bolt, H.W.	AB	190.541
Bowbyes, H.	2/Yeo/Sig	135.887
Boyd, J.	Sto	276.052
Boyes, E.J.	Pte	Po8.679
Brennan, F.W.	AB	190.529
Briggs, J.	Pte	Po5.084
Brown, R.J.	Pte	Po9.583
Burns, H.	Sto	175.441
Burt, S.	Pte	Po4.208
Burtenshaw, G.	PO2	122.618
Butler, J.	Pte	Ch8.249
Byron, W.	Sto	289.795
Campling, W.J.	AB	177.327
Cargill, G.B.	Midn	
Carter, C.J.	Sto	286.002
Carter, H.	Bugler	Po8.394
Case, H.T.	Pte	Po8.774
Cassell, F.	L/Sto	144.869
Chalmers, G.	Pte	Po8.020
Channon, S.G.	AB	180.380
Chittenden, G.	Sto	280.552
Clark, F.	L/Sto	175.923
Clarke, W.	Pte	Po7.082
Clifton, J.	AB	190.114
Collins, J.E.	Pte	Po5.285
Connor, M.	PO1	161.886
Cooke, A.R.	L/Shpwrt	342.332
Cooper, F.	Sto	286.005
Cooper, H.	Sto	286.456
Cooper, J.A.	Pte	Po8.775
Copplestone, J.A.	Sto	286.003
Cotton, J.	AB	196.431
Courtney, T.W.R.	AB	184.658
Cox, P.J.	AB	185.056
Cox, W.	Pte	Po5.596

Bar: RELIEF OF PEKIN *continued.*

Name	Rank	Number
Creedon, J.	Sto	285.447
Cuell, A.J.	Pte	Po7.514
Cullinan, W.F.	Asst/Payr	
Cummings, A.J.	Sto	287.814
Cushion, J.	Sto	350.479
Davis, J.T.	Sto	282.004
Day, H.H.	Sto	284.357
Dear, T.	PO1	138.435
Dedman, F.J.	Pte	Po9.335
Dellow, H.	Pte	Po8.700
Dennis, J.W.	AB	160.938
Dennis, W.F.	AB	190.208
Denny, H.	Pte	Po7.921
Dighton, G.	Pte	Po9.278
Dorling, H.T.	Midn	
Down, R.T.	Midn	
Drummond, J.E.	Lieut	
Dugdale, A.	AB	164.966
Edney, A.W.	AB	197.957
Edwards, W.	Pte	Po8.005
Elliott, W.J.	AB	169.392
Ellis, C.	Pte	Po4.049
Elton, J.	AB	196.240
Farley, E.	Pte	Po5.968
Fayzackerly, A.	Pte	Po5.301
Fegan, J.	AB	187.651
Fisher, F.J.	AB	177.206
Flaherty, D.	AB	188.880
Flyde, F.	Sto	290.017
Foley, W.G.	L/Sto	173.632
Foote, G.	Sto	284.682
Foote, G.	Pte	Po6.339
Forbes, A.	Sto	282.382
Ford, F.M.	AB	189.531
Fowler, W.E.	Sto	173.803
Franklin, T.W.	L/S	170.567
French, C.J.	Sto	284.710
Gardiner, T.R.	L/S	156.072
Gardner, C.A.	Ord	196.628
Gibb, W.	Sto	276.693
Grady, J.	AB	164.960
Gregory, H.	Sto	284.214
Griggs, G.A.	AB	190.174
Gulliver, C.	Pte	Po8.694
Haddrell, P.	Pte	Po6.798
Harding, A.	Sto	287.813
Hardy, W.	Sto	285.886
Harris, H.E.	Pte	Po8.681
Hayes, J.	Pte	Po9.557
Hayson, F.W.	Pte	Po8.702
Herriott, T.A.	L/S	176.477
Hicks, E.L.	AB	167.979
Hide, C.E.	Arm/Crew	341.975
Holland, F.J.	AB	179.145
Holman, C.W.	Sto	284.372
Hook, R.W.	Pte	Po7.591
Hopkins, G.	Pte	Po8.701
Horsley, H.	Pte	Po8.641
Howard, C.	Pte	Po6.267
Hubbard, C.	Sto	288.530
Huckle, F.A.	Sh/Cpl	124.122
Hughes, H.	Ord	190.327
Hutchinson, H.	Act/Lieut	
Hutchinson, R.B.C.	Midn	
Johnstone, J.	L/Sto	158.807
Jones, A.G.	Pte	Po2.466
Jones, H.	AB	195.491
Jones, H.M.	L/Sergt	Po6.718
Jones, J.	Pte	Po2.458
Kemp, T.W.	Sto	286.414
Kewell, G.	PO2	171.125
Kirby, A.G.	AB	192.679
Knight, C.T.	AB	196.264
Knight, W.B.	AB	159.700
Laker, W.	Pte	Po8.773
Lambert, C.E.	Sto	286.421
Lawes, J.	Pte	Po5.613
Lawrie, F.B.A.	Lieut(RMLI)	
Leach, J.	AB	193.075
Legg, W.J.	Pte	Po8.678
Leir, E.W.	Midn	
Lenihan, W.H.	L/S	138.108
Lessay, R.	Pte	Po4.250
Lester, G.F.	Cpl	Po7.513
Lidstone, H.W.	Pte	Po8.761
Light, P.A.	Sh/Std/Asst	341.215
Lock, L.	AB	195.536
Lovelady, H.	AB	161.383
McCormick, T.J.	Sto	289.982
McDonald, J.	Ord	176.515
McLeod, A.	Shpwrt	341.869
Macey, G.A.	Arm/Crew	341.902
Maloney, D.	AB	196.245
Maple, F.W.	Q/Sig	190.263
Marsh, W.H.	AB	182.922
Martin, J.	Sto	286.410
Metcalfe, J.	PO2	166.883
Mills, J.E.	Pte	Po8.675
Morgan, E.	Sto	175.444
Morrison, D.	Sto	287.942
Mullins, G.J.H.	Capt(RMLI)	
Mullis, J.	Act/Ch/PO	137.195
Murphy, J.	Sto	288.644
Neil, A.	AB	180.616
Newland, G.E.	Sto	282.176
Nicholson, S.	Pte	Po9.382
Norman, W.J.	Sto	282.379
Novis, H.A.	AB	156.064
Nowell, H.H.	Pte	Po8.684
O'Mara, F.	Pte	Po7.890
Owens, M.	Sto	285.085
Pagett, J.	Sto	288.497
Pankhurst, J.H.	Sto	282.217
Parker, A.W.	Pte	Po8.680
Pasker, W.J.	Pte	Po6.205
Payne, S.J.	Sto	282.006

Bar: RELIEF OF PEKIN *continued.*

Peck, H.	Sergt	Po2.704	
Penn, W.	Pte	Po7.962	
Pinkerton, S.	AB	160.654	
Pledge, W.J.	L/S	155.047	
Pollard, H.R.	AB	189.966	
Porteous, J.	Cpl	Po9.144	
Porter, J.G.	Sto	281.291	
Prime, A.E.	Pte	Po7.878	
Radcliffe, S.	AB	189.570	
Randall, F.C.	AB	160.726	
Rayner, H.	Ord	197.654	
Rayner, J.M.	Pte	Po5.847	
Reed, W.	AB	166.139	
Rees, W.J.	AB	161.857	
Reilly, F.J.	Pte	Po8.857	
Reinold, B.G.	Midn		
Relf, C.	Pte	Po8.777	
Riley, J.L.	Pte	Po9.400	
Robertson, L.H.	AB	189.945	
Roman, W.	AB	173.878	
Rood, T.H.	L/S	181.095	
Roper, E.	Sergt	Po4.952	K
Roper, W.A.	Pte	Po4.392	
Rose, G.	Pte	Po7.455	
Ross, J.	Sto	282.239	
Rowe, J.	L/S	162.400	
Rudgely, W.E.	Pte	Po8.654	
Sandry, J.A.	AB	169.531	
Scarlett, J.	AB	188.626	
Scott, A.H.	Carp/Mte	151.478	
Seymour, W.	Sto	279.761	
Shepherd, D.	L/S	115.218	
Shepherd, E.C.	AB	187.485	
Sheridan, P.	Sto	276.686	
Sherrin, A.E.	Midn		
Sherwin, H.A.	L/S	173.855	
Silvers, B.	L/Cpl	Po6.330	
Skinner, H.D.	PO2	140.623	
Smith, R.J.	Pte	Po8.783	
Smithen, J.	AB	166.339	
Southard, A.	Pte	Po8.065	
Stanbridge, A.	Cpl	Po4.073	
Stansmore, A.	AB	193.169	
Starck, F.	AB	155.992	
Starling, F.J.	L/S	155.791	
Stevens, A.	AB	190.224	
Stewart, J.	SBStd	121.651	
Stones, A.E.	AB	192.314	
Strickland, H.	AB	195.472	
Strudwick, F.J.	PO1	158.180	
Stubbington, W.H.	Pte	Po8.683	
Sumner, C.G.C.	Midn		
Symons, H.	Act/Ch/PO	146.687	
Thomas, L.	AB	187.923	
Thompson, G.	Pte	Po6.567	
Tompkins, A.H.E.	Pte	Po7.789	
Toms, J.	AB	170.693	
Tovey, A.E.	Pte	Po8.704	
Trengrove, J.	PO1	113.844	
Troup, J.A.G.	Midn		
Tuberfield, H.	Pte	Po8.768	
Tucker, H.W.	AB	176.941	
Underwood, F.	AB	189.143	
Vail, F.	AB	183.656	
Vine, C.A.	Sto	284.691	
Voar, A.J.	Sto	285.274	
Walker, D.McC.	Pte	Po8.695	
Walker, W.	AB	162.563	
Walters, H.A.	Pte	Po8.699	
Warren, S.J.	L/S	166.226	
Watt, S.T.	Pte	Po8.758	
Webster, H.O.	AB	189.798	
Weir, J.McC.	Sto	276.631	
Weldon, E.F.	AB	197.180	
Wells, A.	Sto	285.071	
White, A.H.	L/S	125.048	
White, E.C.	AB	191.331	
White, J.J.	Pte	Po7.070	
Whitlock, C.H.	Arm	340.928	
Whyte, D.S.	AB	189.944	
Wilde, J.S.	Lieut		
Williams, D.	Sto	288.519	
Willoughby, P.F.	Midn		
Wiltsher, W.H.	AB	175.149	
Woodgate, W.A.	Sto	285.092	
Wright, J.	Gunr		K
Wright, P.A.	Pte	Po4.950	
Yeomans, P.	Pte	Po4.326	
York, T.	Sergt	Po4.718	

Duplicate medals:

Barnard, F.R.	L/Cpl	Po8.007
Bell, J.	Sto	283.394
Brennan, I.W.	AB	190.529
Dennis, W.F.	AB	190.208
Drummond, J.E.	Lieut	
Fegan, J.	AB	187.651
Gardner, C.A.	Ord	196.628
Hicks, E.L.	AB	167.979
Horsley, H.	Pte	Po8.641
Hubbard, C.	Sto	288.530
Hughes, H.	Ord	190.327
Laker, W.	Pte	Po8.773
Lenihan, W.H.	L/S	138.108
Maple, F.W.	Q/Sig	190.263
Marsh, W.H.	AB	182.922
Randall, F.C.	AB	160.726
Sheridan, P.	Sto	276.686
Southard, A.	Pte	Po8.065

Bar: RELIEF OF PEKIN *continued.*

Returned medals:

Blake, T.	SBStd	150.291
Clarke, W.	Sto	285.302
Foster, W.	Pte	Po6.920
Houghton, H.	Pte	Po7.387
Saunders, J.	Ord	194.709

NO BAR MEDALS.

Abraham, N.J.	L/S	157.432
Abrahams, G.	Dom	356.356
Aburrow, E.	Sto	148.346
Ackfield, I.	ERA	149.902
Adams, H.	Carp/Crew	341.559
Alexander, A.	AB	183.212
Alexander, W.	AB	195.525
Alford, J.	L/Sto	149.877
Allison, C.	AB	195.542
Alsbury, J.A.	AB	187.203
Alway, F.G.	Ord	194.899
Ames, J.	Band	340.385
Anderson, J.	Pte	Ply3.606
Andrews, H.	Sto	114.603
Armitage, I.	Bugler	Po7.989
Arnell, W.G.	Sto	287.824
Arnold, J.N.	Act/Ch/ Yeo/Sig	146.983
Arthur, W.	Pntr	122.173
Ash, H.W.	Ord	196.034
Astbury, G.E.	Pte	Ply8.901
Atkins, T.	Act/Ch/Sto	148.646
Attree, W.S.	2/SBStd	350.407
Aughton, J.	Sto	172.418
Austin, F.	Sto	280.719
Avery, C.	Pte	Po9.709
Bailey, F.	Sto	166.246
Bailey, H.	L/Sto	138.360
Bainbridge, T.	Pte	Ply7.944
Baker, A.	L/Sto	161.688
Baker, G.	Sto	133.278
Baker, S.	AB	175.064
Baker, W.A.	Sto	284.728
Baker, W.T.	Sto	285.272
Baldwin, T.	Ch/PO	102.545
Ball, G.H.	AB	185.888
Ballard, J.	Sto	293.538
Banbury, R.	Ord	196.380
Barker, J.	Pte	Ply9.690
Barnett, R.	AB	183.983
Barnett, S.J.	Sergt	Ch7.439
Barrett, D.	Blksmth	341.388
Bartlett, E.E.	Asst/Engr	
Bartlett, W.W.	Sto	293.546
Baskerville, H.S.	Fl/Payr	
Bate, W.S.T.	Ch/PO	127.128
Bates, C.	AB	176.403
Bates, J.	Sto	289.961
Beale, W.	Boy	203.457
Beatty, J.E.	PO2	167.835
Belsey, W.J.	Sto	288.518
Bendall, A.E.	Sh/Std/Asst	341.994
Bewers, W.J.	Sto	280.241
Bicker, H.P.	PO1	158.671
Bird, D.S.	PO2	115.186
Bishop, W.J.	Sto	161.281
Black, A.	Sto	281.950
Blackmore, G.A.	PO2	133.591
Blank, C.	Sto	291.469
Blewdon, H.	AB	201.875
Bogle, R.H.	Lieut	
Boland, W.	AB	170.915
Boley, E.	Sto	293.249
Bonnick, F.	AB	197.124
Boobier, J.S.	Pte	Po3.408
Bourne, J.H.	AB	188.443
Bowden, T.	Ord	196.080
Boxall, A.W.	Cpl	Ply7.565
Bradford, J.	Band	166.667
Bradley, C.A.	Pte	Ply8.809
Bray, J.	AB	201.640
Brennan, M.	Ch/Sto	121.124
Brewer, H.E.	AB	195.497
Bright, A.S.	L/S	179.884
Brimble, C.	PO1	110.048
Brindle, E.	AB	189.680
Brock, G.F.	AB	190.418
Brogan, T.W.	AB	193.610
Brown, H.J.	L/Sto	142.435
Brown, H.V.	2/Yeo/Sig	154.374
Brown, J.S.	Sail	195.968
Brown, W.	Carp/Mte	341.022
Browne, C.	Sto	276.425
Browne, E.	Pte	Ply8.925
Bryan, C.	Sto	291.459
Buckett, A.H.	AB	196.213
Bull, E.L.	Sto	286.447
Bullock, E.	Ord	200.196
Bunday, J.	PO1	110.829
Bundy, J.	Sto	280.855
Burke, A.E.	Ch/Arm	133.927
Burn, G.E.	L/Sto	276.407
Burnham, G.	L/S	169.568
Burridge, P.	Sto	284.983
Burridge, R.	Sto	289.789
Bush, G.H.	AB	195.543
Bush, W.J.	Ord	196.047
Butler, A.W.	AB	189.527
Cable, G.W.	Ord	193.685
Caldicott, W.	Sto	119.738
Campbell, J.R.	Sto	278.033
Campbell, R.	Sto	278.706
Caress, W.A.	Sto	281.943
Carey, W.G.	PO1	121.805
Carpenter, W.J.	AB	182.085

NO BAR MEDALS *continued.*

Carr, H.	Sto	278.396
Carver, W.H.	Sto	280.835
Casey, P.	Sto	283.319
Cashman, W.	L/Sto	145.455
Cater, J.S.	PO1	142.742
Caulfield, J.	Pte	Po10.264
Caws, H.	AB	167.423
Challinor, C.	PO1	170.293
Chamberlain, F.J.	AB	188.263
Chambers, W *alias* Bowes.	L/Sto	152.711
Chandler, F.R.	AB	184.023
Chase, J.E.	Fl/Engr	
Childs, C.R.	AB	179.912
Chirnside, H.	Sto	290.799
Chisholm, B.	ERA	268.927
Choi Ah.	Dom	
Christmas, J.	Sto	280.534
Churchman, A.J.	Sh/Cpl	117.542
Clanford, A.	Boy	203.473
Clarke, J.H.	Pte	Po9.531
Clarke, W.O.	L/S	170.363
Cleaves, S.	Ch/Sto	129.513
Clemens, G.	Sto	281.769
Clements, R.	Sto	283.327
Clifton, R.	Sto	157.065
Codd, F.C.	PO2	150.851
Coggins, W.J.	PO1	86.042
Colbourne, J.A.	L/S	158.734
Cole, E.J.	Gunr	
Coleman, W.	Sto	285.885
Coles, F.J.	Ord	196.904
Collenso, J.G.	AB	189.928
Collier, H.B.	Sto	284.117
Collins, J.	ERA	168.187
Collins, W.A.	Sto	285.273
Connell, R.J.	Band	163.330
Cook, R.	Pte	Po9.710
Cook, W.	AB	184.127
Cook, W.A.	Sto	176.609
Cooke, H.	AB	176.138
Cooper, A.E.	PO1	142.526
Cooper, S.	Sto	167.174
Cooper, W.	Sto	290.251
Corfield, F.	Sto	289.742
Cosham, J.	Sto	287.820
Cotcher, W.J.	AB	190.225
Coulson, T.	L/Sto	159.951
Cousins, J.W.	AB	176.413
Couzens, A.G.	Cook/Mte	341.872
Cowell, C.F.	Ord	195.225
Cox, T.F.	Sto	167.140
Crawford, G.	Sh/Cook	100.002
Crees, E.J.	L/Carp/Crew	341.595
Creese, A.E.	AB	191.064
Cripps, H.	L/Sto	131.807
Cripps, W.G.	L/Sto	142.417
Crispin, A.	Sto	289.822
Crougham, H.	AB	177.722
Crowe, G.	MAA	112.100
Cuell, J.A.	Ord	195.551
Cumming, R.	AB	136.507
Cunningham, E.	Ord	201.938
Curtis, C.A.	Sto	285.448
Curtis, E.D.	AB	176.076
Cutler, W.	Ord	201.605 K
Daly, W.	Ord	197.925
Daniells, C.J.	AB	160.778
Daniels, E.	Ch/Sto	136.534
Daniels, W.	L/Sto	152.590
Dart, J.	Ord	194.750
Davidson, F.	AB	184.074
Davie, A.	Ch/ERA	153.706
Davies, A.A.	AB	147.859
Davies, R.	Ord	194.740
Davies, W.	Ord	197.394
Davis, G.	Sto	290.010
Dawson, H.	Carp/Crew	287.857
Deacon, D.	Sto	151.156
Dean, J.	AB	190.199
Delea, E.	Ord	197.699
Denham, H.S.	ERA	269.018
Denzy, R.	Sto	286.518
Dibden, H.E.	AB	171.133
Didcock, F.	Pte	Po6.856
Dillon, A.J.	Sto	284.698
Dobson, G.	Sto	157.068
Donnan, J.	Ord	197.522
Donovan, A.E.	AB	138.255
Downer, E.J.	AB	186.134
Downton, W.J.	ERA	133.008
Doyle, M.J.	Sto	286.197
Draper, W.	PO2	157.590
Driver, W.	Ord	197.941
Dumbleton, C.	Pte	Po6.195
Dummer, H.	AB	177.944
Dunk, C.	Boy	203.453
Dunne, M.	Sto	293.547
Dunvert, J.	Ord	197.715
Dye, H.E.	Ord	194.778
Dyer, G.H.	AB	195.537
Dyer, T.	ERA	269.017
Eames, J.H.	Sto	166.929
Eames, P.	Sto	281.927
Earwaker, T.	Sto	284.741
Easson, R.	AB	186.115
Eaton, A.W.	AB	181.811
Edwards, G.	AB	190.090
Edwards, J.	Sto	136.524
Edwards, J.D.	AB	190.222
Elliott, W.E.	Ch/Wrtr	121.173
Ellis, G.	Pte	Po5.097
Ellis, H.C.	Arm	155.654
Elmes, W.G.	Ord	192.613
Endean, H.	AB	181.829
England, F.H.	AB	189.470

NO BAR MEDALS *continued.*

Name	Rank	No.
England, G.P.	Lieut	
Eustice, T.	AB	129.848
Evans, R.C.	Sto	282.344
Evans, W.	AB	161.370
Everard, W.A.	Pte	Po4.373
Everett, C.E.	Blksmth/Mte	166.975
Farmer, D.	Sto	282.332
Faux, W.H.	Sto	291.558
Fernandez, R.W.	L/Sto	141.392
Ferns, H.J.	AB	196.242
Fielder, H.	AB	193.722
Filbey, G.W.	Pte	Po10.258
Finch, A.	Band	180.234
Fisher, H.A.	AB	181.592
Fitzgerald, M.	AB	145.835
Flynn, Rev. F.	Chaplain	
Foo Ah.	Dom	
Foord, A.	Sto	285.453
Foord, A.	Cook/Mte	340.630
Ford, J.A.	Arm/Mte	340.379
Ford, R.	Bosn	
Forsyth, A.	Sto	174.112
Foster, A.	Sto	285.094
Foster, J.	L/S	130.973
Foyle, R.J.	AB	196.259
Fraley, G.	Sto	292.293
Frood, C.F.	AB	189.006
Froome, C.E.	AB	187.925
Funnell, H.	AB	195.539
Galyer, J.	AB	187.621
Gardiner, G.E.	Ord	193.025
Gardiner, W.	Sto	281.102
Garland, R.	AB	190.110
Garraway, W.B.	Ord	194.901
Geary, A.	AB	151.930
Gibbons, T.	Ch/ERA	142.023
Giddings, C.E.	Bugler	Po7.723
Gilbert, J.	Sto	282.231
Goff, W.V.	Sto	148.679
Goldsmith, W.	Sto	284.554
Goodwin, F.R.	Asst/Engr	
Goodwin, L.H.	AB	187.254
Gordon, J.	Sto	169.344
Gosling, J.	Sto	283.755
Gouge, S.C.	Sto	164.088
Gough, W.G.	Ord	197.771
Goulter, J.G.	AB	166.685
Grant, A.	Sto	281.098
Grant, H.	L/Sto	148.298
Gray, H.P.	AB	186.660
Green, J.	Sto	167.197
Green, L.	Sto	285.998
Greene, G.	Sto	287.735
Greening, A.C.	AB	189.178
Griffiths, F.J.	Plmbr	159.976
Griffiths, J.	Ch/Sto	120.749
Grounds, W.	PO2	180.374
Gun Ah.	Dom	
Gurr, E.	AB	190.323
Haberfield, G.	Sto	289.801
Hall, C.	L/Sto	172.841
Hall, F.	Ord	199.636
Hall, J.T.	Sto	287.899
Hall, R.	AB	190.172
Halligan, J.	Ord	197.706
Hallwright, W.W.	Midn	
Ham, H.	Ord	196.070
Harber, W.J.	Ord	197.768
Harris, G.	Ord	185.125
Hart, E.	Sto	280.274
Hartfield, W.J.	AB	181.819
Harvey, A.	AB	195.473
Harvey, E.A.J.	Carp/Mte	161.650
Harwood, A.J.	Pte	Po5.799
Harwood, G.	Sto	276.877
Hatcher, H.	AB	183.379
Hatt, E.	Band	340.211
Hatterley, W.C.	Ord	196.082
Hawkins, H.	AB	152.138
Hayler, C.	ERA	269.054
Hayles, F.	AB	195.506
Hayman, J.H.	Ord	201.254
Hayter, E.S.	Sto	280.715
Hayward, F.	Cook/Mte	340.938
Hayward, S.	L/Sto	151.716
Heath, W.J.	Ord	195.108
Hefferman, T.	AB	158.031
Helston, H.W.	Pte	Po8.924
Henderson, R.	Pte	Ply8.944
Hendley, L.	Sto	285.452
Henson, G.N.	Midn	
Hewitt, W.	Ch/Sto	119.940
Hill, E.	AB	198.998
Hillman, A.	Sto	284.994
Hirst, S.	PO1	131.398
Hoar, G.	AB	195.470
Hoare, R.	Ord	201.604
Hockaday, C.	Boy	203.470
Hodgson, F.	Act/Gunr	
Hogan, P.	Sto	291.731
Holding, F.	AB	180.369
Holdway, C.	Sto	285.449
Holmes, J.	Pte	Ply6.163
Hong Wing.	Dom	
Honniball, H.	PO1	128.018
Hooker, F.	Sto	168.847
Hookway, H.	2/Cooper	341.345
Hopkins, J.	Sh/Std	101.910
Hoptrough, C.	Sto	146.531
Horne, S.F.	Ord	192.840
House, H.E.	AB	157.391
Hovell, R.	Sto	149.747
Howe, F.H.	AB	189.687
Hughes-Onslow, C.H.	Lieut	
Hung Ching.	Dom	

NO BAR MEDALS *continued.*

Hunt, C.	PO2	155.585
Hunter, F.	AB	170.566
Hurst, A.	Ord	197.980
Hurst, E.	Boy	203.453
Hutchence, A.H.	PO2	136.861
Hutchinson, A.	AB	181.552
Inger, W.B.	ERA	153.143
Ireland, J.	AB	195.555
Janman, H.G.	Sto	276.639
Jeanes, W.J.	Carp/Crew	342.690
Jeffery, J.T.	PO1	151.372
Jenkins, W.	Ord	197.295
Jenner, L.	Boy	202.910
Jennings, W.G.	Sto	293.542
Jennings, W.L.	Ord	199.999
Jerred, W.N.	AB	196.211
Johns, J.	Carp	
Johnson, H.W.	Sto	290.839
Johnstone, J.	Sto	277.758
Jones, C.H.	Sto	285.879
Jones, E.B.	Sto	284.719
Jones, J.	Sto	289.465
Jones, J.A.	AB	197.073
Jones, R.	AB	126.225
Jones, W.	AB	180.379
Jones, W.J.	ERA	268.790
Joy, W.A.	Sto	286.194
Judd, G.H.	AB	196.225
Jupp, F.	Sto	287.771
Kaye, H.A.	Sto	284.742
Kealey, W.	Ord	197.853
Keefe, T.	Sto	285.342
Keeping, C.	Sto	161.295
Kelly, T.	Sto	292.232
Kelly, T.H.	Pte	Ch6.655
Kemp, H.	Ord	201.873
Kendall, J.	AB	174.100
Kennedy, G.	Sto	276.046
Kent, G.	PO1	120.490
Kenyon, H.	AB	181.308
Keohane, C.	AB	190.426
Kerr, D.	2/Cooper	174.490
Kersley, A.	Band	340.183
Kierman, E.	Ord	197.683
Killoran, P.	Pte	Ply8.860
Kimber, R.	AB	192.721
Kimber, W.H.	Sto	285.001
Kinsella, J.	PO1	132.172
Kirby, R.E.W.	Midn	
Knight, J.	Sto	286.222
Knight, W.	Sto	282.342
Knight, W.J.	AB	185.617
Ladd, W.H.	Band	123.226
Lake, F.V.	Sto	281.947
Lam, A.	Dom	
Lane, H.T.	Sto	176.585
Lane, W.H.	Sh/Std/Boy	341.835
Langdon, G.	Sto	285.443
Large, A.	Q/Sig	173.079
Layton, J.	L/Sto	140.895
Leadingham, A.	Sto	282.313
Ledbrook, J.	AB	120.099
Lee, C.	AB	190.167
Lee, P.	Ord	197.690
Lee, T.B.	Ord	199.640
Lee, W.J.	AB	193.808
Lees, A.E.J.	Ord	196.016
Legard, G.P.	Sub Lieut	
Legg, B.	AB	189.247
Lewis, C.	Ord	186.228
Limpus, A.H.	Comdr	
Lindridge, H.	AB	171.713
Lindsay, J.	Sh/Cpl	146.873
Lintern, W.H.	AB	182.999
Linton, H.	L/Sto	109.321
Litchfield, F.S.	Lieut	
Livermore, P.	AB	193.646
Long, A.T.	Sh/Cpl	350.084
Long, F.	AB	188.719
Long, J.	Sto	288.522
Lovell, F.	Pte	Po8.149
Lusty, E.	AB	185.631
Lutman, H.R.B.	AB	185.414
McGrane, E.	Ord	196.180 K
McGuire, P.	Sto	279.968
McKenzie, G.	AB	190.405
McKinlay, W.G.	PO2	151.069
MacMillan, C.C.	Surgn	
McNeil, J.	Sto	284.505
Macer, C.	Ord	199.977
Major, C.G.	Sto	284.724
Major, E.W.	Ord	193.469
Majoram, C.E.	AB	189.641
Maloney, J.	AB	147.347
Man Ah.	Dom	
Manwaring, M.	Sto	281.345
Marsh, F.	Q/Sig	180.550
Marten, G.	Sto	291.772
Mather, W.B.	Gunr	
Matthews, A.O.	AB	189.716
Matthews, F.	Ord	202.213
Mayhew, S.H.	Sto	287.640
Mekin, J.	Pte	Ply2.943
Meredith, O.	Dom	171.454
Middleton, A.	Ord	198.135
Miles, G.T.	Sto	284.727
Millar, T.	AB	165.506
Miller, E.A.	AB	195.845
Miller, E.J.	Ord	195.292
Ming Ah.	Dom	
Mitchell, C.E.	AB	181.742
Mitchell, H.G.	L/S	120.111
Mitchell, R.	PO1	124.007
Mitchell, T.	Ch/Sto	116.737
Moore, A.J.	Sto	115.776
Moore, C.	Sto	127.571

NO BAR MEDALS *continued.*

Moorse, W.	Sto	287.740
Morgan, E.J.	Sto	159.961
Morgan, J.	AB	186.825
Morling, H.W.	Ord	193.202
Morris, J.	Sto	285.994
Moyse, T.J.	Ord	201.872
Munn, W.C.	Ord	196.375
Murch, A.	Ord	201.606
Murdock, R.	Ch/Sto	119.900
Murphy, J.	AB	175.548
Murphy, J.	AB	188.879
Murray, A.E.J.	Engr	
Murray, J.	Sto	282.240
Murray, T.	Sto	280.222
Nash, H.	AB	187.591
Nash, J.	Arm/Crew	154.168
Neiass, T.J.	Ord	194.824
Neil, A.	PO1	152.273
Neil, W.	PO1	119.309
Nend, A.E.	Ord	200.652
Neville, O.	AB	186.015
New, G.W.	AB	179.975
Newcome, S.	Lieut	
Newman, G.	Ord	203.451
Newman, H.	Sto	145.783
Newman, J.W.	Q/Sig	160.203
Newstead, W.J.	AB	192.850
Noble, H. *alias* Nolan.	Sto	161.644
Nunn, F.J.	PO2	169.385
Nunn, W.	Pte	Po10.260
O'Flaherty, J.	Sto	165.222
O'Neill, W.	Sto	291.737
Ogilvy, F.C.A.	Comdr	
Oldbury, C.	L/S	109.701
Oliver, J.	AB	193.784
Orr, W.G.	AB	172.765
Osborne, S.W.	Pte	Po6.402
Otty, F.	Sto	279.961
Ousley, J.	AB	176.409
Pacey, R.	Sto	289.823
Paice, W.J.	AB	183.357
Palmer, A.	AB	189.976
Palmer, C.	Sto	168.207
Pankhurst, T.J.	PO2	145.639
Park, S.	AB	193.787
Parkes, C.	Ord	203.456
Parnell, E.J.	Ord	195.302
Parsons, G.	Sto	173.786
Parsons, H.	Sto	285.270
Pashley, T.J.	Sto	278.379
Payne, W.	Ch/Sto	136.568
Pearce, P.G.	AB	185.415
Peckett, J.H.	PO2	136.844
Pellatt, A.	Carp/Mte	153.885
Pellett, H.	AB	192.931
Phillips, E.W.	AB	183.344
Pillar, J.G.	Ord	196.017
Ping Ah.	Dom	
Plomer, H.	Sto	283.705
Plumb, A.G.	Sto	282.341
Plummer, F.	Ord	193.804
Pocock, W.	Sto	284.706
Pollock, J.	Ord	174.516
Pomeroy, A.	Ord	195.300
Pope, E.	AB	196.251
Porch, F.	PO1	107.694
Porter, W.	Sto	152.581
Powell, E.	AB	174.017
Pratt, H.C.	Pte	Po4.004
Pratt, H.J.	PO1	125.768
Price, J.	Shpwrt	341.650
Prince, G.	PO1	145.605
Prior, W.B.	AB	189.673
Purchase, G.	AB	195.504
Rance, A.	Cpl	Po7.487
Randall, C.W.	AB	196.243
Reading, A.E.	AB	196.257
Redman, F.J.	AB	145.606
Reed, G.G.	Sto	284.989
Reid, A.	AB	179.991
Richards, A.	Sto	284.711
Richards, S.R.S.	Lieut	
Richens, C.	PO1	110.151
Rider, R.T.	Art/Engr	
Robertson, G.	Engr	
Rock, C.B.F. le W.	Asst/Engr	
Rogers, W.E.	Sto	165.929
Ross, E.	Ord	189.507
Rovery, L.	AB	189.144
Rowe, A.	Sto	284.709
Ruider, G.S.	AB	190.359
Ryall, F.W.	L/S	167.799
Sack, F.C.	Sto	165.931
Sales, J.H.	AB	194.564
Salter, M.	AB	201.281
San Wong.	Dom	
Savage, W.	Sto	191.732
Sawyers, C.G.	AB	186.205
Schooley, D.J.	Ord	177.824
Schultz, H.J.	AB	190.734
Scorey, G.H.	AB	196.265
Scott, P.M.	Capt	
Scrivens, B.	Pte	Po8.668
Sears, W.H.	AB	189.442
Self, G.L.	AB	193.634
Sen Ah.	Dom	
Shanahan, H.	Sto	285.998
Shanahan, J.	Blksmth/Mte	340.535
Shannon, J.	Sto	162.609
Sharp, A.M.	AB	190.380
Sheldon, F.	Sto	158.459
Shepherd, G.	2/Wrtr	340.612
Shepherd, H. *alias* Williams.	L/Sto	150.953
Shepherd, R.H.	Sto	280.545

NO BAR MEDALS *continued.*

Sheridan, M.	Ord	197.705
Shirley, E.	Q/Sig	187.399
Shorrock, W.J.	AB	188.174
Silvester, F.A.	Sto	284.205
Simmons, T.E.	AB	183.026
Simmons, W.	Ord	196.064
Sing Ah.	Dom	
Skeene, W.	Sto	283.251
Skene, C.H.	Ord	197.570
Skinner, W.	Sto	276.024
Slater, G.	AB	189.439
Slatter, A.E.	AB	181.543
Sliney, J.	Ord	196.665
Smith, C.	Sto	289.480
Smith, C.W.	Sto	152.689
Smith, E.A.	Pte	Ply9.701
Smith, H.G.	AB	192.680
Smith, J.	Sto	153.587
Smith, T.F.A.	Sto	165.232
Smith, W.J.	AB	193.084
Sow Ah.	Dom	
Sow Ching.	Dom	
Sparkes, A.E.	PO1	129.206
Spindler, W.	Ord	197.582
Spooner, H.	Ord	192.513
Spurgeon, S.T.	L/Sto	156.535
Squire, J.H.	Band	340.489
Squires, R.	PO1	96.834
Stallard, T.	L/Sto	119.744
Standen, A.	Sto	285.277
Standing, W.	Boy	203.454
Staples, A.E.	Sto	148.064
Starling, E.C.	ERA	268.914
Steele, A.E.	Sto	285.271
Stephens, F.	Sto	286.453
Stephens, J.	Sto	291.754
Sterck, R.	Sto	280.535
Stevenson, H.	Sto	152.775
Stewart, C.	Ord	195.035
Stilges, W.H.	Sh/Std/Asst	341.601
Stone, A.E.	Sto	281.344
Street, A.	Sto	281.106
Strickland, W.	AB	141.233
Sullivan, J.	Ord	196.821
Sullivan, P.	Sto	288.520
Sullivan, T.	Sto	288.535
Swaffield, C.	Sto	284.723
Sweeney, E.	Sto	282.583
Swift, G.	AB	189.460
Symes, A.E.	AB	156.916
Talbot, C.H.	AB	187.322
Tame, H.	AB	191.726
Taylor, D.	Ord	197.716
Taylor, P.J.	Pte	Ch10.090
Taylor, T.	PO1	127.142
Teng Ah.	Dom	
Thomas, T.R.	AB	196.258
Thompson, J.R.	Ord	195.039 K
Thornhill, H.	Sto	288.543
Tilden, W.	Boy	203.467
Titheridge, W.H.	Sto	168.871
Tolson, E.	Ord	197.201
Towers, A.	AB	129.226
Treharne, P.	AB	141.551
Trim, H.P.	AB	195.495
Trivett, F.	AB	190.105
Trott, S.E.	Pte	Po9.706
Tuck, F.	AB	190.544
Tull, W.	Pte	Po8.897
Tullis, T.	PO1	110.802
Turner, A.	ERA	269.203
Turner, H.	Pte	Ply5.792
Turrell, A.	Cook/Mte	161.695
Twidale, D.	Sto	289.352
Tyler, G.H.	Pte	Po4.988
Utton, W.	AB	194.028
Vare, G.	Sto	285.884
Varnham, A.E.	AB	162.297
Veness, J.	Act/Ch/PO	128.560
Veness, T.H.	Sto	276.031
Ventham, J.	Act/Band	146.517
Vick, H.	Ch/ERA	128.918
Vickers, H.	Sto	276.635
Vincent, A.	AB	192.829
Vosper, F.J.P.	AB	179.700
Wagg, A.E.	Sto	177.189
Walker, C.	Pte	Ch8.497
Wanless, T.	ERA	269.161
Warburton, C.L.O.	ERA	166.256
Ward, C.O.	Ord	197.950
Ward, G.W.	L/S	156.637
Warne, L.J.	Sto	286.452
Waters, H.	Sto	165.207
Watson, R.	ERA	268.908
Webb, H.W.	AB	189.621
Webster, T.M.	AB	189.466
Wedmore, A.J.	AB	172.073
Weekes, B.	Sto	288.546
Weeks, W.R.	ERA	268.974
Weippert, C.N.	L/S	159.620
Welling, A.	AB	190.133
Wellstead, G.	Boy	203.452
Werndley, F.	Pte	Po8.150
West, G.	Sto	144.775
Whatley, Rev. C.L.	Chaplain	
Wheatley, H.J.	AB	189.438
Wheddon, C.	Boy	202.909
Wheeler, T.	AB	187.062
Whincup, B.	AB	189.550
White, F.C.	Ord	194.780
White, W.	Sto	161.316
White, W.	AB	190.071
Whitmore, G.W.	Pte	Ch10.020
Whitter, W.	Pte	Po6.934
Whyte, A.E.	Sto	281.161
Whyte, H.E.W.C.	Midn	

NO BAR MEDALS *continued.*

Whyte, S.	AB	144.620
Wilkins, A.E.	Sto	287.819
Wilkins, W.	Sto	151.462
Willey, H.	Ord	196.026
Williams, G.E.	L/Sto	159.945
Williams, H.J.	L/Sto	151.931
Williams, J.	Sto	284.984
Williams, J.J.	ERA	268.990
Williams, W.G.	Ord	186.774
Willis, W. *alias* Gentry, W.	Sto	283.708
Wilson, H.	AB	181.351
Wilton, C.	Sto	284.733
Winnett, A.S.	AB	190.101
Wood, E.	AB	190.160
Woolf, T.A.	Clerk	
Woolley, G.A.	Sto	287.898
Wright, B.	PO2	148.262
Wright, E.	Ord	198.997
Wright, J.E.	PO2	128.197
Wright, J.E.	AB	189.969
Wyatt, A.	AB	183.373
Wyman, W.J.	Sh/Cpl	350.038
Yabsley, W.	AB	144.193
Yarham, W.	L/Carp/Crew	341.944
You Ah.	Dom	
Young, H.	Boy	203.474

Duplicate medals:

Bridger, W.J.	Sto	153.637 [1]
Collier, H.B.	Sto	284.117
Couzens, A.G.	Cook/Mte	341.872
Crees, E.J.	L/Carp/Crew	341.595
Curtis, C.A.	Sto	285.448
Doyle, M.J.	Sto	286.197
Dyer, T.	ERA	269.017
Foyle, R.J.	AB	196.259
Gough, W.G.	Ord	197.771
Jennings, W.G.	Sto	293.542
Jones, J.A.	AB	197.073
Kenyon, H.	AB	181.308
Marsh, F.	Q/Sig	180.550
Mayhew, S.H.	Sto	287.640
Millar, T.	AB	165.506
Pillar, J.G.	Ord	196.017
Sheldon, F.	Sto	158.459
Shirley, E.	Q/Sig	187.399
Wheeler, T.	AB	187.062
Wilson, H.	AB	181.351

Duplicate medals - without issue no. on roll:

Coles, F.J.	Ord	196.904
Penny, E.	Ord	195.162
Rance, A.	Cpl	Po7.487
Ward, C.O.	Ord	197.950
White, F.C.	Ord	194.780

Returned medals:

Arthur, J.F.	Engr	
Bone, W.	Sto	153.865
Bourke, J.	AB	181.943
Boyle, W.	Sto	292.158
Bridger, W.J.	Sto	153.637 [1]
Campbell, T.	Pte	Po8.741
Dodd, W.	AB	183.715
Ford, E.	Sto	280.281
Gradden, F.	Sto	125.337
Green, H.	AB	195.493
Hammon, G.	AB	186.724
Harris, W.	AB	189.000
Hawthorne, A.G.	Sto	289.337
Hodson, W.E.	Ord	187.660
Horan, W.	AB	171.337
Johnson, G.	PO1	[2]
Laycock, R.A.	Clerk	
Lee, A.	PO2	132.115
Longworth, A.	Pte	Po7.569
McCoyd, W.	Ord	197.525
Marriott, J.G.	Sto	173.792
Penny, E.	Ord	195.162
Power, R.	Pte	Po8.062
Saunders, W.	Sto	144.501
Smith, H.	L/Sto	151.943
Thompson, R.	Ch/PO	[2]

H.M.S UNDAUNTED.

H.M.S. Undaunted was an Armoured Cruiser of 5,600 tons and 300 x 56 feet. Her armament consisted of 2 x 9.2 in, 10 x 6 in and 10 x 3 pdr guns. The vessel was built by Palmer and launched on 25th November 1886. She was sold on 9th April 1907 to Harris at Bristol.

Bars	*Total*	*Returned*	*Entitled*
None	*537*	*25*	*512*
	537	*25*	*512*

Notes:

K - Medal presented by H.M. The King on 8th March 1902.

1 - The medal was returned on 27/3/11 and the roll endorsed 'Run'. The roll further states, "Restored, sent 26/11/15."

NO BAR MEDALS.

Name	Rank	Number	
Acreman, F.F.	Sto	281.004	
Ahern, J.	AB	183.773	K
Ahern, T.	Sto	280.663	
Akhurst, E.J.	Sh/Std	105.748	K
Allen, S.	Blksmth	114.257	
Anderson, A.	AB	196.432	
Anthony, W.H.	Pte	Ply4.521	
Atkins, A.E.	Engr		
Auger, R.H.G.	Bosn		
Austin, H.A.	ERA	268.398	K
Badge, A.W.	AB	135.780	
Bailey, H.H.	Pte	Ch7.943	
Ball, H.	L/Sto	153.327	K
Ball, W.	Pte	Ply4.229	
Banwell, J.	Sto	277.700	K
Barker, J.	Pte	Ch8.624	
Barley, W.H.	PO2	153.938	
Barnes, W.G.K.	St/Surgn		
Barrett, W.	AB	188.300	
Bawden, F.H.	PO2	162.911	
Beard, T.	Pte	Ply6.313	K
Beattie, J.	Blksmth	113.394	
Behenna, E.C.	L/Shpwrt	159.490	K
Bennett, W.R.	Carp/Mte	140.909	
Bermingham, W.	AB	148.685	
Berry, F.	Pte	Ply5.424	K
Biddick, C.	Carp/Mte	148.192	K
Bird, H.	Sh/Cpl	149.361	
Birt, A.E.	AB	155.013	
Bland, R.	AB	181.955	
Bolter, F.W.	Pte	Ply7.033	
Bone, E.R.	Sto	281.567	
Botright, E.	AB	187.450	
Bowen, A.C.	AB	184.639	K
Bowman, C.	Sto	283.378	
Box, G.H.	AB	189.400	
Bradford, J.	Pte	Ply3.712	K
Bray, H.	AB	184.562	
Breen, T.	AB	183.830	
Brent, A.J.	Sto	277.151	
Brewer, E.	Act/Ch/Sto	148.869	K
Bridges, H.D.	Midn		
Brigstocke, T.H.	L/Sto	146.229	
Broadwater, G.	AB	148.351	
Brodribb, J.	AB	184.507	
Bromley, R.	AB	162.591	K
Brooking, J.	L/Sto	147.005	
Brooking, W.	Ch/PO	126.192	K
Brotherton, A.R.	AB	184.902	
Brotherton, J.	Sto	278.331	
Brown, F.C.V.	Asst/Payr		
Brown, H.A.	AB	151.766	
Buckle, H.C.	Midn		
Budge, T.H.	Sto	280.997	
Burdett, F.	Sto	165.673	
Burke, T.	PO1	134.624	
Burns, A.E.	AB	179.299	
Burton, A.S.	Pte	Ply6.058	
Butterfield, J.	Sergt	Ply2.730	
Cain, J.	Sto	286.618	
Callaghan, J.	Sto	277.742	
Callanan, T.H.	AB	136.688	
Campbell, J.E.	AB	118.845	K
Carne, H.	AB	185.201	
Carroll, H.	L/Sto	152.362	
Carter, A.	Pte	Ch8.503	
Carter, T.G.	PO1	131.284	
Carthew, R.S.	AB	189.410	
Castell, J.E.	AB	184.848	
Cayley, H.P.	Lieut		

NO BAR MEDALS *continued.*

Name	Rank	Number	
Chadwick, S.W.	Pte	Ch8.768	
Chapman, C.E.	PO2	163.309	
Charles, J.P.	AB	176.085	
Chelton, W.	PO1	135.849	
Chetwode, G.K.	Lieut		
Chittenden, S.	AB	181.125	
Chivers, W.G.	AB	130.292	
Clarke, A.	AB	169.152	
Clarke, A.C.	Capt		
Cloonan, M.	Sto	281.649	
Coates, E.	MAA	99.312	
Cobley, C.	AB	177.893	
Cochram, S.	Pte	Ply3.415	
Collins, G.	Pte	Ply5.837	
Collins, R.W.	Sh/Std/Asst	170.926	
Condon, T.	PO2	168.944	
Connell, M.	AB	184.155	
Connor, W.	L/S	176.274	
Cook, H.	Yeo/Sig	115.146	
Cosins, G.J.	AB	179.334	
Cowie, J.	L/S	148.278	
Cowin, W.T.	PO2	155.161	
Cowlard, W.	AB	185.333	
Crawford, J.	L/Sto	162.013	
Crawley, R.	Sto	160.168	
Creamer, P.	AB	127.215	
Crimp, F.	L/Shpwrt	340.713	
Crocker, W.E.	AB	180.914	
Crooke, C.	Sto	283.748	
Crowley, J.	AB	184.888	
Cumming, T.	Band	174.196	
Cunningham, J.	Sto	279.134	
Curry, J.	AB	142.838	
Curtis, B.	Lieut		
Cussen, J.	L/Sto	153.454	
Daly, W.	Sto	280.866	
Daniel, G.A.	AB	184.609	
Darling, A.	Pte	Ply7.336	
Davies, R.I.	AB	195.544	
Davis, J.C.	Bosn		
Davis, J.W.	Pte	Ply6.314	
Dedamess, G.	Cook/Mte	354.438	
Dick, S.R.	Pte	Ch4.743	
Doble, E.	Pte	Ply7.878	
Doidge, A.E.	AB	157.107	
Donnelly, J.J.	AB	174.875	
Donohoe, W.J.	AB	184.619	
Dorsett, J.W.	Band	117.360	
Down, J.G.P.	Sto	161.195	K
Drake, E.P.	ERA	268.813	
Drake, F.	L/S	156.868	K
Driscoll, J.	L/Sto	174.326	
Duff, C.	L/S	126.625	
Dugan, J.	Ord	183.827	
Duke, E.	Sto	281.955	
Dunn, A.	Sto	290.508	
Dunstan, T.A.	AB	184.607	
Dunstone, J.L.	AB	155.674	
Dupuy, F.	Ch/Sto	136.042	
Eadie, W.	Pte	Ply7.895	
Eastaway, T.H.	AB	145.153	
Eastley, J.H.	Sto	279.284	K
Easton, W.H.	L/Sto	147.015	K
Edwards, C.H.	Sto	283.475	
Elliott, J.G.	Sto	158.498	
Ellis, A.J.	PO1	110.147	K
Ellis, C.	Sto	149.192	
Ellison, A.J.	ERA	268.333	
Elmer, H.A.T.	Pte	Ply7.255	
Evans, D.	AB	179.404	
Evans, G.	L/Sto	162.615	
Eyles, A.	PO1	122.937	
Eyres, C.J.	Comdr		
Farrow, F.	AB	194.573	
Fawcett, J.	Sto	281.435	
Fear, R.	PO1	125.777	K
Fegan, T.	PO1	146.357	
Ferris, B.W.	AB	188.319	
Finch, A.J.	AB	182.065	
Fitzgerald, J.	Sto	280.665	
Foo Ah.	Dom		
Forbes, J.P.	AB	104.504	
Forsyth, J.	Sto	283.322	
Foster, F.W.	Sto	283.336	
Fothergill, H.M.	Midn		
Francis, R.W.	Pte	Ply5.528	
Francis, W.H.	Sail/Mte	183.778	
Franklin, J.	Pte	Ply5.967	
Freeman, S.J.	AB	185.576	
Freyberg, G.H.	Midn		
Friend, A.R.S.	Blksmth/Mte	341.204	K
Frost, A.E.	AB	189.782	
Fung Ah.	Dom		
Fury, W.	Pte	Ply6.643	
Gardner, J.	L/Sto	161.275	
Garland, G.	Pte	Ply3.345	
George, F.W.	AB	168.362	
Germain, J.C.	Pntr	158.956	K
Gilbert, E.	AB	189.395	
Gilbert, J.	PO1	181.333	
Gill, M.C.	Arm/Mte	168.557	
Gillard, C.	Sto	281.013	
Glanville, G.J.	SBStd	129.580	
Godfrey, W.	PO1	116.240	
Goodchild, R.	AB	143.861	
Goodman, S.J.	AB	101.723	
Goodwin, W.J.	AB	184.201	
Gore, C.H.	AB	181.608	
Gregory, S.W.	Sto	163.053	
Grimsey, E.	AB	184.592	
Grinter, E.	Sh/Cpl	150.789	
Gulland, A.	Band	355.557	
Gulley, C.J.	Sto	280.131	
Hall, W.J.	L/Cpl	Ply7.834	
Hallahan, T.G.	Arm	144.458	K
Hamilton, G.	Pte	Ch4.766	
Hammond, A.	L/Sto	146.527	
Hammond, A.J.P.	PO1	156.114	

NO BAR MEDALS *continued.*

Name	Rating	Number	
Hannaford, A.	PO1	121.889	
Hannaford, F.G.	Sto	278.946	K
Harnedy, D.	AB	183.388	
Harris, J.H.	L/Sig	155.041	
Harris, W.	Pte	Ply5.218	
Harrison, G.B.	Pte	Ply4.332	
Harrison, J.	Band	177.234	
Hart, J.	AB	185.139	
Harty, E.	Sto	278.606	
Harvey, J.	Dom	132.848	
Hawton, H.J.	Shpwrt	341.460	
Haycock, H.	L/Sto	154.621	
Hayes, B.	PO1	156.571	
Hayes, J.	AB	183.768	
Hayes, J.	Sto	279.576	
Hee Ah.	Dom		
Hellings, R.G.	L/S	157.825	
Hext, T.E.	Arm/Mte	173.337	
Hilson, J.H.	Sto	280.068	
Hing Ah.	Dom		
Hopkins, W.A.	Ch/Sto	146.305	
Hopley, W.	AB	184.030	
Horne, E.	AB	189.388	
Hornsby, W.H.	Ch/Arm	151.414	K
Horrigan, P.	AB	95.216	
Hoskin, G.S.	Act/MAA	128.007	K
Howard, P.T.	AB	189.409	
Howe, H.	Sto	280.065	
Howes, C.	Pte	Ply7.861	
Hughes, G.H.	AB	184.494	
Humphries, K.N.	Midn		
Humphries, R.	AB	180.516	
Hunt, W.J.	AB	136.311	
Hutton, G.B.	Lieut		
Hutton, J.G.	Shpwrt	143.614	
Impey, F.C.	Pte	Ply7.898	
Irwin, E.	Sh/Std/Asst	341.415	
Ireland, W.J.T.	PO1	129.002	K
Jack Ah.	Dom		
Jackett, F.	AB	183.784	
Jackson, G.	PO1	145.842	
Jackson, T.	Sergt	Ply4.823	
Jago, E.	PO1	143.063	
Jago, V.	PO1	118.637	
James Ah.	Dom		
Jarvis, J.R.	Pte	Ply4.670	
Jasper, F.R.	AB	154.999	
Jeanes, G.	Band	177.821	
Johnson, F.J.	Sto	280.692	
Johnson, J.E.	St/Engr		
Jones, A.E.	AB	174.006	
Jones, C.	AB	185.575	
Jones, G.	Sto	280.967	
Jones, J.O.J.	AB	183.185	
Jones, S.	Cpl	Ply6.007	
Jones, W.	Pte	Ply1.592	
Jones, W.P.	AB	102.757	
Judge, T.H.	Pte	Ply7.150	
Kane, R.H.	Midn		
Keetch, S.	Pte	Ply3.091	
Kennedy, W.G.	AB	182.324	
Keogh, W.J.	AB	190.370	
Kettle, R.	PO2	115.138	
King, A.T.	Sto	281.411	K
King, R.W.	AB	188.341	
Kinsella, P.	L/Sto	165.884	
Kirby, T.	AB	179.866	
Kirwan, J.	Q/Sig	178.549	
Kong Ah.	Dom		
Lake, J.A.	AB	169.102	1
Lake, T.	Sto	147.276	
Lamb, E.	SB/Attn	350.274	
Lancaster, E.	Sto	281.003	
Langmaid, J.	L/Sto	153.252	
Lawrence, J.	Sto	278.889	K
Layton, J.	AB	174.797	
Lee Ah.	Dom		
Lee, F.	AB	149.380	
Lee, H.	PO2	145.243	
Lees, J.C.	AB	179.226	
Lewis, E.	AB	178.539	
Ley, M.	2/Yeo/Sig	140.508	K
Lidington, J.	Ch/Sto	138.172	
Liles, F.	2/Yeo/Sig	167.281	
Lines, A.G.	AB	184.174	
Lloyd, E.	Pte	Po1.518	
Loo Ah.	Dom		
Love, S.E.	PO2	161.917	
Loverseed, H.	AB	195.560	
Lucas, T.	Sto	165.374	
Lyons, M.	Sto	277.165	
McBride, J.	AB	184.941	
McBride, J.	AB	187.889	
McCarthy, J.	Sto	278.186	
McCormick, H.	AB	180.308	K
McCoubrey, J.	PO1	110.604	K
McDonald, D.	PO1	156.378	
McDonald, J.	2/Sh/Cook	157.254	
McDonnell, M.	AB	176.796	
McGraw, J.	Band	340.043	
McKnight, W.	AB	188.612	
Maclachlan, C.	Lieut		
Maber, F.E.	AB	181.727	
Macers, D.	AB	152.877	
Mahoney, J.	AB	179.737	
Mahoney, J.	Sto	278.521	
Mann, W.H.	Q/Sig	166.564	
Marsh, E.J.	Sto	280.586	
Martin, A.J.	AB	184.810	
Martin, D.	AB	126.626	
Martin, E.A.	Arm	128.053	
Martin, S.A.	AB	159.131	
Martin, W.J.	AB	169.586	
Martin, W.J.	Sto	281.376	
Mascall, F.	L/Sto	149.695	
Mason, H.	Sto	287.691	

NO BAR MEDALS *continued.*

Massey, E.F.	AB	188.296	
Mathias, F.J.	Ch/ERA	145.735	
Matthews, E.	AB	185.109	
Matthews, H.	AB	183.489	
Mayne, A.J.	AB	184.153	
Melhuish, W.J.	AB	185.141	
Memory, T.H.	AB	183.998	
Mercer, E.N.	Midn		
Mildon, W.	AB	154.985	
Miller, T.	L/Sto	153.187	K
Millington, P.	Band/Cpl	110.806	
Millman, J.J.	Q/Sig	183.909	K
Min Ah (I).	Dom		
Min Ah (II).	Dom		
Mitchell, H.	Pte	Ply7.862	
Mockett, W.S.	AB	184.560	
Moffatt, A.E.	Ch/Cook	122.819	
Moore, A.	AB	179.519	
Moore, C.E.	Sto	112.858	
Moore, R.M.	AB	185.578	
Moores, H.A.	Bugler	Ply6.861	
Moorey, H.	Sto	283.338	
Morgan, G.	L/S	162.897	K
Morgan, P.	AB	137.852	
Morrell, W.J.S.	Act/Carp		
Morris, M.	AB	179.377	K
Moseley, F.	AB	183.965	
Moss, M.W.	L/S	161.780	
Murphy, D.	AB	188.302	
Murphy, J.A.J.	Sh/Std/Asst	341.557	
Mutton, W.T.	Sto	279.444	
Nancollas, F.	AB	126.149	
Nankivell, H.	AB	154.427	
Newman, T.J.	PO2	183.267	
Newton, E.	Plmbr	172.300	K
Nicholls, R.	AB	137.730	
Nightingale, A.H.	AB	155.828	
Nockels, G.W.H.	PO1	147.109	
Norman, R.	AB	195.561	
Normington, F.W.	Act/Ch/Sto	128.050	
Norton, R.	Act/ERA	269.804	
Norwood, A.	AB	174.929	
O'Brien, E.	AB	188.293	
O'Brien, G.	AB	150.648	K
O'Dowd, J.	AB	184.903	
O'Neill, J.	AB	181.525	
Olver, J.	PO2	151.596	K
Openshaw, J.H.	Act/Cpl	Ply7.836	
Owen, B.L.	Midn		
Owens, F.	Sto	281.634	
Paget, H.A.	AB	179.532	
Palmer, W.G.	PO1	114.002	K
Parker, J.	AB	180.662	
Parkinson, J.	AB	181.953	
Parsons, H.	AB	178.401	
Pay, E.	Sto	146.239	
Pearse, W.R.	L/Cpl	Ch8.045	
Peers, W.H.	AB	170.290	
Penhaligon, R.J.	Ch/Sto	132.258	
Percy, A.G.	Pte	Ply6.196	
Perry, C.R.	Sto	278.918	K
Phillips, T.G.	Sto	287.107	
Piggott, J.	PO1	141.480	
Ping Ah.	Dom		
Pithie, D.	Sto	276.799	
Polwin, W.T.	AB	184.564	
Porter, A.A.	AB	183.955	
Porter, G.H.	PO1	139.823	
Porter, W.C.	AB	160.276	
Porter, W.R.	PO1	146.214	
Power, J.	Sto	280.999	
Powsland, H.T.	Pte	Ply5.741	
Priddis, B.G.A.	Bugler	Ply6.655	
Prideaux, F.	AB	184.559	
Punch, J.	AB	184.582	
Quarm, O.J.	Cooper	340.158	
Quinn, M.	AB	184.900	
Rawle, A.H.	AB	178.338	
Rawlings, F.	AB	178.404	
Rawlinson, B.	AB	174.190	
Reddie, C.A.	Pte	Ply7.765	
Reed, R.	Pte	Ply7.828	
Reeves, R.	Band	117.281	
Reid, H.	Pte	Ply2.372	
Rendell, J.	Yeo/Sig	118.347	
Renton, A.	PO2	137.865	
Rice, T.	Pte	Ply7.800	
Rich, C.W.	L/S	157.824	
Riordan, T.	AB	178.648	
Robins, J.E.	Sto	153.832	
Robins, S.	AB	182.712	
Robinson, C.E.	AB	188.609	
Robinson, W.C.A.J.	Fl/Payr		
Robjohns, C.	L/Sto	123.364	
Rock, C.H.	Surgn		
Rockey, F.	AB	182.018	
Rodwell, R.R.	Q/Sig	186.064	
Rogers, S.G.	AB	176.259	
Ross, A.V.	Sub Lieut		
Rowe, T.H.	PO2	123.037	
Rowe, W.	Asst/Engr		
Rundle, E.M.	PO1	154.037	
Rundle, J.T.	Sto	287.298	K
Russell, J.	Ch/ERA	130.768	
Ryan, M.	L/S	149.114	
Saker, F.C.	AB	184.186	
Salisbury, Rev. C.H.	Chaplain & N. Instr		
Saunders, W.H.	Ch/ERA	130.739	
Schutz, G.L.	AB	156.260	
Scripps, J.	Pte	Ply5.876	K
Scrivens, F.J.	MAA	81.096	
Seccombe, A.E.	Ch/Wrtr	133.454	
Semmens, A.J.	AB	184.087	
Sharp, H.	Pte	Po8.258	
Shipley, H.W.	PO1	139.765	

NO BAR MEDALS *continued.*

Name	Rank	Number	
Simmonds, R.J.	AB	189.387	
Sing Ah (I).	Dom		
Sing Ah (II).	Dom		
Sing Yong.	Dom		
Skidmore, D.	AB	176.307	
Skinner, F.	Sail	159.397	
Skuse, A.H.	AB	184.748	
Smith, A.	Pte	Ply6.157	
Smith, S.	AB	185.235	
Smith, T.J.	PO1	114.362	K
Sole, A.G.	AB	195.464	
Sow Ah.	Dom		
Spargo, C.	AB	181.921	
Spenceley, W.O.	Carp/Mte	146.181	
Spencer, A.	Pte	Ply4.871	
Spencer, F.	Pte	Ply7.859	
Squire, A.E.	L/S	123.161	
Stark, H.	AB	177.279	
Stephens, L.	AB	176.897	
Stockwell, H.J.	Sh/Cpl	350.173	
Stubbs, E.C.	Midn		
Stubbs, G.	PO2	169.420	
Sullivan, T.	Band	357.492	
Sutton, S.	L/Sto	277.738	K
Symes, J.	Sto	281.219	
Tam Ah.	Dom		
Tarr, J.	Pte	Ply5.737	
Taylor, F.R.	AB	165.602	
Taylor, W.	AB	184.227	
Taylor, W.	Sto	286.635	
Telford, T.S.	AB	188.935	
Tew, D.	AB	175.792	
Theobald, J.	AB	163.343	
Thomas, W.	Pte	Ply7.285	
Thompson, W.A.	Midn		
Timmins, C.J.	AB	184.901	K
Tinney, E.	AB	188.950	
Tom Ah.	Dom		
Tompkins, F.A.G.	Pte	Ply5.813	
Tottle, J.	L/Sto	143.778	
Trewin, T.H.	Sto	286.045	
Trudgeon, J.	Pte	Ply1.849	
Truscott, H.	PO1	101.058	
Tucker, J.W.	Sto	286.377	
Tung Ah.	Dom		
Turner, A.	Bosn		
Turner, W.	AB	189.417	
Urry, A.E.	AB	195.821	
Velvin, F.R.	AB	185.153	
Venning, T.A.	Asst/Engr		
Vincent, W.	Sh/Cpl	145.928	
Wagner, J.J.	Gunr		
Waldron, W.	AB	181.234	
Walker, T.	L/Sto	146.121	
Wallis, B.	Gunr		
Ward, D.T.	Ch/ERA	154.158	
Warren, F.	L/Sergt	Ply4.795	

Name	Rank	Number	
Waterhouse, G.	AB	185.138	
Waters, A.	Band	355.559	
Watkins, G.W.	Ord	172.001	
Watts, F.	AB	185.144	
Webb, A.	Sto	278.237	
Wellsbury, A.H.	AB	184.221	
West, J.C.	Pte	Ply6.943	
West, R.M.R.	Lieut		
Westlake, E.	PO1	125.572	
Westlake, R.A.	Sto	278.281	
Weymouth, W.	AB	165.512	
Wheaton, A.C.	AB	189.877	
Wheelwright, N.	Midn		
Wilkinson, G.N.	PO1	153.495	
Willes, R.A.	Midn		
Williams, J.H.	AB	181.922	
Williams, J.T.	AB	178.474	
Williams, T.W.	Pte	Ply6.053	K
Williams, W.	AB	175.515	
Wills, L.R.	Pte	Ply4.050	
Wilson, W.J.	AB	182.480	
Winders, C.	PO1	138.105	
Wing Loi.	Dom		
Wise, T.W.	ERA	268.120	
Withey, C.H.	AB	162.853	
Woodrow, E.	Sto	148.822	
Woodward, H.	PO1	130.912	
Woon, E.	AB	184.563	
Worth, S.F.	PO2	147.288	
Wotherspoon, W.	L/Sto	175.692	
Wright, A.	Pte	Ply5.899	
Wright, H.J.	Band/Cpl	158.226	
Wylde, A.W.	Capt(RMLI)		
Yallop, W.C.	AB	162.878	
Yee Ah.	Dom		
Ying Ah.	Dom		

Duplicate medals:

Name	Rank	Number
Atkins, A.E.	Engr	
Badge, A.W.	AB	135.780
Barnes, W.G.K.	St/Surgn	
Bone, E.R.	Sto	281.567
Brodribb, J.	AB	184.507
Cain, J.	Sto	286.618
Collins, R.W.	Sh/Std/Asst	170.926
Cowlard, W.	AB	185.333
Crawley, R.	Sto	160.168
Daly, W.	Sto	280.866
Lees, J.C.	AB	179.226
Mason, H.	Sto	287.691
Morgan, G.	L/S	162.897
Owens, F.	Sto	281.634
Parsons, H.	AB	178.401
Piggott, J.	PO1	141.480
Thomas, W.	Pte	Ply7.285
Waters, A.	Band	355.559
Wellsbury, A.H.	AB	184.221

NO BAR MEDALS *continued.*

Returned medals:

Beach, G.H.	Sto	280.584
Brown, B.J.	AB	188.270
Coram, S.J.	AB	185.314
Cullinane, J.	Sto	153.441
Dagg, R.	AB	134.700
Dunning, C.W.	AB	176.149
Fleming, J.	Sto	277.763
Gahan, J.	Pte	Ply4.455
Harding, T.	Pte	Po4.139
Hill, J.W.	Band	355.558
Jamieson, C.	Pte	Ply4.463
Jenkins, A.	AB	185.601
Kreutzer, W.	AB	184.052
Lovell, J.	Sto	281.475
Marks, W.	Act/Carp	
Murray, G.	AB	183.769
Myson, F.R.	Pte	Ply8.392
Ortheil, C.	L/Sto	174.422
Robertson, C.L.	AB	136.477
Rowe, T.	Pte	Ply6.065
Sloman, J.	Pte	Ply5.916
Vigurs, T.H.	AB	168.266
Walsh, P.	AB	185.111
Walsh, P.	Sto	285.146
Williams, W.	AB	138.822

H.M.S. WALLAROO.

H.M.S. Wallaroo was a 2nd class Cruiser of 2,575 tons and 261 x 45 feet. Her armament consisted of 8 x 4.7 in and 8 x 3 pdr guns. The vessel was built by Armstrong and launched on 5th February 1890. She was named Persian but was renamed on 2nd April 1890. The ship was relegated to Harbour service in 1906. She was renamed again as Wallington on 5th March 1919 then sold on 27th February 1920 to G. Sharpe.

Bars	*Total*	*Returned*	*Entitled*
None	*237*	*18*	*219*
	237	*18*	*219*

Notes:

K - Medal presented by H.M. The King on 8th March 1902.

[1] - Medal roll states, "Run 20/11/05 & 23/12/07. Application for dup. 20/11/11. Duplicate granted on completion of 3 yrs G service.
Dup 1090 sent to Essex 1 Feb 12."

NO BAR MEDALS.

Abbinett, A.	L/Sto	169.345
Abbott, G.W.	Sig	196.991 [1]
Attrell, G.W.	Sto	286.563
Baiss, L.A.	Surgn	
Bamford, H.	AB	183.193
Barry, J.	AB	189.368
Bartlett, A.	Sto	282.575
Bassom, W.C.	Yeo/Sig	139.145
Beams, A.J.	Gunr	
Belling, F.	Payr	
Bennett, F.	Sto	284.347
Bessant, A.	Sh/Cpl	126.767
Biss, J.	AB	178.235
Bissett, H.	AB	145.228
Bolsom, J.	Sto	85.037
Boniface, H.	Sto	284.348
Botham, R.	Pte	Po9.219
Bourne, J.J.	AB	161.808
Box, S.B.	Boy	201.042
Brady, H.	Pte	Po2.055
Brazier, G.	L/Sto	153.668
Bridle, F.	Sto	284.349
Britton, J.T.	AB	181.599
Bromley, B.A.S.	Clerk	
Brown, J.D.	Sto	284.170
Campbell, J.C.	AB	169.395
Cannard, J.	Pte	Po2.089
Card, J.	Sto	291.327
Carpenter, W.	L/S	183.211
Carthy, G.	AB	176.122
Chamberlain, H.A.	AB	157.206
Cherry, A.E.	PO1	125.714
Clarke, D.T.	AB	170.417
Clegg, F.G.	PO1	149.364
Clubb, R.S.	L/Sig	148.499
Coe, J.A.	AB	172.034
Coleman, G.H.	AB	178.243
Collins, J.	PO1	117.110
Cook, C.W.	L/S	161.926
Crawley, P.H.	Pte	Po9.973
Craze, W.E.E.	Pte	Po5.679
Crowley, J.A.	Sto	291.337
Dawson, A.M.	Lieut	
Dewison, J.W.	Sto	290.466
Doel, E.	Sto	290.455
Doidge, J.R.	Ord	198.197
Douglas, J.	Sh/Std	94.910
Dowson, S.	Sto	284.163
Drummond, B.W.	Lieut	
Duffy, J.	PO2	159.861
Dugan, W.H.	Carp/Crew	343.077
Dwyer, M.	Sto	283.594
Dyer, W.G.	Sto	291.331
Eadie, R.	L/Sto	280.565
Ellis, R.	L/Sto	153.153
Featherstone, A.R.	Sto	290.472
Fenney, H.J.	Ord	198.201
Ferguson, J.C.	St/Surgn	
Fletcher, F.	L/Sto	127.488
Folland, S.	Ord	198.195
Forbes, A.	Sig	200.325
Foster, F.	L/Sto	145.729

NO BAR MEDALS *continued.*

Fry, S.	Pntr	342.056
Fugler, W.G.	Ch/Arm	127.754
Gawler, W.	AB	181.987
Gibbs, A.	AB	176.312
Gibbs, H.J.	Sergt	Po4.808
Glazier, J.R.	L/S	166.064
Goodger, F.B.	Ord	198.894
Gosling, A.J.	AB	134.229
Gotts, R.	AB	179.430
Gregory, F.	Ord	198.196
Grist, W.	Ord	201.044
Hackett, J.	Ch/ERA	123.662
Halliwell, T.	Pte	Po9.175
Harris, P.	Sto	290.473
Hart, D.E.	Pte	Ply8.941
Hatchard, G.	Carp/Mte	136.539
Hawkes, H.W.	AB	170.324
Hawksbee, H.W.	PO2	149.600
Hayden, A.J.	AB	175.471
Hayes, M.T.	AB	185.597
Heasman, A.J.	AB	182.401
Hedgeman, W.W.	Sto	290.465
Hedger, T.	L/Sto	131.015
Hillen, J.	Sto	284.208
Holman, H.	AB	142.343
Hopkins, H.	Ord	200.283
Hotson, C.A.	Dom	355.373
Hughes, F.R.	L/Sto	119.764
Humby, H.	ERA	157.717
Ilsey, A.	AB	134.287
Jackett, W.R.	AB	182.439
James, A.E.	Ord	197.468
Jarvis, A.J.	Pte	Ch5.605
Jefferies, J.H.E.	Pte	Po9.974
Johns, S.	Carp/Mte	153.400
Jones, C.	Sto	282.508
Jones, W.	Sto	291.323
Kemp, A.E.	PO1	123.590
Kendall, A.	Sto	282.576
Kenyon, H.	AB	176.509
Kervill, W.J.	Arm/Mte	167.645
Knott, F.H.	AB	158.084
Lasham, W.	Sto	165.979
Lee, W.T.	Ch/Sto	143.260
Lyford, D.E.D.	AB	180.167
McBride, W.	AB	178.862
McCormac, W.	AB	190.047
McDonald, W.D.	AB	176.458
McIntosh, L.S.	Sto	283.715
McRitchie, J.	Sto	290.448
Major, J.T.C.	AB	164.508
Mancey, C.	Pte	Po9.231
Marks, E.	AB	172.646
Martin, J.	AB	157.111
Martin, J.	Sto	283.915
May, G.T.	AB	176.467
Memmen, T.	Pilot	
Merrall, A.H.	Dom	358.043
Miller, W.	ERA	
Monday, J.	Sto	290.252
Moody, J.	Dom	164.101
Moors, G.L.	ERA	172.831
Moss, H.W.	Boy	201.041
Mulcaby, B.	AB	190.049
Nelson, J.W.	Plmbr	165.928
Newton, W.A.	Arm/Crew	341.312
Nineham, A.J.	Sto	282.903
Noble, H.	Sto	170.246
Noel, F.C.M.	Capt	
Odds, H.G.	Dom	135.333
Packham, A.	L/Carp/Crew	133.165
Palmer, A.	Dom	110.963
Passingham, C.	L/Sto	280.547
Paterson, A.	Q/Sig	162.313
Pavey, W.T.	PO1	112.079
Peacock, W.	AB	156.299
Pearce, C.G.	Ord	198.173
Pearson, R.	AB	169.482
Penfold, E.H.	AB	164.324
Pilcher, J.	AB	163.600
Plummer, F.	AB	174.770
Polly, A.	PO2	151.654
Poy Ah.	Dom	
Price, R.	Blksmth	135.507
Priscott, G.P.C.	Ch/Sto	128.434
Prow, E.A.	L/S	164.481
Radham, A.	AB	176.839
Ransom, A.	Sig	192.764
Rathwell, J.G.	AB	176.492
Renyard, H.	AB	182.414
Rice, A.J.	ERA	268.509
Rich, H.J.	AB	165.477
Rich, J.	AB	154.333
Richer, F.	Sto	283.797
Roberts, A.	L/Sto	282.914
Robins, H.T.	Ord	198.202
Rogers, A.S.	AB	176.463
Rumble, W.R.	Dom	358.020
Russell, E.	Ord	204.649
Russell, W.J.	Dom	167.704
Sainsbury, H.W.	Dom	358.021
Sales, J.	Ch/Sto	142.964
Sayce, H.	PO2	132.956
Sayer, E.J.	2/SBStd	350.253
Scarlett, A.E.	Carp	
Scorey, J.W.	AB	166.677
Searley, R.H.	Sh/Cook	144.523
Secretan, E.	Lieut	K
Sedley, W.H.	Sto	291.035
Seward, L.G.	Cpl	Po7.506
Shave, G.E.	Pte	Po6.215
Shipley, T.	ERA	268.487
Shoesmith, W.	Boy	201.040
Shotter, W.A.	Pte	Po8.010
Sills, F.	L/Sig	158.684
Simpson, A.	Ch/ERA	170.043

NO BAR MEDALS *continued.*

Smith, G.	Sto	290.557
Smith, J.	Pte	Po8.570
Smith, P.	Sto	290.471
Smithers, A.E.	AB	156.856
Somerton, C.E.	Sh/Std/Boy	341.939
Stafford, W.	PO1	157.126
Stephens, C.	PO1	154.240
Steward, C.H.	Fl/Engr	
Stubbs, J.	Sto	281.074
Sutton, J.	Act/Ch/PO	107.773
Sykes, G.O.	Sto	284.160
Symes, F.W.	AB	169.476
Talbott, A.	Carp/Crew	342.463
Taylor, F.	Sto	283.717
Taylor, R.	Sto	281.924
Thorne, W.W.	Pte	Ch10.011
Toogood, J.R.	Sto	282.436
Tope, E.	Ord	198.194
Triggs, A.	L/Sto	127.464
Tutt, E.	PO1	113.337
Underwood, G.W.	Sto	290.091
Wadhems, E.	Pte	Po5.827
Walker, F.H.	PO1	113.174
Wallbridge, W.	Sto	284.352
Warton, A.W.	Ord	189.767
Watkins, W.H.	Ord	198.350
Watson, J.J.	ERA	162.608
Watts, A.J.	AB	191.291
Wells, H.	Pte	Po8.732
Westacott, W.H.	AB	201.357
Whatson, J.S.	Ch/ERA	148.571
White, W.	Sto	282.982
Whitlock, G.E.	Ord	196.865
Whitworth, R.	Pte	Po8.253
Wiley, G.F.	PO2	138.652
Williams, F.R.A.	Asst/Clerk	
Wilton, F.	Sto	284.140
Winter, T.	L/Sto	122.817
Wombwell, G.	Pte	Po4.421
Woolley, W.	L/Cpl	Po5.941
Wright, J.	Sto	291.700

Duplicate medals:

Abbott, G.W.	Sig	196.991 *
Gawler, W.	AB	181.987
Hart, D.E.	Pte	Ply8.941
James, A.E.	Ord	197.468
Newton, W.A.	Arm/Crew	341.312
Watson, J.J.	ERA	162.608

* *Two duplicate medals issued.*

Returned medals:

Bain, D.H.W.	Asst/Engr	
Fox, F.	Cooper	141.021
French, H.	AB	182.976
Gilmore, T.	Sto	284.162
Grady, J.	Bugler	Ch4.897
Harris, S.L.	Boy	200.831
Hayes, R.	AB	171.811
Kensett, F.	Ord	200.526
Lowery, J.	Sto	290.248
McGovern, P.R.	Sto	355.481
McRobie, J.	Sto	282.540
Porteous, J.	Sto	290.460
Pybus, C.	Sto	155.356
Shawcross, S.	Sto	290.469
Sillence, W.J.H.	AB	166.346
Turner, A.	Sto	290.254
Watts, W.R.	Pte	Po9.726
Youel, G.F.	Lieut	

H.M.S. WATERWITCH.

H.M.S. Waterwitch was an Iron Screw Survey Vessel of 620 tons and 160 feet in length. The vessel was originally named Lancashire Witch and was purchased on 17th March 1893. She was rammed and sunk on 1st September 1912 while at anchor at Singapore.

Bars	*Total*	*Returned*	*Entitled*
None	*87*	*7*	*80*
	87	*7*	*80*

NO BAR MEDALS.

Name	Rank	Number
Aris, D.	Pte	Po5.059
Atkins, J.H.	Sto	282.189
Austen, W.	AB	165.629
Barton, A.E.	Sto	173.797
Bass, H.	Pte	Po6.800
Bateman, W.J.	AB	129.974
Brett, F.H.	Boy	201.101
Brown, W.H.	ERA	268.130
Caddy, W.	AB	159.720
Callaghan, J.J.	AB	182.408
Campbell, J.	Carp/Mte	132.406
Clarke, W.	Boy	201.115
Connor, T.	Act/Ch/PO	121.073
Constable, E.A.	Lieut	
Coo Ah.	Dom	
Daniells, T.	AB	150.753
Daws, R.E.	Pte	Po7.922
Day, A.E.	AB	167.447
Desbrow, P.	Boy	201.105
Dimes, A.	Pte	Po7.779
Douay Ah.	Dom	
Durkin, J.	Sail/Mte	144.211
Egginton, G.W.	AB	175.518
Fish, F.	Sto	283.286
Ford, H.B.	Pte	Ply8.490
Freemantle, B.J.	AB	157.399
Gee, A.J.	AB	181.658
Glue, P.A.	AB	172.444
Gordon, A.C.	AB	192.992
Hammond, J.B.	PO1	113.158
Hayward, H.W.	PO2	152.133
Hollands, C.	Cpl	Ch3.540
Hood, E.A.	ERA	269.023
Jay, A.H.	AB	190.746
Jemmett, C.F.	2/Sh/Cook	160.488
Jones, K.H.	Surgn	
Kaye, J.W.	AB	151.832
Knight, A.J.	L/Sto	140.147
Langrick, O.F.	Sto	281.976
Larkins, G.	Sto	283.353
Leach, H.	SB/Attn	350.370
Lever, J.	Pte	Po5.675
Loader, W.H.T.I.	Sh/Std/Asst	340.227
Lyne, W.O.	Lieut	
McFarlane, R.McR.	L/S	156.816
MacKenzie-Grieve, A.	Lieut	
Mason, J.W.G.	Arm/Mte	341.456
Mauger, E.F.	L/S	189.799
May, T.H.	AB	164.331
Mussett, E.J.	Ord	206.084
Newman, H.A.M.	AB	179.816
Payne, H.	AB	118.173
Pettit, W.J.P.	Asst/Payr	
Phillips, J.E.	ERA	152.098
Pike, A.J.H.	AB	181.744
Power, P.	Ord	194.871
Pratt, W.J.	L/Carp/Crew	170.477
Price, L.J.	PO2	147.383
Readhead, G.F.	ERA	268.403
Reeds, F.	PO1	130.964
Roberts, W.	PO1	133.916
Sang Pho.	Dom	
Sargent, W.	AB	185.679
Sawle, M.P.	ERA	269.293
Shepphard, H.	AB	146.466
Simson, G.B.S.	Lieut	
Sing Ah.	Dom	
Smith, J.J.	PO2	89.756
Somerville, H.G.C.	Lieut	
States, W.G.	L/S	166.672
Sun Ah.	Dom	
Thomas, E.S.	Blksmth	342.757
Timson, J.H.C.	AB	155.901
Tin.	Smn	
Turner, W.G.	2/Yeo/Sig	148.093
Walsh, P.	AB	194.209
Warburg, H.D.	Lieut	
Willis, R.A.	Boy	201.119
Woo.	Smn	
Yick Chee.	Dom	

Duplicate medals:

Name	Rank	Number
Austen, W.	AB	165.629 *
Desbrow, P.	Boy	201.105

* *Two duplicate medals issued.*

NO BAR MEDALS *continued.*

Returned medals:

Coughlan, J.	Ord	199.431
Durman, A.H.	Sto	276.607
Hayter, J.	AB	183.213
Hazelgrove, W.	Bosn	
Munt, G.H.	AB	166.809
Paterson, R.	Ord	195.608
Wall, C.	AB	171.146

H.M.S. WHITING.

H.M.S. Whiting was a Destroyer of 360 tons and 215 x 21 feet. Her armament consisted of 1 x 12 pdr and 5 x 6 pdr guns and 2 x torpedo tubes. The vessel was built by Palmer and launched on 26th August 1896. She was sold on 27th November 1919 at Hong Kong and later broken up in China.

Bars	*Total*	*Returned*	*Entitled*
TF	*57*	*2*	*55*
None	*9*	*0*	*9*
	66	*2*	*64*

Bar: TAKU FORTS.

Bates, H.F.	Act/ERA	269.362
Broom, F.	Sto	292.737
Butler, H.	L/Sto	130.745
Carr, W.T.	Ch/ERA	141.652
Cole, W.J.	AB	175.469
Cook, W.W.	Sto	282.607
Cullinane, J.	Act/Ch/Sto	142.114
Deed, J.C.	Sto	283.151
Doughty, J.	Sto	279.805
Edwards, W.	PO2	117.357
Fairman, J.	Sto	283.145
Flynn, T.	Sto	292.722
Ford, T.	Sto	292.697
Gayford, A.	L/Sto	153.582
Giles, T.	AB	181.677
Goff, A.	Sto	282.617
Gouren, H.G.	L/Sig	165.308
Grady, J.	AB	182.459
Greenwood, C.	Sto	282.782
Grierson, R.	Sto	282.818
Harding, C.	Sto	283.033
Harris, E.	Sto	282.793
Hayes, C.	Sto	282.801
Jefford, A.E.	Sto	292.741
Jones, J.C.	Sto	282.767
Laver, J.G.	AB	180.252
McGrath, W.J.	Ch/Sto	140.920
Mackenzie, C.	Lieut	
Moreton, J.A.	Lieut	
Neal, J.	Sto	282.807
New, W.	Sto	280.462
Ogden, J.	Q/Sig	190.564
Osbournt, E.A.	AB	176.567
Painter, F.	AB	166.537
Payne, F.	Gunr	
Peat, J.	AB	186.998
Peed, D.	ERA	268.596
Perkins, A.	Sto	282.798
Pilcher, A.S.	Sto	283.130
Ritchie, W.H.	AB	156.952
Roper, R.	Cook/Mte	340.873
Rowe, T.	Sto	290.660
Rushworth, J.	Sto	283.149
Saunders, H.L.	Sto	279.612
Shouler, E.	AB	190.333
Sive Ah.	Dom	
Smith, F.	Sto	282.795
Stearn, W.J.	Engr	
Thomas, A.	ERA	268.017
Thompson, T.	AB	187.274
Townsend, T.W.W.	PO1	135.421
Walton, A.	Sto	277.212
Warn, R.T.	PO1	119.154
Watson, D.	Ch/Sto	141.136
Wood, R.	L/Sto	172.810

Duplicate medals:

Deed, J.C.	Sto	283.151
Fairman, J.	Sto	283.145
Grierson, R.	Sto	282.818 *
Harding, C.	Sto	283.033
Neal, J.	Sto	282.807
Payne, F.	Gunr	
Pilcher, A.S.	Sto	283.130
Saunders, H.L.	Sto	279.612
Smith, F.	Sto	282.795
Thomas, A.	ERA	268.017

* *Two duplicate medals issued.*

Returned medals:

Clorain, T.	Sto	281.299
Neaves, J.H.	AB	178.772

NO BAR MEDALS.

Chang Ah.	Dom	
Flury, W.	AB	187.174
Foster, J.	PO2	117.626
Johnson, J.	AB	165.792
Llewellyn, L.E.H.	Lieut	
O'Norley, T.	Sto	282.754
Sai Tung.	Dom	
Sing Hong.	Dom	
Woolgar, G.T.	Sto	282.756

H.M.S. WOODCOCK.

H.M.S. Woodcock was a River Gunboat of 150 tons and 148½ x 24 feet. Her armament consisted of 2 x 6 pdr guns. The vessel was built by Thornycroft in 1897 in sections and was re-launched in China on 8th April 1898. She was sold in 1927 at Hong Kong.

Bars	*Total*	*Returned*	*Entitled*
None	*46*	*2*	*44*
	46	*2*	*44*

Notes:

† - These men are noted on the Medal Roll as part of the crew for recommission - 28th December 1900.

NO BAR MEDALS.

Ashman, W.	L/Sto	157.684	
Bond, J.	AB	181.860	
Bower, S.	Carp/Mte	144.157	
Braham, E.W.	PO1	125.669	
Ching Ah.	Dom		
Copland, J.	AB	181.631	
Cudbertson, F.	L/Sto	279.002	
Farrier, C.	L/Sto	151.988	
Ford, M.	Ch/PO	121.366	†
Griffiths, E.	AB	171.533	
Hackett, E.C.	Sto	154.769	
Hall, J.	Act/Ch/ERA	159.086	†
Hing Ah.	Sto		
Holmes, T.	AB	178.900	
Hougham, W.	AB	186.388	
Jay Jung	Pilot		
Johnson, A.	Arm/Crew		†
Keith, W.	Surgn		
Kelly, R.E.	Carp/Mte	341.117	†
Kemp, G.	Ch/PO	129.075	
Kemp, T.	AB	156.657	
Kway Yong.	Sto		
Lee Ah.	Dom		
Manthrop, F.L.	ERA	268.515	
Martin, W.	L/Sto	151.203	†
Mortimer, J.	Sto	159.454	
Ogilvie, W.	Arm/Crew	192.321	
Ovenden, W.	PO1	156.410	
Pattle, H.	Sh/Std/Asst	340.152	
Poi Ah.	Dom		
Presnaill, W.	Sto		†
Richardson, W.	AB	166.714	
Sing Ah.	Dom		
Sing Ah.	Sto		
Smith, H.	Sto	278.315	
Sung Yung	Sampan Man		
Tang Wong	Sto		
Tin Ah.	Sto		
Trice, H.	Sto	154.864	
Watson, H.D.R.	Lieut		
Willmott, J.T.	Ch/ERA	141.803	
Wong Ah.	Sampan Man		
Woolley, H.	PO1	129.178	
Yu Chung.	Dom		

Duplicate medal:

Kelly, R.E.	Carp/Mte	341.117	

Returned medals:

Smith, J.H.	Sh/Std/Asst		†
Wyatt, G.	AB	178.167	†

H.M.S. WOODLARK.

H.M.S. Woodlark was a River Gunboat of 150 tons and 148½ x 24 feet. Her armament consisted of 2 x 6 pdr guns. The vessel was built by Thornycroft at Chiswick in 1897 in sections. She was sold in 1928 at Hong Kong.

Bars	*Total*	*Returned*	*Entitled*
None	*37*	*0*	*37*
	37	*0*	*37*

Notes:

K - Medal presented by H.M. The King on 8th March 1902.

NO BAR MEDALS.

Archer, W.	AB	167.726	
Boyden, P.H.	Surgn.		
Cheong La.	Sampan Man		
Ching Sheng.	Dom		
Chung Ah.	Dom		
Clarke, W.	L/Sto	152.417	
Davies, T.	AB	132.510	
Edwards, E.	Sto	280.424	
Fisher, C.	Sh/Std/Asst	340.005	
Friday, G.	AB	152.847	
Grubb, W.	AB	178.782	
Hillman, H.E.	Lieut		
Jay Ah.	Dom		
Jervis, C.	PO1	142.891	K
Kuen Ah.	Sto		
Kuen Kong.	Pilot		
Lae Ah.	Sto		
Mead, F.	ERA	268.938	
Moore, C.A.	Arm/Mte	340.026	
Pallant, H.	AB	186.521	
Palmer, A.J.	AB	176.168	
Pinhey, G.E.	Sto	277.118	
Pope, W.T.	Carp/Mte	158.075	
Pow Ah.	Sto		
Quinhin Ah.	Dom		
Rea, A.W.	Ch/ERA	148.604	
Richardson, S.	Sto	289.429	
Roberts, R.	PO1	132.185	
Rundell, J.	L/Sto	140.265	
Sing Ah.	Sto		
Song Li.	Dom		
Stanley, J.	Sto	282.483	
Sui Ah.	Sto		
Wang Chang Lee.	Dom		
Wilson, W.	PO1	128.831	
Wong La.	Sampan Man		
Yuen Ah.	Sto		

Duplicate medal:

Friday, G.	AB	152.847

Duplicate medal - without issue no on roll:

Jervis, C.	PO1	142.891

LEGATION GUARD, PEKIN.

Bars	*Total*	*Returned*	*Entitled*
DL	*82*	*4*	*78*
	82	*4*	*78*

Notes:

K - Medal presented by H.M. The King on 8th March 1902.

1 - Duplicate clasp only sent to recipient.

2 - The original medal, presented by H.M. The King was returned on 13/9/09; the recipient is noted as RUN on 23/7/09. The medal was finally returned to the Mint in Feb 1922.

DEFENCE OF LEGATIONS.

Alexander, A.	Pte	Ply8.650	
Allin, T.R.	L/Cpl	Ply8.687	
Angel, W.G.	L/Cpl	Ch8.273	
Baker, C.	Pte	Po9.226	
Betts, W.	Pte	Po4.739	
Buckler, J.	Pte	Po9.286	
Cheshire, W.	Pte	Ply5.381	
Cresswell, F.J.	Pte	Ply8.617	
Davis, G.	Pte	Po8.959	K
Dean, J.	Pte	Ply8.665	
Dunkley, A.	Pte	Ply8.654	
Edney, W.	Pte	Po9.331	
Ford, W.	Pte	Po7.036	
Fuller, R.G.	2/SBStd	350.326	K
Goddard, G.	Pte	Po9.255	
Gowney, D.J.	Cpl	Po5.082	K
Grainger, H.	Pte	Ch8.579	
Green, H.J.	Pte	Po9.277	
Gregory, W.	Cpl	Ply6.529	
Haden, S.W.	Pte	Ply8.630	K
Halliday, L.S.T.	Capt(RMLI)		K
Harding, W.R.	Pte	Ply8.623	
Heap, J.W.	Pte	Po8.605	
Hendicott, R.	Pte	Po8.927	K
Hill, D.	Pte	Ply8.684	
Horne, W.	Pte	Po8.816	
Howard, J.G.	Pte	Ch9.451	K
Hunt, W.J.	Pte	Po8.879	
Johnson, C.	Pte	Ply8.677	
Johnson, J.	Cpl	Po5.819	
Jones, A.	Pte	Po8.885	
Jones, A.	L/Cpl	Ply8.601	
Jones, G.T.	Pte	Ch8.798	K
King, K.	Pte	Ply8.333	
Layton, A.J.	Pte	Ch9.640	
Lister, G.	Pte	Po9.081	
Marriott, J.	Pte	Po9.243	
Masters, J.	Pte	Ch9.676	K
Mayo, A.G.	Pte	Ch9.642	K
Mears, J.	Pte	Po8.603	
Mellows, S.	Pte	Ply8.622	
Murphy, J.	Sergt	Ch5.376	
Murray, J.	Pte	Ply8.653	
Newland, J.D.	Pte	Po9.344	
Ormiston, J.	Pte	Po9.346	
Phillips, C.W.	Pte	Ch9.065	
Pitts, J.F.	Pte	Po8.924	
Powell, E.E.	Pte	Po8.932	
Preston, J.E.	Sergt	Po7.358	
Roberts, A.S.	Pte	Ply8.649	
Roe, W.G.	Pte	Po8.935	
Rose, P.A.	Pte	Po9.290	
Rumble, J.	Pte	Po9.008	
Salvin, H.J.	L/Cpl	Po5.186	
Sands, H.	Pte	Ch6.471	K
Saunders, A.E.	Sergt	Ch4.932	K
Sawyer, A.G.	Pte	Po8.526	
Scadding, A.	Pte	Ply8.683	
Sheppard, G.	Cpl	Po6.830	
Shilliam, G.	Pte	Ply8.679	
Smith, F.G.	Pte	Po9.239	
Smith, W.	Pte	Po9.258	
Sparkes, W.J.	L/Cpl	Po8.604	
Strouts, B.M.	Capt(RMLI)		
Swannell, H.	L/Sig	178.253	
Tanner, F.	Pte	Po8.912	
Taylor, W.A.	Pte	Po9.195	
Thomas, J.T.	Arm	146.882	K
Tickner, A.J.	Pte	Ch9.672	K
Turner, W.	Pte	Ch7.695	
Viney, W.	Pte	Ply8.611	
Walker, J.W.	Pte	Po9.251	
Webb, A.E.	Bugler	Po3.155	
Webb, E.	Pte	Po5.308	
Webster, H.A.	Pte	Ply8.688	K
Westbrook, A.E.	Pte	Po9.113	

DEFENCE OF LEGATIONS *continued.*

Woodward, W.T.	Pte	Po8.926	K
Wray, E.	Capt(RMLI)		K

Duplicate medals:

Jones, G.T.	Pte	Ch8.798
Mears, J.	Pte	Po8.603
Thomas, J.T.	Arm	146.882
Webb, A.E.	Bugler	Po3.155 [1]

Returned medals:

Forrester, G.	Pte	Ply8.669	
Greenfield, J.	Pte	Ch9.675	K[2]
Myers, J.A.	Pte	Ply8.698	
O'Neill, E.G.	Pte	Ch9.635	

NORTH WEST FORT, TAKU.

Bars	*Total*	*Returned*	*Entitled*
None	*197*	*3*	*194*
	197	*3*	*194*

Notes:

K - Medal presented by H.M. The King on 8th March 1902.

NO BAR MEDALS.

Name	Rank	Number	
Allen, R.	Pte	Ch10.106	
Allison, G.H.	Gunr	RMA7.075	
Allport, W.A.	Cpl	RMA3.230	
Andrews, F.	Gunr	RMA4.709	
Appleby, J.R.	Pte	Ply9.662	
Armstrong, A.	Gunr	RMA7.631	
Aylott, F.O.	Gunr	RMA4.925	
Bailey, W.	Act/Bombdr	RMA5.560	
Bakhurst, H.	Pte	Ch8.964	
Bates, S.G.	Pte	Ply7.223	
Beare, A.D.	Pte	Ch6.283	
Benfield, T.E.	Gunr	RMA7.649	
Biles, H.	3/Wrtr	340.113	
Bilney, T.	L/Sergt	Ch5.655	
Bissett, W.	Pte	Ch10.246	
Blackledge, J.	Gunr	RMA6.104	
Blair, D.	Gunr	RMA6.661	
Blair, G.	Gunr	RMA5.626	K
Bowen, H.	Pte	Po10.256	
Bowers, S.J.	Gunr	RMA7.955	
Brighty, G.	Pte	Ply9.663	
Brooks, R.	Pte	Ch10.622	
Brothwell, A.H.	Gunr	RMA7.930	
Budden, A.W.	Gunr	RMA7.931	
Burridge, R.A.M.	Asst/Payr		
Butler, J.H.	Gunr	RMA5.710	
Button, E.	Gunr	RMA4.558	
Cairns, J.	Pte	Ply8.879	
Cairns, J.	Pte	Ply9.440	
Carey, W.	L/Sig	166.679	
Carter, P.	Pte	Ch10.265	
Chapman, E.W.P.	Pte	Ply9.688	
Childs, G.W.	Pte	Ch10.633	
Chiverton, J.	Col/Sergt	Po10.167	
Clark, A.G.	Pte	Ch8.282	
Clark, W.	Gunr	RMA4.068	
Clark, W.	Gunr	RMA7.927	
Clarke, J.	Pte	Ply8.927	
Cleary, D.	Sto	294.594	
Coleman, A.E.	Gunr	RMA6.264	
Coles, G.	SB/Attn	150.876	
Coles, W.E.	Pte	Ply9.680	
Connew, T.F.	Gunr	RMA7.763	
Cooney, H.A.	Pte	Ply9.676	
Cooney, J.	Pte	Ply9.665	
Cousins, J.R.	Gunr	RMA7.541	
Cowtan, F.R.	Gunr	RMA5.992	
Cummins, H.A.	Gunr	RMA7.839	
Cummins, P.J.	Pte	Ply9.686	
Dennett, W.H.	Pte	Ply9.696	
Diamond, G.H.	Pte	Ch8.932	
Dodge, A.	Sergt	Ply3.989	
Downing, W.E.	Gunr	RMA6.339	
Duncan, J.W.	Gunr	RMA7.891	
Dunn, J.C.	Cpl	Po7.770	
Dyer, T.W.P.	Capt(RMA)		
Eldridge, F.C.	Pte	Ply8.903	
Elson, C.	Pte	Ch5.470	
Falconer, J.	Gunr	RMA5.462	
Fitzpatrick, J.	Gunr	RMA6.099	
Forbes, R.	Act/Bombdr	RMA5.553	
Forrest, T.	Pte	Ch10.995	
Fowler, H.	Gunr	RMA7.910	
Frace, W.H.	Pte	Ply9.683	
Francis, E.F.	Act/Bombdr	RMA7.621	
Francis, W.J.	Gunr	RMA7.817	
Frost, W.J.	L/Sergt	Ply5.908	
Gibbons, G.W.W.	Sergt	RMA2.192	
Gibbons, T.	Pte	Ch8.762	
Goldstraw, H.S.	Pte	Ply9.700	
Goodwin, T.	Pte	Ply9.657	
Goshawk, S.W.E.	Pte	Ch10.561	
Grady, J.J.	Pte	Ply7.671	
Green, D.	Gunr	RMA7.886	
Green, F.	Pte	Ply8.815	
Green, F.A.	Gunr	RMA7.884	
Green, R.J.H.	PO1	126.711	
Gregory, H.	Gunr	RMA5.893	
Grimley, E.	Pte	Ply9.401	
Grimmett, P.V.G.	Gunr	RMA7.913	
Gutteridge, J.G.T.	Gunr	RMA5.490	
Hall, J.	L/Sergt	RMA5.008	
Ham, T.W.	Pte	Ply9.679	
Hancock, A.	Pte	Ply7.694	
Hanson, G.	Pte	Ply8.882	
Harmsworth, G.H.	Pte	Ply8.795	
Harris, C.J.	Pte	Ply9.681	
Harvey, W.J.	Gunr	RMA5.693	
Hatherall, J.W.	Gunr	RMA7.017	
Hawkes, T.	Pte	Ch2.604	

NO BAR MEDALS *continued.*

Name	Rank	Number	
Hawkins, W.C.	Pte	Ch9.428	
Hawks, T.	Pte	Ch6.979	
Hayes, C.L.	Gunr	RMA5.972	
Hendy, G.	Pte	Ply8.955	
Higgins, C.S.	L/Cpl	Ch10.603	
Hoare, W.T.	Pte	Ch8.333	
Howell, H.T.	L/Sergt	Ch3.923	
Hunter, J.T.	Pte	Ply9.661	
Husband, J.	Gunr	RMA6.966	
Ifoald, F.G.	Gunr	RMA7.073	
Ivory, W.T.	Pte	Ch5.004	
Jeffery, H.W.	Gunr	RMA7.896	
Johnstone, J.	Pte	Ply8.923	
Jones, J.	Gunr	RMA7.860	
Judd, A.C.	Gunr	RMA5.203	
Kappey, F.G.	Major(RMA)		K
King, J.C.	Gunr	RMA5.439	
Kneller, G.	Pte	Po10.262	
Landsdell, W.J.	Pte	Po10.259	
Lawes, P.	Gunr	RMA7.756	
Lawrence, H.W.	Gunr(RN)		
Lee, H.	L/Cpl	Po5.123	
Lendon, J.	Sergt	Ply3.873	
Lewis, G.E.	Gunr	RMA7.814	
Love, A.	Pte	Ply9.326	
Lyon, J.	Act/Bombdr	RMA8.060	
Macdonald, W.	Gunr	RMA5.475	
McKay, A.	Gunr	RMA7.847	
McKinstry, J.	Gunr	RMA6.348	
McLennan, T.H.	L/Cpl	Ch6.553	
Maher, D.J.	Gunr	RMA6.638	
Mahon, G.B.	L/Sergt	Ply5.743	
Mastin, A.A.	Col/Sergt	RMA2.223	
Mearchant, W.J.de	Gunr	RMA7.970	
Meech, W.O.	Pte	Ch9.253	
Moore, A.	Pte	Ch10.271	
Morris, C.L.	Bugler	RMA6.096	
Murray, M.P.	Arm/Crew	176.743	
Neller, J.G.H.	Gunr	RMA7.974	
Nethersole, J.	Gunr	RMA5.807	
Nevill, G.B.	Gunr	RMA6.291	
Norris, J.E.	Bugler	RMA5.725	
Owen, J.A.	Pte	Ch9.282	
Page, T.W.H.	Pte	Ch8.894	
Perkins, W.	Pte	Ply8.907	
Pettit, H.H.	Gunr	RMA6.109	
Phillpot, R.	Gunr	RMA6.857	
Pickworth, A.E.	Gunr	RMA5.347	
Pomeroy, A.E.	Pte	Ply9.705	
Powell, E.D.	Gunr	RMA7.898	
Proctor, F.	Pte	Ch6.959	
Ralph, C.	Gunr	RMA6.073	
Randell, H.	Pte	Po10.263	
Ray, G.J.	Pte	Po8.345	
Reading, A.E.	Gunr	RMA2.916	
Rees, F.E.J.	Cpl	Ply4.820	
Rendall, F.	Pte	Ply9.694	
Rennie, A.P.	Pte	Ply9.666	
Richards, E.G.	Pte	Ply8.785	
Richards, G.H.	Sh/Std	173.231	
Richmond, H.S.H.	Lieut(RMLI)		
Riggs, J.A.	Pte	Ch8.576	
Roades, A.	Pte	Ch6.816	
Robinson, G.	L/Cpl	Ply9.560	
Roche, N.J.	Surgn		
Rogerson, W.	Sergt	RMA2.971	K
Rutherford, G.	Pte	Ply9.659	
Ryan, E.J.	Gunr	RMA7.906	
Searle, A.	Pte	Ch9.075	
Shaw, L.	Gunr	RMA5.703	
Sinnock, W.	Pte	Ch5.990	
Sissons, A.	Gunr	RMA5.774	
Smith, J.G.	Gunr	RMA6.087	
Sostman, H.	Pte	Ch10.748	
Spencer, A.G.	Pte	Ply8.980	
Stone, E.H.	Pte	Ply8.801	
Stride, F.	Pte	Po9.524	
Targett, A.	Pte	Ch8.383	
Taylor, J.W.	Gunr	RMA4.796	K
Thompson, J.	Gunr	RMA6.311	
Tickner, H.A.	Pte	Ch8.392	
Timpson, A.E.	Pte	Ply8.939	
Townsend, J.H.	Pte	Ch7.312	
Trenfield, R.	Pte	Ply8.928	
Turpie, R.E.	Gunr	RMA6.309	
Underwood, H.	Gunr	RMA7.849	
Walker, F.	Pte	Ply8.959	
Wallis, S.T.	Pte	Ply9.703	
Warner, E.	Gunr	RMA6.266	
Webber, J.	Pte	Ply9.687	
Weekes, P.B.	Cpl	Po8.071	
West, F.	Gunr	RMA6.925	
Westbury, G.E.	Gunr	RMA7.926	
White, J.	Gunr	RMA7.819	
Whitestone, W.T.	Pte	Ply9.702	
Whitney, E.C.	Gunr	RMA5.649	
Wibberley, H.	Gunr	RMA4.592	
Wilde, W.G.	Pte	Ch10.269	
Wiles, H.H.	Gunr	RMA7.045	
Wilkins, W.	Gunr	RMA5.678	
Williams, E.	Pte	Ch3.014	
Woodcock, A.	Gunr	RMA6.903	
Wrigley, T.	Pte	Ply9.685	
Wyatt, W.	Pte	Ch10.717	

Duplicate medals:

Name	Rank	Number
Budden, A.W.	Gunr	RMA7.931
Degnan, J.	Pte	Ply9.643
Dennett, W.H.	Pte	Ply9.696
Ham, T.W.	Pte	Ply9.679
McKinstry, J.	Gunr	RMA6.348
Moore, A.	Pte	Ch10.271
Wilde, W.G.	Pte	Ch10.269

NO BAR MEDALS *continued.*

Duplicate medals - without issue no on roll:

Frace, W.H.	Pte	Ply9.683
Hawks, T.	Pte	Ch6.979
Kneller, G.	Pte	Po10.262

Returned medals:

Clark, N.	Pte	Ch7.811
Degnan, J.	Pte	Ply9.643
Pratt, A.J.	Gunr	RMA4.013

NAVAL DEPOT, WEI-HAI-WEI.

Bars	*Total*	*Returned*	*Entitled*
RP	*74*	*2*	*72*
None	*106*	*7*	*99*
	180	*9*	*171*

Notes:

K - Medal presented by H.M. The King on 8th March 1902.

1 - Also noted on the Medal Roll of H.M.S. Terrible.

† - These names are noted on the Medal Roll as the same recipient.

Naval Personnel.

Bar: RELIEF OF PEKIN.

Name	Rank	Number	
Adams, A.	Pte	Ch9.571	
Adams, J.	Pte	Ply8.604	
Adcock, A.	Bugler	Ch4.888	
Anderson, J.	Pte	Ch9.539	
Andrews, A.	Pte	Ply8.615	
Atkins, J.E.	Pte	Ply4.974	
Ball, J.W.	Pte	Ch9.895	
Barr, W.C.	Pte	Ch9.576	
Bell, C.R.	Pte	Ch8.882	
Bell, W.C.	Pte	Po8.945	
Bland, A.	Pte	Ch9.625	
Boyle, J.	Pte	Po1.080	
Brooks, B.	Pte	Ply8.619	
Carey, A.W.T.	Pte	Ply8.685	
Churchill, C.	Cpl	Ch7.847	
Clarke, W.	Pte	Ply8.643	
Cowell, J.	Pte	Ch6.170	
Cowling, P.	Pte	Ply8.645	
Darke, W.C.	Pte	Ch8.832	
Dawes, H.	Pte	Ply5.358	
Dean, W.B.	Pte	Po8.866	
Dodd, J.H.	L/Sergt	Ply2.782	
Dunkley, F.	Pte	Ch8.926	
Dunnett, J.W.	Pte	Po8.697	
Dustan, J.W.	Capt(RMLI)		
Eades, W.G.	Pte	Ply7.291	
Farmborough, J.	Pte	Po8.928	
Fletcher, A.	Pte	Po4.505	
Good, R.	Pte	Ch6.887	
Gray, A.H.	Pte	Ply8.598	K
Hammond, H.S.J.	Pte	Ch9.679	
Handford, W.	Sergt	Po2.379	
Harmer, C.D'O.	Lieut(RMLI)		K
Harries, C.	Pte	Ply8.666	
Harris, W.A.	Capt(RMLI)		
Hart, M.P.	Act/Sgt/Mjr	Ch2.330	
Hooten, H.	Pte	Po8.933	
Inch, F.A.	Pte	Ch9.636	
Ireland, W.L.	Pte	Ch9.391	
Johns, W.	Pte	Ch9.578	
Lawson, A.	Pte	Po8.923	
Lord, W.	Pte	Po8.961	
McKay, D.	Pte	Ply8.618	
McLeod, H.E.	Pte	Ch7.592	
McLoughlin, J.F.	Pte	Po8.873	
Maclurcan, J.L.R.	Major(RMLI)		
Mayhew, C.L.	Lieut(RMLI)		
Moloney, M.	Pte	Po8.954	
Moore, H.	Pte	Ply8.674	
Neller, F.J.	Pte	Ch7.612	
Padgett, L.	Cpl	Ch8.712	
Philbrick, A.	L/Cpl	Ch2.155	
Phillimore, S.	Pte	Po8.931	
Polkinghorne, E.F.	Bugler	Ch9.943	
Randall, T.L.	Pte	Ch9.629	
Reeve, A.M.	Cpl	Po7.060	
Rogers, J.	Pte	Ch3.421	
Rudgeley, F.	Pte	Po7.792	
Rushman, A.	Pte	Ply8.277	
Sibley, J.	Pte	Ply1.872	
Smith, C.J.	Pte	Ch8.796	
Snook, C.	Pte	Ch8.875	
Sparrow, H.S.R.	St/Surgn		K
Spooner, W.	Pte	Ch9.381	
Stansfield, T.	Pte	Ch8.751	
Tassell, C.	Pte	Ch5.673	
Thatcher, E.C.	Sergt	Ply3.421	
Thompson, W.G.	Pte	Ch7.225	
Tidmas, G.	Pte	Po7.148	
Timms, G.	Pte	Ch4.604	
Tulk, A.	Cpl	Po8.858	
Wood, F.G.	Pte	Ply8.657	

Naval Personnel *continued.*

Bar: RELIEF OF PEKIN *continued.*

Duplicate medals:

Cowling, P.	Pte	Ply8.645
McLeod, H.E.	Pte	Ch7.592
McLoughlin, J.F.	Pte	Po8.873
Padgett, L.	Cpl	Ch8.712

Returned medals:

Lee, A.J.	Pte	Ch9.678
Middleton, A.	Pte	Ch9.574

NO BAR MEDALS.

Amy, J.	2/SBStd	150.473
Bentley, F.	Cpl	Ply6.270
Bevis, C.	2/Wrtr	161.203
Biddiss, W.	Pte	Ch8.179
Blackler, R.G.	2/SBStd	350.381
Borg, J.	Dom	356.079
Bowring, W.H.	L/Sto	157.923
Bowyer, J.T.	L/Sto	140.600
Brown, F.W.	Cpl	Ch10.352
Byatt, C.T.	Sto	153.783
Ching, H.	Cpl	RMA5.724
Clatworthy, J.T.	2/Wrtr	340.594
Cooper, H.	Pte	Ply8.589
Dimond, H.	Sergt	Ply2.110
Draper, W.	Dom	355.534
Dyer, F.J.	Dom	173.488
Elliott, H.	Act/Sgt/Mjr	Ch1.546
Ellis, J.	Dom	356.209
Farwell, H.	2/Wrtr	152.511
Fielder, B.J.	Pte	Ply8.684
Fielding, D.	Pte	Ply8.676
Foo Ah.	Dom	
Gaskell, A.	Surgn	
Gaunt, E.F.A.	Comdr	
Gibson, G.	Pte	Ply8.588
Goodwin, W.	Pte	Ply3.185
Gough, W.J.	Bosn	
Guyer, T.	Ch/Engr	
Haley, T.J.	L/S	163.619
Hayes, W.	ERA	269.064
Hearn, J.	Bugler	Ply7.832
Homan, P.W.	Pte	Ply8.678
Horwood, W.	L/Sto	141.595
Hutchinson, W.	L/Sto	144.800
Jones, S.	SBStd	133.066
Kee Eu.	Dom	
Kersey, A.C.	Pte	Ply8.668
King Li.	Dom	
Kirby, T.T.	Cpl	Ch9.588
Lacy, T.	Pte	Ply7.857
Leburn, G.	PO1	129.770
Locock, W.	Pte	Ply5.971
Lu Wong Foo	Dom	
Luke, R.	L/Sto	141.077
McNerney, J.	Dom	358.431
Mace, J.W.	Pte	Ply6.958
Maxted, F.	Pte	Ch3.481
Munday, R.C.	Surgn	
Osborne, W.	Pte	Ch9.667
Palmer, W.	Pte	Ply8.652
Penniall, J.	Pte	Ch9.673
Powell, J.S.	Pte	Ch9.038
Prince, J.H.	ERA	131.785
Randall, G.H.B.	Pte	Ch7.957
Reeby, F.	SB/Attn	353.717
Renno, J.A.	Pte	Ch3.749
Reypert, J.	Carp	
Rundle, G.C.	Sh/Std	119.094
Savage, E.	L/Sto	162.100
Schembri, F.	Dom	356.314
Scott, J.	Pte	Ply8.644
Shin Kiung.	Dom	
Skinner, G.J.	Bugler	Ch9.078
Slowman, J.	Pte	Ply6.832
South, G.B.	2/Wrtr	340.555
Stafford, G.	L/S	166.378
Stewart, R.	Pte	Ply8.580
Swan, J.	Pte	Ply8.597
Sweeney, P.	Pte	Ply6.469
Sylvester, S.	ERA	158.759
Toleman, J.H.	Sh/Std/Asst	340.039
Tyler, T.	Pte	Ply8.587
Warren, G.	Pte	Ply3.914
Wright, J.T.	Asst/Payr	
Wright, W.H.	Sto	167.116

Duplicate medals:

Reeby, F.	SB/Attn	353.717
Sylvester, S.	ERA	158.759

Returned medals:

Dawson, C.H.	Pte	Ch8.136
Feaver, W.G.	Pte	Ch7.404
Griffiths, C.P.	Pte	Po8.848
Kelly, J.	Pte	Ply8.612
Moodie, D.	Pte	Ch9.566
O'Connell, D.J.	Dom	355.206
Trainor, M.	Pte	Ch9.621

NAVAL DEPOT, WEI-HAI-WEI.

Civil Practitioners & Nurses employed at Wei-hai-wei.

NO BAR MEDALS.

Name	Role	Name	Role
		Haslake.	Lady Nurse †
		Jones, H.M.	Lady Nurse
Barr, F.M.	Lady Nurse	Laws, A.F.	Male Nurse
Batchelor, H.	Lady Nurse	Makeham, E.	Lady Nurse
Burnham, M.L.	Lady Nurse	Mills, L.	Lady Nurse
Cameron, M.E.	Lady Nurse	Peill, A.D.	Doctor
Cheeseman, C.	Male Nurse	Timmis, M.M.	Lady Nurse
Funk, M.A.	Lady Nurse	Unwin, E.	Lady Nurse
Gladwell, A.F.	Lady Nurse	Wallace, M.S.	Lady Nurse
Gough, E.	Lady Nurse	Wills, W.A.	Male Nurse
Hanzlik, L.C.	Lady Nurse †	Young, W.	Doctor

Wei-hai-wei Dockyard Staff served in Wei-hai-wei Volunteers.

NO BAR MEDALS.

Name	Role	Name	Role
Coverly, W.	Dredger Service	Thompson, R.	Dredger Service [1]
Johnson, G.L.	Dredger Service [1]	Trew, G.H.M.	Asst/Civil/Engr

NEW SOUTH WALES NAVAL DEFENCE FORCE.

Bars	*Total*	*Returned*	*Entitled*
None	*257*	*7*	*250*
	257	*7*	*250*

NO BAR MEDALS.

Adams, S.M.	PO1	214
Aird, F.J.	AB	131
Albone, D.W.	AB	146
Allen, J.	Ch/PO	22
Ambrose, F.N.	AB	148
Archibald, W.G.	AB	160
Armitage, J.D.	AB	99
Armsby, T.	AB	161
Arthur, H.A.	L/S	90
Atkinson, H.J.	Ch/PO	244
Bain, K.R.	AB	104
Ballerum, F.	AB	178
Barnett, J.J.	L/S	11
Barrett, A.E.	AB	183
Beale, H.E.	AB	81
Bennett, A.J.	PO2	7
Beynon, J.	AB	117
Bickley, F.	AB	58
Biddall, J.	AB-Sig	72
Binkins, A.	L/S	65
Black, B.	Sub Lieut	
Blacker, J.	PO2	76
Blanchard, J.A.	AB	49
Blyth, B.	Sergt/Mjr	M11
Bones, C.E.	AB	113
Boutell, C.	AB	75
Bracegirdle, L.S.	Midn	
Brown, J.H.	AB	137
Bruton, C.	AB	239
Bull, R.A.	AB	142
Burdett, C.F.	PO2	5
Burgess, G.N.	AB	187
Cahill, T.	AB	193
Calcraft, W.F.	AB	27
Cale, R.	AB	115
Callie, R.	AB	247
Cane, E.T.	PO1	106
Carr, W.J.	AB	157
Chambers, E.A.	AB	221
Chester, J.	AB	26
Clarke, G.J.	Ch/PO	54
Clemson, G.	AB	139
Clinton, J.M.	AB	201
Coates, W.H.	AB	120
Connor, E.R.	Comdr	
Connor, H.O.	L/S	53
Conwell, T.	AB	80
Cooper, H.	AB	20
Coppock, A.H.	AB	232
Corben, H.	L/S	111
Creer, R.C.	Sub Lieut	
Croke, J.	AB	207
Cryer, F.D.	AB	10
Daggar, D.A.	AB	32
Daid, J.R.	AB	140
Dalby, J.	AB	234
Davies, A.A.	AB	85
Davis, J.J.	AB	250
Degan, H.O.	AB	179
Dennis, G.E.B.	AB	134
Donochie, R.	AB	31
Dorey, A.C.	AB	203
Dunn, A.W.	AB	109
Earley, C.	AB	200
Edmond, T.D.	AB	37
Elders, W.R.	AB	33
Empson, J.	AB	94
Evans, R.	AB	199
Eves, A.T.	AB	124
Ferns, J.H.	Pte	M16
Field, L.G.	AB	47
Flemming, E.	AB	138
Ford, J.	AB	262
Fox, J.	AB	83
Foy, E.	Pte	M3
Frekleton, S.	Bugler	163
Fuller, H.W.	AB	225
Garwood, R.	Sh/Cpl	17
Gascoine, J.N.	AB	184
Geddes, A.	AB	21
Geddes, A.	AB	125
Giblin, W.J.	AB	127
Gillam, O.N.	Sub Lieut	
Gillespie, A.	Capt	
Gleen, A.	Pte	M21
Golden, F.	AB	143
Good, J.	AB	145
Gould, W.E.	AB	86
Goulstone, A.	Pte	M34
Graham, W.S.	AB	159
Grey, C.	AB	112
Griffiths, J.	AB	252
Groves, C.	AB	122
Hart, J.	Pte	M23
Hartnett, A.	Pte	M4
Harvison, G.L.M.	SBStd	63
Healey, J.	AB	100
Hearne, S.A.	AB	82
Hendy, H.S.	Ch/Arm	66
Hentsch, C.	Pte	M13

NO BAR MEDALS *continued.*

Hicks, J.T.	AB	186
Hidden, R.F.	AB	219
Hilliard, H.	AB	220
Hinnew, W.	PO2	116
Hixson, H.O.N.	Lieut	
Holloway, F.	AB	43
Holmesby, H.A.	AB	259
Hood, J.	AB	6
Horden, C.	AB	56
Horner, W.H.	L/S	107
Hughes, J.G.	AB	77
Hurley, J.	AB	202
Ingram, A.W.	AB	9
Jackson, J.H.	AB	132
Johnson, G.H.	Pte	M24
Jones, G.L.	AB	16
Jones, H.	AB	152
Jones, W.J.	AB	205
Kingsford, J.J.	AB	28
Knowles, E.	AB	191
Lambton, R.S.	Lieut	
Larsen, C.J.	AB	59
Lavette, J.	Pte	M15
Laycock, W.	AB	3
Lea, R.	Pte	M22
Lee, W.J.	AB	245
Leheman, F.	Sh/Cook	233
Leslie, W.	AB	190
Lindeman, Y.G.	Sub Lieut	
Lindley, J.L.	AB	254
Lindsell, J.C.	AB	29
Lodge, M.A.	AB	92
Lofts, H.E.	Lieut(RMLI)	
Luscombe, F.W.	AB	1
McConnell, J.	Pte	M19
McDonald, A.E.	AB	165
McDonald, C.A.	AB	166
McFarlane, J.R.	AB	30
McGovern, E.	AB	55
McGowan, R.S.	AB	151
McKenzie, A.	AB	103
McMenemy, H.	AB	128
Madden, E.T.	AB	189
Maguire, W.C.	AB	256
Malone, R.S.	Ch/PO	19
Maloney, J.V.	AB	228
Matthews, A.E.	AB	136
Matthews, C.D.	AB	105
May, H.J.	Yeo/Sig	182
Mercer, S.	Bugler	M33
Miller, S.	AB	262
Milton, W.C.	AB	242
Mooney, J.	Pte	M5
Morgan, W.F.	AB	251
Morrell, W.F.	AB	74
Murnin, C.E.	Midn	
Murphy, A.H.	AB	42
Murray, C.	AB	78
Naylor, F.W.	AB	216
Nicholas, C.	AB	230
Nicoll, C.	AB	73
Nixon, H.G.	Pte	M9
Noble, J.	AB	4
O'Connell, E.	AB	215
Oliver, A.	AB	213
Oliver, A.W.	Pte	M18
Parker, W.R.	L/S	57
Pascoe, F.J.	AB	44
Patterson, S.	AB	98
Payne, H.	AB	18
Pearce, T.W.	Sig	70
Pickering, J.	AB	8
Pittaway, E.T.	AB	69
Plagmann, H.C.R.	AB	38
Pollard, J.	AB	119
Potts, H.	AB	36
Praill, W.	AB	68
Price, A.	AB	24
Priest, S.H.	AB	197
Prothero, J.	AB	71
Puddephatt, E.S.G.	PO1	84
Quilly, H.J.	AB	257
Reed, A.E.	L/S	79
Reynolds, J.	AB	141
Riddell, C.J.	AB	34
Roberts, F.	Pte	M10
Roberts, M.A.	Lieut	
Robertson, G.	L/S	114
Robinson, W.	AB	96
Rogers, R.	Sergt	M2
Rose, E.	AB	188
Ross, E.	AB	173
Ross, J.	AB	133
Sale, G.J.	AB	217
Sapsted, A.H.	AB	196
Sayers, H.T.	AB	101
Share, A.	AB	97
Sharman, G.	AB	195
Shepherd, A.G.	AB	194
Sippe, J.T.	AB	48
Smart, S.M.	Pte	M11
Smart, W.C.	Pte	M6
Smith, A.	AB	35
Smith, W.	AB	229
Spain, S.W.	Lieut	
Sparkes, J.G.	Ch/PO	102
Steel, J.J.	St/Surgn	
Stone, A.E.	AB	64
Storey, T.W.	AB	88
Sturch, F.	AB	204
Sullivan, D.	L/S	253
Surreane, W.W.	AB	156
Symonds, T.C.	Cpl	M12
Tate, A.	AB	87
Thomas, W.	AB	130
Tipper, E.J.	Pte	M26

NEW SOUTH WALES NAVAL DEFENCE FORCE.

NO BAR MEDALS *continued.*

Troke, S.G.	AB	13
Tyrrell, F.W.	AB	249
Upton, P.W.	AB	12
Vine, W.H.	Dom	258
Waite, G.	AB	208
Walker, A.L.	Midn	
Walker, T.F.	AB	41
Walker, W.J.	Arm/Mte	147
Wallace, J.R.	Asst/Payr	
Wallwork, J.B.	AB	61
Walsh, J.	Sig	25
Walsh, W.	AB	62
Watson, E.E.	AB	108
Watson, G.	AB	14
Watts, W.	AB	180
Weedon, W.	Pte	M35
White, E.P.	Ch/PO	23
White, H.C.	Sub Lieut	
Whiteley, C.E.	AB	52
Whiting, W.	AB	118
Whitwell, F.E.	AB	210
Whytelaw, W.	AB	46
Wiggins, J.	AB	192
Williams, C.	AB	2
Williams, R.	AB	235
Williams, W.H.	AB	60
Wills, J.H.	AB	39
Woodcock, J.E.	AB	218
Woodcock, W.E.	AB	40
Woods, W.J.	AB	237
Wright, P.E.	AB	121
Wright, R.H.	Sig	246
Wynne, G.W.	Asst/Payr	
Young, B.	Shpwrt	45

Duplicate medals:

Fuller, H.W.	AB	225
McFarlane, J.R.	AB	30
Matthews, C.D.	AB	105
Milton, W.C.	AB	242
Payne, H.	AB	18

Returned medals:

Coe, E.	Cpl	M20
Denney, A.	AB	248
Forbes, D.	AB	181
Foster, F.M.	Pte	7
Hamilton, J.	AB	95
Rogers, T.J.	Pte	M28
Thompson, R.	AB	209

SOUTH AUSTRALIA NAVAL DEFENCE FORCE.

H.M.S. PROTECTOR.

H.M.S. Protector was a Cruiser of 920 tons and 188 x 30 feet. Her armament consisted of 1 x 8 in and 5 x 6 in guns. The vessel was built by Armstrong and launched in 1884. She was renamed Cerberus on 1st April 1921 when she was on harbour service; she reverted to Protector in 1924. She was sold on 10th September 1924 to J. Hill at Melbourne; she was resold in 1931 and renamed Sydney.

Bars	*Total*	*Returned*	*Entitled*
None	*103*	*1*	*102*
	103	*1*	*102*

NO BAR MEDALS.

Aitkin, R.C.	Sto
Allen, S.	Ch/Sto
Argent, E.	Ch/Gunr
Austin, W.	Sto
Baker, R.	AB
Barr, J.	PO1
Batson, W.N.	AB
Beare, H.	Ord
Beck, R.	AB
Blake, W.H.	Ch/Gunr
Brown, W.H.	AB
Brown, W.J.	AB
Burch, J.	AB
Butler, R.	Sto
Cameron, A.S.	AB
Carr, C.T.	AB
Carr, W.	Sto
Carrison, G.	PO1
Carter, F.C.P.	AB
Clare, C.J.	Comdr
Clarkson, W.	St/Engr
Cougliano, J.	AB
Creswell, W.R.	Capt
Darnody, F.C.A.	AB
Davies, J.J.	Cook/Mte
De Longville, C.	AB
Deane, J.	ERA
Deers, L.	AB
Duncan, R.C.	Art/Engr
Edwards, W.T.	AB
Ellis, C.	AB
Ewens, D.A.	AB
Fenwick, R.W.	Boy
Fulton, R.	MAA
Gill, J.H.	AB
Gilles, J.	AB
Gillespie, J.	PO1
Grady, E.O.	Ord
Grant, R.	AB
Halton, J.	AB
Hayter, J.J.	Sto
Healy, J.	AB
Hibbs, W.	Sto
Hill, W.H.	AB
Horricks, W.H.	Sto
Jeanes, S.	Ch/Carp/Mte
Jeffery, G.F.	AB
Johnson, B.	AB
Johnson, G.	PO1
Johnson, L.	Sto
Joss, G.T.	Bosn
Knowles, T.H.	AB
Lacerda, H.	AB
Lamb, J.C.	AB
Lewis, H.	Sto
Lloyd, B.	L/Sto
Lucas, R.	PO1
Luckett, G.E.	PO1
McEachern, J.	PO1
McLean, H.	L/Sto
Mackay, A.	AB
Malloney, T.	AB
Moon, A.	AB
Morris, B.H.	St/Surgn
Morrison, J.P.	AB
Murch, R.	AB
Murison, J.S.	ERA
Murphy, D.	PO1
Neilson, A.	Ord
Norman, J.	AB
Norton, E.C.	Asst/Payr
Owen, T.	AB
Oxley, A.J.	AB
Parrott, F.W.	Dom
Perry, H.	PO1
Perryman, H.	AB
Robins, P.	L/Sto
Rogers, J.	Sto

SOUTH AUSTRALIA NAVAL DEFENCE FORCE.

H.M.S. PROTECTOR.

NO BAR MEDALS *continued.*

Scott-Cameron, A.	AB
Shaw, G.	Sto
Silver, J.	AB
Smith, B.S.	PO1
Smith, C.	Dom
Smith, C.E.	Dom
Stevens, A.	Ord
Stuart, G.	L/Sto
Sutherland, R.	Ch/Arm
Taylor, W.	AB
Thompson, H.	Ord
Thornton, C.	AB
Ticklie, J.	AB
Ticklie, W.H.	AB
Turner, J.D.	Gunr
Turner, P.	Sh/Cook
Weir, P.	Lieut
White, J.E.	Sto
Willis, W.	L/Sto
Winchester, G.	PO1
Wood, W.	PO1
Woodman, J.F.	PO1
Wooley, A.J.	AB
Wylie, R.	Dom

Duplicate medals:

Knowles, T.H.	AB
Thompson, H.	Ord

Returned medal:

Duncan, R.	Dom

VICTORIAN NAVAL DEFENCE FORCE.

Bars	*Total*	*Returned*	*Entitled*
None	*198*	*1*	*197*
	198	*1*	*197*

NO BAR MEDALS.

Name	Rank	No.
Adams, J.J.	Dom	186
Albon, J.F.	AB	88
Aldridge, G.E.	AB	73
Alexander, G.	AB	96
Alford, G.	AB	137
Allen, W.	AB	118
Anderson, A.	AB	131
Anderson, A.	AB	149
Anderson, H.A.	AB	125
Anderson, J.	AB	140
Andrew, J.F.	AB	89
Barry, D.	L/S	75
Bassett, W.T.	L/S-Sig	53
Bates, J.A.	Gunr	
Bates, W.H.	AB	91
Beaumont, F.W.	AB	101
Bertotts, W.T.	AB	49
Beverley, J.D.	Sh/Cook	184
Biddlecombe, J.	Lieut	
Brown, J.W.	AB	135
Bryan, W.	AB	113
Burford, O.L.A.	Sub Lieut	
Bury, A.H.	L/S	25
Carter, T.	AB	160
Charles, J.	AB	173
Churchill, B.F.	AB	119
Claringbold, H.S.	Gunr	196
Coffey, J.	AB	26
Cole, W.	AB	106
Compton, A.	L/S	28
Connell, B.	AB	32
Cooper, E.	AB	176
Cooper, H.W.	Sig-AB	59
Cumming, W.	Dom	185
Cunningham, C.H.	AB	175
Currer, A.	AB-Sig	8
D'Elton, G.	AB	123
Davis, W.M.	Sto	117
Dunn, J.W.	AB	5
Eastwood, A.T.	AB	116
Elkins, G.H.	AB	139
Elso, E.	AB	95
Evans, J.	L/S	178
Farrington, R.H.	L/S	61
Fitzpatrick, M.	Ch/PO	33
Fletcher, H.W.	AB	99
Ford, F.	AB	144
Foster, J.	AB	138
Fox, A.J.	AB	92
Franscombe, T.	AB	2
Fraser, W.	L/S	66
Fredrickson, C.F.	AB	142
Freeman, W.M.	Sto	35
Gabriel, J.	AB	63
Gibbs, A.A.	Boy	48
Goding, T.W.	Ch/PO	14
Gordon, C.W.	AB	166
Grant, D.	AB	44
Greer, G.	AB	114
Gries, F.C.R.	AB	39
Griffiths, E.E.	AB	11
Hale, G.A.	AB	15
Hamerton, R.B.	Sto	126
Hampton, R.J.B.	L/S	38
Hansen, R.A.	AB	156
Hansen, R.B.	PO1	57
Harding, J.	AB	147
Harris, F.W.V.	Sig-AB	6
Harris, S.	AB	82
Harty, M.	L/S	20
Harvey, C.W.	AB	55
Hayes, E.G.	AB	81
Hayes, H.	AB	90
Hearn, W.	Gunr	192
Hedford, L.M.	AB	168
Heffey, C.	AB	109
Henningsen, H.	AB	161
Henwood, J.	AB	102
Hogg, J.M.	AB	167
Holmes, C.E.	Boy	71
Honey, C.M.	AB	83
Hooper, R.M.	AB	134
Hughes, J.E.	AB	115
Hunter, E.	AB	85
Inglis, D.G.	Gunr	197
Irons, W.H.J.	Sig-AB	41
Jackson, A.F.	AB	10
James, W.	Sto	130
Jamieson, J.C.	L/Sto	133
Jamieson, J.E.	AB	120
Jones, O.	PO1	24
Jones, T.R.	AB	87
Kean, H.	AB	98
Kearns, R.	Gunr	
Kelson, C.H.	AB	40
Kennedy, W.A.	L/S	22
Kenny, R.G.	Sto	141
King, F.	AB	97
Laing, W.	AB	162
Lake, J.A.	PO1	56

VICTORIAN NAVAL DEFENCE FORCE.

NO BAR MEDALS *continued.*

Laws, G.A.	AB	154
Livingstone, A.J.	ERA	181
Lock, H.B.	AB	152
Lusch, E.	Sto	78
Lyle, J.	Sig-AB	47
McAllister, J.A.	AB	43
McCarthy, J.M.	AB	52
McConnell, J.	AB	163
McDiarmid, D.	Ch/PO	23
McDonald, A.	AB	104
McDonald, D.	AB	153
McInnes, A.B.	AB	67
McIntosh, W.	AB	72
McKay, A.	AB	17
McKenzie, J.P.	AB	159
McKenzie, M.	Ch/PO	27
McLeod, D.	PO1	58
McNaughton, J.	Sto	13
McPherson, D.	AB	150
Mangan, J.	Sto	100
Marwood, J.H.	Gunr	193
Miller, J.	AB	122
Montague, A.	L/S	64
Monteith, W.G.	PO1	16
Mooney, T.E.	Ch/PO	3
Morgan, J.	AB	143
Morris, F.R.	Sig	51
Morris, G.	Sig-AB	76
Morrison, N.	L/S	36
Muir, J.	AB	174
Mumford, H.	AB	69
Murdock, G.	Sto	21
Mutton, E.S.	Ch/PO	18
Nagell, W.C.F.	AB	103
Nelson, C.	AB	158
Nelson, J.	AB	105
Nicholls, R.	AB	171
Nugent, A.	Sig-AB	74
O'Neill, M.J.	AB	1
Pagan, D.C.	AB	157
Page, C.E.	AB	65
Parry, W.	Sto	7
Patchett, W.S.	SBStd	188
Patterson, W.	AB	146
Pettersen, H.	PO1	42
Petterson, S.C.	AB	93
Pike, S.	AB	107
Pilgrim, A.G.	AB	31
Pilling, E.	Sto	136
Pope, M.	AB	29
Pope, W.H.	AB	86
Prideaux, G.	Ch/Arm	37
Quinlan, J.	AB	172
Raeymackers, G.	AB	169
Rasmussen, C.M.	Sig-AB	54
Reid, R.	PO1	45
Roach, E.	AB	151
Roberts, J.	L/S	19
Robertson, A.	Sig-AB	9
Robertson, W.	PO1	50
Robertson, W.G.	Engr	190
Roche, T.	AB	30
Rogers, W.M.	Carp/Mte	179
Salmon, L.	L/Sto	127
Sarsfield, J.	AB	111
Sheaf, S.G.	AB	108
Sheddon, W.	Sto	128
Shenn, P.	PO1	60
Silvester, J.	AB	164
Sinclair, A.	Sto	34
Slade, W.	AB	129
Smith, J.	AB	110
Smith, T.A.	AB	121
Smith, T.J.	AB	84
Stevens, W.H.	AB	177
Stevenson, A.G.	AB	79
Stewart, C.A.	St/Engr	207
Stewart, G.	AB	68
Stonely, S.H.	Sig-AB	12
Summerfield, J.	AB	70
Sweetman, W.L.	Sto	62
Tickell, F.	Capt	
Tonkin, J.M.	AB	155
Treacy, A.M.	Payr	
Tyrrell, J.	AB	46
Underwood, W.	PO1	148
Varey, A.H.	ERA	182
Wade, F.H.	AB	165
Walker, J.	Carp/Mte	180
Walters, G.	AB	132
Watson, J.	AB	170
White, J.	Gunr	
White, J.H.	Dom	187
Whiting, A.	AB	112
Wilson, J.	AB	94
Young, E.L.T.	AB	4
Young, F.	L/S	80

Duplicate medals:

Jones, T.R.	AB	87
Shenn, P.	PO1	60

Returned medal:

Beadles, H.J.	AB	124

ROYAL INDIAN MARINE.

R.I.M.S. CANNING.

R.I.M.S. Canning (ex Golconda) was a Troopship of 2,246 tons and 370 x 36 feet. She was built by Inglis and launched on 15th November 1882.

Bars	*Total*	*Returned*	*Entitled*
None	*143*	*0*	*143* *
	143	*0*	*143*

Notes:

* - This total includes 10 BRONZE No Bar Medals.

Recipients of BRONZE No Bar Medals are indicated in the following text by the use of *italics*.

NO BAR MEDALS.

Abbas, Sk.	Lascar
Abbas, Sk.	Sto
Abdoolla, C.	Sto
Abdooraman, Sk.M.	Lascar
Adam, M.	Lascar
Adam, Sk.B.Sk.	Sto
Ahman, Sk.	G.M. Servt
Ahmed, Sk.	Sto
Ahmed, Sk.	Sto
Ahmed, Sk.	Sto
Ahmed, Sk.O.Sk.	Cassaub
Allen, W.F.P.	Asst/Engr
Alli, G.H.	Seacunny
Alli, O.	Comdr/Servt
Alli, Sk.	Lascar
Alli, Sk.	Lascar
Alli, Sk.	Lascar/Boy
Alli, Sk.	Lascar/Boy
Alli, Sk.	Tindal of Sto
Alli, Sk.A.	Lascar
Amien, Sk.A.Sk.	Lascar
Amien, Sk.E.	Lascar
Amiensab, Sk.H.	Sto
Ayan, J.	Carp/Mte
Baba.	*Officer/Servt*
Baba, Sk.A.	Seacunny
Baba, Sk.B.	Seacunny
Baben, M.	Seacunny
Bala, Sk.H.	Lascar
Balamea, M.S.	Sto
Baloo, Sk.H.Sk.	Tindal Of Lasc
Bapoo, Sk.B.	Cassaub
Barnes, J.C.	Gunr
Bawa, Sk.	Lascar
Bawa, Sk.A.Sk.	Seacunny
Bawa, Sk.N.	Lascar
Bawa, Sk.O.	Lascar
Bawa, Sk.S.	Lamptrimmer
Bhamboo, P.	Lascar
Bhica, M.	*Officer/Servt*
Bicoo, Sk.	Lascar
Bicoo, Sk.	Lascar
Borges, S.M.	G.M. Servt
Buksh, I.	*Officer/Servt*
Carneiro, P.S.	Cook/Mte
Carvalho, J.	Topass
Cassim, M.	Bhandarry
Cassim, M.	Sto
Castelino, I.C.	G.M. Butler
Colkers, J.A.	Asst/Surgn
Cumroodin.	Sto
D'Souza, A.	Plmbr
D'Souza, F.	*Officer/Servt*
D'Souza, J.	Carp/Crew
D'Souza, J.A.	W.O.M. Servt
D'Souza, S.	Engr/Butler
Dawood, Sk.	Lascar
Dawood, Sk.	Lascar/Boy
Dawood, Sk.	*Officer/Servt*
Dawood, Sk.	Sto
de Souza, P.A.	Masal
Ebram, Sk.	Lascar
Ebram, Sk.	Lascar/Boy
Ebram, Sk.B.Sk.	Lascar
Esack, Sk.	Lascar
Esack, Sk.I.M.	Sto
Esool, Sk.	Lascar
Esool, Sk.	Lascar

ROYAL INDIAN MARINE.

R.I.M.S. CANNING.

NO BAR MEDALS *continued.*

Fernandes, A.	*Officer/Servt*
Fernandes, B.	Topass
Fernandes, C.	Topass
Fernandes, M.	E.M. Servt
Fernandes, N.	*Officer/Servt*
Fernandes, N.	Topass
Fernandes, N.C.	G.M. Std
Fernandes, S.	Topass
Ferrao, B.C.	Cook/Mte
Ferrao, C.	Cook
Gomes, F.	Topass
Gulam, Sk.	Lascar
Gunny, A.	Sto
Hamilton, A.H.J.	Sub Lieut
Hassan, Sk.	Lascar/Boy
Husain, F.Sk.	Lascar
Husain, Sk.	Tindal of Sto
Husain, Sk.A.G.	Lascar
Husain, Sk.D.G.	Lascar
Husain, Sk.G.	Lascar
Husain, Sk.G.	Lascar
Husain, Sk.G.	Lascar
Hutchinson, F.J.B.	Sub Lieut
Ishamudin.	Sto
Ismail, M.	Sto
Ismail, Sk.	Lascar
Isoof, Sk.	Sto
Jaffer, M.	Bhandarry
Jainudin, Sk.E.	Lascar/Boy
Jeewa, K.	*Officer/Servt*
Jones, B,H.	Lieut
Khan, S.	Lamptrimmer
Khan, Y.	Syrang of Lasc
Mahomed, Sk.	Lascar
Mahomed, Sk.	Lascar
Mahomed, Sk.	Lascar/Boy
Mahomed, Sk.	Lascar/Boy
Mascarculas, K.P.	Sh/Std
Mendouca, B.	G.M. Servt
Meya, Sk.	Syrang of Sto
Mohidin, Sk.B.	Lascar
Monteers, C.F.	Cook
Moosein, Sk.	Lascar
Nakwa, Sk.	Lascar
Nakwa, Sk.	Lascar
Nooroodin, Sk.	Lascar/Boy
Nooroodin, Sk.	Tindal of Lasc
Nurudin, Sk.M.	Lascar
Oosman, Sk.	Lascar
Palowji, Sk.A.	Sto
Piffard, A.J.G.	Comdr
Rahamon, A.	Sto
Rainudin, Sk.E.	Sto
Rodrigues, T.	Clerk
Rooknoodin.	Sto
Sallia, M.	Sto
Sallia, M.	Sto
Sallia, M.	Sto
Santos, J.	G.M. Servt
Sherfoodin.	Sto
Shirasdin, Sk.A.	Sto
Soma.	*Officer/Servt*
Sudroodin,	Sto
Sumsoo, Sk.	Lascar
Sumsoodin, Sk.M.	Lascar/Boy
Thyne, W.K.	Sub Lieut
Tulsiram.	*Officer/Servt*
Tyre, Sk.A.M.	Lascar
Vaz, S.	Baker
Wakefield, T.R.	Engr
Walker, R.	Ch/Engr
Wheatley, W.	Asst/Engr
Yacoob, S.	Seacunny
Yacoub, Sk.	Lascar
Yates, J.G.	Asst/Engr

ROYAL INDIAN MARINE.

R.I.M.S. CLIVE.

R.I.M.S. Clive was a Troopship of 3,570 tons and 300 x 45½ feet. She was built by Laird and launched on 15th November 1882.

Bars	*Total*	*Returned*	*Entitled*
None	*185*	*0*	*185* *
	185	*0*	*185*

Notes:

* - This total includes 10 BRONZE No Bar Medals.

Recipients of BRONZE No Bar Medals are indicated in the following text by the use of *italics*.

NO BAR MEDALS.

Abbas, Sk.	Sto
Abbott, E.R.	Asst/Engr
Abdoola, Sk.	Sto
Ahmed, Sk.	Lascar
Ahmed, Sk.	Lascar
Ahmed, Sk.	Sto
Ahmed, Sk.	Sto
Ahmed, Sk.E.Sk	Sto
Alli, E.	Lasc
Alli, E.M.	Lascar/Boy
Alli, M.	Tindal of Sto
Alli, Sk.	Lascar
Alli, Sk.	Lascar
Alli, Sk.	Lascar
Alli, Sk.	Lascar/Boy
Alli, Sk.	Tindal of Lasc
Alli, Sk.	Tindal of Sto
Alvares, M.	*Officer/Servt*
Ameen, Sk.B.	Lascar
Ameen, Sk.H.	Lascar
Azavedo, P.	Clerk
Baba, A.C.	Sto
Baba, S.C.	Sto
Baba, Sk.	Seacunny
Baba, Sk.E.	Seacunny
Baba, Sk.G.	Lamptrimmer
Balkoo, Sk.A.	Lascar
Balla, Sk.H.	Carp/Crew
Bapoo, Sk.	Lascar
Bapoo, Sk.	Lascar
Baugh, G.J.	Comdr
Bawa, Sk.	Bhandarry
Bawa, Sk.	Cassaub
Bawa, Sk.	Lascar
Bawa, Sk.	Lascar
Bawa, Sk.	Lascar
Bawa, Sk.	Sto
Bawa, Sk.A.	Seacunny
Bawa, Sk.E.	Lascar
Bawa, Sk.N.	Lascar
Belton, W.R.	Gunr
Bhicoo, M.	Lascar/Boy
Bhicoo, Sk.	Lamptrimmer
Bhicoo, Sk.	Seacunny
Blunt, C.C.	Carp
Bowden, A.St.C.	Lieut
Brumby, W.N.K.	Asst/Surgn
Carneiro, M.A.	E.M. Butler
Cassim, M.	Tindal of Sto
Chedee, Sk.	Lascar
Dadumia, N.	Sto
Dawood, Sk.	Lascar
Dawood, Sk.	Lascar
Dawood, Sk.	Lascar/Boy
Dawood, Sk.	Sto
Dawood, Sk.E.Sk.	Lascar
de Costa, L.	G.M. Servt
de Cruz, S.	Cook
de Gama, I.	*Officer/Servt*
de Souza, C.P.	G.M. Servt
de Souza, R.F.	Sh/Std
Dharmo, Sk.M.	Sto
Dias, J.P.	Baker
Dias, M.S.	Topass
Ebrahim, Sk.	Lasc
Ebram, M.S.	Sto
Ebram, Sk.	Lasc
Ebram, Sk.	Lasc

ROYAL INCIAN MARINE.

R.I.M.S. CLIVE.

NO BAR MEDALS *continued.*

Ebram, Sk.	Lascar
Ebram, Sk.	Lascar
Ebram, Sk.	Lascar
Ebram, Sk.	Lascar/Boy
Ebram, Sk.E.Sk.	Sto
Edroos, Sk.	Sto
Ellis, J.F.	Engr
Essack, Sk.	Lascar
Essoop, Sk.	Lascar
Essoop, Sk.	Sto
Essoop, Sk.M.	Lascar/Boy
Fackir, Sk.	Lascar/Boy
Fackir, Sk.	Lascar/Boy
Fackir, Sk.	Lascar/Boy
Fackir, Sk.A.R.Sk.	Lascar/Boy
Fernandes, A.	Topass
Fernandes, A.C.	Cook/Mte
Fernandes, F.	Carp/Crew
Fernandes, G.	Topass
Fernandes, G.L.	G.M. Butler
Fernandes, J.	Masal
Fernandes, N.	G.M. Servt
Fernandes, V.	*Officer/Servt*
Garoo, S.	Lascar
Gomes, G.A.	G.M. Servt
Guppy, E.	Asst/Engr
Hosein, G.	Sto
Hosein, M.	Lascar
Hosein, Sk.	Lascar
Hosein, Sk.	Seacunny
Hosein, Sk.	Sto
Hosein, Sk.	Sto
Hosein, Sk.G.	Lascar
Hosein, Sk.G.	Lascar
Hosein, Sk.J.G.	Lascar
Hussain, Sk.	Lascar
Hussain, Sk.G.	Lascar
Jaffer, Sk.	Sto
Jainoodeen.	Bhandarry
Jainoo, Sk.	Lascar
Jainoo, Sk.	Lascar
Jainoo, Sk.B.	Lascar
Jainoo, Sk.K.	Lascar/Boy
Jamaloodin.	Sto
Jamaloodin, M.	Sto
Kadeer, A.	Sto
Kurbudin.	Sto
Lamb, F.S.	Ch/Engr
Lobo, C.M.	Cook
Mahomed, C.	Cassaub
Mahomed, Sk.	Lascar
Mahomed, Sk.	Lascar
Mahomed, Sk.	Lascar
Mahomed, Sk.	Lascar
Mahomed, Sk.	Lascar/Boy
Mahomed, Sk.	Lascar/Boy
Mahomed, Sk.	Sto
Mahomed, Sk.	Sto
Mahomed, Sk.	Syrang of Sto
Mendouca, B.	*Officer/Servt*
Menezes, J.S.	G.M. Std
Miah, H.	Plmbr
Misquita, T.V.	G.M. Servt
Mohideen.	Sto
Mohideen, M.	Lascar/Boy
Mohideen, Sk.	Lascar/Boy
Mohideen, Sk.	Seacunny
Moilliet, H.M.K.	Sub Lieut
Nakwa, Sk.	Lascar
Nakwa, Sk.	Lascar
Nakwa, Sk.	Lascar
Narudin, Sk.	Lascar/Boy
Norauha, C.	*Officer/Servt*
Nurudin, Sk.	Lascar
Nurudin, Sk.	Lascar/Boy
Nurudin, Sk.	Sto
Nutter, J.N.	Engr
Pagurear, B.	Lascar
Pereira, A.	Topass
Rahaman, A.	Lascar
Rama.	*Officer/Servt*
Ranched, S.	*Officer/Servt*
Rayman, Sk.B.A.	Sto
Raymon, A.	Lascar
Raymon, A.	Lascar/Boy
Raymon, Sk.A.	Lascar
Relelo, J.	W.O.M. Servt
Rodrigues, A.F.	Comdr/Servt
Rodrigues, C.V.	*Officer/Servt*
Rodrigues, J.	Topass
Rodrigues, R.	Cook/Mte
Runched, M.	*Officer/Servt*
Saldanha, C.R.	Cook
Salia, M.	Sto
Salia, M.	Sto
Salia, M.	Sto
Salia, Sk.A.M.	Sto
Sena, P.	*Officer/Servt*
Sidoo, Sk.	Tindal of Lasc
Sidoo, Sk.G.N.	Lascar
Silveira, B.	G.M. Servt
Siqueira, A.J.	Clerk
Siqueira, B.	Topass
Siqueira, C.	E.M. Servt
Stocken, E.	Lieut
Sumsudin, Sk.A.	Sto
Sumsudin, Sk.N.	Lascar
Tyer, M.	Bhandarry
Walker, T.J.	Lieut
Wazoodeen.	Seacunny

ROYAL INDIAN MARINE.

R.I.M.S. CLIVE.

NO BAR MEDALS *continued.*

Wazoodeen.	Sto
Wazoodeen, Sk.	Lascar
Wazoodin.	Lascar
Wazoodin, Sk.	Lascar
Whish, E.V.	Sub Lieut
Yacoob.	Seacunny
Yacoob, Sk.	Lamptrimmer

ROYAL INDIAN MARINE.

R.I.M.S. DALHOUSIE.

R.I.M.S. Dalhousie was a Troopship of 1,960 tons and 239 x 36 feet. Her armament consisted of 6 x 6 pdr guns. She was built by Laird and launched at Greenock on 5th June 1886.

Bars	*Total*	*Returned*	*Entitled*
None	*118*	*0*	*118* *
	118	*0*	*118*

Notes:

* - This total includes 6 BRONZE No Bar Medals.

Recipients of BRONZE No Bar Medals are indicated in the following text by the use of *italics*.

NO BAR MEDALS.

Name	Rank
Abdoola, Sk.D.	Sto
Adam, Sk.E.Sk.	Seacunny
Ahmed, Sk.	Carp/Mte
Ahmed, Sk.	Lascar
Ahmed, Sk.	Lascar
Ahmed, Sk.	Sto
Ahmed, Sk.A.Sk.	Sto
Alfonso, P.	Masal
Alli, Sk.	Cassaub
Alli, Sk.	Lascar
Alli, Sk.	Lascar
Alli, Sk.E.	Lascar
Ameen, D.	Bhandarry/Mte
Ameen, Sk.A.	Lascar
Ameen, Sk.M.Sk.	Lascar
Andeen, G.F.	Asst/Surgn
Baba, N.	Lascar
Baba, Sk.	Lascar
Baba, Sk.	Lascar/Boy
Baba, Sk.	Seacunny
Baba, Sk.D.Sk.	Lascar
Babajee, N.	*Officer/Servt*
Bagwan, S.	*Officer/Servt*
Balla, S.	Bhandarry
Balla, Sk.	Cassaub
Balla, Sk.	Lascar
Balla, Sk.B.	Tindal of Lasc
Balla, Sk.N.	Lascar
Balloo, Sk.N.	Lascar
Baptista, B.	Topass
Baptista, J.	W.O. Servt
Bawa, Sk.	Lascar/Boy
Bawa, Sk.J.Sk	Lascar
Bawoodeen, M.	Sto
Bawoodin.	Lamptrimmer
Bawoodin, Sk.	Lascar
Bhicoo, Sk.	Lascar
Brebner, B.R.M.	Asst/Engr
Continho, A.	G.M. Servt
Currim, Sk.	Carp/Mte
D'Souza, A.	G.M. Std
D'Souza, E.	Comdr/Servt
D'Souza, N.	Engr/Butler
Dawood, Sk.	Syrang of Sto
de Abreu, F.C.	Sh/Std
Dennis, J.A.	*Officer/Servt*
Dhurmoo, B.	Sto
Dhurmudin, Sk.D.	Sto
Ebram, Sk.	Lascar/Boy
Ebram, Sk.	Lascar/Boy
Emam, Sk.	Sto
Eroos, Sk.	Lascar
Esmael, A.R.Sk.	Sto
Esmail, Sk.E.Sk.	Lsac
Essack, Sk.	Tindal of Lasc
Essoob, Sk.	Lascar/Boy
Essoob, Sk.	Sto
Fakrudeen, Sk.A.	Plmbr
Fernandes, C.	Cook/Mte
Fernandes, C.	G.M. Servt
Fernandes, L.	Topass
Fernandes, M.	G.M. Servt
Frazer, F.T.	Asst/Engr
Goldsmith, O.	Lieut
Harnae, N.	Lascar
Hoosein, B.S.	Sto
Hordern, E.J.C.	Lieut
Hussain, Sk.	Lascar

R.I.M.S. DALHOUSIE.

NO BAR MEDALS *continued.*

Hussain, Sk.	Sto
Hussain, Sk.G.	Lascar
Hussain, Sk.M.G.	Sto
Hyder, Sk.	Sto
Jainoodin, Sk.A.	Lascar
Kadir, A.L.A.	Sto
Kadir, H.A.	Tindal of Sto
Kanchoo, Sk.B.	Lascar
Kanjoo, Sk.	Seacunny
Kendall, C.J.C.	Lieut
Khan, A.	Sto
Kurrim, A.	Sto
Kurrim, M.S.A.	Sto
Lal, Sk.	Sto
Lobo, N.	Cook
Lobo, P.P.	Cook/Mte
Macdonald, A.A.	Engr
Mahomed, H.K.	Sto
Mahomed, Sk.	Lascar
Mahomed, Sk.	Lascar/Boy
Mahomed, Sk.	Sto
Mahomed, Sk.N.	Tindal of Sto
Manwar, Sk.	Sto
Mendouca, C.	G.M. Butler
Mendouca, M.F.	Topass
Menezes, J.	Topass
Mohideen, Sk.	Lascar
Mohideen, Sk.	Syrang of Lasc
Mohideen, Sk.B.	Lascar
Moosa, Sk.E.	Sto
Morha, N.	*Officer/Servt*
Mungloo, Sk.	Tindal of Sto
Newman, W.W.	Ch/Engr
Nizamoodin.	Bhandarry/Mte
Nunes, D.M.	Clerk
Nuruddin, Sk.	Lascar
Oosmon, Sk.	Sto
Pereira, D.	Topass
Pereira, V.M.	Cook/Mte
Rajac, A.	*Officer/Servt*
Raymon, A.	Sto
Raymon, Sk.A.	Sto
Saldanha, V.M.	*Officer/Servt*
Shaboodin, J.	Lascar
Sulliman, Sk.M.	Sto
Thompson, J.	Gunr
Vibart, J.F.	Sub Lieut
Wazuddin, Sk.	Seacunny
Wood, G.E.	Asst/Engr
Yaub, Sk.	Bhandarry

ROYAL INDIAN MARINE.

SHIP - Not Specified.

Bars	*Total*	*Returned*	*Entitled*
RP	*10*	*0*	*10*
None	*14*	*0*	*14*
	24	*0*	*24*

Note:

1 - This officer also appears on the roll of R.I.M.S. Clive.

Bar: RELIEF OF PEKIN.

Bapoo, Sk.	Syrang of Lascars
Bawa, Sk.	Lascar
Elderton, F.H.	Comdr
Hoosein, C.G.	Lascar
Hoosein, Sk.	Lascar
Ismail, M.	Lascar
Khan, Y.	Lascar
Monteiro, D.	Comdr/Secretary
Perrett, C.F.	Clerk
Vale, S.D.	Lieut

NO BAR MEDALS.

Abranches, C.F.C.	Dom
Acheson-Gray, R.	Lieut
Ally, M.	Engr/Dom
Bawa, Sk.	Lascar
Bawa, Sk.	Sto
Bawa, Sk.	Tindal of Lascars
Harold, A.E.	Lieut
Headlam, E.J.	Lieut
Laxton, R.W.	Sub Conductor
Makadam, M.I.R.	Dom
Mohomed, SK.	Lascar
Mascarenhas, D.C.	Dom
Rowand, A.	Lieut
Stocken, E.	Lieut [1]

Duplicate medal:

Abranches, C.F.C.	Dom

MISCELLANEOUS.

The following is a list of recipients of the China War Medal who do not appear on other Naval medal rolls in ADM 171.53.

Bars	*Total*	*Returned*	*Entitled*
RP	*3*	*0*	*3*
None	*5*	*0*	*5*
	8	*0*	*8*

Notes:

1 - Presented through the British Embassy in Washington 11.6.03.

2 - Presented by the Embassy at Berlin 10.6.03.

3 - Roll states, "Medal damaged in post. Fresh one to be issued on ret. of damaged one."

Bar: RELIEF OF PEKIN.

Bellingham, A.W.M.	M.I.C.E.
McCalla, B.H.	Capt(U.S. Navy) [1]
Von Usedona, Sir G.	Capt(Imperial German Navy) [2]

NO BAR MEDALS.

Carles, W.R.	Consul General - Tientsin
Home, W.E.	St/Surgn - SS Jelunga
Johnston, W.S.	Interpreter - Taku Forts
McMillan, J.P.	Ch/Engr - SS Pioneer
Tamplin, L.H.	Capt - SS El Dorado

MEDALS PRESENTED BY H.M. THE KING.

The list of recipients of the medals presented by H.M. The King is given in The Naval & Military Record of March 13 1902. The following is an alphabetic list of those recipients; as usual there are differences in spelling between some of the names found on the medal rolls and the corresponding names reported in The Naval & Military Record.

> " The Royal Naval Barracks, Keyham, was the scene of a very interesting and imposing ceremony on Saturday, at noon, when his Majesty King Edward VII presented 280 China and 60 South Africa medals, and other decorations, to officers, petty officers and men of the Royal Navy ....
>
> The distribution of medals by the King was at once proceeded with, Capt. Fortescue, equerry, handing the medals to his Majesty, and Lieut. Preston, R.N., reading out the list of recipients as they approached in single file. The medals were handed to them in cardboard boxes, each recipient saluting his Majesty with his left hand and receiving his medal in his right."

Notes:

Some recipients of the China medal have their entitlement entered on the medal roll of different ships as follows:-

α - H.M.S. Isis, β - H.M.S. Terrible, λ - Defence of Legations, ϕ - North West Fort, Taku.

List of Recipients.

Ahern, J.	AB	Undaunted	Bickford, S.	L/Sto		Bonaventure
Akhurst, E.J.	Sh/Std	Undaunted	Biddick, C.	Carp/Mte		Undaunted
Alton, F.C.	Fl/Payr	Centurion	Bigg, F.W.	AB		Centurion
Armstrong, H.G.B.	Lieut(RMLI)	Barfleur	Bignell, W.J.	Sto		Bonaventure
Arnold, W.	Pte	Aurora	Blades, T.J.	Sto		Hermione
Arthur, J.	Sto	Dido	Blair, G.	Gunr	ϕ	Phoenix
Ash, W.	Sto	Bonaventure	Bradford, J.	Pte		Undaunted
Attrill, J.	Ch/Carp	Centurion	Bragg, S.J.	AB		Bonaventure
Austin, H.A.	ERA	Undaunted	Brewer, E.	Act/Ch/Sto		Undaunted
Babbage, W.H.	PO1	Hermione	Brien, J.	Sto		Centurion
Bailey, G.W.	Gunr	Barfleur	Bromley, R.	AB		Undaunted
Bailey, S.R.	Sub Lieut	Centurion	Brooking, W.	Ch/PO		Undaunted
Baker, G.W.	Ord	Centurion	Browne, R.H.J.	St/Surgn		Alacrity
Baker, J.	Sto	Hermione	Browne, W.E.	ERA		Hermione
Ball, H.	L/Sto	Undaunted	Bruce, Sir J.A.T.	Rear Admiral		Barfleur
Banwell, J.	Sto	Undaunted	Bryant, J.H.	AB		Plover
Barrett, D.	Sto	Bonaventure	Buckingham, T.	Ch/Sto		Bonaventure
Bassett, E.W.T.	L/Sto	Hermione	Burt, E.H.	2/Wrtr		Hermione
Beard, T.	Pte	Undaunted	Burt, G.H.	ERA		Peacock
Beatty, D.	Capt	Barfleur	Button, H.	Ord		Centurion
Behenna, E.C.	L/Shpwrt	Undaunted	Buzzo, A.E.	PO1		Bonaventure
Behennah, S.	Ch/Cook	Hermione	Caley, H.E.	PO1		Barfleur
Bennett, W.H.	Blksmth	Hermione	Callaway, H.C.B.	Gunr		Centurion
Berry, F.	Pte	Undaunted	Campbell, J.E.	AB		Undaunted
Berry, T.	ERA	Bonaventure	Canley, A.R.	PO1		Peacock
Bettinson, J.	Ch/Sto	Bonaventure	Christmas, W.J.	PO1		Barfleur

MEDALS PRESENTED BY H.M. THE KING.

Name	Rank	Ship
Clarke, J.	Pte	Algerine
Cobb, E.W.	Gunr	Barfleur
Cockey, G.H.	Engr	Centurion
Coggins, R.S.	Sto	Barfleur
Coleman, T.	PO2	Hermione
Collins, W.J.	Sto	Hermione
Cooper, G.F.	Sergt	Aurora
Costello, J.P.	AB	Bonaventure
Cottam, S.	AB	Centurion
Coussins, R.J.	L/S	Bonaventure
Cradock, C.G.F.M.	Capt	Alacrity
Crennell, J.	AB	Hermione
Currie, S.	L/Sto	Centurion
Cutcliffe, E.G.	PO1	Phoenix
Cutler, W.	Ord	β Barfleur
Davies, W.H.	Sergt	Centurion
Davis, G.	Pte	Legation Gd
Davis, J.C.	Midn	Centurion
Dickson, C.B.	Sub Lieut	Aurora
Dinwoodie, J.	Sto	Centurion
Donovan, R.	Sto	Barfleur
Down, J.G.P.	Sto	Undaunted
Downley, W.J.	Sto	Bonaventure
Drake, F.	L/S	Undaunted
Drew, J.W.	PO1	Barfleur
Duckworth, F.	ERA	Centurion
Eastley, J.H.	Sto	Undaunted
Easton, W.H.	L/Sto	Undaunted
Edwards, J.L.	Bugler	Centurion
Edworthy, J.A.	AB	Barfleur
Efford, E.A.	AB	Hermione
Ellis, A.J.	PO1	Undaunted
Ellis, G.	Bosn	Centurion
Esau, T.	L/Carp/Crew	Barfleur
Ettie, O.R.B.	Bugler	Orlando
Fanshawe, G.D.	Sub Lieut	Endymion
Fear, R.	PO1	Undaunted
Field, F.L.	Lieut	Barfleur
Finch, A.E.	AB	Barfleur
Finegan, D.	Sto	Bonaventure
Fitzgerald, T.	AB	Hermione
Flahive, J.	Sto	Hermione
Floyd, S.	Sto	Centurion
Foreman, A.G.	Ch/PO	Centurion
Foster, A.J.	2/Wrtr	Bonaventure
Friend, A.R.S.	Blksmth/Mte	Undaunted
Fuller, R.G.	2/SBStd	Legation Gd
Galliford, J.T.	Cpl	Endymion
Gallop, J.	AB	Hermione
Gater, W.J.	Sto	Bonaventure
George, H.	L/S	Orlando
Germain, J.C.	Pntr	Undaunted
Gibbs, V.F.	Sub Lieut	Barfleur
Gipps, G.	Sub Lieut	Orlando
Goard, H.W.	Sto	Hermione
Golden, P.	AB	Barfleur
Gomm, A.E.	AB	Hermione
Goodban, J.	AB	Centurion
Gowney, D.J.	Cpl	Legation Gd
Granville, C.D.	Capt	Centurion
Gray, A.H.	Pte	Wei-hai-wei
Greasley, G.W.	Sto	Centurion
Greenfield, J.	Pte	Legation Gd
Gregory, J.J.	PO1	Centurion
Gunn, S.	Sergt	Centurion
Guy, B.J.D.	Sub Lieut	Barfleur
Haden, S.W.	Pte	Legation Gd
Haine, H.	Sto	Bonaventure
Hall, C.	PO1	Bonaventure
Hallahan, T.G.	Arm	Undaunted
Halliday, L.S.T.	Major(RMLI)	Legation Gd
Hannaford, F.G.	Sto	Undaunted
Harding, W.G.	PO2	Hermione
Harmer, C.D'O.	Lieut(RMLI)	Wei-hai-wei
Harris, S.H.	Sto	Bonaventure
Hart, W.H.	AB	Centurion
Hayes, J.	PO1	Aurora
Hayward, G.H.	Sto	Bonaventure
Healy, C.R.	PO1	Bonaventure
Hellyer, A.J.	Carp/Mte	Centurion
Hendicott, R.	Pte	Legation Gua
Hexter, W.	L/S	Bonaventure
Hickey, H.	PO2	Hermione
Hill, J.	PO2	Bonaventure
Hill, S.W.	PO2	Centurion
Hollinsworth, C.J.	Ch/ERA	Barfleur
Holmes, W.J.	PO1	α Bonaventure
Hornsby, W.H.	Ch/Arm	Undaunted
Horswell, J.	ERA	Peacock
Hoskin, G.S.	Act/MAA	Undaunted
Howard, J.G.	Pte	Legation Gd
Howell, E.A.	L/S	Hermione
Hulbert, A.R.	Comdr	Endymion
Ireland, W.J.T.	PO1	Undaunted
Ivery, G.	Pte	Centurion
Jago, F.	L/Sig	Centurion
Jarman, C.H.	Ord	Aurora
Jarvis, C.	PO1	Woodlark
Jellicoe, J.R.	Capt	Centurion
Johns, W.	Sto	Hermione
Johnstone, J.R.	Lieut Col	Centurion
Jones, A.	Sto	Bonaventure
Jones, G.T.	Pte	Legation Gd
Jupp, W.H.	Gunr	Centurion
Kappey, F.G.	Major(RMA)	ϕ Centurion
Keohane, D.	AB	Bonaventure
Keyes, R.J.B.	Comdr	Fame
King, W.E.	Col/Sergt	Barfleur
Kingsley, J.	AB	Aurora
Knott, A.	AB	Bonaventure
Ladlow, J.R.	Pte	Peacock
Lawrence, J.	Sto	Undaunted
Legg, H.	Sto	Dido
Lepine, R.J.	Pte	Centurion
Lewin, W.H.	Sto	Bonaventure
Ley, M.	2/Yeo/Sig	Undaunted
Littledale, H.F.	Midn	Orlando
Littlejohns, W.G.	Asst/Payr	Centurion

MEDALS PRESENTED BY H.M. THE KING.

Livermore, A.G.	L/S	Centurion
Longhurst, G.F.	Midn	Barfleur
Lowe, J.	AB	Bonaventure
Lucid, M.	Sto	Bonaventure
Luke, E.V.	Major(RMLI)	Barfleur
Luttrell, J.L.F.	Lieut	Centurion
McCormick, H.	AB	Undaunted
McCoubrey, J.	PO1	Undaunted
McElligott, M.	L/S	Centurion
McGeorge, J.W.	L/Shpwrt	Centurion
McGrane, E.	Ord	β Barfleur
McKensie, J.	Pte	Centurion
McLean, W.G.	SB/Attn	Centurion
McLeod, A.	Cooper	Bonaventure
Madge, L.J.H.	PO1	Centurion
Mahoney, M.	Sto	Centurion
Marshall, W.H.	Sto	Bonaventure
Martin, A.	Sto	Barfleur
Masters, W.J.	Pte	Legation Gd
Matthews, G.	PO1	Peacock
Mayne, R.C.	Sub Lieut	Barfleur
Mayo, A.G.	Pte	λ Centurion
Messenbird, G.H.	Sergt	Barfleur
Metcalf, C.H.	Pte	Centurion
Miller, H.C.	L/Sergt	Centurion
Miller, T.	L/Sto	Undaunted
Millman, J.J.	Q/Sig	Undaunted
Mills, J.C.	Sto	Centurion
Mintram, A.S.	AB	Centurion
Moore, W.	AB	Centurion
Morgan, G.	L/S	Undaunted
Morris, M.	AB	Undaunted
Moull, W.D.	2/SBStd	Centurion
Mulcahy, E.	Sto	Centurion
Newton, E.	Plmbr	Undaunted
Norton, J.E.	Plmbr	Bonaventure
O'Brien, G.	AB	Undaunted
Olver, J.	PO2	Undaunted
Palmer, W.G.	PO1	Undaunted
Parsonage, W.	AB	Aurora
Paul, C.	Sto	Hermione
Payne, A.E.	Sto	Peacock
Payton, J.H.	PO2	Plover
Pemble, E.H.	PO1	Centurion
Perry, C.R.	Sto	Undaunted
Peters, H.G.	Sto	Bonaventure
Pickthorn, E.B.	St/Surgn	Centurion
Pomeroy, J.	Sh/Cpl	Aurora
Pomeroy, W.J.	PO2	Bonaventure
Potter, C.J.	Sto	Bonaventure
Read, J.	PO1	Hermione
Read, T.B.	Pte	Centurion
Reeve, A.D.	AB	Centurion
Regis, H.W.	Act/Bosn	Centurion
Roberts, R.	Sto	Bonaventure
Robins, S.	Sto	Hermione
Rogerson, W.	Sergt	φ Phoenix
Roper, E.	Sergt	Terrible
Rundle, J.T.D.	Sto	Undaunted
Sands, H.	Pte	Legation Gd
Saunders, A.E.	Sergt	Legation Gd
Scripps, J.	Pte	Undaunted
Scuttling, J.C.	Sto	Hart
Seymour, Sir E.H.	Admiral	Centurion
Shaughnessy, J.	L/Carp/Crew	Isis
Shea, D.	Sto	Dido
Shepherd, J.	Pte	Aurora
Shilston, E.A.	PO1	Centurion
Sims, W.H.	Sto	Barfleur
Small, A.	L/S	Centurion
Smith, E.C.	Asst/Engr	Barfleur
Smith, F.	Pte	Centurion
Smith, M.	Arm	Centurion
Smith, T.J.	PO1	Undaunted
Smyth, A.P.	AB	Hermione
Smythe, D.W.	PO1	Centurion
Sparrow, H.S.R.	Fl/Surgn	Wei-hai-wei
Squires, F.J.	AB	Hermione
Staughton, A.W.	Pte	Aurora
Steed, W.G.	Sto	Hermione
Stewart, R.H.J.	Capt	Algerine
Stocker, S.J.	Sto	Bonaventure
Sutton, S.	L/Sto	Undaunted
Swiggs, A.E.	AB	Centurion
Taylor, J.W.	Gunr	φ Phoenix
Thomas, J.	Arm	λ Orlando
Thompson, J.R.	Ord	β Barfleur
Tichborne, G.M.	Chaplain	Barfleur
Tickner, A.J.	Pte	Legation Gd
Timmins, C.J.	AB	Undaunted
Todd, T.A.	AB	Hermione
Toms, J.H.	MAA	Hermione
Torrington, B.	L/Sto	Centurion
Trenaman, J.	Pte	Bonaventure
Tristram, H.J.	Pte	Barfleur
Underhill, C.	PO1	Snipe
Venton, L.	Sto	Centurion
Vine, W.G.	L/S	Centurion
Vosper, W.T.	L/S	Hermione
Warrender, G.J.S.	Capt	Barfleur
Waterman, J.J.	Arm/Mte	Hermione
Waters, J.	Sto	Centurion
Webber, F.A.	Dom	Centurion
Webster, H.A.	Pte	Legation Gd
Whibley, E.E.	AB	Barfleur
White, W.	Sto	Bonaventure
Whitecross, P.A.	AB	Centurion
Willcox, O.H.	Gunr	Centurion
Williams, G.	AB	Centurion
Williams, T.W.	Pte	Undaunted
Wood, H.	Pntr	Hermione
Woodward, W.T.	Pte	Legation Gd
Wray, E.	Capt(RMLI)	Legation Gd
Wright, J.	Gunr(RN)	Terrible
Wrottesley, F.R.	Lieut	Barfleur
Young, M.	Sto	Centurion

MEDALS PRESENTED BY H.M. THE KING.

The following recipients are noted on their respective ship's medal rolls as having received their China medals from His Majesty The King; however, their names are not noted in the list of recipients reported in The Naval & Military Record of March 13th 1902.

Bowen, A.C.	AB	Undaunted	Jellicoe, E.H.	Lieut	Barfleur
Brooke, B.V.	Lieut	Bonaventure	King, A.T.	Sto	Undaunted
Finnimore, J.G.	Sto	Isis	Secretan, E.	Lieut	Wallaroo
Gardner, T.	Act/SBStd	Barfleur			

ANALYSIS OF BARS & MEDALS.

SHIP / UNIT	BARS					TOTAL
	DL	TF&RP	TF	RP	None	
H.M.S. Alacrity		42	8	1	87	138
H.M.S. Algerine		9	94	1	9	113
H.M.S. Arethusa					306	306
H.M.S. Aurora		46	10	258	231	545
H.M.S. Barfleur		70	22	272	398	762
H.M.S. Bonaventure					342	342
H.M.S. Centurion		20	8	390	332	750
H.M.S. Daphne					136	136
H.M.S. Dido					460	460
H.M.S. Endymion		25	10	280	288	603
H.M.S. Esk					95	95
H.M.S. Fame		3	58	1	3	65
H.M.S. Goliath		1		1	760	762
H.M.S. Hart					56	56
H.M.S. Hermione		1			332	333
H.M.S. Humber					103	103
H.M.S. Isis					432	432
H.M.S. Linnet					95	95
H.M.S. Marathon					226	226
H.M.S. Orlando		81	35	194	220	530
H.M.S. Peacock		1			81	82
H.M.S. Phoenix				13	102	115
H.M.S. Pigmy					74	74
H.M.S. Pique					289	289
H.M.S. Plover					74	74
H.M.S. Redpole					72	72
H.M.S. Rosario					109	109
H.M.S. Snipe					20	20
H.M.S. Terrible				263	706	969
H.M.S. Undaunted					512	512
H.M.S. Wallaroo					219	219
H.M.S. Waterwitch					80	80
H.M.S. Whiting				55	9	64
H.M.S. Woodcock					44	44
H.M.S. Woodlark					37	37
Legation Guard	78					78
N.W. Fort, Taku					194	194
Naval Depot, Wei-Hai-Wei				72	99	171
New South Wales Naval Defence Force					250	250
South Australian Naval Defence Force					102	102
Victorian Naval Defence Force					197	197
R.I.M.S. Canning					143	143
R.I.M.S. Clive					185	185
R.I.M.S. Dalhousie					118	118
R.I.M. Ship not specified				10	14	24
Miscellaneous				3	5	8
TOTAL	78	299	245	1814	8646	11082

CASUALTIES.

The following list of casualties has been almostwholely been derived from official documents, previously unpublished, which are in the possession of the Ministry of Defence. Additionally, we have consulted the official despatches published in the London Gazettes of October and November 1900 and other relevant sources.

We acknowledge with thanks the Ministry of Defence for permission to use this material and to Mr R Broad for his valuable assistance.

Summary of Casualties:

SHIP	*KILLED*	*DIED OF WOUNDS*	*WOUNDED IN ACTION*
Alacrity	0	0	3
Algerine	0	0	8
Aurora	6	0	24
Barfleur	7	3	59
Centurion	20	8	61
Endymion	10	0	39
Orlando	7	0	48
Terrible	0	1	21
Legation Guard	2	2	19
Wei-Hai-Wei	1	0	8
TOTALS	53	14	290

Note - The casualty rolls show only those officers and men who were killed or injured as a result of offensive action against the enemy. Men who died of disease, without having previously been injured, are not included.

KILLED IN ACTION:

Name	Rank	Number	Ship	Place	Date	Details
Barton, R.	Pte	Po9573	Endymion	Hsiku	23 June	Bullet wound to brain.
Berry, H.	Ord	197904	Orlando	Langfang	18 June	Bullet wound to brain.
Beyts, H.	Capt(RMA)		Centurion	Hsiku	23 June	Bullet wound to brain.
Bing, W.J.	Ord	188203	Barfleur	Taku	17 June	Bullet entered mouth & lodged in base of skull.
Bone, S.	AB	158529	Centurion	Peitsang	21 June	Bullet wound to spine.
Brown, J.	AB	187333	Barfleur	Tientsin	13 July	Killed in action.
Bryan, H.W.	Pte	Po9576	Endymion	Hsiku	23 June	Bullet wound to brain.
Bryson, J.	Ord	198639	Centurion	Hsiku	22 June	Bullet wound to brain.
Chandler, W.	Pte	Ch9131	Endymion	Tientsin	27 June	Killed in action.
Charlo, H.	PO2	152172	Endymion	Hsiku	23 June	Bullet wound to abdomen.
Clayton, J.	Sto	285520	Centurion	Tientsin	9 July	Shell wound causing fractured skull.
Craddock, E.H.	Ord	193819	Orlando	Langfang	18 June	Shot through skull - bullet through brain.
Davies, T.	Pte	Ply5816	Aurora	Hsiku	22 June	Body not seen - killed on railway line at night.
Eddiford, H.	Pte	Ply4814	Aurora	Tientsin	27 June	Wound to heart.
Edwards, W.	Sto	282137	Centurion	Hsiku	23 June	Bullet wound to lung.
Ellis, A.E.	Pte	Po8634	Centurion	Hsiku	22 June	Bullet wound to abdomen.
Flory, W.	AB	147621	Endymion	Tientsin	27 June	Killed in action.
Foster, F.H.	Pte	Ply8594	Centurion	Hsiku	22 June	Bullet wound to lung.
Frisby, E.	Pte	Po3599	Centurion	Hsiku	23 June	Bullet wound to thigh.
Gigg, A.H.	Pte	Ply7271	Aurora	Hsiku	22 June	Probably hacked to pieces by the enemy; killed on railway line, body not seen.
Gingell, W.T.	Sergt	Ply3769	Orlando	Langfang	18 June	Bullet wound to abdomen.
Greaves, F.A.	AB	187078	Barfleur	Tientsin	13 July	Killed in action.
Hawes, G.H.	Pte	Po8906	Centurion	Hsiku	22 June	Bullet wound to brain.
Johnson, J.W.	L/S	156990	Orlando	Tientsin	9 July	Shell wound of abdomen & left thigh.
Kane, F. alias G.B.Cree	Pte	Ply8529	Aurora	Langfang	18 June	Bullet wound to neck.
King, J.	AB	162904	Barfleur	Tientsin	13 July	Killed in action.
Lee, A.J.	Pte	Ch9678	Wei-Hai-Wei	Tientsin	27 June	Killed in action.
Lloyd, H.T.R.	Capt(RMLI)		Aurora	Tientsin	13 July	Wound to neck.
Lloyd, W.T.	Ord	190614	Centurion	Hsiku	23 June	Bullet wound to brain.
Lunn, E.	Gunr	RMA5767	Centurion	Hsiku	23 June	Bullet wound to thigh.
McCarthy, T.	AB	182293	Barfleur	Tientsin	13 July	Killed in action.
McIntosh, D.	Sto	285206	Endymion	Hsiku	25 June	Shell wound to head.
Mills, H.T.	AB	179839	Orlando	Langfang	18 June	Shot through chest.
Noble, A.	Coop/Crew	278052	Centurion	Tientsin	11 July	Shell wound to abdomen.
O'Brien, J.	AB	187456	Barfleur	Hsiku	23 June	Wound to heart.
Parker, J.	Pte	Po9565	Endymion	Hsiku	23 June	Bullet wound to spleen.
Parsons, R.	AB	184683	Centurion	Peitsang	21 June	Bullet wound to brain.

Phillips, C.W.	Pte	Ch9065	Legation Guard	Pekin	29 June	Killed in action.
Restall, T.J.	L/S	151659	Centurion	Peitsang	21 June	Bullet wound to brain.
Robinson, H.	Pte	Po8934	Orlando	Langfang	17 June	Bullet wound through brain - fractured skull.
Scadding, A.	Pte	Ply8683	Legation Guard	Pekin	22 June	Killed in action.
Sharpe, F.	AB	188893	Centurion	Tientsin	27 June	Bullet wound to abdomen.
Skipsey, R.	AB	143729	Centurion	Tientsin	7 July	Shell wound to head - fractured skull.
Spillaine, J.	Sto	278528	Aurora	Tientsin	27 June	Wound to heart.
Spiller, G.	PO1	124233	Centurion	Langfang	17 June	Bullet wound to brain.
Stanford, W.	Pte	Ply7749	Endymion	Hsiku	23 June	Bullet wound to brain.
Townsend, T.	AB	174826	Centurion	Hsiku	22 June	Bullet wound to abdomen.
Wallace, F.	AB	188772	Barfleur	Tienstin	13 July	Bullet wound to brain.
Watson, D.	Ord	192403	Endymion	Lofa	14 June	Bullet wound to lung.
Wheeler, R.G.	AB	188651	Orlando	Langfang	18 June	Shot through chest.
Wooldridge, S.E.	PO1	139778	Endymion	Langfang	18 June	Bullet wound to abdomen.
Wyatt, E.S.	Ch/PO	104052	Centurion	Hsiku	23 June	Bullet wound to abdomen.
Yates, J.T.	Gunr	RMA5890	Centurion	Hsiku	22 June	Bullet wound to brain.

DIED OF WOUNDS:

Beaumont, A.	Sto	149838	Centurion	Tientsin	7 July	Died of wounds at Wei-Hei-Wei - 17 July.
Bolton, H.S.	AB	183671	Centurion	Hsiku	22 June	Shell wound to head; died at Tientsin - 6 July.
Briggs, F.W.	Pte	Po8239	Centurion	Hsiku	23 June	Bullet wound to chest & lung and wounded right arm, died at Tientsin - 30 June.
Cufley, J.	AB	184373	Centurion	Tientsin	10 July	Bullet wounds to back, chest, lower jaw & scapula, died at Wei-Hai-Wei - 15 August.
Curtis, J.W.	Arm	143242	Centurion	Langfang	19 June	Accidental bullet wound to left knee, died - 30 July.
Donaldson, A.P.	Midn		Barfleur	Langfang	19 June	Wounds to neck & chest, died at Tientsin - 3 July.
Esdaile, F.	Midn		Barfleur	Tientsin	6 July	Bullet wounds to chest, spine & shoulder, died at Tientsin - 7 July.
Grover, W.	Ord	188808	Barfleur	Tientsin	27 June	Wounded in chest, died at Tientsin - 27 June.
Howard, C.	Pte	Po6267	Terrible	Tientsin	9 July	Died of wounds.
Sawyer, A.G.	Pte	Po8526	Legation Guard	Pekin	24 June	Died of wounds.
Strouts, B.M.	Capt(RMLI)		Legation Guard	Pekin	16 July	Died of wounds.
Thompson, A.C.	Sto	176043	Centurion	Hsiku	23 June	Bullet wounds to left arm, left thigh, right shoulder & right thigh, died at Wei-Hai-Wei - 27 July.
Turner, E.	L/S	179102	Centurion	Tientsin	7 July	Shell wound to head fracturing skull, died at Wei-Hai-Wei 28 July.
Wright, T.	L/S	161349	Centurion	Hsiku	23 July	Shell wound to right knee, bullet wounds in chest, left hand & left thigh, died at Wei-Hai-Wei - 27 July.

WOUNDED IN ACTION:

Name	Rank	No.	Ship	Place	Date	Wound
Adams, H.C.	Ord	188899	Barfleur	Hsiku	23 June	Bullet wound to right forearm.
Adams, J.J.	AB	148437	Centurion	Hsiku	22 June	Bullet wounds to left elbow & thigh.
Allin, T.R.	L/Cpl	Ply8687	Legation Guard	Pekin	26 June	Shell wound to left shoulder.
Anwyle, F.	Sto	283173	Centurion			Shell wound to foot.
Ashley, C.R.	Pte	Ply8820	Aurora	Tientsin	13 July	Bullet wound to right foot.
Aymer, F.	AB	161550	Orlando	Langfang	18 June	Bullet wound to right shoulder.
Bailey, G.	Gunr	RMA6505	Barfleur	Tientsin	12 July	Bullet wound to right shoulder.
Bamber, W.L.	Lieut		Centurion	Peitsang	21 June	Bullet wound to buttock.
Barge, L.	AB	185726	Orlando	Langfang	18 June	Shell wound to penis & pubic region.
Barrett, J.	AB	144271	Terrible	Tientsin	8 July	Shell wound to right arm (shattered).
Bastard, G.	AB	183036	Centurion	Peitsang	21 June	Bullet wounds to right arm & right hand.
Bate, A.	AB	180843	Aurora	Hsiku	22 June	Bullet wound to hip.
Beach, H.	AB	176923	Centurion	Hsiku	23 June	Bullet wound to left calf.
Beatty, D.	Comdr		Barfleur	Langfang	19 June	Wounds to left hand & shoulder.
Bevis, A.	AB	183480	Centurion	Peitsang	21 June	Bullet wounds to head & right side of face, causing total loss of sight in both eyes.
Bicknell, D.	AB	147106	Orlando	Langfang	18 June	Bullet wound to left arm.
Bigg, F.W.	AB	185001	Centurion	Hsiku	22 June	Bullet wound to left forearm.
Bone, E.	AB	184684	Centurion	Tientsin	27 June	Bullet wound to abdomen.
Bonner, W.	AB	190471	Orlando	Tientsin	27 June	Superficial wound of abdomen.
Bowden, J.J.	Pte	Ch5943	Barfleur	Langfang	17 June	Wound to right ankle.
Bowhey, A.	Ord	192846	Endymion	Tientsin	27 June	Bullet wound to right leg.
Braithwaite, L.	Sub Lieut		Endymion	Hsiku	22 June	Bullet wounds to face & tongue.
Breeds, F.	Ord	191559	Centurion	Peitsang	21 June	Bullet wound to left thigh.
Brennan, F.W.	AB	190529	Terrible	Tientsin	9 July	Shell wound to head & right eye.
Brien, J.	Sto	286629	Centurion	Peitsang	21 June	Bullet wound to chest.
Brewster, J.R.	Pte	Ply3436	Barfleur	Tientsin	13 July	Bullet wounds to both hands.
Bridges, G.	Blk/Mte	340374	Centurion	Tientsin	3 July	Bullet wound to right leg.
Brown, A.	L/Cpl	Ply6094	Aurora	Langfang	18 June	Bullet wound to buttock (flesh wound).
Browne, G.C.	Midn		Barfleur	Langfang	18 June	Wound to right thigh.
Browne, R.J.	Pte	Po9583	Terrible	Tientsin	13 July	Wounds to right thigh & left leg.
Buchan, M.	Gunr	RMA5217	Barfleur	Langfang	17 June	Wound to right leg.
Buck, J.B.	AB	179110	Barfleur	Langfang	18 June	Bullet wound to right foot.
Buckler, J.	Pte	Po9286	Legation Guard	Pekin	1 July	Wounded in action.
Burke, C.D.	Midn		Centurion	Peitsang	21 June	Bullet wound to right thigh.
Butler, E.	Ord	188464	Barfleur	Langfang	18 June	Wound to neck.
Button, H.	Ord	193432	Centurion	Tientsin	4 July	Bullet wound to right hand.
Carter, H.	Bugler	Po8394	Terrible	Tientsin	27 June	Bullet wound to leg.
Catlin, E.	Ord	197796	Aurora	Tientsin	27 June	Bullet wounds to both thighs.
Chapman, W.C.	PO1	124133	Centurion	Hsiku	23 June	Bullet wounds to right ankle & right arm.

Charles, G.	PO1	129795	Endymion	Langfang	18 June	Bullet wound to left leg.
Christie, J.	Sto	287577	Endymion	Hsiku	23 June	Wound to left thigh,
Clapson, G.	Gunr	RMA5734	Centurion	Tientsin	27 June	Bullet wound to left thigh.
Clark, A.V.	AB	190788	Orlando	Langfang	18 June	Wounded behind left ear.
Clark, G.	AB	103747	Centurion	Hsiku	23 June	Bullet wound to left leg.
Cole, E.	AB	171400	Orlando	Langfang	18 June	Bullet wound to left scapula.
Coleman, W.	AB	196191	Centurion	Hsiku	23 June	Bullet wound to left arm.
Coles, H.	AB	187899	Orlando	Langfang	18 June	Bullet wound to right elbow.
Collett, J.E.	AB	188370	Barfleur	Langfang	18 June	Bullet wounds to face & right foot.
Collier, R.K.	AB	183066	Barfleur	Tientsin	13 July	Bullet wound to right heel.
Colomb, H.W.	Lieut		Endymion	Peitsang Tientsin	21 June 27 June	Bullet wound to face. Bullet wounds to right leg & hip.
Conning, H.R.	L/Shpt	340653	Barfleur	Hsiku	23 June	Wounds to right elbow & leg.
Cooper, A.	AB	189055	Barfleur	Tientsin	11 July	Shell wound to left side.
Cooper, G.F.	Sergt	Ply4978	Aurora	Tientsin	13 July	Bullet wound to left thigh.
Cooper, J.	Pte	Po8775	Terrible	Tientsin	27 June	Bullet wound to leg.
Corber, S.S.	AB	163298	Algerine	Taku Forts	17 June	Shell wound to chest.
Corbett, G.	Sto	282964	Centurion	Hsiku	22 June	Bullet wound to left shoulder.
Cowell, J.	Pte	Ch6170	Wei-Hai-Wei	Tientsin	11 July	Shell wound to face & lower jaw.
Crews, W.J.	Ord	203576	Algerine	Taku Forts	17 June	
Crockford, A.J.	Sto	288538	Orlando	Langfang	18 June	Wound to right ankle & heel.
Cudd, J.A.	AB	162488	Aurora	Tientsin	4 July	Shell wound to face (loss of right eye).
Cuell, A.J.	Pte	Po7514	Terrible	Tientsin	13 July	Wound to left hand.
Culmer, A.H.	AB	193079	Barfleur	Tientsin	13 July	Wound to left thigh.
Cunningham, J.	AB	186540	Orlando	Langfang	18 June	Bullet wounds to left leg & right forearm.
Curtis, J.E.	Ord	191750	Endymion			
Dale, W.T.J.	AB	187093	Barfleur	Langfang	18 June	Bullet wound to face.
Davey, J.	AB	184706	Centurion	Tientsin	2 July	Bullet wound to scalp.
Dean, T.	PO1	138435	Terrible	Tientsin	11 July	Bullet wound to right thigh.
Deane, J.	Pte	Ply8665	Legation Guard	Pekin	1 July	Bullet wound to left side.
Derkin, J.H.	AB	150763	Centurion	Hsiku	22 June	Bullet wound to neck.
Divers, H.T.	Sto	276104	Barfleur	Peitsang	21 June	Bullet wound to right thigh.
Downes, J.	AB	174723	Barfleur	Tientsin	13 July	Bullet wound to left foot.
Dunleavy, J.	Ord	188878	Orlando			Wound to leg.
Durrant, H.	Sto	281076	Barfleur	Peitsang	21 June	Wound to left foot.
Eastman, G.	L/Cpl	Po8976	Endymion	Hsiku	23 June	Bullet wound to left leg.
Edwards, J.	Sto	279781	Orlando	Hsiku	22 June	Shell wound to right cheek & bullet wound to left cheek.
Edwards, W.	Pte	Po8005	Terrible	Tientsin	13 July	Bullet wound to right shin.
Ellis, C.	Pte	Po4049	Terrible	Tientsin	13 July	Bullet wounds to both thighs.
Ellis, G.	Bosn		Centurion	Tientsin	9 July	Shell wound to right leg.

Evans, T.	Sto	281659	Centurion	Hsiku	23 June	Bullet wound to left shoulder.
Facey, A.J.	Sto	158342	Endymion			Bullet wound to left ankle.
Fair, G.McK.	Lieut		Centurion	Tientsin	9 July	Shell wound to left arm
Farley, J.R.	Pte	Po5968	Terrible	Tientsin	13 July	Wound to left arm.
Farmer, A.	AB	156955	Barfleur	Tientsin	13 July	Wound to left arm.
Farrant, W.H.	Pte	Ply7805	Aurora	Hsiku	23 June	Shell wound to left leg.
Fazackerley, J.	Sto	290674	Barfleur	Hsiku	23 June	Wounds to left elbow & back.
Felton, I.	Pte	Po8250	Centurion	Hsiku	23 June	Bullet wound to left elbow.
Field, F.L.	Lieut		Barfleur	Tientsin	13 July	Wound to scalp.
Field, G.H.	AB	149938	Barfleur	Hsiku	23 June	Wound to scalp.
Field, V.E.	Ord	197306	Barfleur	Langfang	18 June	Bullet wound to lower jaw.
Fitz, H.P.	AB	171632	Orlando	Langfang	18 June	Wounds to neck & chest.
Fletcher, C.	AB	187913	Orlando	Tientsin	13 July	Bullet wound to leg (fractured fibula).
Fleullen, H.	Ord	192781	Endymion	Tientsin	27 June	Bullet wound to shoulder.
Ford, W.	Ord	197743	Endymion	Langfang	18 June	Bullet wound to chest.
Fryer, G.	AB	125018	Centurion	Tientsin	7 July	Shell wound to right foot.
Gagg, C.	AB	153942	Aurora	Tientsin	13 July	Bullet wound to leftside of head.
Gardner, D.C.	AB	188610	Centurion	Hsiku	23 June	Bullet wound to right arm.
Garrod, F.	Gunr	RMA4835	Barfleur	Tientsin	27 June	Bullet wound of hip.
Gibbs, V.P.	Midn		Barfleur	Peitsang	21 June	Wound to scalp.
Gill, S.	Pte	Po9554	Endymion	Hsiku	23 June	Bullet wound to right leg.
Glew, J.	Ord	194653	Orlando			Wound to chest wall.
Goddard, G.	Pte	Po9255	Legation Guard	Pekin	24 June	Wounded in action.
Godfrey, W.J.	Sto	276417	Orlando	Langfang	18 June	Bullet wound to right leg (fractured femur).
Golden, P.	Ord	193873	Barfleur	Langfang	19 June	Wound to left thigh.
Good, R.	Pte	Ch6887	Wei-Hai-Wei	Langfang	18 June	Bullet wound to right arm.
Gordon, F.	PO1	101621	Endymion	Peitsang	21 June	Bullet wound to right shoulder.
Gowney, D.J.	Cpl	Po5082	Legation Guard	Pekin	3 July	Shell wound to left arm.
Green, G.H.	Ord	187014	Barfleur	Tientsin		Struck by a stray bullet, left side of vertex.
Greenfield, J.	Pte	Ch9675	Legation Guard	Pekin	9 July	Wound to scalp.
Gregory, W.	Cpl	Ply6529	Legation Guard	Pekin	3 July	Wound to right foot.
Gunn, S.	Sergt	Ply5107	Centurion	Hsiku	23 June	Bullet wound to left thigh.
Haden, S.W.	Pte	Ply8630	Legation Guard	Pekin	1 July	Bullet wound to right thigh.
Hagger, E.	AB	184736	Centurion	Hsiku	22 June	Bullet wound to left knee.
Haines, J.	Pte	Po8757	Endymion	Hsiku	23 June	Bullet wounds to both thighs.
Hales, F.L.	PO2	127090	Algerine	Taku Forts	17 June	Shell wound to right elbow.
Hall, H.F.	Cpl	Ply6863	Aurora	Langfang	18 June	Bullet wound to right forearm (flesh wound).
Hall, J.	Ord	192113	Orlando			Shell wound causing general contusions.
Halliday, L.S.T.	Capt(RMLI)		Legation Guard	Pekin	24 June	Wound to left shoulder.
Hammond, H.	Pte	Ch9679	Wei-Hai-Wei	Langfang	18 June	Bullet wound to right shoulder.
Hargreaves, H.J.	Asst/Payr		Algerine	Taku Forts	17 June	Shell wound to abdomen, right hand & left leg.

Name	Rank	No.	Ship/Unit	Place	Date	Wound
Harries, C.	Cpl	Ply8666	Wei-Hai-Wei	Langfang	18 June	Bullet wound to right elbow
Harvey, F.	Sto	286335	Barfleur	Tientsin	27 June	Bullet wounds to left knee & left leg.
Harvey, W.	AB	143475	Barfleur	Tientsin	13 July	Bullet wound to cheek & shoulder. Later died of dysentery 30 July.
Hawkes, W.	Ord	185260	Barfleur	Tientsin	13 July	Wounds to face, jaw & thigh.
Heald, B.	PO1	127109	Barfleur	Tientsin	11 July	Shell wound to right leg.
Heap, J.W.	Pte	Po8605	Legation Guard	Pekin	1 July	Wound to left thigh.
Helyar, J.	Pte	Ply8828	Aurora	Tientsin	13 July	Bullet wound to left arm.
Hill, S.	PO2	165126	Centurion	Tientsin	9 July	Shell wound to left leg.
Hoare, F.	AB	143508	Aurora	Tientsin	27 June	Bullet wound to thigh.
Hodges, T.	AB	156375	Endymion	Tientsin	27 June	Bullet wounds to shoulder & neck.
Holmes, J.N.	AB	197100	Orlando	Langfang	18 June	Wound to right shoulder.
Holness, A.	AB	169063	Barfleur	Tientsin	5 July	Bullet wound to back.
Homan, E.A.	Midn		Endymion	Peitsang	21 June	Bullet wound to left calf.
Hood, F.G.K.	AB	158460	Orlando	Langfang	18 June	Bullet wound to neck(thyroid).
Horne, W.	Pte	Po8816	Legation Guard	Pekin	30 June	Wounded in action.
Hosier, T.	AB	150891	Centurion	Peitsang	21 June	Bullet wounds to right thigh & right buttock.
Howard, T.	Sto	288981	Orlando	Langfang	18 June	Bullet wound to left leg.
Hunt, G.S.	Pte	Ply8831	Aurora	Tientsin	13 July	Bullet wound to back.
Hussey, F.J.	AB	178735	Orlando	Langfang	17 June	Wounds to chest, shoulder & thigh. Noted as died 30 October, but cause of death not stated.
Hutton, A.J.	Pte	Ch10298	Aurora			Bullet wound to left foot.
Ivery, G.	Pte	Po8878	Centurion	Hsiku	23 June	Bullet wound to left leg.
Jellicoe, J.R.	Capt		Centurion	Peitsang	21 June	Bullet wound to left leg.
Jennings, A.	Sto	286340	Centurion	Hsiku	22 June	Bullet wounds to left leg & left hand.
Jones, A.	Pte	Po8209	Endymion			
Jones, A.	Pte	Po2466	Terrible	Tientsin	4 July	Wounds to left elbow caused by gun explosion.
Jones, E.	L/S	169432	Endymion	Hsiku	22 June	Bullet wound to left arm.
Jordan, J.	AB	173932	Centurion	Peitsang	21 June	Bullet wound to right thigh.
Jordan, J.F.	AB	170312	Alacrity	Taku Forts	17 June	Bullet wounds to right arm & nose.
Kerwin, H.J.	AB	179577	Barfleur	Tientsin	13 July	Bullet wound to left arm.
Kinch, G.	Ord	196771	Endymion	Langfang	18 June	Bullet wound to left ankle.
King, G.	Sto	162648	Orlando			Wound to left shin.
King, K.	Pte	Ply8333	Legation Guard	Pekin	1 July	Bullet wound to left side.
Kingsley, J.G.	AB	156151	Aurora	Tientsin	8 July	Bullet wound to right foot.
Kippen, C.	Pte	Po6974	Centurion	Tientsin	27 June	Bullet wounds to back, side & right arm.
Kite, H.	Sto	169059	Endymion	Langfang	18 June	Bullet wound to left arm.
Lawrie, F.B.	Lieut(RMLI)		Terrible	Tientsin	23 June	Wound to right thigh.
Layton, A.T.	Pte	Ch9640	Legation Guard	Pekin	4 July	Wounds to face & neck.
Leaney, J.	Sto	253190	Barfleur			Bullet wound to left leg.
Lewis, A.	AB	157596	Centurion	Peitsang	21 June	Bullet wounds to chest & left thigh.
Livermore, A.	AB	183633	Centurion	Hsiku	22 June	Bullet wound to chest.

Lockyer, W.	AB	182455	Centurion	Tientsin	7 July	Shell wound to left leg.
Logan, W.	Pte	Po9558	Endymion	Hsiku	23 June	Bullet wound to left forearm.
Lowen, H.	Pte	Po9567	Endymion			Bullet wound to left knee.
Luke, E.V.	Major(RMLI)		Barfleur	Tientsin	5 July	Bullet wound to scalp.
McDonald, J.	Sto	288492	Orlando	Tientsin	9 July	Wound to neck.
McElligott, M.	AB	151904	Centurion	Peitsang	21 June	Bullet wounds to chest.
McKee, G.	AB	186414	Centurion	Hsiku	23 June	Bullet wound to abdomen.
Marr, J.E.	Pte	Po6918	Orlando	Langfang	19 June	Wounds to right shoulder, neck & chest.
Martin, W.H.	AB	187098	Barfleur	Tientsin	13 July	Bullet wound to right arm.
Mason, E.	AB	188006	Orlando	Hsiku	22 June	Bullet wounds to chest, right hand & shoulder.
Mason, J.W.	AB	184515	Orlando			Wounds to both hands.
Massey, F.T.	AB	184357	Orlando	Hsiku	23 June	Abrasion to left shoulder.
May, W.	Gunr(RN)		Alacrity	Tientsin	27 June	Bullet wound to right foot.
Meerin, W.	AB	160692	Endymion	Taku Forts	17 June	Bullet wound to left arm.
Merchant, R.	AB	188076	Barfleur	Taku Forts	17 June	Bullet wound to right thigh.
Merritt, C.W.	Sig	191274	Endymion	Langfang	18 June	Shell wound to right knee.
Merwood, F.	AB	191041	Orlando	Langfang	18 June	Bullet wound to right arm.
Mesor, C.	Sto	285199	Endymion	Langfang	18 June	Bullet wound to left thigh.
Miller, H.C.	Sergt	RMA3413	Centurion	Hsiku	23 June	Bullet wounds to right thigh & scrotum.
Milroy, W.	Sto	282207	Orlando	Langfang	18 June	Bullet wound to right foot.
Mintram, A.	Ord	186700	Centurion	Hsiku	22 June	Bullet wounds to left thigh & right shoulder.
Mitchell, G.	AB	170362	Endymion	Langfang	18 June	Bullet wound to left breast.
Morgan, W.	AB	182941	Centurion	Hsiku	23 June	Bullet wound to left hand.
Mowatt, W.H.T.	L/S	160158	Orlando	Langfang	18 June	Wound to chest.
Mulford, B.	L/Sto	158581	Orlando	Langfang	18 June	Bullet wound to left leg.
Mullins, G.	Capt(RMLI)		Terrible	Tientsin	6 July	Wounds to left arm caused by gun explosion.
Munro, A.	AB	183981	Barfleur	Tientsin	13 July	Bullet wound to right calf.
Murrell, W.	Sto	281335	Orlando	Langfang	18 June	Bullet wounds to both thighs.
Negus, C.	Ord	187722	Centurion	Peitsang	21 June	Bullet wound to right foot.
Nethercott, C.	Ord	193431	Endymion	Langfang	18 June	Bullet wound to right shoulder.
Newcombe, W.	PO1	155132	Barfleur	Langfang	19 June	Wound to right leg.
Norman, W.C.	AB	169038	Orlando	Langfang	18 June	Wound to left knee.
Oakley, J.	L/Cpl	Ch7612	Endymion	Hsiku	23 June	Bullet wound to left leg & shell wound to right knee.
Oliver, J.	AB	173838	Algerine	Taku Forts	17 June	Shell wound to right elbow.
Ott, G.	AB	185259	Barfleur	Langfang	19 June	Wound to left leg.
Parks, A.E.	Ch/PO	125081	Barfleur	Taku Forts	17 June	Bullet wound to left thigh.
Parsonage, W.	AB	185723	Aurora	Langfang	19 June	Wound to left thigh (flesh wound).
Parsons, E.J.	AB	181553	Barfleur	Hsiku	23 June	Wound to right leg.
Parsons, G.	Ord	195630	Endymion	Langfang	18 June	Bullet wound to thigh.
Parsons, J.H.	Sto	288549	Orlando			Wound to ankle.
Payne, T.C.	AB	147713	Orlando			Wound to right shoulder.

Peck, H.	Sergt	Po2704	Terrible	Tientsin	4 July	Shell wound to back.
Pittock, W.C.	AB	183712	Barfleur	Langfang	19 June	Wound to nose.
Plant, F.	Ch/PO	117099	Barfleur	Tientsin	13 July	Bullet wound to left thigh.
Polkinghorne, E.F.	Bugler	Ch9943	Wei-Hai-Wei	Tientsin	13 July	Bullet wound to left arm.
Powell, G.B.	Lieut		Aurora	Langfang	19 June	Wound to chest.
Prynn, T.	AB	178330	Aurora			Bullet wound to right side of abdomen.
Quaife, A.	Pte	Po7958	Endymion	Hsiku	23 June	Bullet wound to left leg.
Reddan, P.	AB	195969	Endymion			Wounded in action.
Rees, J.	AB	185409	Orlando	Tientsin	9 July	Shell wound to left leg.
Reeve, A.	Cpl	Po7060	Wei-Hai-Wei	Langfang	18 June	Bullet wound to left leg.
Riseborough, J.	AB	180352	Barfleur	Tientsin	13 July	Wound to left foot.
Robertson, L.H.C.	Ord	189945	Terrible	Tientsin	13 July	Wound to right knee.
Robinson, E.G.	Midn		Endymion	Tientsin	27 June	Wound to left arm.
Roe, W.	Pte	Po8935	Legation Guard	Pekin	16 July	Wound to left shoulder.
Rogers, W.H.	L/S	157415	Centurion	Peitsang	20 June	Bullet wound to right shoulder.
Roper, E.	Sergt	Po4952	Terrible	Tientsin	27 June	Bullet wound to head (Injury to brain & right eye).
Rose, C.	L/S	160886	Endymion	Taku Forts	17 June	Bullet wound to right arm.
Roskelly, J.	Ord	193310	Endymion	Langfang	18 June	Bullet wound to buttock.
Roskruge, S.	AB	194507	Aurora	Peitsang	20 June	Bullet wound to left knee (flesh wound).
Rudgely, W.E.	Pte	Po8654	Terrible	Tientsin	13 July	Wound to left thigh.
Salter, E.C.	Ord	187300	Barfleur	Langfang	19 June	Bullet wound to right shoulder.
Samphier, H.	L/S	137166	Centurion	Hsiku	22 June	Bullet wound to left arm & breast.
Samways, G.	AB	153532	Orlando	Hsiku	23 June	Bullet wounds to chest, arm, back & left wrist.
Schiller, F.O.von	AB	187161	Barfleur			Bullet wounds to scalp & scapula.
Searle, J.	Pte	Ch8612	Centurion	Hsiku	23 June	Bullet wound to abdomen.
Shailer, T.	Sto	111634	Centurion	Langfang	14 June	Bayonet wound to left thigh.
Shea, J.	AB	195886	Orlando	Hsiku	22 June	
Shea, R.	AB	179757	Aurora	Tientsin	27 July	Bullet wound to thumb.
Shepherd, J.	Pte	Ply8814	Aurora	Langfang	18 June	Bullet wound to right arm (flesh wound).
Sherwin, H.	AB	173855	Terrible	Tientsin	3 July	Superficial wound to back.
Shilston, A.	PO1	121405	Centurion	Tientsin	4 July	Shell wound to back.
Shore, L.	Midn		Barfleur	Tientsin	25 June	Bullet wound to thigh.
Simmons, J.W.	AB	190465	Endymion	Peitsang	21 June	Shell wound to left shoulder. Died of tetanus 30 June.
Smith, F.	Pte	Ply4983	Centurion	Hsiku	23 June	Bullet wound to right shoulder.
Smith, J.	Ord	191864	Centurion	Hsiku	22 June	Bullet wound to right thigh.
Smith, M.	Arm	129367	Centurion	Hsiku	22 June	Bullet wounds to chest, left hand & left thigh.
Smyth, W.	AB	151609	Aurora			Shell wound to left wrist.
Snook, C.	Pte	Ch8875	Wei-Hai-Wei	Tientsin	27 June	Bullet wound to both legs.
Solen, J.T.	Pte	Po4379	Centurion	Hsiku	23 June	Bullet wound to right thigh.
Sparkes, W.J.	L/Cpl	Po8604	Legation Guard	Pekin	27 June	Wound to left eye.
Stanbridge, A.	Cpl	Po4073	Terrible	Tientsin	13 July	Bullet wound to right hand.

Staples, E.	Sig	185724	Orlando	Peitsang	21 June	Shell wound to right arm.
Staughton, A.	Cpl	Ply8216	Aurora	Tientsin	27 June	Bullet wounds to both legs.
Stirling, A.J.B.	Lieut		Barfleur	Langfang	19 June	Fractured right thigh.
Sumpter, T.	Pte	Ply7390	Aurora	Hsiku	22 June	Bullet wound to right forearm.
Swallow, J.H.T.	Sto	286323	Barfleur	Hsiku	23 June	Wound to scalp.
Sweeney, P.	Sto	281630	Algerine	Taku Forts	17 June	
Symes, F.	L/S	165132	Endymion	Langfang	18 June	Bullet wound to right knee.
Symes, T.	AB	173324	Orlando	Langfang	18 June	Bullet wounds to both thighs.
Tabuteaux, A.E.	Clerk		Centurion	Peitsang	21 June	Bullet wound to right leg.
Taylor, A.	Pte	Po9241	Orlando	Tientsin	13 July	Bullet wounds to right arm & foot.
Taylor, R.	Ord	189229	Barfleur	Tientsin	13 July	Shell wounds to hip & right shoulder(amputated).
Thom, A.	Ord	186919	Barfleur	Langfang	19 June	Bullet wound to left leg.
Thomas, F.	L/Sig	162913	Algerine	Taku Forts	17 June	
Thomas, H.	PO1	126498	Orlando	Langfang	18 June	Wounds to face & neck.
Thompson, W.	AB	169625	Orlando			Contusions to right knee.
Thurger, C.	PO1	113132	Barfleur	Tientsin	11 July	Bullet wound to right side.
Tickner, A.J.	Pte	Ch9672	Legation Guard	Pekin	30 June	Wounds to both legs.
Tidmas, G.	Pte	Po7148	Wei-Hai-Wei	Langfang	18 June	Bullet wounds to left arm & thigh.
Toal, J.W.	Sto	282730	Centurion	Hsiku	23 June	Bullet wound to back.
Tooze, S.J.S.	PO1	156075	Centurion	Hsiku	22 June	Bullet wound to left breast.
Townsend, W.	AB	169987	Alacrity	Tientsin	27 June	Bullet wound to right foot.
Tubby, C.W.	Ord	188805	Barfleur	Langfang	19 June	Bullet wound to leftside of neck.
Versey, J.	AB	185307	Barfleur	Langfang	18 June	Wound to left elbow joint.
Wakefield, J.	Pte	Ch8812	Barfleur	Langfang	17 June	Wound to right axilla.
Walker, D.	Pte	Po8695	Terrible	Tientsin	4 July	Shell wound to right knee.
Walsh, T.	Ord	194545	Endymion	Tientsin	27 June	Bullet wound to head.
Watson, G.W.	Ord	194444	Orlando	Tientsin	24 June	Bullet wounds to abdomen & right forearm.
Watt, S.	Pte	Po8758	Terrible	Tientsin	13 July	Bullet wound or graze above right ear.
Wellard, H.	AB	117015	Orlando	Tientsin	8 July	Shell wound to right side.
Westbrook, A.E.	Pte	Po9113	Legation Guard	Pekin	13 July	Wound to left forearm.
Whaley, W.	PO1	102529	Centurion	Hsiku	22 June	Bullet wound to right arm.
White, F.J.	Ord	191558	Barfleur	Terrible	13 July	Bullet wound to right achilles tendon.
Whitmore, A.	AB	162314	Orlando	Langfang	18 June	Wounds to both thighs.
Wilkinson, F.W.	Sto	282983	Centurion	Hsiku	23 June	Bullet wound to face.
Wilson, F.	Midn		Centurion	Peitsang	21 June	Bullet wounds to left elbow & back.
Wilson, W.	AB	139993	Centurion	Peitsang	21 June	Bullet wounds to both hands & left breast.
Wiltshire, H.W.	Ord	190171	Algerine	Taku Forts	17 June	Shell wound to right arm & foot.
Wood, S.	AB	178503	Orlando	Tientsin	13 July	Wound to front of abdomen.
Woodward, W.T.	Pte	Po8926	Legation Guard	Pekin	3 July	Wound to left eye.
Wrangles, G.	Gunr	RMA4790	Barfleur	Tientsin	6 July	Wounds to right arm & left hand caused by gun explosion resulting in amputation.

Wray, E.	Capt(RMLI)		Legation Guard	Pekin	2 July	Bullet wound to left shoulder.
Wright, P.N.	Lieut		Orlando	Langfang	19 June	Shell wound to skull. Died in London 27 June 1901 after an operation.
Wright, R.	AB	167503	Endymion	Langfang	18 June	Bullet wound to right leg (fractured tibia).
Wyatt, E.J.	AB	171606	Endymion	Taku Forts	17 June	Bullet wound to thigh.
Wynn, W.J.	Pte	Ply8839	Aurora	Tientsin	13 July	Bullet wound to right forearm.
Yates, B.	Ord	192941	Endymion	Langfang	18 June	Bullet wound to left knee.
Young, D.O.G.	Ord	187771	Barfleur	Hsiku	23 June	Bullet wound to back.
Young, F.	Pte	Po9347	Orlando	Langfang	17 June	Wound to left foot.

The London Gazette.

Published by Authority.

Admiralty, 1st October 1900.

Despatches of which the following are copies, have been received from the Commander-in-Chief and the Rear Admiral on the China station, relative to the attempted relief of the legations at Peking; the capture of the Taku forts; the operations at Tientsin:-

Letter No. 384, from Commander-in-Chief on the China Station, dated 27th June 1900.

Combined Naval Expedition to attempt the Relief of Legations at Peking. No. 384.

Sir, **Tientsin, 27th June 1900**

With reference to my Submission No. 336 of 30th May forwarding copies of telegrams I had received from H.M. Minister on the above subject, I have the honour to report the course of events since that date.

On 29th May I received a telegram from H.M. Consul at Tientsin reporting that Fengtai, the railway station next to Peking, had been burnt, also five stations on the Peking-Hankau line, and on the following day (30th) H.M. Minister at Peking informed me that the situation there was "extremely grave", the soldiers mutinous and people very excited," and that European life and property was in danger.

Both the "Orlando" and "Algerine" were then at Taku, and thirteen ships of various nationalities. The "Algerine" on her arrival on 30th had immediately disembarked twenty-five marines, who had been sent up as a guard for the Legation at Peking before it was known that affairs had assumed such a serious aspect. On the following day the "Orlando" landed fifty marines and sixty-seven seamen and the "Algerine" ten seamen. The "Algerine's" men were subsequently sent back to their ship, from which they could not well be spared, and were replaced on 4th June by a field gun's crew from "Centurian".

The men were disposed as follows:- Captain Bernard M. Strouts, R.M.L.I., commanding Tientsin Winter Guard; Captain Lewis S.T. Halliday, R.M.L.I. H.M.S. "Orlando"; Captain Edmund Wray, R.M.L.I., Wei-hai-wei detachment; 25 marines, Tientsin Winter Guard; 26 marines, H.M.S. "Orlando"; 25 marines, Wei-hai-wei detachment; making a total of 79 officers and men at Peking, and 104 seamen and marines at Tientsin.

The guards for Peking arrived there on 31st May by train, the total number of all nationalities forwarded to Peking being 337.

After receiving the Minister's telegram before mentioned, I decided, in view of the gravity of the situation, to proceed off Taku myself, and left on the afternoon of 31st with "Whiting" in company, leaving the Rear-Admiral (H.M.S. "Barfleur") at Wei-hai-wei, with orders to send on "Endymion", which was expected there the next day, and also the "Fame."

On arrival off Taku (13 miles distant from the anchorage) on 1st June, I telegraphed at once to H.M. Minister and informed him I was prepared to land two hundred more seamen and marines, and awaited an intimation of his wishes. On 2nd June a telegram from him was received (dated the previous day) stating that the guards had arrived at Peking without any opposition, and that affairs were quieter, at the same time asking if I was coming up. This I could not do, but on 3rd June I landed at Tongku and went to Tientsin by train to see the arrangements made for our guards, and also to have some conversation with our Consul, and learn as far as I could the actual state of affairs at Tientsin and in the neighbourhood.

While there, I heard that an attack had been made a day or two previously on an armed party of over thirty Belgians who were coming in with their families from Pao-ting-fu, on the Peking-Hankau railway line now under construction. It was supposed that some of the party had been killed as nine were missing.

I was also informed of the murder of an English missionary, Mr. Robinson, and the abduction of another, Mr. Norman, at Yung ching, some thirty miles from Tientsin. Bishop Scott asked me to send out a party to attempt to rescue Mr. Norman, but before any action could be taken it was ascertained that he too had been murdered.

The situation at the Palace was said to be strained, the Dowager Empress being credited with a wish to put down the Boxers, but not daring to do so on account of their numbers and support by some of the princes. It was rumoured that she contemplated withdrawing from Peking to the ancient capital, Sian Fu, in Shensi Province. My object in going to Tientsin was also partly to return to Taku by river in order to know something about it in case we required to use it for transport, etc. This I did and returned to my flagship.

On 4th June a gun's crew and gun were sent up from "Centurion" to Tientsin in response to a request from the Consul, and on 5th a force of one hundred men from "Centurion" was sent to H.M.S. "Algerine" in the river off Taku to be ready for immediate landing if required, as the distance at which the ships lie from Taku, about thirteen miles, causes great delay in receiving messages; and sending in men such a long distance over a bar, which can only be crossed even by a steamboat at near high-water, loses several hours.

Matters remaining serious and the gravity of the situation in no way abated, but likely to increase, the Chinese Government being up to this time quite inactive, although the "Boxers" were near Tientsin in force and had committed outrages such as destroying property and burning railway in several places, I proposed to Rear-Admiral Courejolles (French), then the next Senior Naval Officer present on the 5th instant, that the Senior Naval Officers should meet together to discuss the situation and arrange for mutual action. Rear-Admiral Courejolles agreed, and suggested that the meeting should be held on board "Centurion", in which I acqueisced, and at 4 p.m. the same day our first meeting took place, officers of seven nations besides our own being present The proceedings were marked by great unanimity.

On 5th June I received a requisition from H.M. Consul at Tientsin for a vessel to protect Pei-tai-ho (a watering place a few miles south of Shan-hai-kuan) as several British subjects and much British property were there. I informed him that I would send a ship there to protect lives of Europeans and to embark them if necessary, but that I was unable to give protection to property, and that British subjects if in danger should embark and go to Chifu. The "Humber", then at Wei-hai-wei, was ordered to proceed there, taking twenty-five marines in addition to her own crew. I sent her partly because she has accommodation for people.

The "Aurora", which had arrived at Wei-hai-wei on 4th June, was ordered to Taku in case a larger landing force became necessary, and arrived on 7th.

Having received a message from H.M. Consul requesting an increase in guard, fifty seamen of "Centurion" were sent to Tientsin on 6th, and also seventy-five marines. The latter were to be sent on to Peking if required by H.M. Minister, from whom I have received an inquiry whether that number could be spared, without stating whether they were actually required or whether he was only making an inquiry in case of further developments.

On the 5th June the Consul in a telegram advocated permission being given to guards "to take active measures of hostility", but this I did not accede to, my view being that our mission here was solely for the protection of European lives, and property also, as far as might be, with which my colleagues concurred.

On 6th a meeting of the Senior Naval Officers was again held, and it was generally agreed that in case communication with Peking became cut off it should be reopened, using whatever force was necessary with this object.

The Austrian Captain informed me that he would be glad if his men at Tientsin might be placed under the orders of the Senior British Naval Officer at Tientsin. I thanked him for the honour he paid me by making this request, and I instructed the officer in charge of our guards accordingly.

Rumours were afloat that the Boxers intended to attack the Foreign Settlements at Tientsin on 19th June, the aniversary of the massacres there in 1870. If this was to have been carried out the community should have been fully prepared to meet them.

On 7th June I received intelligence that General Nich, who had been ordered by the Chinese Government to march on the rebels then assembled in great force twenty miles from Tientsin, had an engagement and had killed five hundred. It appears from subsequent information that this number was greatly exaggerated.

On the morning of 9th June another conference of the Foreign Senior Naval Officers took place. On the same day, at about 11.30p.m., I received an urgent telegram from H.M. Minister informing me that unless those in Peking were relieved soon it would be too late. I immediately acquainted my colleagues with the tenor of the telegram, at the same time informing them that I was starting with all our available men at once, and expressed a hope that they would co-operate.

The officers and men of the squadron were then sent in to Tongku, in "Fame", "Whiting" and a tug, and about 6 a.m. were entrained and reached Tientsin about 7.30 a.m. After paying a visit to H.M. Consul, the train started about 9.30 a.m. for Peking. The numbers in the train were as follows:- 300 British, 112 United States, 28 Austrian, and 40 Italian.

The train proceeded without any obstacle beyond Yungtsun, near which there was a camp of four thousand Chinese troops under General Nich. About 3.30 p.m. the train had to be stopped for repair of damages to railway a few miles this side of Lofa, and remained for the night.

Two more trains joined here, bringing up the total force to (62 officers, 640 seamen, and 213 marines) 915 British, 25 Austrian, 40 Italian, 100 French, 450 German, 54 Japanese, 112 Russians, 112 United States.

Early next mroning (June 11th) the trains proceeded to Lofa Station, where the engines were watered.

A fourth train joined here with two hundred Russians and fifty-eight French, making a total force of over two thousand. The train proceeded at 11.30 a.m. A guard of one officer and thirty men (afterwards reinforced to sixty) was left at Lofa to protect the line.

About 6 p.m. when beyond some three miles short of Langfang Station, some "Boxers" were seen approaching; they had previously endeavoured to cut off an advanced party with railway repairing gear, but had failed, and now came to the attack of No. 1 train; they advanced in skirmishing order, and were soon repulsed by our rifle fire, leaving about thirty-five killed.

All trains proceeded to Langfang (June 12th) as soon as the line was repaired. It was found that the line beyond had been much cut up, the damage being apparently done recently by bodies of men as we approached, and evidently not far ahead. As some time would have to be spent at Langfang repairing bridges etc., Lieutenant Smith of "Aurora", commanding her men, was sent with a party of three officers and forty-four men to try to get, if possible, to Anting, thirteen miles on, to prevent more damage being done to the line, and to hold the railway station there. He occupied a village on the line the following morning, and early in that morning was attacked by Boxers three times in succession, who, however, retreated on a few volleys being fired, with a loss of fifteen men. At 10.30 a final and more determined attack was made by about four hundred and fifty Boxers, who charged in line with great courage and enthusiasm, but were repulsed with heavy loss, estimated (with those killed in previous attacks) to be about 150. The party then being short of ammunition, Lieutenant Smith wisely decided to return, and rejoined at 2.30 p.m.

Major Johnstone, R.M.L.I., was sent forward in the afternoon (June 13th) with sixty men towards Anting, to try to prevent the line being broken up ahead. He was attacked by the Boxers in a village adjoining the railway a few miles on the railway, which had been destroyed for about a mile, and the sleepers etc., carried away. The "Boxers" lost about twenty-five killed, and there were no casualties on our side. He returned on the evening of 14th.

Langfang:- At about 10.15 a.m. (June 14th) the outposts were seen running in and reported the Boxers close to in great numbers; they were closely followed by the Boxers, who made a most determined rush at the fore part of the train which was then drawn up alongside a well, where many of our men were engaged in watering. They came on in great numbers in loose formation and with the utmost courage under a withering fire, some of them even reaching the train before they were killed. They did not retreat until they had suffered a loss of about one hundred. I regret to say that we have to deplore the loss of five Italians, who formed the picket near a deserted village, which was used by the Boxers to conceal their approach. At 5.30 p.m. a messenger arrived on a trolley from Lofa Station to report that the guard there was being attacked by a large body of the enemy. No. 2 train then being ready, I took it down the line at once to assist the Lofa guard. On arrival it was found that the brunt of the attack was over, the "Boxers" then being on the retreat; they were harrassed in their retreat by the reinforcements, and left about 100 killed behind. Two small canon were taken from them. I regret to say that two seamen belonging to H.M.S. "Endymion" were here wounded, one seriously, and the other dangerously, who has since died.

The trains remaining at Langfang (June 15th) while the line ahead was being repaired, a strong guard being detached with the construction train to protect the workers. A train which had been sent back to Lofa returned and reported that the line we had repaired had been much broken up again below that place. Later on, the officer of the station guard at Lofa came up with an engine and reported that he thought that an attack in force by the Boxers might be expected, and he had seen three large bodies moving about in the distance. They eventually moved off without attacking, being probably only making for the lower line to break it up towards Yungstun.

A train left at 4 p.m. (June 16th) to endeavour to get through to Tientsin, but came back at 3 p.m., having found the line too much destroyed to repair with their resources. It being evident that the line was much damaged between Yungtsun and Lofa, I decided to return and investigate, and left Langfang in No. 1 train at 4 p.m. Nos. 2 and 3 remained at Langfang, and No. 4 at Lofa, to follow later on if the development of affairs at those places seemed to render such a course desirable. It appeared to me probable that the attempt to relieve Peking might have to be made by river for the following reasons:-

1. We were so much delayed that more provisions were required by many of the force, and would in a very few days run short. Ammunition was also getting short.
2. It seemed unlikely we could get nearer Peking than Anting, or a little beyond it; some transport would be needed, and we could not go without it.
3. That we were quite cut off from our base, and ignorant of what was happening there having had no communication since 13th.
4. It was necessary to take some steps to protect the line in our rear as trains had ceased to run.

On the night of 16th-17th, No. 1 train remained on the line between Lofa and Yangtsun, and in the morning, as soon as repairs were effected, reached the latter place, where the station was found to be entirely demolished, communication by rail with Tientsin impossible to re-establish with the resources at disposal, and, consequently, no possibility of obtaining any supplies or necessaries.

A few days previously I had endeavoured to send down orders to Tientsin for junks, provisions, and ammunition to be sent to Yungtsun with a view to establishing a base there from which to start, if found desirable, by river to Tungchow, marching thence to Peking, as our alternative route. Not one of these couriers reached Tientsin, the surrounding country being at that time overrun with Boxers or hostile Chinese, but had they done so it would have been impossible to have complied with my requisition, owing to the state of affairs at Tientsin which was itself then in a state of siege and being bombarded by the Chinese. Of this I was in complete ignorance at the time, as no news whatever from outside reached me between 13th and 26th June. I had also tried to get messages to the General at Hong Kong to send immediately all available troops, having at the commencement of the march to Peking, when the hostility of the Chinese authorities and their active support of the Boxers was not known, only asked for the troops (650) then ready, whom it was intended to employ as guards at the railway stations selected to be held against attack by Boxers and for guard at Peking to enable men of the Fleet to return to their ships.

On 17th messages were sent back to Lofa and Langfang to recall Nos. 2, 3 and 4 trains, it being evident that the advance by rail was impossible, and the isolation and seperate destruction of the trains a possibility. No.3 returned on the afternoon of the 18th June, and in the evening Nos. 2 and 4 from Langfang. Captain Von Usedom (His Imperial German Majesty's Navy), the senior officer present with Nos. 2 and 4 trains, reported that they had had a severe engagement with the enemy, who unexpectedly attacked them at Langfang about 2.30 p.m. on that day (18th) in great force estimated to be fully 5,000 men (including cavalry), large numbers of whom were armed with magazine rifles of the latest pattern. The banners captured show them to have belonged to the army of General Tung Fu-Hsiang, who commands the Chinese troops in the Hunting Park outside Peking, and it was thus definitely known for the first time that Imperial Chinese troops were being employed against us. The attack was made in front and on both flanks, the enemy pouring in a heavy fire on the allied forces coming out to engage them; they were driven off with much loss, but when they saw our forces retiring towards the trains they rallied and made another attack; a halt was then made and the men were once more beaten off with greater loss than before, and then finally retreated. In this action the Chinese lost over 400 killed, the Allied forces 6 killed and 48 wounded.

While at Yangtsun we had endeavoured to open friendly relations with the headmen of the town (distant one mile), but their promises to furnish supplies were not fulfilled, probably owing to pressure from Boxers, who seemed to be in strength in the locality.

At a conference of the officers commanding, of various nationalities, it was decided on 19th June to desert the trains and withdraw to Tientsin, marching by the left bank of the river and conveying the wounded and necessaries in junks, four of which had been taken by the Germans from some Boxers below Yangtsun on the previous day.

Preparations were rapidly made, and the wounded having been safely embarked and made as comfortable as possible under the circumstances, a start was made at 3 p.m. Soon afterwards some delay was caused by the junks grounding in a shallow reach of the river, but when this difficulty had been overcome satisfactory progress was made and we bivouacked for the night 2½ miles down the river without further incident. A six-pounder Q.F. gun of "Centurion" had been thrown overboard to lighten one of the junks before she would float off.

Early on 20th June the march was resumed, progress being regulated by the speed of the junks with wounded, and none of our men being skilled in handling such craft, and Chinese being impossible to get, their movements retarded the advance of the forces on the river bank. At 9.15 the enemy opened fire on our approach to one of the villages; they were driven out after some resistance falling back on the next in our line of advance. Several villages in succession had to be carried either by rifle-fire, or, failing that, at the point of the bayonet. The charge with bayonets was always very effective, the cheers of the men as they advanced appearing to intimidate the Chinese, who without waiting to receive the charge, would fall back immediately. In the afternoon a one-pounder Q.F. gun was brought into action by the enemy for the first time, and although not much damage was actually done by it, the effect of its fire was harassing to those on the march, especially when an exposed space had to be crossed. Its position could not be accurately located as the nature of the country and the use of smokeless powder enabled them to mask its position both on this and subsequent occasions. After fighting during the whole day a suitable place for bivouac was selected at 6 p.m. The distance was made good during the day was estimated to be about eight miles.

March was resumed at 7.30 a.m. (June 21st). About an hour later a body of from 150 to 200 cavalry was observed in the distance on our left flank of advanced guard. At first it was hoped they might be Cossacks coming to our relief, but as they approached nearer to reconnoitre it was seen that they were Chinese troops. After satisfying themselves they withdrew, but hovered about the left flank for the remainder of the day, firing when favourable opportunities offered several well directed shrapnel from the nine-pounder did much to discourage them and to keep them at a distance.

A few minutes after the withdrawal of the cavalry referred to above the enemy opened fire with a field gun and one-pounder Q.F. Their fire was returned by our nine-pounder and machine guns, and the position of their field gun being disclosed by its smoke our fire was successful in checking it; although it was brought into action again during the day from time to time, but with the same result as soon as its position was known.

Fighting was carried on continuously throughout a succession of villages and in the town of Peitsang, which is the chief place between Tientsin and Yungtsun, and at 6 p.m., the enemy being then in a very strong position from which we were unable to dislodge them during the evening, a halt was made, and further movements considered. It was then decided that after supper and two or three hours' rest the forces should make a night march, starting after midnight as our best chance of getting through.

Our advance during 21st was probably not more than six miles owing to the stubborn resistance of the enemy and their increased gun power.

The field and machine guns had to be placed in a junk taken on the previous day, and at 1 a.m. (June 22nd) the march commenced. As we passed along fires were seen at one or two places a little distance off the river bank, evidently signalling our advance, but nothing occurred until about 1½ miles had been covered, when heavy fire was opened on the advance guard from a village about two hundred yards off in the direct line of advance. The marines then fixed bayonets and carried the position without further opposition.

The lighter containing our guns filled and sank about this time, probably owing to the fire of a field piece from ahead of us, and so had to be abandoned, the maxims only being saved.

At 4 a.m. we arrived opposite what proved to be the Imperial Chinese Armoury near Hsiku (on right bank of river). Two unarmed soldiers were seen coming out of a house one hundred yards from the bank, evidently to communicate. A halt was made to hear what they had to say, which was some simple enquiries as to who we were and where we were going etc. These advances seemed perfectly friendly and the men walked leisurely back to the house, which they had no sooner reached than a heavy fire was opened on us from rifles and several guns. Fortunately good cover was close at hand in a village, and behind the river embankment, which was immediately taken advantage of. The rear columns had not come up, nor the junks with the wounded, but the latter were carried down by the river before they could be brought up, and although placed in the best position possible under the circumstances could not be entirely sheltered and were occasionally struck.

Rifle fire was directed to a 47mm. Hotchkiss gun at the north corner of the armoury, and two 10cm guns on the river front. Some of the men at the guns were killed and others driven from them. Major Johnstone, R.M.L.I., of "Centurion", was then sent higher up the river to cross over unobserved with a party of 100 marines and seamen to rush the position at the north corner. There is a village about 150 yards from this which enabled the attacking force to come up without being seen until they emerged from it, when they charged with a cheer joined in by those on the other side of the river, and the Chinese in that part of the armoury fled precipitately. At the same time, lower down the river, a German detachment crossed over and captured two guns (10 cm. Krupp) in their front, and subsequently several others. The marines also took two more guns (47 mm. Krupp). The two detachments then cleared the whole armoury grounds.

In the afternoon the Chinese made a most determined but unsuccessful attempt to retake the armoury trying to drive us from the place by shell fire and to carry it by assault. Their losses were heavy, but we also suffered severely, losing, amongst others, Commander Bucholtz, Imperial German Navy, a valuable officer whose death was a blow, not only to the Germans, but to the whole force.

The main body of the forces and wounded crossed the river at 3 p.m., and occupied quarters in the armoury. Conditions and prospects were now somewhat better than they had been, as the place could be defended by the captured guns, but as provisions for only three days at half-allowance remained we were still in a somewhat precarious position.

The importance of communicating our position to our forces in Tientsin was urgent, as, to proceed by water was impossible, and to carry our wounded would take nearly all our force and leave no one to protect them. I had sent various messengers without success, and therefore on the eve of the 22nd, ordered Captains Richard O.M. Doig and Henry T.R. Lloyd, R.M.L.I., with 100 marines to start after dark and try to make their way into the foreign Settlement by a detour to the northward and along the railway. This was the route recommended by Mr. A. Currie C.E., of the Imperial Chinese railway, who accompanied our force for the repair of the line. Mr. Currie now gave his services as a guide. The party reached the railway and at once encountered active resistance, the alarm bugles sounded in various places, and having lost four of their number they had no option but to return to us.

At daylight (June 23rd) the Chinese made another unsuccessful attempt to retake the armoury which was continued until nearly 8 a.m. Captain Beyts, R.M.A. ("Centurion"), was killed while defending the east front, and there were several other casualties.

When everything was quiet and only a desultory shell fire kept up, a thorough search of the contents of the various buildings was made, about fifteen tons of rice being found. In the "armoury" we discovered immense supplies of guns, arms, ammunition, and war material of latest pattern. Their discovery gave us what we most needed, viz., food and ammunition, and enabled us, if need be, to hold out there for several days. The necessity of carrying our wounded - now 200 in number - prevented our forcing our way down to Tientsin. Efforts were made to convey there information of our position and condition, but the couriers were at first killed or stopped.

Several guns were mounted on the various fronts, and in the afternoon we assumed the aggressive by bombarding a Boxer stronghold near the armoury and a Chinese fort lower down the river. This seemed to have an excellent effect, as we were afterwards but little troubled by the enemy.

A native courier sent out this day managed to get through to Tientsin and give an account of our condition. He had been captured by Boxers and tied to a tree, but, having destroyed his message before being taken, nothing incriminating was found upon him, and he was eventually released; his life was for some time in danger, and after escaping from the Boxers he had some difficulty in getting safely inside the lines round Tientsin Settlement. None of the couriers previously sent had got through, the surrounding country being so closely watched.

A Chinese soldier, wounded and captured while trying to enter the armoury (June 24th), stated that General Nieh's army were much discouraged at their want of success, and that the attempts to retake the armoury were made with twenty-five battalions (nominally, of 500 men each, but probably not more than 300 to 400 men). During the day the Chinese fort was again bombarded.

Early in the morning (June 25th) one of the guns in the fort below the armoury was observed to be firing towards Tientsin, and to create a diversion two of our guns were got into position and bombarded it. The gun then turned its fire towards the armoury.

About 6 a.m. European troops were reported to be in sight, and at 7 a.m. a relief column under the Rusian Colonel Shirinsky, composed of forces of the various nations, arrived outside the armoury.

Preparations were then made -

1. For the evacuation of the armoury; the wounded were transported across the river in the afternoon, the whole force following later and bivouacked on the river bank for the night.
2. To set on fire and destroy this very important arsenal, said by some who should know, to contain £3,000,000 worth of warlike stores.

At 3 a.m. on 26th the return march with the relieving column commenced, and the combined forces arrived at Tientsin about 9 a.m. without further incident. The wounded were immediately placed in the hospitals, and the various detachments joined their respective forces in Tientsin.

After the return march had commenced, Lieutenant Edward G. Lowther-Crofton and Mr. Charles Davidge, Acting Gunner of H.M.S. "Centurion", remained behind to set fire to the ammunition and other storehouses in the armoury. Fires were lit in five separate places, and judging by the great volume of smoke continually rising, with occasional explosions, the destruction must have been fairly complete. After doing their work these officers crossed the river, mounted ponies which were waiting for them, and rejoined the main body.

During the expedition the hostile villages, which afforded shelter to the enemy from which to attack the force, had to be burnt and destroyed as a matter of military necessity.

The number of enemy engaged against us in the march from Yungtsun to the armoury, near Hsiku, cannot be even estimated; the country alongside the river banks is quite flat, and consisted of a succession of villages of mud huts, those on the outskirts having enclosures made of dried reeds; outside, high reeds were generally growing in patches near the villages, and although trees are very scarce away from the river, along-side it they are very numerous; these with the graves, embankments for irrigation and against flood, afforded cover to the enemy, from which they seldom exposed themselves, withdrawing on our near approach. Had their fire not been generally high it would have been much more destructive than it was. The number of the enemy certainly increased gradually until the armoury, near Hsiku, was reached, when General Nieh's troops and the Boxers both joined in the attack.

In the early part of the expedition the Boxers were mostly armed with swords and spears, and not with many firearms; at the engagement at Langfang, on 18th June, and afterwards, they were armed with rifles of late pattern; this, together with banners captured and uniform worn, shows that they had either the active or covert support of the Chinese Government, or some of its high officials.

The primary object of the expedition , viz., to reach Peking and succour the Foreign Legations had failed. Success was only possible on the assumption that the Imperial troops, with whose Government we were not at war, would at least, be neutral; their turning their arms against us, and certainly conniving in the destruction of the railway (probably actually joining in it), made failure inevitable.

For the undertakings of the expedition, for its conduct and its issue, I am responsible.

The destruction of the valuable "armoury", near Hsiku, may be regarded as some object at least gained.

When the somewhat unusual character of the force, viz., the combination of eight different nationalities, is considered, it may, I think, be conceded that their harmonious action reflects credit on the various members of the expedition, and I venture to think it will tend to foster international sympathies.

I have with pleasure to acknowledge my gratitude to the various commanding officers for their hearty co-operatioon and accordance to my wishes, which is the more creditable to them as our position was often an anxious one.

Both officers and men have suffered a good deal of pecuniary loss of clothes, etc., as we had to leave behind in the trains nearly all that we could not personally carry, yet no want of cheerfulness was observable. As regards to our own service, I shall submit claims for compensation for the above to their Lordships.

I have written officially to the respective Admirals or Senior Naval Officers of the several foreign nationalities present to thank them for their cordial co-operation throughout our short campaign, and to express my sense of the service rendered by the officers and men in question.

I have especially referred to Captain von Usedom, of the Imperial German Navy, who was senior officer present after myself. I nominated this officer to direct the expedition should I fall; and after I was deprived of the services of my Flag Captain by his wound at the battle of Pietsang, I requested Captain von Usedom to act as my Chief of the Staff, in which capacity he rendered very valuable service, and I beg to submit the same to their Lordships, Captain von Usedom was slightly wounded at Langfang.

I must also specially refer to Captain B.H. McCalla, of the U.S. Navy, who was of the greatest value to me and to all concerned. He was slightly wounded in three places and well merits recognition.

Before closing my despatch I have the very pleasing duty of reporting to their Lordships that the officers and men landed from H.M. ships, and present with me, acted throughout, as regards energy, courage, and cheerfulness, in a manner well worthy of the high traditions of H.M. Navy. I might with truth mention favourably all names; it is hard justly to discriminate, and there are probably others who deserve special mention fully as much as those named below.

I feel it is right specially to recommend for their Lordships favourable consideration the following officers:-

Captain John R. Jellicoe, my Flag Captain, who was, as always, of most valuable help, both by his judgment and action, till disabled by a serious wound at the battle of Peitsang on 21st June.

Commander Charles D. Granville, of my Flagship, who ably commanded the Naval Brigade with me after my Flag Captain was wounded.

Commander William O. Boothby, of H.M.S. "Endymion", in command of the seamen from that ship, and at times, of others also. He was in every engagement, and I specially noted his energy and activity.

Lieutenant George M.K. Fair, of my Flagship, employed on my Staff in Intelligence Department, etc, but diverted as required to other duties, such as the very important one of getting along with the junks with wounded.

Lieutenant Horatio W. Colomb, of H.M.S. "Endymion", was twice slightly wounded on different days. He had charge of Lofa Station Fort, defended it against various attacks, and showed good judgment while in separate command.

Lieutenant Edward G. Lowther-Crofton, of my Flagship, most intelligent and active; with great risk to himself he remained behind in the Hsiku Armoury on 26th instant, when we left for Tientsin, to set fire to and destroy it, having made the preparations for so doing, which were carried out by him most satisfactorily. This important service reflects very great credit on him.

Lieutenant Arthur G. Smith, of H.M.S. "Aurora", led and commanded an advanced post above Langfang, on the line towards Peking, with zeal and good judgment.

Midshipman William B.G. Jones of H.M.S. "Centurion", who took command of Lieutenant Wyndham L. Bamber's company in the operation on 21st June, after the latter officer was wounded.

Mr. Charles Davidge, Acting Gunner of "Centurion", who ably assisted Lieutenant Crofton in the destruction of Hsiku Armoury, and shared the risks with him - they two being alone.

Major James R. Johnstone, R.M.L.I., of "Centurion", has been most active throughout. He often commanded all the marines present. He kept pushing ahead of the trains on our advance, to clear and protect the line. He it was who led the storming party, I sent round on 22nd June to carry the north angle of the armoury, near Hsiku, and he has rendered very good service.

Captain Richard O.M. Doig, R.M.L.I., H.M.S. "Endymion", has been very active throughout, and commanded the night expedition of one hundred men, on 22nd June, sent from the armoury to try and communicate with Tientsin, which attempt he made with skill and credit.

Mr. Francis C. Alton, my secretary, has been near me throughout, and, as at all times, was of the greatest assistance and value by his grasp of matters and good judgment and sence.

Mr. Charles J.E. Rotter, Assistant Paymaster of my Flagship, was in charge of the commissariat arrangements, a most difficult task under the circumstances, but performed by him with constant efforts and all possible success. To this, having regard to our foreign allies, Mr. Rotter's knowledge of German, and well known tact and good temper, much contributed.

Fleet-Surgeon Thomas M. Sibbald, H.M.S."Centurion", has had charge of the hospital arrangements throughout, and has also been much under fire. His activity, attention, and constant cheerfulness have gone far to mitigate the sufferings of the wounded, and have met with my entire approval.

Mr. George H. Cockey, Engineer, H.M.S. "Centurion", took over the duties of company officer of the "Centurion's" marine detachment after Captain H.W.H. Beyts, R.M.A., fell on 23rd June, until their arrival at Tientsin, 26th June, and was of the greatest assistance to Major Johnstone, R.M.L.I.

Mr. Arthur E. Cossey, Assistant Engineer, H.M.S. "Aurora", at much risk to himself returned from our most advanced post towards Anting Station to bring important news.

Mr. Clive Bigham, late Grenadier Guards, honorary attache to H.M. Legation, at Peking, has been attached to me as Intelligemce Officer, and shown much zeal and ability as such; he has been of great value to me.

Mr. Archibald Currie, C.E. B.Sc., resident engineer in charge of railway line between Tientsin and Peking, came with us to take charge of the trains and their personnel, and to repair the line. In this he worked with a skill and energy not to be surpassed. He acted in opposition to the Chinese director-in-chief of the railway, for our benefit, and H.M. Service and the Allies owe him a debt of gratitude which I submit must be acknowledged and repaid. He has lost his home and nearly all his worldly possessions out here, destroyed by the Chinese.

Mr. C.W. Campbell, H.M. Consul for Wuchow (on leave), accompanied us as interpreter, and was of the utmost value by his knowledge both of the language and customs of the Chinese. He showed untiring zeal, and I would submit him for the decided acknowledgement of H.M. Government.

When the fact of the Chinese having beheaded anyone they got is considered, the conduct of such offficers or men as risked themselves to such capture is to be praised far more than if against a civilised foe.

I have, etc.,
E.H. SEYMOUR,
Vice-Admiral.

The Secretary, Admiralty.

* * * * *

List of officers who accompanied Expedition, and guns:-

H.M.S. "Centurion": Sir Edward H. Seymour, K.C.B., Vice-Admiral; Fredk. A. Powlett, Flag Lieutenant; Francis C. Alton, Secretary; Wm. G. Littlejohns, Secretary's Clerk; Hy. W.E. Manisty, Secretary's Clerk; John R. Jellicoe, Flag Captain, wounded 21 June, Peitsang; Charles D. Granville, Commander; George M.K. Fair, Lieutenant; Edwd. G. Lowther-Crofton, Lieutenant; John L.F. Luttrell, Lieutenant; James M. Fairie, Lieutenant; Wyndham L. Bamber, Lieutenant, wounded 21 June, Peitsang; Claud H. Sinclair, Lieutenant; Jas. R. Johnstone, Major R.M.L.I.; Herbert W.H. Beyts, Captain R.M.A., Killed 23 June, Hsiku; Rev. Ernt. F. Harrison Smith, M.A., Chaplain and Naval Instructor; Thomas M. Sibbald, Fleet Surgeon; Morris E. Cochrane, Sub-Lieutenant; Edward B. Pickthorn, Surgeon; Charles J.E. Rotter, Assistant Paymaster; George H. Cockey, Engineer; George H. Starr, Assistant Engineer; Charles Davidge, Acting Gunner (T); Frank Sammels, Acting Gunner (Q.D.D.); James Attrill, Carpenter; Hector Boyes, Mipshipman; Wm. B.C. Jones, Midshipman; Charles D. Burke, Midshipman, wounded 21 June, Peitsang; Sidney R. Bailey, Midshipman; St. Andrew St.John, Midshipman; Guy B. Alexander, Midshipman; Hardinge L. Shepard, Midshipman; Philip W. Douglas, Midshipman; Robert L. Jermain, Midshipman; Edwd. O.B.S. Osbourne, Midshipman; Frank O.B. Wilson, Midshipman, wounded 21 June, Peitsang; John C. Davis, Midshipman; Augustus E. Tabuteau, Clerk, wounded 21 June, Peitsang.

H.M.S. "Aurora": Arthur G. Smith, Lieutenant; Hy. T.R. Lloyd, Captain, R.M.L.I.; Arthur E. Cossey, Assistant-Engineer; Thomas R. Fforde, Midshipman; Charles B. Dickson, Midshipman; George M. Hill, Midshipman.

H.M.S. "Orlando": Francis E.M. Garforth, Lieutenant; Edward F. Murray, Assistant Paymaster; Patrick McGuire, Gunner; Cloudesley V. Robinson, Midshipman; Herbert F. Littledale, Midshipman; Charles P. Dumaresq, Midshipman.

H.M.S. "Endymion": Wm. O. Boothby, Commander; Horatio W. Colomb, Lieutenant, wounded 21 June, Peitsang, (wounded 27 June, Tientsin Arsenal); Frank Powell, Lieutenant; Richard O.M. Doig, Captain, R.M.L.I.; Revd. John C. Leishman, Chaplain; Lawrence W. Braithwaite, Sub-Lieutenant, wounded 22 June, Hsiku; Eric D. Macnamara, B.A., Surgeon; Ethelbert S. Silk, Engineer; Henry J.S. Brownrigg, Midshipman; Guy D. Fanshawe, Midshipman; Eric G. Robinson, Midshipman; Edwin A. Homan, Midshipman; Norman M.C. Thurston, Midshipman; Fras. S. McGachen, Midshipman; Herbert R. McClure, Midshipman; Stuart E. Holder, Midshipman.

Numerical Strength of Expedition:

Austrian: 1 officer, 24 men, Lieutenant Prochasca in command. British: 62 officers, 640 seamen, 213 marines, 1 6-pr. Hotch Q.F., 3 9-pr. M.L., two .45 Maxim, six .45 Nord., Vice-Admiral Sir Edward H. Seymour, K.C.B., in command. French: 7 officers, 151 men, 1 field gun, Captain de Marolles in command. German: 23 officers, 427 men, 2 Maxims, Captain von Usedom in command. Italian: 2 officers, 38 men, 1 Maxim, Lieutenant Sirianni in command. Japanese: 2 officers, 52 men, Captain Mori in command.

Russian: 7 officers, 305 men, 1 field gun, Commander Chagkin in command. United States: 6 officers, 106 men, 1 13-pr., 1 Colt automatic, Captain B.H. McCalla in command; making a total of 110 officers, 1,956 men, and 19 guns. (All the officers in command were naval officers.)

Casualty List.

British: "Centurion", officers, wounded, 5; seamen, etc. killed 9; wounded 36; Marines, killed, 1 officer and 6 men; wounded, 7. "Aurora", seamen, etc., wounded, 2; Marines, killed, 3; wounded, 5. "Orlando", seamen, etc., killed, 1; wounded, 13. "Endymion", officers, wounded, 3; seamen, etc., killed 5; wounded, 15; Marines, killed 5; wounded, 6. Wei-hai-wei detachment, Marines, wounded, 5; making a total of officers, wounded, 8; seamen, etc., killed, 15; wounded, 23. Foreign: Austrian, seamen, etc., killed, 1; wounded, 1. French, seamen, etc., killed, 1; wounded, 10. German, officers, killed, 1; wounded, 6; seamen etc., killed, 11; wounded, 56. Italian, seamen etc., killed 5; wounded 3. Japanese, seamen etc., killed, 2; wounded, 3. Russian, officers, wounded, 4; seamen etc., killed, 10, wounded, 23. United States, officers, wounded, 2; seamen etc., killed, 4; wounded, 25; making a total of officers, killed, 1; wounded, 12; seamen etc., killed, 34; wounded, 121; making a grand total of officers, killed, 1; wounded, 20; seamen etc., killed, 49; wounded, 187; Marines, killed, 1; officer and 14 men; wounded 23.

Summary

Killed: 2 officers, 63 men, total 65; wounded: 20 officers, 210 men, total 230; making a grand total of 295 officers and men killed and wounded.

* * * * *

Copy of Letter despatched to the Commander-in-Chief or Senior Officer of each Nationality on the Expedition's return to Tientsin.

YOUR EXCELLENCY (or Sir), **Tientsin, 27th June, 1900.**

THE late allied Naval Expedition for the attempt to reach Peking and succour our respective Legations in that city having now terminated, I have the honour, as the Senior Naval Officer of the various National Forces engaged therein to address your Excellency (or you) on that subject.

First, to officially thank your Excellency (or you) for sending the officers and men belonging to the (nation) in company with those of Her Majesty the Queen of England, to act in concert with them.

Secondly, to express to your Excellency (or you) my highest sense of-

1. The valuable, cheerful and constant co-operation and assistance I received from (Commanding Officer's name), and all others under his command.
2. The unfailing energy and zeal displayed, under somewhat trying circumstances by (nation) officers and men, whose courage was worthy of their high traditions, and requires no words of mine to describe.

Thirdly, to ensure your Excellency (or you) of my sincere belief and hope that the above expedition, though both small and not of long duration, will help to cement between our respective nations that mutual good feeling and respect which happily now exists between our Sovereigns (or Governments), and which, especially in China, is now so desirable in all the best interests of civilisation and advancement.

(The following additions were made to the letters to respective nationalities):-

To His Excellency, Vice-Admiral Bendemann, Commander-in-Chief, His Imperial German Majesty's Ships, China Station.

Though it might seem out of place for me to report on the conduct of an officer not placed under my command, yet I cannot close this letter without sir, expressing to your Excellency both my personal admiration of the ability and unfailing energy which Captain von Usedom, of His Imperial German Majesty's Ship "Hertha", displayed throughout the expedition, and also my high sense of the value of his services. The Allied Forces at the battle of Langfang, on 18th instant, was under his command, I myself being some miles away at the time. In this determined attack on us, the first in which the Chinese Imperial troops joined with the "Boxers", Captain von Usedom was wounded. To his skilful conduct and arrangements for withdrawing the trains when it had become necessary, the avoidance of a disaster then should be ascribed.

As second to myself in rank of all officers present, I often consulted him with much benefit, and I also officially nominated him to succeed me in the direction of the expedition should I fall, and then felt our general interests would not suffer.

When my Flag-Captain was disabled by a wound, I requested Captain von Usedom to do me the honour to act as Chief of my Staff, which he acceded to, and was of the greatest value to me.

As regards the courage and high discipline shown by all His Imperial Majesty's officers and men accompanying us, I can only say they were well worthy of the high traditions of the great German Empire.

I have, etc.
E.H. SEYMOUR,
Vice-Admiral.

To His Excellency, Rear-Admiral Courejolles, Commander-in-Chief, French Squadron, China Station.

THOUGH it may seem out of place for me to report on the conduct of an officer not placed under my command, yet I cannot close this letter without, your Excellency, expressing my high sense of the valuable co-operation and support I received from Captain de Marolles, of the "D'Entrecasteaux", and all under his command; that in the various engagements they acted with us in a manner worthy of the high traditions of the great National French Navy was only what I felt sure I might expect, yet may be allowed with pleasure to dwell on.

When in the west armoury, near Hsiku, Captain de Marolles took the honourable part of occupying and holding the arsenal there, which, being most advanced towards Tientsin and also full of combustibles, with a fire of shell from the enemy's guns at times upon it, was a decided post of danger and honour. Captain de Marolles also undertook, with his men only, a reconnaissance on the 25th instant towards the railway.

I would request your Excellency to express my thanks to Captain de Marolles for his cordial co-operation throughout our short campaign, which reminded me of our happy alliance with your great nation, both in the Crimea and out here. May I add my hope that it may, though of small degree, help to draw together in friendship France and England, a thing certainly desirable for the civilisation of the world.

I have, etc.
E.H. SEYMOUR,
Vice-Admiral.

To Rear-Admiral Kempff, Second in Command, United States Squadron, China Station.

I cannot conclude my letter without expressing to you, sir, the high admiration I have for Captain B.H. McCalla, who accompanied us in command of your officers and men. Their post was usually in the advanced guard, where their zeal and go was praised by all. I regret to state that Captain McCalla was wounded in three places, but considering the gallant way in which he exposed himself, I am only equally surprised and thankful that he is alive.

Had he been thoroughly British he could not have more kindly and loyally stood by me in every way and carried out any wish I expressed. I may, indeed, say the same for all those under his command.

I hail this experience as a further proof of the real good feeling so happily existing between our nations, which is by no one more valued than by your brother sailors of our Navy.

I have, etc.,
E.H. SEYMOUR,
Vice-Admiral.

To Capitano di Frigato Casella, Senior Italian Naval Officer, Taku.

PERMIT me sir, to express the pleasure I have felt in co-operating with the officers and men belonging to H.M. Royal Navy, and allow me to add my tribute to the energy and readiness they have shown throughout to assist the expedition.

I have, etc.,
E.H. SEYMOUR,
Vice-Admiral.

To Captain Thoman von Montalmar, S.M.S. "Zenta" (Austrian) (No special addition).

To His Excellency Vice-Admiral J. Hiltebrandt, Commander-in-Chief, His Imperial Russian Majesty's Ships, China Station.

In conclusion, pray let me express to your Excellency my high sense of the valuable service rendered to our joint expedition by Captain Chagkin of His Imperial Majesty's Navy, who was always ready, always to the front, and did me the honour to as exactly carry out any wish I expressed to him as if he had belonged to our own Navy.

I have, etc.,
E.H. SEYMOUR,
Vice-Admiral.

To Captain Shimamura, Senior Japanese Naval Officer, Tientsin.

Pray allow me, sir, in conclusion, to express my satisfaction at this opportunity of sharing our efforts with officers and men belonging to His Imperial Majesty's Navy, who showed that energy and mobility which is well known to characterise the Japanese nation. I trust this may prove an instance of the friendly feeling now happily existing between our respective Services and the forerunner of long good fellowship between them.

I have, etc.,
E.H. SEYMOUR,
Vice-Admiral.

YOUR EXCELLENCY, **Tientsin, 27th June, 1900.**

I CANNOT let the present occasion pass without doing myself the honour of addressing you, to thank you from myself, and feel sure I may add, also for the other commanding officers of the various national forces engaged in the late expedition towards Peking, for the very prompt and throughly efficacious way in which you, sir, organised, and Colonel Shirinsky, in charge of the relieving force, carried out, on 25th and 26th instants, the arrangements for our return from the west armoury near Hsiku, to Tientsin, with the large number of wounded by whom we were encumbered.

It is not for me as a sailor to give any opinion on a military land movement, yet, as an officer of some experience, I am be permitted to express my admiration of the arrangements of Colonel Shirinsky, and I would request you, as you feel right, to express the same.

Such events are what help to draw nearer to each other civilised nations like our own, and this occasion is, I feel sure, as much a source of gratification to your Excellency as to myself.

I have, etc.,
E.H. SEYMOUR,
Vice-Admiral.

His Excellency Major-General Stessel, Commanding Imperial Russian Troops, Tientsin.

* * * * *

Letter No. 4 from the Rear-Admiral on the China Station, dated 17th June 1900. No.4.

"Barfleur" at Taku.
17th June, 1900.

SIR,

I HAVE the honour to report, for the information of the Lords Commissioners of the Admiralty, that on my arrival here on the 11th instant I found a large fleet, consisting of Russian, German, French, Austrian, Italian, Japanese, and British Ships, and that in consequence of an urgent telegram from Her Majesty's Minister at Pekin, Vice-Admiral Sir Edward H. Seymour, K.C.B., Commander-in-Chief, had started at 3 o'clock the previous morning (10th June) taking with him a force of 1,375 of all ranks, being reinforced by men from the allied ships as they arrived, until he commanded not less than 2,000 men.

At a distance of some 20 to 30 miles from Tientsin - but it is difficult to locate the place, as no authentic record has come in - he found the railway destroyed and sleepers burned, etc., and every impediment made by supposed Boxers to his advance.

Then his difficulties began, and it is supposed that the Boxers, probably assisted by Chinese troops, closed in on his rear, destroyed railway lines, bridges, etc., and nothing since the 13th instant has passed from Commander-in-Chief and his relief force and Tientsin, nor vice versa, up to this date; nor has any report whatever, to my knowledge, come in as to his movements, and the last we heard was that the British and German advanced party, probably about 500 men, had left the railway about 40 miles from Tientsin (Long Fa) for the purpose of making forced marches the rest of the distance (30 to 35 miles) to the relief of Pekin.

During the night of the 14th, instant, news was received that all railway carriages and other rolling stock had been ordered to be sent up the line for the purpose of bringing down a Chinese army to Tong-ku.

On receipt of this serious information a council of Admirals was summoned by Vice-Admiral Hiltebrandt, Commander-in-Chief of the Russian Squadron, and the German, French, United States Admirals, myself, and the Senior Officers of Italy, Austria, and Japan attended; and it was decided to send immediate orders to the Captains of the Allied Vessels in the Peiho River (3 Russian, 2 German, 1 United States, 1 Japanese, 1 British ("Algerine") to prevent any railway plant being taken away from Tong-ku, or the Chinese Army reaching that place, which would cut off our communication with Tientsin; and in the event of either being attempted they were to use force to prevent it, and to destroy the Taku Forts.

By the evening, and during the night of 15th instant, information arrived that the mouth of the Peiho River was being protected by electric mines.

On receipt of this, another Council composed of the same Naval Officers was held in the forenoon of 16th June on board the "Rossia", and in consequence of the gravity of the situation, and information having also arrived that the Forts were being provisioned and reinforced, immediate notice was sent to the Viceroy of Chili at Tientsin, and the Commandant of the Forts, that in consequence of the danger to our forces up the river, at Tientsin, and on the march to Peking, by the action of the Chinese Authorities, we proposed to temporarily occupy the Taku Forts, with or without their good will, at 2 a.m. on the 17th instant.

Necessary orders were given to the Captains of the allied ships in the river, acting under command of the Russian Post Captain of the "Bohr".

At 0.50 a.m. of Sunday, 17th June, the Taku Forts opened fire on the allied ships in the Peiho River, which continued almost without intermission until 6.30 a.m. when all firing had practically ceased, and the Taku Forts were stormed and in the hands of the Allied Powers, allowing of free communication with Tientsin by water, and rail when the latter is repaired.

In forwarding the reports of Commander Robert Hathorn Johnston Stewart, Commanding H.M.S. "Algerine" and Commander Christopher George Francis Maurice Cradock, who commanded the allied landing force, I wish to bring most strongly to the notice of their Lordships that the brilliant manner in which Commander Stewart handled his ship, immensely contributed to the success achieved, which at one time was extremely doubtful, and his putting her so close under the Forts that most of their shot went over him, accounts for his small loss. He and the Captain of the German Vessel "Iltis" were always contending for the post of danger, and the German officer is, I regret to say, severely wounded in several places.

The Japanese and British stormed the North-West Fort together, and the Japanese Commander was, I believe, the first man in and then assisted Commander Cradock up, when I much regret to say that the Japanese Commander was killed.

Four Destroyers of the Chinese Navy were boarded and captured by Lieutenant and Commander Roger John Brownlow Keyes of the "Fame" and Lieutenant and Commander Colin MacKenzie of the "Whiting" which was done by towing a boat astern with boarders under the command of Lieutenants John Alfred Moreton and Wilfred Tomkinson of the "Whiting" and "Fame" respectively, who boarded and captured two Destroyers each. I intend handing over three of the Destroyers to the Admirals of our Allies, viz: the Russian, German, and French.

In the action slight damage was done to the "Algerine" by shell fire, principally to ventilators, etc., and a shell passed through the hull of the "Whiting" which necessitates her being sent to Nagasaki for repairs.

I regret to have to report that during the action William Theodore Bing, Ord. O.N. 188203, H.M.S. "Barfleur", was killed, and Mr. Herbert J. Hargreaves, Assistant Paymaster in charge H.M.S. "Algerine" and 12 men were wounded; but, owing to the lack of any communication with the shore today (18th June) on account of the weather, I have not received any details.

I have, etc.
JAMES BRUCE,
Rear-Admiral.

The Secretary of the Admiralty.

* * * * *

Enclosure in Letter from Rear-Admiral, China Station. (Dated 17th June, 1900. No.4.)

SIR, **Taku, 17th June, 1900.**

I HAVE the honour to report, that in conjunction with the Allied Forces on shore, the British Force, which, I have the honour to command, stormed and assisted to take the North-West Fort of Taku, at 5 o'clock this morning after which the outer North and South Forts were respectively occupied.

I regret to state that in the capture of the North-West Fort, W.T. Bing O.S., of H.M.S. "Barfleur" was killed, and six other men of the British Force were wounded, the Foreign Forces on shore had also, I am sorry to say, some casualties, including amongst the killed the Japanese Commander.

The North-West Fort was first attacked. Half the British Force, the Russians on the left and the Italians on the right, composed the firing line, the other half were deployed to act as a close support.

The resistance at the North-West Fort was severe, other Forts were occupied with but slight opposition.

On the junction of the Allied Forces this morning, the German and Japanese Commanders were pleased to propose that I should take command of the proceedings of the combined forces, which I did.

At a meeting held by the Foreign Representatives after the operations, it was decided that the several Nations should each occupy a fort; in consequence the British Force, under my command, take charge of the North-West Fort. The entire force had been landed as a result of fears expressed by the conference as to the descent of Boxers on Taku in large numbers at night, and I am endeavouring to place the Fort in such a state of defence that danger of its being rushed by weight of numbers will not be probable.

Machine guns are wanted, and also, more rifle and pistol ammunition.

I have, etc.,
CHRISTOPHER CRADOCK,
Commander.

Commanding the Allied Forces on shore at the attack on Taku Forts. To Rear-Admiral James Bruce.

* * * * *

Enclosure in Letter from Rear-Admiral, China Station. (Dated 17th June, 1900. No. 4)

H.M.S. "Algerine", Taku.
SIR, **17th June, 1900.**

I HAVE the honour to report that after receiving your orders of yesterday's date, I attended a conference of the Allied Squadron of Men-of-War inside the bar, when it was decided that we should take up our appointed positions by 4 a.m., and open fire on the Forts at that hour, should they not be surrendered before then.

I took up my position at once, shifting berth at 8 p.m., and prepared for action. At 1.30 a.m., I ordered the Destroyers "Fame" and "Whiting" to seize the Chinese Destroyers alongside the government yard.

At 12.50 a.m. all the forts opened fire, and we engaged the enemy. At about 1.30 Commander Cradock and his landing party were landed on the north bank, and at about 5 o'clock the fire of the North-West Fort was, except for field and machine- guns, practically silenced, and the Fort taken by the landing party.

At 6 o'clock the Allied Ships weighed and proceeded down the river, I anchored again, and it was not until 7.10 a.m. that the Chinamen finally abondoned their guns and the Forts were occupied.

No damage has been done to the hull of the ship but there are several holes in the cowls, and one in the steam cutter.

A list of casualties will follow with a detailed report.

Reports from Lieutenants Keyes and MacKenzie as to their proceedings will be sent in with the detailed report, observing that the Chinese Destroyers are all in our possession.

At a conference of Commanding Officers held this morning, it was decided that the British Forces should occupy the North-West Fort, the Japanese the North Fort, and the Russians and Germans the South Fort.

Our wounded have been landed and the Taku Hotel pretty well taken for them.

Captain Cradock will detail a guard for the hospital.

I have, etc.,
R.H. JOHNSTON STEWART,
Commander.

To Rear-Admiral James Bruce, H.M.S. "Balfleur".

* * * * *

Letter No. 385 from Commander-in-Chief on the China Station, dated 4th July.

SIR,

Tientsin, 4th July, 1900.

I HAVE received from Rear-Admiral Bruce, Second in Command, a copy of his letter of 17th June (No.4) reporting to their Lordships the taking of the Taku Forts, and of the Chinese Dockyard with four destroyers there on that day.

It is my pleasing duty to inform their Lordships that these operations meet with my entire approval. In my opinion they were skilfully planned and executed in a most gallant manner, worthy of the highest traditions of our Service.

I concur in the Rear-Admiral's commendation of those concerned, and would specially mention Commander Johnston Stewart, of H.M.S. "Algerine", the Senior Naval Officer present at Taku, (The Rear-Admiral being in his Flagship outside the Bar, 12 miles off). Commander Stewart directed our part of the operations, and well and ably handled his ship under heavy fire from the forts in a most gallant and seamanlike way, and I desire to submit his name to their Lordships for their very favourable notice.

I have, etc.
E.H. SEYMOUR,
Vice-Admiral.

The Secretary of the Admiralty.

* * * * *

Letter No. 388 from Commander-in-Chief on the China Station, dated 8th July 1900.
Affairs at Tientsin between 10th and 26th June 1900. No. 388.

SIR,

Tientsin, 8th July, 1900.

I HAVE the honour to report, for the information of the Lords Commissioners of the Admiralty, the following occurrences at Tientsin between 10th June, the date of the departure of the expedition to attempt the relief of Peking, until its return on 26th June.

Captain E.H. Bayley, of H.M.S. "Aurora", who was left in charge of the British forces at Tientsin found immediately after my departure that the Chinese authorities were doing all they could to prevent trains being sent forward with reinforcements, and to keep up communication. Large and threatening mobs of Chinese came to the railway station to obstruct the work, but trains were with some difficulty sent through as required until 14th, when the tearing up of the line prevented further communication in advance.

On 10th June, Lieutenant C.D. Roper with 50 men was sent from Tientsin to Tongshan to protect British railways employees there, at the earnest request of Mr. Kinder, the Engineer-in-Chief. They remained until 16th June, when, finding the position untenable, they withdrew with the European residents to Peitaho, and embarked on 21st in H.M.S. "Humber" for Taku.

On 11th June the Chinese began to leave the Settlement and shops to close. Reinforcements of 150 seamen and marines, under Commander Beatty (H.M.S. "Barfleur"), arrived on that day, and on 13th some 1,600 to 1,800 Russians with cavalry and field guns.

A courier arrived from Peking on 14th with news that the Summer Legation and all mission houses at the western hills had been destroyed.

15th June - Some mission houses in the French Settlement and the cathedral in the Native City were burnt and telegraphic communication with Taku interrupted. A search-light train patrolled the line between Tientsin and Tongku all night, and a guard of 200 Russians was left at Chun Liang Cheng, a station midway between.

16th June - The first attack on the Settlement was made by some Boxers, who set fire to several stores and houses before they were driven out, they also attacked the railway station held by the Russians.

A train for repairing the up line was prepared with search-light and a 6.8 gun mounted; work had to be commenced within a half a mile of the station. A train sent down to Tongku was fired at by the forts as it approached and returned to Tientsin next morning.

17th June - Some Chinese were observed gathering together to destroy the line 1½ miles away; the repairing train was sent out with a small force under Mr. Henry C. Halahan, midshipman, to drive them off. Outside the station they came across a body of Chinese troops (80 to 90) who opened fire on the train; the fire was returned, and after losing a few men, the Chinese made off.

The Russians afterwards went out with a force of 200 men and one of our 6-pr with crew, under Lieutenant G.B. Powell, of "Aurora", and engaged the enemy.

The Military College on the river opposite the British Concession was taken by a party of the Allied Forces under Major Luke, R.M.L.I. ("Barfleur"); the guns found there were destroyed and the building also. The British loss was one killed and four wounded.

The bombardment of the Settlement by guns in the Native City commenced.

18th June - A train under Lieutenant Field ("Barfleur") started with a Russian force to bring back the 200 Russians from Chun Liang Cheng, but found the line badly damaged and failed to reach that place. They were heavily engaged by the enemy and returned in the afternoon in time to help, by a flank attack, to repulse the Chinese troops then attacking the railway station. During the engagement two British companies, under Commander Beatty, with a 9-pr. field gun under Lieutenant P. Wright ("Orlando"), reinforced the Russians and did excellent service.

19th June - Two Chinese field guns were placed near the railway embankment opposite the British Concession and opened fire. Commander Beatty, with three companies of seamen, crossed the river and manoeuvred to within 200 or 300 yards in the hope of capturing them with a rush; some Russians moved out at the same time to co-operate. While our men were waiting for the Russians to come up, a large force of Chinese appeared to the right behind a mud wall and poured in a heavy fire, wounding Commander Beatty, Lieutenants Powell ("Aurora") and Stirling ("Barfleur"), Mr. Donaldson, midshipman ("Barfleur") (the latter died on 3rd July of his wounds), and 11 men. The force then retired.

A 9-pr. gun was brought up to the Bund outside the British Consulate and succeeded in throwing shell close in front of the guns, upon which the Chinese brought up horses and withdrew them. During this action a piece of shell from one of the enemy's guns struck Lieutenant Wright, who was on the roof of the Consulate directing the fire of his guns, inflicting dangerous wounds on the head and arms.

Mr. J. Watts, of the Tientsin Volunteer Corps, undertook to ride to Taku with despatches, and left at 9.30 p.m. with a guard of only 3 Cossacks. Mr. Watts knows the country thoroughly well and succeeded in getting through; his action was most gallant and is well deserving of official recognition, as the whole country was swarming with Boxers and Imperial troops.

20th-21st June - Only small attacks and skirmishes took place, but the Concession was still bombarded from the Native City.

22nd June - Troops were seen in the far distance advancing from Tongku. A courier from Peking arrived with a message that all Europeans had been ordered to leave within 24 hours.

23rd June - A column, composed of 250 seamen and marines, 300 Royal Welsh Fusiliers, 40 Royal Engineers, 150 United States marines, and 23 Italians (in all about 763), arrived from Tongku about noon. They left Tongku three days previously, under the command of Commander Cradock, of H.M.S. "Alacrity", and had not met with much opposition from the enemy until nearing Tientsin, when at the last bridge before coming to the Settlement they encountered a heavy fire. This was checked by a 3-pr. field gun, lent by the Americans, assisted by the artillery of a Russian force (about 1,200) also advancing to Tientsin, and the enemy driven off. During this last part of the advance the British force lost two killed, five wounded, from a galling flank fire.

The Russian force camped on the leftbank of the river, opposite the Settlement, where it still remains. Major-General Stessel is in command.

24th June - Detachments of the Chinese Regiment and 50 men from "Terrible" with a 12-pr. arrived. In the afternoon the 12-pr., in conjunction with a 6-pr. on the wall, shelled the Western Arsenal and set it on fire. It contains a great quantity of small-arm ammunition, and some explosions took place.

Arrangements were made by Captain Bayly with the Russian General for the despatch of a force to relieve the Peking Expeditionary Force, then in the armoury near Hsiku, about five miles distant, from whom a messenger had arrived on the 24th asking for assistance. The Russian General provided 1,000 men with two guns, and 900 men were furnished by the remainder of the garrison at Tientsin (600 being British) with two maxims, the whole force being under the command of Colonel Shirinsky, of the Russian Army. The various divisions met at a rendezvous on the left bank of the river at midnight, and after a night march arrived soon after daylight of the 25th outside the armoury. Next day (26th June) the combined force returned to Tientsin without incident.

On 25th June the "Terrible's" 12-pr. was placed in position, on the river bank, to shell the fort in the City which had been bombarding the Settlement; the position of the gun (or guns) was not known, but by careful watching in the evening the flash was detected and the gun located. By directing the fire from the roof of some houses near, the direction and range was obtained and after a few minutes the gun was silenced. This accounts for the return of the forces from Hsiku to Tientsin on the following day having been unmolested.

Since the 14th June Captain Bayly, as commandant of the British Settlement, has been ably assisted by Captain Burke, of H.M.S. "Orlando", whom I placed, and who still remains, in command of the Naval Brigade.

I am highly satisfied with the behaviour of all employed in these operations, which reflect very great credit on all concerned, but I desire to bring specially to their Lordship's favourable notice the conduct of the following officers and men:-

(1) Captain Edward H. Bayly, of H.M.S. "Aurora", whose duties were most constant, harassing, and onerous. He displayed throughout great calmness, energy, and good judgment, and a tact and temper quite remarkable. He is now performing the same duties with equal efficiency and also those of Chief

of my Staff, which combination he has proved himself quite equal to.

(2) Commander David Beatty, D.S.O. of H.M.S. "Barfleur", although suffering from two wounds only partially healed, one of which is likely to cause him considerable suffering and inconvenience for some time, begged to be allowed to accompany the expedition for the relief of the forces under my command. He is thoroughly deserving of any mark of appreciation of his services.

(3) Lieutenant Philip N. Wright's (H.M.S. "Orlando") services have been of a most arduous nature and of the highest character. His coolness and gallantry on every occasioon merit the highest praise. Lieutenant Wright's very dangerous wound caused a severe loss to the whole force, which was felt by everyone. I have recently ventured by telegraph, to recommend this officer for special immediate promotion, and feel sure that if granted it will give pleasure and satisfaction to the whole force who served with him.

(4) Lieutenant Herbert du C. Luard, of H.M.S. "Barfleur", who took on the duties of inspection of defences after Lieutenant Wright had been wounded, and the defence of the line - a very long and troublesome one, constantly "sniped" by night - has been most indefatigable.

(5) Lieutenant Frederick L. Field, of H.M.S. "Barfleur", deserves mention for his very excellent and arduous services with the repairing and other armed trains, having been hard at work for almost 48 hours continuously on one occasion.

(6) Major Edward V. Luke, R.M.L.I., of H.M.S. "Barfleur", whose excellent leading and handling of his men at the attack on the Military College contributed very largely to the success of the operation. After Commander Beatty had been wounded, Major Luke assumed the duties of that officer with regard to the military work of the British Defence Force.

(7) Surgeon J. Falconer Hall, of H.M.S. "Barfleur", whose devoted care and attention to his patients (as well as his professional skill) during a most trying time have been the admiration of all.

(8) Mr. George Gipps, midshipman, of H.M.S. "Orlando", has been almost continuously in charge of a gun at an outlying and dangerous portion of the defences, and has displayed at all times great coolness and ability, calmly waiting the arrival of the enemy within effective range, when he has invariably dispersed them with a few well-directed shell.

(9) William Christmas, P.O. 2 cl., of H.M.S. "Barfleur", for coolness and gallantry during the British attack on the Chinese field guns, on 19th June, when he carried Mr. Donaldson, midshipman, severely wounded, on his back out of the firing line while exposed to a heavy rifle fire.

(10) Patrick Golden A.B. of H.M.S. "Barfleur", on the same occasion asssited to carry Lieutenant A.J.B. Stirling, severely wounded, across an open ground, swept by rifle fire, and was himself wounded in so doing.

(11) William Parsonage, A.B. of H.M.S. "Aurora", on the same occasion, assisted to carry Lieutenant G.B. Powell, wounded, to the rear, over open ground swept by rifle fire, and was wounded in so doing.

Many of the civilian residents have been most helpful, working hard continuously and unselfishly for the benefit of the community. Their kindness and generosity to the regular forces have been great. Mercantile and private houses have been placed at the disposal of officers and men.

Our relations with the representatives and commanding officers of other nations have been most cordial.

I have etc.,
E.H. SEYMOUR,
Vice-Admiral.

The Secretary, Admiralty.

* * * * *

Enclosure to Letter from Commander-in-Chief, China Station. (Dated 8th July, 1900. No.388)

APPROXIMATE numerical strength of forces in Tientsin on 24th June, 1900: - Austrian, original force present during seige, 50. British, original force present during seige, 393; relief force from Taku, 590; total, 983. French, original force present during seige, 50. German, original force present during seige, 110. Italian, original force present during seige, 40; relief force from Taku, 23; total, 63. Japanese, original force present during seige, 50. Russian, original force present during seige, 1,800; relief force from Taku, 1,200; total, 3,000. United States, original force present during seige, 43; relief force from Taku, 150; total, 193; making a grand total of 4,499.

Enclosure to Letter from Commander-in-Chief, China Station. (Dated 8th July, 1900. No. 388)

ABSTRACT of casualties between 10th and 25th June at Tientsin:- "Barfleur", officers, killed, 1; wounded, 5; seamen, etc. killed, 1; wounded, 23; marines, wounded, 3. "Aurora", officers wounded, 1; seamen, etc., wounded, 1. "Endymion", seamen etc., wounded 1. "Orlando", officers, wounded, 1; seamen, etc., killed, 3; wounded, 15; marines, killed, 1; wounded, 1; making a total of 6 killed and 51 wounded.

Enclosure to Letter from Commander-in-Chief, China Station, dated 8th July, 1900. No. 388.

List of Naval and Marine Officers present in Tientsin between 10th and 25th June, 1900.

H.M.S. "Barfleur" : David Beatty, D.S.O., Commander, wounded 19th June; Herbert du C. Luard, Lieutenant; Frederick L. Field, Lieutenant; Valentine E.B. Phillimore, Lieutenant; Anselan J.B.

Sterling, Lieutenant, wounded 19h June; Edward V. Luke, Major R.M.L.I.; Harold G.B. Armstrong, Lieutenant, R.M.L.I.; Edward C. Kennedy, Sub-Lieutenant; John F. Hall, Surgeon; Harry G. Wilson, Assistant Paymaster; Edgar C. Smith, Assistant-Engineer; Valentine F. Gibbs, Midshipman, wounded 21st June; Archibald B. Donaldson, Midshipman, wounded, 19th June, died 3rd July; Ronald C. Mayne, Midshipman; Charles C. Dix, Midshipman; Harold L. Carmichael, Midshipman; George C.Browne, Midshipman, wounded 18th June; Francis N.A. Cromie, Midshipman; Basil J.D.Guy, Midshipman; James S.C. Salmond, Midshipman; Richard B. England, Midshipman; Gerald F. Longhurst, Midshipman; Frank S.D. Esdaile, Midshipman, wounded 6th July, died 7th July; Hamilton C. Allen, Midshipman; Lionel H. Shore, Midshipman, wounded 25th June; William E. Cornabe, Midshipman.

H.M.S. "Centurion": Robert Kilpatrick, Assistant Engineer; Edgar W. Riley, Assistant Engineer; George H. Borrett, Lieutenant (T); Colpoys C. Walcott, Sub-Lieutenant; Cecil B. Prickett, Midshipman; John W. Dunstan, Captain, R.M.L.I.; William A. Harris, Captain, R.M.L.I.

H.M.S. "Aurora": Edward H. Bayly, Captain; Thomas W. Kemp, Lieutenant; George B. Powell, Lieutenant, wounded, 19th June; Charles D. Roper, Lieutenant, detached to Tongshan; Charles F. Ballard, Sub-Lieutenant; Edward F. Power, Surgeon; Augustus P. Hughes, Assistant Paymaster; Francis C. Hanning-Lee, Midshipman; Robert H. Clark-Hall, Midshipman, detached to Tongshan, 12th June; Cecil R. Hemans, Midshipman, detached to Tongshan; Henry C. Halahan, Midshipman; Arthur F. Crutchley, Midshipman.

H.M.S. "Orlando": James H.T. Burke, Captain. Arrived prior to 10th June, Philip N. Wright, Lieutenant, wounded 19th June; Herbert M. Perfect, Lieutenant; Frederick C. Fisher, Sub-Lieutenant; Edmond A.B. Stanley, Midshipman; George Gipps, Midshipman; John A. Collett, Midshipman; George W. Taylor, Midshipman; Dennis de C.A. Herbert, Midshipman. 14th June, John H. Young, Midshipman.

H.M.S. "Terrible": John E. Drummond, Lieutenant (C); Joseph Wright, Gunner (Acting); Alexander G. Andrews, Lieutenant-Surgeon; George J.H. Mullins, Captain, R.M.L.I.; Frank B.A. Lawrie, Lieutenant, R.M.L.I.; Alwyne E. Sherrin, Midshipman; Henry T. Dorling, Midshipman.

H.M.S. "Alacrity": Christopher G.F.M. Cradock, Commander; Eric Charrington, Lieutenant; Robley H.J. Browne, Surgeon; William S. May, Gunner, wounded 27th June.

* * * * *

Letter No. 402 from Commander-in-Chief on the China Station of 12th July 1900.

Affairs at Tientsin, 27th June to 11th July, 1900. No. 402.

H.M.S. "Centurion" off Taku.
12th July, 1900.

SIR,

I HAVE the honour to report, for the information of the Lords Commissioners of the Admiralty, the following account of occurrances at Tientsin since my return of 26th June.

I found the Settlement presenting a very desolate appearance, the railway station wrecked, the mud huts or cottages of the labouring (but hostile) Chinese round the Settlement burnt to prevent the enemy taking cover there; many of the houses in the Settlement closed or unoccupied; the buildings generally more or less injured by shell fire, which had evidently been heavy, and some by incendiaries; the streets barricaded with bales of wool, rice, etc., and trade entirely suspended both in the Settlement and on the river.

Some of the residents had previously taken the precaution to send their families away, but many women and children still remained. Their number has since been much reduced by sending them, as opportunities offered, to Tongku to wait on board Her Majesty's or other ships until they could be sent away. Several of the ladies have cheerfully devoted themselves to nursing the wounded, and have well fulfilled their self-imposed task.

On the forenoon of 27th June the Russian forces began bombarding the large arsenal two miles east-north-east of the British Concession. Before doing so, the Russian General had asked me if I could send a British force to act as a reserve, and support the Russian attack, if necessary. This I consented to do, and sent out a force of seamen under Commander Cradock, and marines under Major Johnstone, R.M.L.I., about 600 strong, the whole under the command of Captain Burke. They were brought into action directly they arrived, and ordered to advance parallel to the left face of the arsenal, the Russians taking the centre and right face. When about 200 yards from the face a heavy rifle fire was opened on them, and they had to push forward on a flat plain for a considerable distance under a flanking fire, until they could turn and face the arsenal, when they advanced towards it subjected to a harassing shrapnel fire from a field gun at the left corner of the arsenal.

At about 250 yards from the arsenal our men fixed bayonets and charged, the enemy then quickly cleared out; the marines were left outside to fire at them while flying across the plain.

The Russians on their side had also succeeded in gaining entrance, and drove the enemy out from their end. As they then no longer required assistance, our force returned to Tientsin, and the arsenal was destroyed.

The British casualties were seven killed and twenty-one wounded, the latter number including two officers. The bearing of our men under a heavy flanking fire was all that could be desired, and they worked splendidly.

On 28th June a courier arrived from Sir Robert Hart, and another on the following day both with messages from Peking of the same date (8 a.m., 24th June), "Our case is desperate, come at once".

The Chinese of this day flooded a part of the country near the western quarter of the native city by opening the Grand Canal, whether for their own protection or with a view or injuring us is uncertain, but we have not suffered in consequence, as the floods are of small area, and near the native city.

On 4th July, at 5 a.m., the Chinese opened fire from several guns which had been mounted near the railway bridge over a canal. About noon large bodies of troops were seen moving towards the western arsenal, but on being shelled kept at a distance out of range. About 4 p.m. Chinese troops on the other side of the river attacked the railway station, but were repulsed.

On 4th July two additional 12-pr. guns were received from "Terrible" and two 9-pr. (about) Krupp, guns from forts at Taku to oppose the enemy's guns, our guns up to this time being one 12-pr. Q.F., two 9-pr. M.L. field guns, and three 6-pr. Hotchkiss.

On the forenoon of 6th July an attempt was made to take a small gun (about 1-pr Q.F.) which had been pushed up within short range of the settlement, and whose position had been discovered. The attempt would have been quite successful, the Chinese being taken by surprise, but it was found to be on the opposite side of the river, and the nearest bridge was too much exposed to risk crossing it.

About noon a bombardment of forts in the native city and of the arsenal, took place, the two 12-pr guns of "Terrible" being assisted by the French and Japanese field guns. The guns in the Chinese forts were silenced by our guns, the French guns set fire to the Viceroy's Yamen, and the Japanese guns shelled the arsenal, where two guns were mounted and kept them from firing at the 12-prs. while they were engaged with the forts in the city.

In the afternoon Major Bruce, 1st Chinese Regiment, volunteered to make an attempt to silence the 1-pr. Q.F. gun above-mentioned by the fire of a 9-pr. which he said could be taken by a road he knew, sheltered from the enemy's fire, to within close range. The road was found to be too narrow for the gun, and it was then unfortunately decided to use the main road, which was swept by the enemy's fire. The gun and rifle fire was too heavy for the 9-pr. to be brought into action, and the force retired with the loss of two killed and five wounded, the latter including Major Bruce and Mr. F. Esdaile, midshipman, of H.M.S. "Barfleur", both severely.

On 7th July at noon another bombardment was made as on the previous day, partly to keep down the incessant Chinese shell fire on the European settlements. Our fire was returned by various guns, mostly very difficult to locate, the flash being amongst ruined houses. For half an hour the enemy's practice was very good.

Meanwhile a Japanese cavalry reconnaissance was made to the south-west towards the race-course, which at once unmasked a heavy rifle fire from that position. The Chinese for the last day or two had evidently been trying to work round to the west and south from the native city, perhaps with a view to cutting our communications by river.

On 8th instant it was arranged that a combined movement of Japanese, British, Russian and American forces should be made at daylight next morning (9th July) to clear the enemy out of their position near the race-course. A force of nearly 1,000 British (400 naval), under the command of Brigadier-General Dorward, was sent as supports; the Americans sent 150 and the Russians 400, the latter being in reserve; the whole being under the command of the Japanese general (Brigadier-General Fukushima).

Before daylight on 9th July this force moved in a southerly direction and then wheeled to the right; the Japanese then brought their field guns and those of the Hong Kong Artillery into action against the Chinese, who occupied a village near the race-cource. The Japanese cavalry on the left came on a body of Boxers, whom they charged and dispersed, killing about 200; the infantry in the meantime advanced to some earthworks and captured four 3-pr. Krupp guns and about fifty rifles. The force then continued its advance in a northerly direction and occupied a village immediately south of the arsenal, and afterwards advanced towards the arsenal; a gun in the south-west corner of the city opened fire, but was silenced. At the same time a Japanese naval force and American marines advanced along Sankolin's Wall from the Settlement, and entered the western arsenal from that direction at the same time as the forces from the west. The arsenal was found to be evacuated, but two guns, about 9-pr. Krupp, were taken in it. The Japanese advanced beyond the arsenal towards the south wall of the city, but the Chinese troops were collected in force, and a heavy fusillade with gun fire and "sniping" rendered it inadvisable to continue, and later burning the arsenal - which was decided to be untenable by us, and rendering it so by the Chinese, the Forces returned. It is estimated that the Chinese lost about 300 to 400 in killed. Our casualties (naval) were one killed and three wounded.

The Russians during the 10th constructed some pontoons, intending that night to convey them to the Lutai Canal (north-east from the city) to enable them to cross and attack the Chinese on their left flank on the other side, about a mile from the city, where they had made a strong position for themselves with several guns. The co-operaton of the other Allies was asked, and parties told off from each nationality as supports and in reserve, but late that night it was discovered that the pontoons were not fit for the work intended. This is to be regretted, as a successful attack on the left bank following up that on the right two days previously would have had an excellent effect and done much to discourage the Chinese. I hope it is only postponed for a short time.

Early on the morning of the 11th July a most determined attempt was made by the Chinese, in force, to take the railway station, which has always been one of their main points of attack, either to destroy the rolling stock or to acquire a near position from which to bombard the Settlement. The fight lasted for three hours and was stubbornly contested, when the Chinese were finally driven out; the losses of the Allies in killed and wounded were fully 150, principally between the French and Japanese. The Chinese loss must have been very heavy, but cannot be accurately given.

About midday the forts in the native city were bombarded for one hour by British and French guns. The "Terrible's" 12-prs. and one of the "Algerine's" 4-inch Q.F. did good work, and demolished the pagoda in the fort used as a look-out place. The enemy's reply was not so vigorous as usual.

The numbers of Chinese to the west of the native city have increased either by reinforcements or by withdrawal of troops formerly on the other side. With Boxers, their numbers cannot now be less than 20,000 men. The forces of the Allies are:- Austrian, 50; French, 2,160; Great Britain, 1,420; German, 400; Italian, 40; Japanese, 3,090; Russian, 4,450; United States, 360; total, 12,170.

The operations of the Allied Forces, owing to want of numbers and guns, have been limited to what is necessary for protection of the troops and defence of the Settlement.

The most difficult positions to defend have been the railway station, and the French Settlement. The former was held by a mixed force of 100 seamen or marines in turn, 100 French, and 100 Japanese or more, as their General feels able to add to them. all these nations forming a reserve for their own men. At first the Russians held it, but declined to do so after the 4th instant. The French Concession is that part nearest to the Chinese city, hence its danger. It is mainly held by the French troops, but we and the Japanese offered protection also. The south-east part, so called German Concession, has been quite quiet.

The river has been open throughout and traffic undisturbed; there has been no difficulty in forwarding supplies as far as lighter accommodation admitted. The railway is being repaired by the Russians, and should be open in a day or to.

With the foregoing exceptions the operations have not been of importance. Frequent small attacks on our defences have been made by the Chinese and repelled, and they have been continually "sniping" from cover near, and every day for some hours shelling the Settlement, occasional outbursts being followed by a corresponding lull.

Before closing my despatch I feel it right specially to recommend for their Lordships' favourable consideration the following officers:-

Lieutenant Thomas W. Kemp, H.M.S. "Aurora" has been brought very favourably to my notice by Commander Cradock in the advance to Tientsin. I can also recommend him for zeal and usefulness, and his services as Russian interpreter have been of very great assistance.

Lieutenant John E. Drummond, of the "Terrible" in command of guns on and near south wall of defences, a very important and exposed position. He was, with all under his command, rendered most valuable service there, and merits their Lordships' recognition.

Lieutenant Frederick A. Powlett, my Flag Lieutenant, was with me throughout the expedition towards Peking, and since. He has been most useful at Tientsin, in addition to his other duties, in arranging the signals and communications with the tower and our batteries for firing on the Chinese guns. also in trying to surprise and capture Chinese signallers at night.

Sub-Lieutenant Edward G. Kennedy, H.M.S. "Barfleur", recommended by Major L.W.F. Waller, United States marines. Placed himself under Major Waller with a maxim, and was most useful firing on the enemy or Chinese guns of the arsenal as they retreated.

Mr. George Ellis, signal boatswain of "Centurion". With me through all the operations hitherto and has shown the zeal he always does; he was slightly wounded at Tientsin.

Mr. Joseph Wright, gunner (act.) "Terrible", with Lieutenant Drummond. I have noticed the great coolness, energy, and valuable service performed by this officer.

Mr. Edward O.B.S. Osbourne, Midshipman, of "Centurion", has been with me the whole time, and shown great zeal, coolness, and courage.

Mr. James Attrill, carpenter, of H.M.S. "Centurion", has been with the expedition towards Peking and at Tientsin, and showed great zeal and energy, first working hard at repairs to railway; secondly in the mounting of guns. He has been very often under fire.

On the evening of 11th July, the Allies having received reinforcements of United States and Japanese troops, the officers and men of "Centurion" were sent back to their ship, and I then returned with my staff to the flagship outside Taku bar.

I have, etc.
E.H. SEYMOUR,
Vice-Admiral.

The Secretary, Admiralty.

* * * * *

Statement of Casualties, 26th June to 11th July, 1900.

"Centurion": officers, wounded, 2; seamen, etc. killed, 5; wounded, 10; Marines, wounded 2.
"Barfleur": officers, killed 1; wounded, 1; seamen etc., killed, 1; wounded, 5; Marines, wounded 2.
"Terrible": officer, wounded, 1; seamen etc., wounded, 4; Marines, killed, 1; wounded, 6.
"Aurora": seamen etc., killed 1; wounded, 5; Marines, killed, 1; wounded, 1.
"Orlando": seamen etc., killed, 1; wounded, 5.
"Endymion": officer, wounded, 1; seamen etc., killed 1; wounded, 4; Marines, killed, 1.
"Alacrity": officer wounded, 1; seamen etc., wounded, 1. Wei-hai-Wei detachment, Marines, killed 1; wounded, 2; making a total of officers, killed 1; wounded 6; seamen etc., killed, 9; wounded, 34; Marines, killed, 4; wounded, 13.

Summary

Killed: 1 officer, 13 men, total 14; wounded: 6 officers, 47 men, total 53; making a grand total of 67 officers and men killed and wounded.

* * * * *

Letter No. 429 from the Commander-in-Chief on the China Station, dated 23rd July, 1900.

Report of Occurrences in connection with the Attack on the Native Walled City of Tientsin on 13th and 14th July, 1900.

The attached reports are submitted for information. The following officers and men have been brought to my notice on this occasion:-

Lieutenant Valentine E.B. Phillimore H.M.S. "Barfleur", who commanded A Company, went to the support of one half-battalion of American Marines, who had so many wounded that they would have been unable to save themselves had it not been for the able and timely support which he gave them.

Mr. Basil J.D. Guy, Midshipman, H.M.S. "Barfleur", for the great coolness and bravery he displayed in stopping with and attending to a wounded man under an excessively hot fire, eventually assisting to carry him in across a fire-swept zone.

Ernest Whibbley, Ordinary Seaman, H.M.S. "Barfleur", for the great coolness and gallantry, he displayed in assisting to carry in three men across a heavy fire-swept zone.

Thomas Gardner, Sick Berth Steward, H.M.S. "Barfleur", for the great coolness and attention he displayed whilst attending to and caring for the wounded (including the Americans) under a very heavy fire.

James Drew, Petty Officer, 1st Class, H.M.S. "Barfleur", for his coolness and attention to the wounded under a very heavy fire.

To those names I should also have added that of Captain Henry T.R. Lloyd, R.M.L.I., had he lived. This officer was with me in the advance towards Peking, and was engaged in every action, showing on all occasions great courage and zeal.

E.H. SEYMOUR,
Vice-Admiral.

* * * * *

Enclosure to letter from the Commander-in-Chief on the China Station. (No. 429 of 23rd July, 1900)

H.M. Naval Brigade,
Tientsin, 15th July, 1900.

SIR,

I HAVE the honour to forward for your information the following details regarding the operations of the 13th and 14th instant, resulting in the complete capture of the native walled city and forts by the allied forces.

Early on the morning of the 13th a large force of Russians accompanied by some Germans and French, attacked on the E. and N.E., while the remainder of the forces from the Settlement marched out of the Taku gate and proceed to make a detour to the west, in preparation for an attack on the south gate of the city.

By request of General Dorward, I directed all the naval guns, including the 4-inch and 12-pr. guns mounted close to the Russian camp, under the direction of Lieutenant Luard, of H.M.S. "Barfleur" and those in the Meadows Road, near the wool mill, and on the mud wall, to be in readiness to open fire at 4 a.m. The fire of these batteries I personally controlled by means of telephone from the signal tower on the Gordon Hall, some of them being, unable to actually see the object aimed at from their positions.

Owing to the darkness and mist, fire was not opened until nearly 4.30 a.m.

The guns in the native city immediately replied by shelling the Settlement heavily for some time, one shell wrecking a portion of the hospital, established in the Tientsin Club, from which, fortunately, nearly all the wounded had been removed on the previous day.

As the attacking columns advanced on their respective sides, the Russians soon came into conflict with the enemy, whom they steadily drove back towards the city.

At about 5 a.m. a tremendous explosion took place near the right flank of the Russians. This was caused by the blowing up of a magazine, said to be full of brown powder, close to the Lutai Canal, which had been set on fire by a shell from a French field gun.

A volume of black smoke was thrown up into the air for a height of at least 600 feet.

Much glass was broken in the Settlement, and the signal tower rocked heavily for some seconds.

No deaths or severe casualties resulted from the explosion, but very many Russians who were nearest to it were thrown from their horses, and the general in command received a blow on the head and arm from some falling debris.

Soon after this the attack on the left was perceived by the Chinese, and a heavy fire opened from some of the guns in the city.

Both attacks were steadily pressed home until the Chinese were driven under the walls, after some very heavy fighting, as the casualty lists show.

During the time of the advance a heavy fire was kept up, by my direction, from all our guns, both on the east and west, on the forts and guns which seemed to be firing most heavily on the attacking columns.

After the Russian attack had closed in near the city, I ordered Lieutenant Luard's 4-inch and 12-pr. guns in the Russian camp to direct their fire on the fort in the city.

I may here state that the outlying guns were all captured by the Russians.

A most destructive fire was kept up by all the guns to the westward, under Lieutenant Drummond, of H.M.S. "Terrible", on the south wall the city as the attacking force appraoched from the S.W., with the view of keeping down the enemy's fire, which was poured heavily from the wall on either side of the south gate when our troops had once passed the western arsenal.

Large portions of the wall were swept away, and the fire was considerably subdued, when a signal reached me from the general to request that all guns might cease fire on the wall, as the Japanese had entered the city. This subsequently proved not to have been the case, and was due to some misunderstanding of a report.

During the time the fire of the guns was taken off the south wall, the Chinese re-manned the battlements, and poured in a very heavy rifle fire, until the guns once more received permission to re-open on the wall, which they did with great effect.

The Chinese most gallantly stuck to their positions, keeping up a heavy rifle fire until literally swept away, wall and all.

It was then past midday, and all our forces on the west were lying down under such shelter as was obtainable from houses and walls near the native city, and the arsenal walls in the case of the supports.

Killed and wounded have been brought in in great numbers; the Americans lost very heavily in proportion to numbers engaged, but, naturally, the Japanese losses were actually very great, they having such a large number under fire.

In fact, search parties were employed yesterday evening in bringing them in, many of them having been shot in the long grass to the N.W. of the canal.

The troops remained in position for the night, food and water being sent out to them.

At daylight next morning there was a little sniping from the walls, but nothing more.

The Japanese sappers blew in the first gate and climbed over and opened the next.

The enemy by this time had, it was found, practically quitted the city during the night, a large body being observed from the Gordon Tower to the N.W.

All the south side of the city was in possession of the allied forces by 6 a.m.

The large fort to the N.E. had not then been captured, but was subsequently taken by the Japanese about midday, and the whole of the place was divided into four districts, to be held by the foreign troops as detailed, the British holding the N.W. portion.

About 200 junks and a very useful stern-wheel steamer were captured in the canal to the north of the city, and will all be very useful later for water transport.

I have the honour to enclose despatches from Captain Burke and a letter from General Dorward, which will convey to you fuller details of the operations of the naval and marine brigade, about 300 strong.

The casualties in this force amounted to six killed and 38 wounded, the former including, I deeply regret to say, Captain H.T.R. Lloyd, R.M.L.I., of H.M.S. "Aurora", who has been engaged in every action with the marines with the force under your command on its march to Pekin, and in the vicinity of Tientsin since your return.

I have, etc.
EDW. H. BAYLY,
Captain and Senior Naval Officer, Tientsin.

Vice-Admiral Sir E.H. Seymour, K.C.B.
Commander in Chief.

* * * * *

Enclosure to Letter from the Commander-in-Chief on the China Station. No. 429 of 23rd July, 1900.

Report of Operations carried out by Naval Brigade against Tientsin (Walled) City on 13th and 14th July 1900.

SIR, **Tientsin, 14th July, 1900**

I HAVE the honour to report that, at 3.30 a.m. on 13th instant, the Naval Brigade, numbering a little over 300 bluejackets and Royal Marines, marched out of the European settlement by the Taku Gate, and joined the left attacking column to support the Japanese in the attack on the southern gate of Tientsin (Walled) City.

After passing the end of a deserted village at 4 a.m. the head of the column turned to the right in the direction of the western arsenal. The British naval guns on the mud wall now opened fire on the arsenal and city. Soon after the Japanese had reached the plain they deployed, and immediately came in contact with a body of Imperial Chinese troops, whom they soon drove back with apparently slight loss to themselves. The column then advanced until the bridge leading to the front gate of the western arsenal was reached. This was at about 5 a.m., when a halt was made to permit the Japanese to repair this bridge, which had previously been destroyed by fire on the 9th instant. The Naval Brigade was extended and ordered to lie down and maintained this position for some time when the Chinese small-arm men on the City Wall got the range very accurately and caused many casualties in our ranks, including the death of Captain Lloyd, R.M.L.I., H.M.S. "Aurora", and James Brown, A.B. H.M.S. "Barfleur". I then moved the brigade some distance to the right, and it was some little time before the enemy again obtained our range, when their fire was again very destructive.

At about 7.15 a.m., the Japanese, having completed the repair of the bridge, the whole column advanced over it, the Japanese entering the arsenal, and the remainder taking cover under its mud wall. Here we remained without further casualty until noon, when the Japanese had cleared the arsenal and commenced the attack. Shortly after this the American marines joined in the attack, and were reinforced by our "A" Company of seamen.

About 1 p.m. our "B" Company and all our marines advanced under a heavy fire in support of the Japanese centre, and took cover as supports in a village, and remained there for the rest of the day.

At 8 p.m. the remaining two companies of our seamen went out to occupy two large houses on our left to prevent this occupation by snipers, and an hour later were reinforced by 100 French marines. All these men returned to the mud wall shortly after daybreak on the 14th inst. At 10 p.m. (13th) our "A" Company returned from the firing line, bringing in the American wounded, who were very numerous.

At 3.45 a.m. (14th) the Japanese succeeded in blowing in the Outer Southern Gate of the city, and opened the Inner Gate and entered, supported by our "A" Company and Marines. They then occupied this gate. The remaining three companies of our seamen advanced at 5 a.m., entered the city and cleared the main road and side streets between the South and North Gates. Outside the latter were several junks in the canal, which were seized by us.

The behaviour of our officers and men was admirable under very trying circumstances, in which we lost very heavily.

An abstract of casualties is attached.

I have, etc.,
J.H. BURKE,
Captain Commanding Naval Brigade.

Captain Edward H. Bayly, R.N.
Senior Naval Officer, Tientsin.

* * * * *

Enclosure to Letter from the Commander-in-Chief on the China Station. No. 429 of 23rd July 1900.

To Captain Burke, R.N. commanding Naval Brigade on 13th and 14th inst. Through the Senior Naval Officer, Tientsin. From Brigadier-General Dorward, Commanding British Forces, Tientsin.

SIR, **Tientsin, 15th July, 1900.**

I WISH to express my deep sense of the honour done to me by having under my command the officers and men of the Naval Brigade during the long and hard fighting of the 13th inst., which resulted in the capture of Tientsin city.

The success of the operations was largely due to the manner in which the naval guns were worked by Lieutenant Drummond, R.N., the accuracy of their fire alone rendering steady fire on the part of the troops possible against the strong Chinese position, and largely reducing the number of casualties.

The delicate operation of withdrawing troops from advanced positions at nightfall, to strengthen other parts of the line, and the bringing back of the wounded could not have been effected without the aid of the well-directed fire of the guns.

I desire to place on record my appreciation of the gallantry and fine spirit of the men, and to join in their regret for the heavy loss in killed and wounded, and particularly with the Royal Marines in regret for the death of Captain Lloyd.

The Naval Brigade had their full share in the fighting at the centre and right of the position, and had the honour of being among the first troops to enter Tientsin. The succour they brought under a heavy fire to the hard pressed American troops on the right was highly appreciated by the 9th Regiment United States Infantry, who found themselves unexpectedly under the heaviest fire of the day, and were much heartened by the arrival of Lieutenant Phillimore, R.N., and his men. It will be my honour to bring their conduct to the notice of the Secretary of State for War.

I join with them in their admiration for the gallantry, soldierly spirit, and organisation of our comrades of the Japanese Army.

I have the honour to thank you particularly for the ready and unquestioning assistance which you personally gave me at all times during the progress of the operations, and for the cheerful co-operation of your officers and men in instantly carrying out any duty assigned to them.

I have, etc.
A.R.F. DORWARD,
Brigadier-General.

* * * * *

Abstract of Casualties.

Killed: "Barfleur", seamen, 4. "Aurora", officer, 1; total 5. Died of wounds: "Barfleur", seaman 1. Wounded: "Barfleur" officers, 2; seamen, 14; marine, 1. "Terrible", seaman, 1; marines, 8. "Aurora", seamen, 1; marines, 6. "Orlando", seamen, 3; marine, 1. Wei-hai-wei guard, marine, 1; total 38; making a grand total of 44.

J.H. BURKE,
Captain Commanding Naval Brigade.

Tientsin, 14th July, 1900.

* * * * *

Letter No. 24 from the Rear-Admiral on the China Station, dated 27th June 1900. No. 24

H.M.S. "Barfleur", at Taku.
27th June, 1900.

SIR,

IN continuation of my letter of the 17th instant, No. 4, I have the honour to report the following for the information of their Lordships:-

1. Communication with the shore was cut off the whole of Monday the 18th on account of the weather, but heavy firing was heard in the direction of Tientsin during the night of the 17th, and on the 19th a letter was received from Captain Bayly, H.M.S. "Aurora", who is in command at Tientsin stating that the Chinese troops had openly appeared on the 17th, and had fired on a party sent out to drive off rail wreckers, subsequently shelling the foreign settlement, and a series of skirmishes or small engagements took place during the whole day.

The Chinese Military College was taken and destroyed that afternoon; of our forces, 48 marines, under Major Luke and Lieutenant Armstrong, of the "Barfleur", were engaged. Major Luke received a graze on the cheek from the bullet which killed Private Henry Robinson, R.M.L.I., of the "Orlando".

On the 20th a cypher message from the Consul at Tientsin, asking for reinforcements, was brought down by runner, and H.M.S. "Terrible", having arrived on the morning of the 21st with 350 officers and men of the Royal Welsh Fusiliers and Royal Engineers, they were landed as soon as possible, and sent on by train to join up with a party of seamen under Commander Cradock, which had started from the N.W. Fort at five that morning for the relief of Tientsin.

A strong party of Russian troops, with a party of Americans, had previously advanced, but fell into an ambush some few miles from Tientsin, and were repulsed with some loss; they eventually joined up with our men, who reached Tientsin on the 23rd, having engaged the enemy with the loss of one bluejacket killed and some wounded.

Commander Cradock reports that the British bluejackets were in Tientsin 20 minutes before any of the others arrived. The Consul at Tientsin, writing on the 25th, says that news had been received from Sir Robert Hart, dated 19th instant, saying that the foreign Ministers had been ordered to leave Pekin within 24 hours; nothing has since been heard from them.

He further informs me that the Commander-in-Chief was a few miles to the north of Tientsin, very short of provisions, and that on the morning of the 23rd he had 40 killed and 70 wounded, but does not say what communication has been made with him.

A force of 2,000 men started to the relief of the Commander-in-Chief from Tientsin on the * , and at the time he wrote an action was taking place in that direction.

A large fort on the south bank of the Peiho, above Tong-ku, was reconnoitred yesterday and being found deserted, Lieutenant and Commander Keyes, of H.M.S. "Fame", proceeded there this forenoon, and destroyed it by exploding the magazine.

This fort, which was armed with 6-inch guns, commanded the river, which is now believed to be open for connection with Tientsin.

In view of the probable number of wounded being too great for the medical staff of Her Majesty's ships to cope with, I have engaged two civillian doctors to serve where required; one I have sent to Wei-hai-wei in charge of the sick quarters there, and the other is serving in the base hospital, which has been established at Tong-ku.

I received a signal from the Russian Admiral this evening to the effect that the Commander-in-Chief was "disengaged", and I hope to be able to telegraph tomorrow that he has been relieved, but up to the present have had no confirmatory news from Tientsin.

I forward herewith printed copies of the protocols drawn up at meetings of the Allied Admirals held on the 17th,20th and 23rd instant.

I also enclose detailed reports from Commanders Stewart and Cradock of the attack on the Taku forts on the 17th instant, and the capture of the four torpedo boat destroyers of the Hai-lung class on the same date.

As previously reported, I have turned over a destroyer to the Russian, German and French Admirals; the one retained for H.M. service having been re-named the "Taku". Her boilers were found to be in need of cleaning and overhaul, but she will be ready for service in a few days.

A list of guns captured in the north-west fort at Taku is forwarded herewith.

I have, etc.,
JAMES BRUCE,
Rear-Admiral.

To the Secretary, the Admiralty.

* Probably 24th June.

* * * * *

Enclosure in Letter of Rear-Admiral, China Station, dated 27th June, 1900. No. 24

Submitting Reports of Proceedings from H.M. Torpedo Destroyers "Fame" and "Whiting".

H.M.S. "Algerine", Taku.
June 19th, 1900.

SIR,

I HAVE the honour to submit the reports of proceedings of H.M. ships "Fame" and "Whiting" during the operations for the reduction of the Taku forts on the morning of 17th June.

I take this opportunity of bringing to your notice the very able and gallant manner in which Lieutenant and Commander Roger Keyes carried out my orders, and also the brilliant way in which both Lieutenant and Commander Keyes and Lieutenant and Commander Mackenzie handled their vessels under a heavy fire.

I have, etc.,
R.H. JOHNSTON STEWART, Commander.

To Rear-Admiral James Bruce,
H.M.S. "Barfleur".

Enclosure in Letter of Rear Admiral, China Station, dated 27th June, 1900, No.24

H.M.A. "Fame", Taku.
June 17th.

SIR,

IN compliance with your order of 16th instant to take H.M.S. "Whiting" under my command and capture the four Imperial Chinese destroyers lying between Taku and Tongku, so as to ensure the safe passage of the "Iltis", "German", and "Lion", French gun vessels at 3 a.m., I beg to report that, having visited the place during the evening with Lieutenant and Commander Mackenzie of H.M.S. "Whiting", and found them moored head and stern in single line off the south steep-to bank with wire hawsers laid out from each bow and quarter, I arranged as follows:- That the "Fame" should weigh at 2 a.m. followed by the "Whiting" at a distance of about 1½ cables (the distance between the fourth and second destroyers). Each vessel to tow a whaler with a boarding party of 12 men under Lieutenants Tomlinson of H.M.S. "Fame" and Moreton of H.M.S. "Whiting". That we should pass well out in the stream to give them the idea we were proceeding up the river, and when the "Fame's" bow was abreast of No. 4 and the "Whiting's" abreast of No. 2, sheer in and board them over the bow, each whaler boarding the next astern, and each boarding party being covered by a rifle party and the guns.

When the forts commenced the heavy firing about 0.45, both ships being in a very exposed position and the necessity of clearing the river, immediate, I directed the "Whiting" to weigh and proceed as arranged. This was effected most successfully. After a slight resistance and the exchange of a few shots, the crews were driven overboard or below hatches; there were a few killed and wounded; our casualties nil. No damage was done to the prizes, the "Fame's" bow was slightly bent when we closed to board, and the "Whiting" was struck by a projectile about 4 to 5 inches abreast a coal bunker. This was evidently fired from a mud battery on the bend between Taku and Tongku, which fired in all about 30 shots at us, none of the others striking, though several coming very close. I could not reply for fear of striking the Russian gunvessels lying behind it. There was a good deal of sniping from the dockyard, so I directed all cables of the prizes to be slipped and proceeded to tow them up to Tongku. At this point, Mr. Macrae, the manager of the "Tug and Lighter Company", came to my assistance; I cannot speak too highly of this gentleman's assistance, he took one destroyer off my hands, as did another of the same company's tugs for the "Whiting". In the former case Mr. Macrae had to use force, with the assistance of one of my men, on the Chinese crew, most of whom tried to jump overboard when we came under the fire of the mud battery. In the latter case, Mr. Mayne, Midshipman of the "Barfleur" was in command of a guard of seamen with a maxim, and also did very well. So soon as the destroyers were captured, the "Iltis" and "Lion" passed. The torpedoes were in the tubes, but war heads were not fitted. Ammunition for Q.F. guns in two destroyers was on deck.

By 5 a.m. they were securely berthed at Tongku. It was not a good position, owing to the exposure to shell passing over the bombarding ship, but the best I could find under the circumstances. Fortunately no damage was done.

Mr. Mayne, Midshipman in charge of a tug with despatches and stores for Tientsin informed me that his Chinese crew would not pass a fort 12 miles up the river at Lun Chang. So I proceeded in company with the "Whiting" to force a passage if necessary; finding no opposition I returned as directed by you to Taku.

Lieutenant Commander Mackenzie is forwarding a seperate report. I can only say he did most excellently, as did Lieutenant Tomkinson in charge of the whaler boarding party, and Mr. Mascull, gunner, who took charge of the other destroyer. Mr. Knight, engineer, was of the greatest assistance in charge aft when I was left with a very small crew and no executive officer.

I have, etc.,
ROGER KEYES,
Lieutenant and Commander.

Commander R.H. Johnston Stewart, R.N.,
H.M.S. "Algerine".

* * * * *

Enclosure in Letter of Rear-Admiral, China Station, dated 27th June, 1900. No. 24.

H.M.S. "Whiting", Taku.
17th June, 1900.

SIR,

I HAVE the honour to report that, having received your order to attack and capture the four Chinese destroyers moored off the dockyard at Taku, acting in conjunction with H.M.S. "Fame" last night, I boarded and captured the two lying down stream at about 1.30 a.m., and as soon as prize crews were got on board and the four wires hawsers, with which each was secured, either cut, or the anchor attached to it weighed, I towed one to Tongku out of reach of the shell-fire of the forts, and was just returning to tow the other up (she had great difficulty in weighing her anchor) when she came in sight, in tow of the tug "Fa Wan".

The capture of the destroyers was effected without any casualties on our side and without much resistance.

In towing one of the prizes to Tongku, a mud fort hitherto silent, opened a hot fire on us, and the "Whiting" received one 5" shot in the hull just forward of engine-room bulkhead, starboard side, passing through bunker (full), carrying away wing-door of boiler and damaging several tubes and putting No.4 boiler out of action, otherwise not causing any more damage.

After placing the captured destroyers in a place of safety at Tongku with a skeleton crew in charge, I proceeded in company with the "Fame" to escort the tug "Fa Wan" past the fort at Sheng Shing, meeting with no opposition.

I beg to recommend to your notice Lieutenant Moreton of this ship, who carried out the operation of boarding the first destroyer in a very able manner, and succeeded in raising steam and going to quarters for action in about two hours from time of boarding.

I have, etc.,
C. MACKENZIE,
Lieutenant and Commander.

Commander H.J. Stewart, R.N.,
H.M.S. "Algerine".

* * * * *

Enclosure in Letter of Rear-Admiral, China Station, dated 27th June, 1900. No.24.

North West Fort, Taku.
20th June, 1900.

SIR,

I HAVE the honour to lay before you a further despatch with inclusive details of the operations conducted by the allied forces on shore, when capturing the Taku Forts.

The British Force detailed for the purpose, embarked in the tug from the outer anchorage, and at 3 p.m. on 16th June each man, having been supplied with 100 rounds of ammunition and three days' provisions, proceeded to H.M.S. "Algerine" for the purpose of being berthed, prior to being landed.

Immediately on arrival at Taku on the same evening, a conference was held on board the Russian gunboat "Bohr", among the commanding officers of the several allies, and a plan of attack for the shore forces was prepared.

It was arranged that the British landing party was to land abreast of H.M.S. "Algerine" at a certain hour, and meet the other forces marching from Tongku at the rendezvous on the military road.

The Chinese opened fire on the ships rather earlier than was expected, but the proposed meeting was satisfactorily accomplished, and the men were put into the boats at the commencement of the bombardment to clear the "Algerine's" decks. Each man of the force received a ration of optional cocoa, handed down into the boats before shoving off, and this was consumed before the boats were allowed to leave.

Landing occupied half-an-hour, and was completed under heavy shell fire by 2.30 a.m. without mishap.

Allied forces consisted of:-

British: 23 officers, 298 men, Commanding officer, Commander C. Cradock, H.M.S. "Alacrity"; total 321.

German: 3 officers, 130 men, Commanding officer, Commander Pohl, H.M.S. "Hansa"; total, 133.

Japanese: 4 officers, 240 men, Commanding officer, Commander Hattori, I.J.S. "Kasagi"; total, 244.

Russian: 2 officers, 157 men, Commanding officer, Lieutenant Stankewitch, 12th Regiment Triailleurs, "D'Orient", Lubrie; total, 159.

Italian: 1 officer, 24 men, Commanding officer, Lieutenant J. Tanca, I.M.S. "Calabria"; total,25.

Austrian: 2 officers, 20 men, Commanding officer, Lieutenant Ernt. Tatniams Qenta; total 22 - making a total of 904 officers and men.

It was arranged that, after an effective bombardment, the N.W. fort should be the first to be attacked, then the N. fort (on same side of the river), and finally, the long string of south forts on the other bank; before the advance, it was agreed that half the British should leave the firing line with the Italians on the left, Germans, Japanese, and that the other half of the British, the Russians and Austrians, should form the supports and reserves.

The German and Japanese commanders were pleased to propose that I should direct proceedings, which I had the great honour to do.

At 2.45 a.m., when some 250 yards from the north face of the fort, the advance commenced, deploying from the right, which flank rested on the river bank; the whole ground a thousand yards this side of the fort was hard mud, but unfortunately quite flat, without a vestige of cover.

The objective of the British was to force or scale the west gate, and this done, to endeavour to gain an entrance into the inner fort, by means of another gate, the whereabouts of which was not quite clear. To do this they were to advance in skirmishing order, to within 50 yards of the moat on the north face, then close on the right, and swinging round the corner of the fort along the military road, the right flank leading in loose formation, seeking what cover the right bank might afford, and charge on the west entrance.

The advance continued until within 1,000 yards of the fort, when I could plainly see that, owing to the darkness, it had suffered little from gun fire, and was practically intact, no guns being silenced. I therefore halted the men and returned myself to consult the other commanding officers as to continuing; it was at once unanimously agreed, that to take it in its present condition, all its guns being still in action, would entail a serious and unnecessaryloss of life, and it was therefore decided to retire slightly for the cover afforded by a bend in the river, and wait until the fort was further reduced.

It was not until 4.30 a.m. half-an-hour after dawn, that the heavy ordnance was finally silenced by the ships, although two field guns which had been previously silenced, now commenced to play on the attacking party.

The second formation of attack was different to the first; on the previous retirement the "Alacrity" and the "Endymion's" men had been ordered to remain 300 yards to the front, as an observation party. They were under cover of a small rising, and shortly before the advance were joined by the Russians on the left.

In the firing line were the "Alacrity's" and "Endymion's" on the right, Russians on the left, and Italians in loose formation immediately on the right flank, the military road slightly interfering with their getting into line. The "Barfleur's" closed in the rear of the fighting line, reinforcing while the charge was sounded. The foreign forces and the remainder of the British were in close support, the Russians inclining to the left to make their attack on the right rear.

When the charge was sounded the Japanese doubled up from the supports in column of route along the road, and raced with the British along the intervening 300 yards to the west gate, the two nations scaling the parapet together.

Part of the British force also gained an entrance through two gun ports, and over a low part of the ramparts to the right of the gates which were held by my officers through the instrumentality of Lieutenant Duncan of H.M.S. "Algerine", who from previous observation on shore had found these weak spots.

The inner and second gate was forced by rifle fire from the British and Japanese, and this done the fort was practically ours.

As mentioned in my previous despatch the remaining forts were taken with slight resistance, and after the north fort was captured, the British and Germans were each able to turn and work one of the fort's guns on the still active artillery in the south fort across the river.

Enclosed is a despatch I have the honour to forward.

I have the honour to enclose letter received from Lieutenant Jno. Tanca, I.M.S. "Calabria", whose force of 25 men had been linked with the British, which he has insisted I should forward, and I have therefore given him a letter couched in similar terms.

I cannot close this despatch without mentioning the capital behaviour of the men more especially as there were amongst them many ordinary seamen and lately joined stokers. I would especially remark on the fine examples set by Lieutenant Eric Charrington of H.M.S. "Alacrity", and Lieutenant R. Hulbert, of H.M.S. "Endymion", in the firing line, both being worthy of the highest praise. I would also respectfully bring before your notice the pluck and ability of my two A.D.C.'s, Midshipman Dennis Herbert, H.M.S. "Orlando", and Midshipman Lionel Shore H.M.S. "Barfleur", also the conduct of Midshipman C. Dix, H.M.S. "Barfleur", who undoubtedly saved his lieutenant's life.

Surgeon Robley Browne, H.M.S. "Alacrity", was quick in his aid and assiduous in his attention to the wounded.

I have, etc.,
CHRISTOPHER CRADOCK,
Officer Commanding British Landing Force, Taku.

To Rear-Admiral J. Bruce,
H.M.S. "Barfleur".

* * * * *

Enclosure in Letter of Rear-Admiral, China Station, dated 27th June, 1900. No.24.

To Commander C. Cradock, Commanding the Naval Brigade.

I HAVE the honour to report to you that in the fight of this morning round the Taku forts, no casualty happened among my 24 men. I have also the honour to thank you very much for your kindness, in the same time that I cannot find sufficient words to praise the conduct and direction of your troops, which I tried, though very poorly, to emulate. Hoping that in any other occasion may I have the honour to be put under your orders, and to fight side by side with the gallant British sailors.

I remain, dear sir, with kind regards, yours,
Lieutenant, JOHN TANCA.

On board the "Algerine", 17th June, 1900.

* * * * *

Enclosure in Letter of Rear-Admiral, China Station, dated 27th June, 1900. No. 24.

"Algerine", at Tongku,
22nd June, 1900.

SIR,

I HAVE the honour to submit a full report of the operations for the reduction of the Taku forts, which took place on the morning of the 17th June.

Having, about 6 p.m. on the 16th instant, received your instructions, and a landing party of 350 men, under Commander Cradock, from the ships outside, together with 20 Italians from the "Elba", having arrived, Commander Cradock and I attended a Conference on board the Russian ship "Bohr", when it was decided that if the forts were not surrendered by 2 a.m. on the 17th, the allied squadron should bombard them. It was also arranged that the bombardment should commence at 4 a.m., and that the ships should by that hour be in the positions assigned to them. The "Algerine" was at the position next above her the German "Iltis", then the Russian ships "Bobr", "Koreytz", and "Gilyak", the French gunboat, "Lion" and the Japanese "Atago", the U.S.S. "Monocacy" remaining at Tongku to look after the railway and the various landing parties.

On my return from the conference at about 8 p.m., I shifted berth to my allotted position, and found there the "Bobr", "Koreytz" and "Gilyak", the forts taking no notice of my movements.

I instructed Lieutenant and Commander Keyes, of H.M.S. "Fame", to take the "Whiting" under his orders and seize the four Chinese torpedo-boat destroyers moored alongside their Government yard, at 1.30 a.m., so that they should not interfere with the passage of the "Iltis" and "Lion" to their allotted positions.

At 12.50 a.m., when all the ships, except the "Iltis" and "Lion", were in position, and I had the landing party on my upper deck, the forts opened an almost simultaneous and heavy fire, which was replied to almost at once by the allied ships. I directed my fire with 4-inch guns on the north-west fort, but finding that much ammunition was being expended, and that the shooting in the moonlight was not very accurate, I simply kept one 4-in.firing. I did not use my searchlight, as I judged that it would only draw the fire of the south fort on the ship.

At 1.30 a.m. the "Iltis" took up her position, followed shortly afterwards by the "Lions". As soon as possible the tug "Fan Wan", which was alongside, shoved off and proceeded up the river to Tientsin, and the landing party were got into the boats, and disembarked at about 2°'clock at a previously selected point a short distance below the ship on the north bank of the river.

At about 2.45 a.m. I received a message from Commander Cradock that the landing party were about to assault the north-west fort, and requesting the ships not to fire on it, which message was passed on to the other allied ships by boat, and the fire continued on the south and north forts. At about 3.45 another message was received from Commander Cradock to the effect that the north-west fort was practically untouched and too strong for them to assault. It was now daylight, and I opened fire on the fort with all my starboard 4-in.guns, together with the "Iltis", whose firing was very well directed. By about 4.30 the return fire had practically ceased, and shortly afterwards the fort was carried by assault.

At 5 °'clock I hoisted the pre-arranged signal, and when it had been repeated by the foreign ships, I weighed at about 5.30, and, closely followed by the "Ilitis" and the other ships, except the "Gilyak", which had a compartment full of water, and could not move, I led the squadron down the river firing on the north fort with my forecastle guns, and engaging the south forts with the remainder of my starboard broadside. The north fort made no return, and had been deserted by the garrison, but the fire from the south fort was very heavy, and it was only by God's mercy that we were not hulled. It was at this period that all our casualties occurred.

At about 6.20 a.m. I anchored in position C, and the "Iltis", which had followed me closely, passed ahead and anchored about a ship's length from us, the remainder of the foreign ships being some way astern. At about 6.55 a magazine blew up after which there was practically no return to our fire, and at 7.10 I ceased firing.

A list of casualties is attached, and I submit that H.M. ship under my command, though always in the thick of it, was extremely lucky in not suffering more damage, three or four shots through cowls, one through our steam cutter at the davits, and some standing and running rigging shot away, being the extent of the damage.

The behaviour of officers and men was admirable, and where all did their duty it is difficult to particularise, Lieutenants Chambers and Duncan were indefatigable in the performance of their duties and in superintending the firing, while Lieutenant Robinson navigated the ship down the river as coolly as if nothing was going on.

Commander Cradock is sending in a separate report of the operations of the land forces.

The ships engaged were the Russian vessels "Bohr", "Koreytz", and "Gilyak", the German "Iltis", and the French "Lion".

The reports of Lieutenant and Commander Keyes of the "Fame", and Lieutenant and Commander Mackenzie of the "Whiting" have already been submitted, and I have nothing to add to my remarks already made thereon, except cordially to endorse Lieutenant and Commander Keyes' remarks as to the indefatigable manner in which Mr. A.J. Macrae, of the Taku Tug and Lighter Company, assisted us by every means in his power, both before and during the operations, and I respectfully submit that his services are deserving of some recognition.

The ship which suffered most was the Russian "Gilyak", which had 10 men killed, and two officers and 47 men wounded. She was disabled by a shot which severed one of her steam pipes and most of her casualties were caused by a shell which penetrated one of her smaller magazines, and exploded some charges in it. She also had one or two below the water line.

The "Iltis" also lost her gunner and seven men killed, while the Captain and about 30 men were wounded. The manner in which this ship was fought was the admiration of the whole squadron.

The "Lion" had one man wounded, since dead. The "Koreytz" had two officers and several men killed and wounded. The "Bobr" had no casualties.

I have, etc.,
R.H. JOHNSTON STEWART,
Commander

Rear-Admiral James A.F. Bruce,
Commanding H.M. Ships and Vessels at Taku.

* * * * * *

Enclosure in Letter of Rear-Admiral, China Station, dated 27th June, 1900. No. 24.

List of Guns captured in North-West Fort, Taku, 17th June.

Number.	Calibre, etc.	Description.
4	12 c.m.	Krupp, B.L.
4	12-pr.	Smooth bore, M.L.
8	40-pr.	Rifled, M.L.
2	5-in.	Vavaseur, B.L.
4	8 c.m.	Krupp field guns, B.L.
3	4-in.	Brass, Rifled, M.L.

cont/......

Number.	Calibre, etc.	Description.
3	8 c.m.	Krupp, iron carriages, B.L.
4	6-pr.	Smooth bore wooden carriages M.L.
	Guns bearing on the River.	
4	12 c.m.	Krupp, B.L.
5	40-pr.	Smooth bore, M.L.
2	5-in.	Vavaseur, B.L.
2	8 c.m.	Krupp, on field carraiges.

Chinese killed at N.W. Fort.

Found dead, 450. Estimated by prisoner to have been thrown into moat by Chinese, 50.

* * * * *

Letter No. 26 from the Rear-Admiral on the China Station, dated 11th July, 1900. No. 26.

"Barfleur", at Taku.
11th July, 1900.

SIR,

IN continuation of my General Letter No. 24, of 27th June, I have the honour to report the following proceedings at this port.

The Councils of Admirals sat on the 5th and 6th instant.

I forward a report from Lieutenant and Commander Keyes, H.M.S. "Fame", of the destruction of the Hsin Cheng Fort.

This fort commanded the river, and it most important that it should have been destroyed.

It is with much pleasure I forward to their Lordships a letter received from the Russian Admiral, conveying the appreciation expressed by Captain Dobrovolsky, who commanded at Taku during the attack on the Taku forts, for the services of the British on that occasion; my reply to Admiral Hiltebrandt is also enclosed.

H.M.S. "Whiting" returned from Nagasaki on the 9th July, her repairs having been expediously and efficiently executed by the Nagasaki Dock Company, and I have asked Her Majesty's Consul at that port to convey to the directors my thanks, they having put aside other work in order to hasten her.

A composite squadron was despatched to Shan hai kwan on the evening of the 8th instant. The decision to send this squadron was reached at the Council of 5th July.

The squadron consisted of:- 1 German (Hansa, Senior Officer); 1 French; 1 Japanese; 1 Russian; 1 British ("Aurora").

This squardon returned to Taku to-day.

I have, etc.
JAMES BRUCE,
Rear-Admiral.

The Secretary, the Admiralty.

* * * * *

Enclosure to letter from the Rear-Admiral on the China Station, dated 11th July, 1900. No. 26.

Reporting the Destruction of the Hsin Cheng Fort.

H.M.S. "Fame", at Taku.
26th June, 1900.

SIR,

I HAVE the honour to report that, in accordance with your order of the 25th instant, to reconnoitre, and if possible destroy all munitions of war in the Hsin Cheng Fort, I embarked Lieutenant Duncan and 12 men of H.M.S. "Algerine", at 6 a.m. this day, and proceeded up the river.

On arriving there I anchored the "Fame" in the most suitable position for covering the operations and landed with 32 men, 24 being armed with rifles, the remainder with cutlasses and pistols. After posting sentries and taking every precaution against surprise I entered the fort without opposition and blew up the magazine and disabled the guns.

The guns disabled were six in number, and were 15 cm. Krupp B.L. on recoil mountings; these guns command the river and Tientsin Road, and if they were properly manned the passage of the river would be extremely difficult to force. They were in excellent order.

A 2½-lb. charge of guncotton was placed under the trunnions of each gun with the result that the carriage was shattered and bent and the gun rendered unserviceable, but except in one case when a primer was also placed in the breech of the gun, the guns themselves were not permanently injured should they be required for Her Majesty's Service.

The magazine contained about 50 tons of powder pebble, prism, black and small grain.

The explosion was very severe, and though I took every precaution to ensure the safety of my men and the villagers, I regret to have to report that two men were slightly injured by the falling debris at a distance of a quarter of a mile from the magazine.

It is possible that there is more ammunition in the fort, but the time at my disposal was limited and did not admit of a systematic search being made. The 6-in. B.L. shell room was not discovered.

On the outside, to the eastward of the fort, there is a large store of projectiles (round) for the numerous obsolete guns which evidently were mounted all round the ramparts and in the three cavaliers; also some hundreds of war rockets, and the carriages and limbers of 27 field pieces - the guns for these could not be found.

I would submit that further investigation be made, as munitions of war must presumably still remain there in large quantities.

Mr. Baldwin (the manager of the mining company), who accompanied me, acted as interpreter, and his services were invaluable.

Lieutenant Duncan was in charge of the guncotton party; he performed the work with celerity and great success.

I have, etc.,
ROGER KEYES,
Lieutenant and Commander.

To Captain George Warrender,
Commanding Naval Brigade at Tongku.

* * * * *

Enclosure to Letter from the Rear-Admiral on the China Station, dated 11th July, 1900. No. 26.

Imperial Russian Pacific Squadron.

No. 1648

Taku Roads,
9th July, 1900.

SIR,

CAPTAIN DOBROVOLSKY, who commanded the combined column of gunboats during the bombardment of the Taku Forts, expresses the highest praise of the gallant conduct of Commander Stewart, the officer and crew of H.M.S. "Algerine", and Lieutenants and Commanders Keyes and Mackenzie of the torpedo-destroyers "Fame" and "Whiting", which took part in the action and did good business under fire of the forts.

I am glad to be able to state this to you, sir, and on behalf of the Russian Fleet to acknowledge that we are proud to co-operate with the British Navy.

I am, etc.,
J. HILTEBRANDT,
Vice-Admiral.

His Excellency Rear-Admiral Bruce.

* * * * *

"Barfleur", at Taku.
10th July, 1900.

SIR,

I HAVE much pleasure in acknowledging your kind letter in which you express the appreciation of Captain Dobrovolsky, who commanded the combined column of gunboats at the attack on the Taku Forts, of the gallant conduct of Commander Stewart, the officers and crew of H.M.S. "Algerine", and Lieutenants and Commanders Keyes and Mackenzie of the torpedo-boat destroyers "Fame" and "Whiting" on that occasion.

In thanking you, sir, for your letter of appreciation of the services of the officers and men of the British Fleet who assisted at the capture of the Taku Forts, I have the honour to inform you, sir, that the British Navy are proud to have co-operated with the Russian Navy, and been under the command of Captain Dobrovolsky.

I have, etc.,
JAMES BRUCE.
Rear-Admiral.

To His Excellency Admiral Hiltebrandt,
Commanding the Imperial Russian Squadron at Taku.

* * * * *

In connection with the operations referred to in the foregoing despatches the Lords Commissioners of the Admiralty have caused a letter, of which the following is a copy, to be sent to the Commander-in-Chief on the China Station:-

Admiralty,
1st October, 1900.

SIR,

MY Lords Commissioners of the Admiralty having had before them your letter of the 27th June last, No. 384, reporting the proceedings of the allied forces in the gallant attempt to relieve the Legations at Peking, desire me to convey an expression of their high appreciation of the tact and judgment displayed by you on that occasion, which contributed so greatly to the harmonious feeling that prevailed between the various sections under your orders

Their Lordships consider that, having been suddenly called upon to assume command of a mixed force comprising representatives of almost every nation, great credit is due to you for the rapidity with which this force was organised, and for the manner in which the expedition was conducted, in view of the great difficulties necessarily attending it, and the overwhelming numbers of the opposing forces.

My Lords have read with pleasure your testimony to the courage shown, and the hardships cheerfully endured by Her Majesty's officers and men during the period in question, and they desire that you will express to Captain Jellicoe (your Flag Captain); Commander Granville, of H.M.S. "Centurion"; Major Johnstone, R.M.L.I., of H.M.S. "Centurion"; and to all concerned, their unqualified satisfaction at receiving this high commendation of their conduct.

The further reports contained in your letters of the 8th, 12th, and 23rd July, Nos. 388, 402, and 429, respecting the state of affairs at Tientsin during your absence and subsequent to your return, have also been laid before their Lordships, and they desire that you will inform Captain Bayly, of H.M.S. "Aurora", whose tact and untiring energy contributed materially to the successful defence of that place; Captain Burke of H.M.S. "Orlando", who ably assisted him; Commander Beatty of H.M.S. "Barfleur"; Lieutenant (now Commander) Wright, R.N., of H.M.S. "Orlando"; Major Luke, R.M.L.I., of H.M.S. "Barfleur", and the officers and men under their orders, how fully their Lordships recognise the valuable services rendered by them during a time of great peril and anxiety.

My Lords, having had before them a letter from the Rear-Admiral, dated the 17th June, No. 4, containing reports on the storming and capture of the Taku forts, desire that you will convey to Commander (now Captain) Stewart, of H.M.S. "Algerine", who most ably handled and fought his ship; to Commander Cradock, of H.M.S. "Alacrity", who skilfully led the allied landing force; to Lieutenants and Commanders Keyes and Colin Mackenzie, who did good service in the "Fame" and "Whiting" respectively, especially in their smart cutting out of four Chinese Destroyers, and to the other officers and men engaged, an expression of their thorough approbation of the gallantry displayed by them during these successful operations which their Lordships are pleased to find from your letter No. 385 of the 4th July, have met with your entire concurrence.

Further letters from the Rear-Admiral dated the 27th June and 11th July, Nos. 24 and 26, have also been received relating to other events which occurred whilst you were on shore, and their Lordships wish to take this opportunity of recording their appreciation of the manner in which Rear Admiral Bruce conducted the important duties which developed upon him during your enforced absence, and of the excellent relations which he maintained with his foreign colleagues throughout a period of exceptional gravity.

I am to inform you that the Secretary of State for Foreign Affairs entirely concurs in the expressions of approval which it has given their Lordships great pleasure to signify in this letter.

The despatches will be published in the "London Gazette" with the names of the officers and men of the Royal Navy and Royal Marines specially recommended.

My Lords cannot conclude without expressing their deep regret at the casualties which have occurred amongst the officers and men in the various engagements and operations, especially at the valuable lives which have been lost to Her Majesty's Service, notably that of Captain H.T.R. Lloyd, Royal Marine Light Infantry, mentioned favourably on several occasions; and I am to add that they have caused expressions of sympathy to be conveyed to the relatives of those who have fallen.

I am, etc.,
EVAN MACGREGOR.

Vice-Admiral Sir Edward H. Seymour, K.C.B.,
Commander-in-Chief of H.M. Ships and Vessels, China Station.

* * * * *

THE LONDON GAZETTE - TUESDAY, NOVEMBER 6, 1900

War Office, November 6, 1900.

The following Deespatches have been received by the Secretary of State for War:-

From the General Officer Commanding in China and Hong Kong to the Secretary of State for War.

SIR, **Hong Kong, July 5, 1900.**

I HAVE the honour to forward herewith a despatch received by me to-day from Major F.Morris, 2nd Battalion Royal Welsh Fusiliers, by which it would appear that his small force was fortunate enough to have been the means of at any rate assisting to open out the relief of Tientsin.

The reason this despatch was addressed direct to me was no doubt the fact that Major Morris had been detailed by me to command the force sent from Hong Kong, and it was only after he had left Hong Kong, and when all telegraphic communication with the north was interrupted, that I learnt that Colonel Dorward had been appointed to the command. Colonel Dorward had not joined at the time this despatch was written.

From what I learn, both Her Majesty's ship "Terrible" in which Major Morris and this force went up, and the transport in which the remainder left, encountered such severe weather as to delay their arrival at Taku; Her Majesty's ship "Terrible" though leaving Hong Kong a day later than the hired transport, arriving first at Taku. As troops were urgently needed, Major Morris started with his party, leaving the rest of the force sent by me to follow as soon as they landed. I learn, from unofficial sources, that these latter joined him later on, and the whole are now under the command of Brigadier-General Dorward.

It will, I think, be a source of satisfaction to you to know that the arrival of a British force enabled the relief to be successfully carried out.

I have, etc.,
W.J. GASCOIGNE, Major-General,
Commanding in China and Hong Kong.

* * * * *

From Major F. Morris, Royal Welsh Fusiliers, Commanding North China Field Force, to the General Officer Commanding, Hong Kong.

SIR, **Tientsin, June 24, 1900.**

I HAVE the honour to make the following report with reference to the relief of Tientsin:-

On 21st June I arrived in Her Majesty's ship "Terrible" at Tongku at 5 a.m., with details as per margin,* and left by train a few hours later for the front. I was joined by Captain Craddock, R.N.,

Royal Welsh Fusiliers, Officers 7, rank and file 328.
Royal Engineeers, Officers 1, rank and file 32.
Royal Army Medical Corps, Officers 1, rank and file 9.
Army Service Corps, Officers 1.
Army Pay Department, Officers 1, rank and file 1.

with the Naval Brigade. We proceeded to Chunlienshang Station, our advance being greatly retarded owing to the two leading trucks being derailed and overturned at some points, and also through having to repair the line where the sleepers had been burned. At Chulienshang we encamped for the night, and found a combined force of Russians and United States Marines,(²) who, on the previous day, had attempted to enter Tientsin, but had been repulsed with the loss of their gun. Major Waller, in command of the United States Marines, informed me that the position was too strong to take without guns, I, therefore, in consultation with Captain Cradock, R.N., agreed that it was advisable to delay a day till a Russian Field Battery should arrive. In the meantime my force was occupied in clearing the line of communications of Boxers and other Rebels; this was carried out completely, and a base for stores, etc., established at a place 10 miles west of Tientsin, where the line was so much destroyed that it was impossible for the train to advance further.

On 23rd June a Russian force (³) joined the British force, the latter consisting of seven Officers and 287 non-commissioned officers and men of the Royal Welsh Fusiliers, under myself, and the Naval Brigade, under Captain Cradock, R.N., and advanced to the attack of Tientsin at 4 a.m. The whole advanced along the railway line, the Russians were on the right, and the British and Americans on the left.

At a distance of about 6 miles from Tientsin the attack was opened and a heavy fire returned by the enemy. From this point the Russians made the railway station their objective, and I was ordered by the Russian General in command to diverge, and in conjunction with the Naval Brigade and American Marines, attack the military School. For about 5 miles the force fought its way under a very heavy rifle fire; many villages were rushed and taken at the point of the bayonet. The Military School was not strongly held, and was easily cleared of the enemy, who retreated out of it, leaving 25 killed and wounded. This school was the enemy's strongest position holding the European settlement, the relief of which was effected at 1 p.m., the inhabitants pouring out of their entrenchments to greet our soldiers and sailors as they crossed the river. I wish to testify to the great steadiness of my force under a very heavy fire and the heroic manner in which the various villages were assaulted and the enemy driven out. I attribute my casualties being small to the fact that the men availed themselves of cover on every possible occasion.

The following are my casualties:-

Killed
3752 Private F. Power
Wounded
4977 Private J. Jones, gunshot wound in knee. 4017 Private G. Martin, gunshot wound in thigh
Self slightly.

I wish to bring to your notice the names of the following Officers for favourable consideration:-

Captain J.H. Gwynne, Royal Welsh Fusiliers. This Officer has done most excellent work, and was conspicuous in leading some of the principal attacks on the various villages.

Lieutenant F.J. Walwyn, Royal Welsh Fusiliers. This Officer managed, under great difficulties, to make local arrangements to bring up the reserve ammunition into the firing line and assisted in saving the killed and wounded from falling into the hands of the enemy.

Lieutenant O.S. Flower, Royal Welsh Fusliers, afforded me valuable assistance as Staff Officer.

Major Watson, Royal Army Medical Corps, performed excellent work under great difficulties.

In forwarding this despatch, I should like to point out the difficulties under which I laboured.

The whole of my stores, reserve ammunition, stretchers and medical comforts were on board the chartered steamer "Hansing", which did not arrive till four days after me, so that I had to borrow ammunition and food in small quantities from the Royal Navy at different times.

There is no transport of any kind available, except a few odd mules and donkeys found in the country, but they have no saddlery or gear.

I am now organizing a company of Mounted Infantry, under Lieutenant Walwyn, 100 strong. The ponies and saddlery are provided by the civilians in Tientsin.

I find that the number of Officers under my command is inadequate, and I request that you will send me four more for duty with the present detachment, and one more complete company of 100 men, to include as many men as possible who have been through a course of Mounted Infantry.

I have, etc.,
FRED. MORRIS, Major,
Royal Welsh Fusiliers,
Commanding North China Field Force.

* Military Force.
Naval Force - About 150 strong.
(²) Russians about 300, United States Marines about 100.
(³) Infantry, Artillery, 4 guns, 1,500.

From the General Officer Commanding North China British Field Force to the Secretary of State for War.

SIR, **Tientsin, July 11, 1900.**

I HAVE the honour to submit the following report on the action which took place near here on the 9th instant:-

2. At 3 a.m. on 9th July a combined force of Japanese, Russian, American, and British troops moved out from the Taku Gate at the southern end of the Foreign Settlements with the object of clearing the Chinese Imperial troops and Boxers and their guns from the villages south of the Mud Parapet and also from the Western Arsenal.

3. The force consisted of 1,000 Japanese, including three troops of Cavalry, a battery of Mountain Artillery, and a party of Engineers, under General Fukushima, and of 950 British* 400 Russians, and 200 American troops under my command.

4. The whole force, with the exception of the Americans, who advanced on the Arsenal along the Mud Parapet, proceeded south by the main road for one and a half miles to the village of Tung Lou; there the force turned to the west and half a mile further on deployed, when opposition from the enemy was met with, the Japanese being on the left and the British troops on the right. The Russians acted as reserve to the British Column.

5. Four guns, that for several days had annoyed the Settlements by their fire from the village of Hei-niu-Chuang, were quickly silenced and captured, and the Japanese Cavalry were able to execute three successful charges among a considerable body of flying enemy, who had made but slight resistance to our attack.

6. The line then wheeled to the right and attacked the Western Arsenal.

7. The Japanese Engineers had to make a bridge across a small stream before the Artillery could advance. The bridge was made under cover of our combined Artillery fire, slowly replied to by the enemy's guns left at the Arsenal.

8. At 7.30 a.m. the Artillery crossed the stream and took up positions on the further side; the remainder of the force followed, the left of the line resting on the road leading to the Arsenal and the city. The whole of the country to the west of the road had been flooded by the enemy and rendered impassable for troops.

9. The Arsenal was quickly captured by a rush of the Japanese and Americans, and was entered at 9 a.m. by the combined forces, which also spread along the Mud Parapet to the west. Artillery was brought up close to the Parapet and a heavy fire opened on the city, which was answered with vigour by the enemy.

10. It had been intended to leave a force to prevent the reoccupation of the Arsenal by the enemy, but, owing to its gutted condition and exposed position, it was considered untenable. The houses surrounding it, which might give cover to guns or snipers, were burned, and the bridge leading to the city from the south destroyed.

11. The combined forces then returned along the Mud Parapet to the Settlements.

12. The success of the attack has relieved our batteries in the British Settlement from both direct and enfilade fire to which they had been exposed and has also diminished the number of guns bombarding the Settlements.

13. The most arduous work in the day was done by the Chinese Regiment, who, as escort to the guns, worked indefatigably in getting them over broken and swampy country.

14. The casualties in the British Force were - 1 private Royal Welsh Fusiliers, 1 private Royal Marine Light Infantry, and 1 Chinese hospital attendant, killed; 3 privates Royal Welsh Fusiliers, 1 private Chinese Regiment, and 1 Chinese hospital attendant, wounded. The Americans and Russians had no casualties. The Japanese lost 50 killed and wounded.

15. The Chinese lost 350 killed and the number of their wounded must have been considerable. As a result of the action, General Nich, one of the best of the Chinese generals, is reported to have been killed or to have committed suicide.

I have, etc.,
A.R.F. DORWARD,
Brigadier-General.

* 2 companies 2nd Battalion Royal Welsh Fusiliers, 2 2.5-in guns, 2 Maxims of the Hong Kong Royal Artillery, ½ company Hong Kong Regiment, 2 companies 1st Chinese Regiment, 400 Marines & Bluejackets.

* * * * *

From the General Officer Commanding British Forces, Tientsin, to the Secretary of State for War.

SIR, **Tientsin, July 19, 1900.**

ON the afternoon of the 11th instant I arranged with General Fukushima, Commanding the Japanese Forces, to carry out as soon as possible the capture of Tientsin City. Owing to our heavy losses during the bombardment of the Settlements we considered this movement necessary.

2. The Russian General was approached on the subject and said he would co-operate in the movement by an attack on the Chinese batteries and fort to the north-east of the city. He desired to get his pontoon train in readiness and said that as soon as he had done so he would give me notice of his readiness to move. His Staff Officer gave me that notice at 5 p.m. on the 12th instant, and it was arranged that the Russian Forces, who had the longer march, should move in time to deliver their attack on the batteries about 10 a.m., on the following day, and that the Japanese-British Forces should deliver their attack on the city as early as possible, in order to attract the bulk of the

Chinese troops to their side and so facilitate the capture of the batteries by the Russians.

3. I then called on Colonel de Pelacot, Commanding the French Forces, and Colonel Meade, commanding the American Forces, and together with them visited General Fukushima to discuss the plan of operations.

4. It was decided that the Allied Forces would parade at 3 a.m. and move in three columns - about 500 yards apart - on the Western Arsenal.

5. The French force 900 strong was to form the right column and. crossing the Mud Parapet in the British Extra Concession, was to move on the south side of it and under its cover direct on the Arsenal, timing its movement to agree with that of the other columns. Two companies were detailed to advance from the French Settlement and clear the houses between it and the city of troops. They were unable, however, in the face of a heavy fire to make much headway.

6. The Japanese column 1,000 strong under General Fukushima was to move out from the Settlement by the Race Course Gate at 3.20 a.m. and move parallel to the Mud Parapet about 500 yards from it.

7. The left column, consisting of 800 British troops (500 military and 300 naval), 900 Americans and 30 Austrians, moved out of the Taku Gate at 3.30 a.m. under my command and marched parallel to the Japanese column and about 500 yards from them. About 500 yards on the left of the left column was the Japanese Cavalary 150 strong.

8. The left column was somewhat delayed in clearing the villages of small parties of the enemy, and its head arrived at the road leading to the Arsenal and South Gate of the city about a quarter of a mile behind the head of the Japanese column.

9. The French column suffered a check at a bridge in the Mud Parapet about a quarter of a mile from the Arsenal, in crossing over which their troops were exposed to fire. The Arsenal was cleared of the enemy principally through the agency of the Japanese troops.

10. The advanced British troops, consisting of the detachment 2nd Battalion Royal Welsh Fusiliers, and the American Marines moved forward and lined the Mud Parapet west of the Arsenal, the 9th American Infantry being also brought forward under the parapet as support. The reserve, consisting of two companies Chinese Regiment and the Naval Brigade, were halted about 2,500 yards from the city and suffered some loss from long-range fire.

11. All the artillery of the combined force, consisting of mountain guns with the exception of three 3.2-inch guns belonging to the Americans, formed up a short distance south of the Mud Parapet and bombarded the city (5.30 a.m.).

12. One 4-inch gun three 12-pr. and a few 9-pr. and a 6-pr, worked by the Navy from a position in the British Extra Concession, did excellent service in keeping down the fire from the city walls.

13. After about an hour's bombardment it was decided to attack. The French were to be on the right, the Japanese in the centre, and the British on the left, the centre of the attack being the south gate. Owing to the attack being pushed on somewhat too hurriedly in the centre the Fusiliers and American Marines had to move forward rather too quickly under a heavy fire to get into their position on the Japanese left (7.15 a.m.).

14. General Fukushima had asked me to give some support to the left of his line during the attack and the 9th American Infantry was directed by me to give this support and also to support the attack of the Fusiliers and Marines.

15. When the 9th regiment had crossed the Mud Parapet, a body of men estimated at 1,500 strong, made up of cavalry and infantry, appeared about 2,500 yards away from our extreme left. I directed the detachment of the Hong Kong Regiment, who up to this time had been acting as escort to the guns, to take up a favourable position at a bend in the Mud Parapet about one mile from the Arsenal to meet any attack. They had no difficulty in repulsing this threatened attack with the aid of two Maxim guns sent to assist them as soon as possible.

16. The Japanese attack extended considerably more to the left than had been intended so that the Fusiliers and Marines were pushed more to the left than had been contemplated and brought close to heavy enfilade fire from the suburbs south of the south-west croner of the city. They faced that fire in the steadiest way, taking up a position under fairly good cover, and during the whole day prevented a large body of the enemy from making any forward movement.

17. Meanwhile seven or eight guns of the enemy's artillery were replying to our artillery fire from a fort about 1¼ miles west of the West Gate of the city.

18. The reserves were ordered up to take cover under the Mud Parapet and the whole of the artillery moved inside the parapet and took up the best positions obtainable to continue the bombardment.

19. Moving back from the Hong Kong Regiment position I could see nothing of the 9th American Infantry, but when I reached the Arsenal I saw that only a few Japanese troops were extended on the right of the road, and that the French troops were all in compact bodies in the villages on the road leading to the south gate behind the Japanese, from which I judged that the fire on the right hand had been so heavy that the French attacking line could not be formed.

20. At the Arsenal I met the Acting Adjutant of the 9th Regiment, who said he had been sent back with news that his regiment were in a very exposed position, which from his description I made out to be near the French settlement, and that they had lost heavily, their Colonel amongst others being mortally wounded. He said he had been ordered to ask for reinforcements, and I directed 100 men of the Naval Brigade under Lieutenant Phillimore, R.N., to proceed to their assistance.

21. I signalled in to Lieutenant-Colonel Bower, who was in command of the forces left in the Settlement, to send me out two more companies of the Chinese Regiment with all the stretchers he could collect and on their arrival sent the stretchers forward carried by the men of the regiment under Major Pereira. Major Pereira made two trips out to the American position and brought back many of their wounded under a very heavy fire, losing several men and being himself wounded. He told me

on returning from his second trip that the Americans and the men of the Naval Brigade had got into a fairly safe position, so I decided to leave them there till nightfall. They detained a considerable body of the enemy in front of them and prevented any attack being made on the right flank of the Japanese.

22. Major Pereira also informed me that the Americans were very badly off for ammunition, so I directed Captain Ollivant and a party of the Chinese Regiment to take a further supply to them. While performing this service I regret to say that Captain Ollivant was killed.

23. A Japanese Staff Officer afterwards told me that he had seen the 9th Regiment moving along the right rear of the Japanese attack in column of fours, and that he was afraid they must have suffered heavy loss.

24. The naval guns were all this time making splendid practice keeping down the fire from the city walls, and we were anxiously waiting for the sound of the explosion which would tell that the Japanese sappers had reached the city gate and blown it in. Shortly after 1 p.m. I received the following note from the Japanese Chief Staff Officer:-

"Mon General. Nos Soldats sont deja entres dans la cite. Je vous done de faire cosser le feu de vos canons immediatement. ASKI, Lieutenant-Colonel."

25. Orders were accordingly given for the cessation of all artillery fire and the advance of all our troops to support the assault on the city. The advancing troops were met with a very heavy fire from the walls, which continued to increase in intensity, and it soon became apparent that the Japanese troops had not entered the city. The troops were then forced to take cover close to the canal round the city. I shortly afterwards heard from the Japanese General that he had been misinformed and that his troops had not entered the city.

26. Orders were sent for all guns to open fire again and owing to the beautiful practice of the naval guns very little loss was suffered by the troops in the advanced trenches.

27. Towards evening the 1,500 troops on the left flank again advanced and began preparing a long line of shelter trenches. I received a request from General Fukishima asking me if I could undertake arrangements for the protection of his troops and the French, while in their advanced positions, from attack from the left flank or rear, as his Cavalry had informed him that bodies of the enemy were threatening us from those directions.

28. The naval guns were then requested to direct their whole fire on the enemy facing the extreme left of our position and, under cover of that fire and of volleys from the detachment, Hong Kong Regiment, directed on the various points from which the enemy were harassing the retirement, the Fusiliers and American Marines were withdrawn with very slight loss and formed up behind the Mud Parapet. The movement reflected great credit on Colonel Meade, commanding the Marines, and Captain Gwynne, commanding the Fusiliers.

29. The more delicate manoeuvre of withdrawing the 9th American Infantry and the Company of the Naval Brigade had then to be undertaken. The naval guns were directed to sweep the barriers constructed along the fringe of houses between the French Settlement and the city from which the fire on the American troops proceeded. The American troops themselves were only about 300 yards from this fringe and there was great danger of the fire from the naval guns injuring them as well as the enemy. The dead and wounded, of which the Americans had still a considerable number with them, were brought back with the assistance of the Company of the Naval Brigade, and shortly afterwards the 9th Regiment arrived at the Mud Parapet in safety. I would specially bring to notice the conduct of Major Jesse Lee during the retirement; in him the regiment possesses an Officer of exceptional merit.

30. The whole force is under the greatest obligation to Captain Bayly and Lieutenant Drummond, Royal Navy, for their working of the naval guns.

31. After posting troops to secure our flank and rear from attack, the troops turned in for the night, during which there was some rain.

32. About 3 a.m. next day the Japanese sappers, crossing the canal by a bridge they had made during the night, blew in the South Gate and in less than half an hour, after some desultory street fighting, the city was in our possession.

33. The British force seized a large number of junks and one small steamer on the canal north of the city, which will be useful when we advance on Pekin, and also the eight guns which had kept up a steady fire on our artillery throughout the previous day.

34. News was then received that the Russian attack on the other side of the city had been delayed by unforeseen causes, but when made had proved very successful, resulting in the complete rout of the Chinese and the capture of 11 guns; the Russian loss was about 120 killed and wounded.

35. The losses of the Allied Forces in the attack on the South Gate were as follows:-

Royal Marine Light Infantry. - Killed, Captain Lloyd; slightly wounded, Major Luke; wounded, 16 men.

Royal Navy. - Slightly wounded, Lieutenant Field; killed, 5 men; wounded, 19 men.

Royal Welsh Fusiliers. - Killed, 5 men; wounded, 12 men.

Hong Kong Regiment. - Wounded, 8 men, of whom 1 afterwards died.

Hong Kong Companies, Royal Artillery. - Killed, 2 men; wounded, 5 men.

Chinese Regiment. - Killed, Captain Ollivant; slightly wounded, Major Pereira and 1 European non-commissioned officer; killed, 3 men; wounded, 13 men, of whom 1 died afterwards.

American Forces, 9th Infantry. - Colonel Liscum and 22 men killed; 3 Officers and 70 men wounded. Marines 5 killed and 27 wounded.

French Forces. - 110 killed and wounded. Japanese Forces. - 400 killed and wounded.

Austrians. - 5 wounded. The Austrians were my personal escort during the greater part of the day and were sent forward to enter the city with the advanced troops.

36. On returning to the Settlement it was found that 7 men of the Royal Welsh Fusiliers had been wounded, and 1 American killed, and 4 wounded by a shell at the railway station on the 13th instant.

37. Among many instances of personal bravery in the action, I would specially bring to notice the conduct of First Lieutenant Smedley D. Butler, United States Marine Corps. in bringing in a wounded man from the front under heavy and accurate fire. Lieutenant Butler was wounded while so doing, and was himself carried out of the firing line by the Adjutant First Lieutenant Henry Leonard, who, I regret to say, was dangerously wounded in so doing.

38. Captain Lawton, Acting Adjutant of the 9th Regiment, brought me news of their condition under a heavy fire and, when returning with the reinforcements to guide them to his regiment, was severely wounded.

39. The Royal Welsh Fusiliers were well handled throughout the day by Captain Gwynne; they were very careful of their ammunition and wasted less than any other body of troops on the ground.

40. No. 5653 Private Doodson of the Royal Welsh Fusiliers volunteered to carry back to medical assistance - across 300 yards of open and fire-swept space - Lance Sergeant Pearce of the same regiment, who was severely wounded; this he successfully accomplished and afterwards brought back a severely wounded Japanese soldier from the advanced trenches to medical assistance and safety.

41. No. 4617 Private Crew of the Royal Welsh Fusiliers attempted to carry back Private Bonner over the same ground; Private Bonner was hit twice during the attempt and Private Crew was shot dead.

42. I would also bring to notice the brave and collected conduct of No. 4575 Sergeant C.W. Taylor of the same regiment, throughout the day. He was prominent in bringing in the wounded men and was generally a splendid example to the half company of which he was in charge.

43. Captain Watson of the Chinese Regiment led his men well and the two companies with him were among the first troops to enter the city. He has specially brought to my notice the conduct of No.94 Serjeant Gi-Dien-Kwee, who was in command of a half company without any European.

44. The artillery under Major St.John were very well handled and managed to make their ammunition last considerably longer than the artillery of the other nations did. As they were firing black powder, they were at a distinct disadvantage with the artillery of the enemy, which was using smokeless powder, thus rendering the exact location of their guns very difficult. Major St.John has specially brought to my notice the coolness and accuracy of fire of No. 353, Havildar Roshan Khan, who succeeded in putting out of action in four rounds an enemy's gun which had done us much damage.

45. The Naval Brigade under Captain Burke, R.N., had their full share of the fighting in the centre and right of the position and had the honour of being among the first troops to enter the city. The Companies were splendidly led by Commander Beatty and Lieutenant Phillimore, and nothing could have been finer than their spirit and conduct. I have already brought to notice the exceptionally fine work done by Captain Bayly and Lieutenant Drummond, R.N., and the naval guns. I received at all times the most ready and unquestioning assistance from Captain Burke.

46. The medical arrangements for the treatment, care and removal of the wounded reflected great credit on Major Watson, R.A.M.C., and his subordinates. Not only were those arrangements sufficient for the British wounded, but he was also able to take medical charge of American, French and Japanese patients and to send them into hospital. Captain Prynne, R.A.M.C., and Assistant-Surgeon Pullen, S.M.D., were in the advanced fighting line all day dressing cases under fire. They are both valuable Officers, always cool and collected.

I have, etc.,
A.R.F. DORWARD,
Brigadier-General.

* * * * *

India Office, November 6, 1900

The following Despatch has been received by the Secretary of State for India from Lieutenant-General Sir Alfred Gaselee, K.C.B., Commanding the British Contingent, China Expeditionary Force:-

Despatch from Sir A. Gaselee, General Officer Commanding China Expeditionary Force, dated Peking, 19th August, 1900.

No. 36 S.

Head-Quarters,
China Expeditionary Force, Peking,
August 19, 1900.

MY LORD,

NOW that the first and paramount duty of relieving the Legations has been successfully performed, I am in a position to address to your Lordship a preliminary Despatch, describing the operations of the British forces in Northern China from the 27th July, the date I arrived at Tientsin, to the 14th August, the date on which we entered Peking.

2. On my arrival at Tientsin I at once put myself into communication with the General Officers commanding the American and Japanese forces, and soon came to a satisfactory understanding with them. We decided to collectively impress upon the Allied Commanders the absolute necessity of pressing forward towards Peking at the earliest possible moment, and happily our views were eventually accepted.

At a confernece held on the 3rd August it was arranged to commence the advance on the 4th, with approxiamtely 20,000 men, viz:-

10,000 Japanese with 24 guns.
4,000 Russians with 16 guns.
3,000 British with 12 guns.
2,000 Americans with 6 guns.
800 French with 12 guns.
200 Germans.
100 Austrians and Italians.
20,100 with 70 guns.

3. The Chinese were believed to occupy a strongly intrenched position near Pei-tsang, astride the Pei-ho. It was decided to force this position and push on to Yang-tsun, so as to secure the passage of the river at that important strategical point. The general idea was that the Japanese, British, and Americans should operate along the right bank of the river, the other allies along the left bank. It was then settled in direct communication with General Chaffee, United States Army, and General Yamagutchi, Japanese Army, that, as regards the left attack, i.e., that on the right bank of the river, the movement should be of a turning nature along the embankment marked A........B in the attached sketch, the Japanese leading, followed in succession by the British and Americans. The turning movement to commence at 2 a.m. on the 5th.

4. In pursuance of the above agreement, the British troops marginally noted* moved from Tien-tsin to Hsi-ku on the afternoon of the 4th and bivouacked in the area marked C. Annexure A (Field Force Order No. 140) shows the arrangements for the march. The British were followed by the Americans and Japanese, who bivouacked at the points marked D and E.

5. As arranged, in the early hours of the 5th instant, the turning movement commenced. At day-break the column came under heavy fire from the right front and the action began with a vigorous forward movement of the Japanese against the entrenchments, supported on the right by the British. The brunt of the action fell on the Japanese, who attacked and stormed line after line in the most gallant manner. Our troops, in consequence of their position, scarcely fired a shot, and I readily accord to the Japanese the whole credit of the victory. Their loss was, I understand, about 300 killed and wounded, while ours was only 25 (vide Annexure B). The Chinese rout was complete, and before noon they had entirely disappeared, having fled to the left bank of the river. The other allied forces were scarcely engaged at all and practically had no loss.

6. After the victory at Pei-tsang we pushed on for a mile or two along the right bank, but, being stopped by inundations, were compelled to return to Pei-tsang, and cross over to the right (sic) bank, where we bivouacked for the night, covered by a strong outpost, two or three miles in advance.

7. On the 6th instant the whole of the allied forces marched on Yang-tsun by the right bank, with the exception of about 6,000 Japanese, who continued to advance by the left bank. Owing to the direction taken by the several columns the British troops were leading along the direct road when we came in sight of Yang-tsun, the Americans being on our right flank. The enemy's main position was apparently along the railway embankment, with one flank resting on a village close to the Pei-ho railway bridge. It was at once, arranged to attack this position with one Russian battalion on the left, the British troops in the centre, and the Americans on the right, while the 1st Bengal Lancers covered the extreme right flank. I thereupon directed the 1st Sikh Infantry to extend for attack, supported by the Royal Welsh Fusiliers, and the 24th Punjab Infantry, the advance to be covered by the fire of No. 12 Battery Royal Field Artillery. The remainder of our troops were too far in rear to be utlized at the moment. The advance to attack was made in beautiful order over about 5,000 yards of level plain, covered with high crops. At about half this distance the troops came under a hot shell and musketry fire, nevertheless, owing to the open order in which we worked, the British loss was comparatively small. The further advance was a rapid one, and the embankment was carried by a rush of the 1st Sikh Infantry and 24th Punjab Infantry. The Welsh Fusiliers, owing to the conformation of the ground, were rather wedged out of the assaulting line. This practically ended the fight, as the Chinese fled precipitately in all directions. The enemy's guns were in a retired position, and thus escaped capture. Our loss on this occasion was as shown in Annexure C.

8. On the 7th instant the allies halted to bring up supplies, and on the 8th the movement was continued. On the 9th, at Ho-hsi-wu, a squadron off the 1st Bengal Lancers caught up some retreating Tartar cavalry, inflicting on them heavy loss, and on the 12th Tung-chao was occupied without opposition. At a conference held on that day it was decided to send forward strong reconnoitring forces on the 13th, to concentrate on a line about five miles from Peking on the 14th, and to attack on the 15th. The positions of the several forces were assigned, the British taking the extreme left. On the 14th, however, owing to the premature advance of a battalion of one of the allied forces, the intended concentration was abandoned, and the troops all hurried forward to assault the city of Peking.

9. I have above endeavoured to give a connected account of the military operations preceding the attack on Peking, and I will now try to briefly relate what occurred on the 14th, so far as Her Majesty's troops are concerned. Our forces on the night of the 13th were concentrated on the river south-east of Tung-chao, about 15 miles from Peking, with two guns, the 1st Bengal Lancers and the 7th Bengal Infantry about nine miles in advance as an observation force. At 2.30 a.m. on the 14th, hearing heavy firing in the direction of Peking, I caused the rouse to be sounded and marched without delay towards the supposed scene of action. About 7 a.m. I reached the point held by my advanced force, and at once pushed on with the troops there available, directing the main body to follow after an hours' rest. About noon I got into touch with the Americans, who were on the south bank of the canal, and as they and the French were preparing to assault the Tung Tien Gate, I decided to push straight on and assault the south-east gate of the Chinese city, Sha-chia-men. Here I met with no

opposition, and about 1 p.m. the British troops passed through the city wall. I then ordered the 1st Bengal Lancers and the 24th Punjab Infantry to march straight to the Temple of Heaven Park, which I wished to secure as a camping ground, and also as a protection to my left and rear, while with the rest of my available troops I pushed on through streets and alleys towards the water gate of the Tartar City, a point which I had learnt from a cypher message from Sir. C. Macdonald would probably be the most vulnerable. Our troops were much exhausted by the long march and intense heat, and were much scattered in groups, but they struggled gamely on without attempting to reply to the desultory and ineffective fire of the enemy. At a few minutes before 3 p.m., I, with a few officers of my staff and about 70 men of the 1st Sikhs and 7th Bengal Infantry, reached a point opposite the water gate. The British flag was still flying on that portion of the Tartar wall which we knew the Legations had occupied, but an ominous silence made us fear that the worst had occurred, and that the flag was only a ruse to lure us on; when suddenly to our great relief, we saw a flag signal being made, "Come up sluice street by water gate". Our small party at once rushed across the almost dry canal, and entered into the Legation zone through the water gate under the Tartar wall. As we crossed a hail of ill-aimed fire was directed on us from the Ilata-Men gate, but not a man was touched, and at 3 p.m. Her Majesty's troops has the supreme gratification of finding that they were the first to relieve the sorely pressed beleaguered garrison.

10. Our loss * during these operations was quite insignificant, which may be attributed to the fact that the enemy had never expected attack from this quarter, and had concentrated their defence on the eastern wall of the Tartar city, where the resistance was, I understand, of a most obstinate description.

11. The operations I have described have, happily, not been attended with the loss that might have been expected; nevertheless, the troops engaged have been subjected to a severe strain on account of the intense heat, the want of good water, the heavy mud or dust which characterises the roads in this country, and, above all, the want of sufficient rest. The patient endurance and ardour of the troops has, however, more than compensated for these difficulties, and I am proud of the manner in which Her Majesty's British and Indian troops have acquitted themselves.

12. In conclusion I do not propose in this despatch to bring specially to your Lordship's notice the services rendered by many Officers of this force, but I take the opportunity of mentioning the names of those few who had a special opportunity of distinguishing themselves at the action of Yang-tsun. They are:-

Major T.E. Scott, D.S.O., 1st Sikh Infantry (attached).

Lieutenant W.F. Bainbridge, 1st Sikh Infantry.

Captain J.H. Gwynne, Royal Welsh Fusiliers.

No. 4995, Private Jackson, Royal Weslh Fusiliers, whose commanding officer reports that "as some shells from one of the batteries engaged were taking our troops and the Americans in reverse, he volunteered to get up on the embankment and tried to communicate with the battery." While doing so, he was exposed to fire from both sides.

I would also like to mention the names of two American Officers who gallantly supported our fighting line, viz:-

Major William Quinton, 14th United States Infantry.

Captain J.R.M. Taylor, 14th United States Infantry.

As regards other officers and men, I deem the conclusion of the campaign to be the most fitting moment to bring their services to your Lordship's notice.

I have, etc.,

ALFRED GASELEE, Lieutenant-General,

Commanding China Expeditionary Force.

The Right Honourable, The Secretary of State for India.

* Naval Brigade, 4 guns; Royal Marine Light Infantry, 300; 12th Battery Royal Field Artillery, 6 guns; Hong Kong Artillery, 2 guns, 4 Maxims; Detachment Royal Engineers, -; 1st Bengal Lancers, 400; Royal Welsh Fusiliers, 300; 7th Bengal Infantry, 500; 24th Punjab Infantry, 300; 1st Sikh Infantry, 500; Hong Kong Regiment, 100; Chinese Regiment, 100.

* * * * *

ANNEXURES

Annexure A. China Expeditionary Force Orders, Tientsin, 4th August, 1900.

140. Movements. - The enemy is in position in the direction of Pei-Tsang on both banks of the Pei-Ho. The position is believed to be entrenched with outposts thrown forward.

(ii) The Russian, French, and German Forces will operate on the left bank of the River Pei-Ho.

- - -

* Vide Annexure D.

the British, Americans, and Japanese on the right bank.

(iii) The British Forces will march to Hsi-Ku to day, where they will bivouac for the night.

(iv) The British Forces will march in the order given below:-

Royal Welsh Fusiliers with advance guard of one Company.

Detachment Royal Engineers.

One Field Troops 1st Bengal Lancers.

Head-Quarters Staff of Division.

One half Company 1st Sikhs (General Officer Commanding's escort).

12th Battery Royal Field Artillery.
R.7 Ammunition Column Unit.
Hong Kong Royal Artillery.
1st Brigade Staff.
7th Rajputs, less one Company.
1st Sikhs.
Chinese Regiment.
1st Bengal Lancers.
Divisional and Brigade Head-Quarters Transport.
Commissariat and Transport.
Field Hospitals.
Rear Guard one Company 7th Rajputs.

(v) The route will be by the Temperence Hall on the Taku road, through the Chinese City entering by the South Gate and over the Iron Bridge to Hsi-Ku. The road to be followed will be shown by the Deputy-Assistant Quartermaster-General for Intelligence, who will lead the column.

(vi) The troops will keep closed up as much as possible, water bottles are to be filled with boiled water or tea, and all mussacks filled with good water.

(vii) The head of the column will leave the Temperance Hall at 2.30 p.m. Officers commanding units will hold their units in readiness to join the line of march in the order detailed above. No intervals between units.

(viii) Camp Colour men of all units and one officer or non-commissioned Officer per unit will accompany the advance guard.

(ix) No fires or cooking will be allowed in bivouac to-night.

(NOTE. - All units not mentioned in paragraph iv had marched to Hsi-Ku the previous evening.)

By order,
E.G. BARROW, Major-General,
Chief of the Staff,
China Expeditionary Force.

All transport of units will march immediately in rear of their own units.

- - -

Annexure B.
Detail of Casualties in the Action at Pei-tsang.

British non-commissioned Officers and Men, slightly wounded, 4.

Native Officers, slightly wounded, 3.

Native non-commissioned Officers and Men, killed, 1; dangerously wounded, 1; severely wounded, 9; slightly wounded, 7.

Total: killed, 1; dangerously wounded, 1; severely wounded, 9; slightly wounded, 14.

- - -

Annexure C.
Detail of Casualties in the Action at Yang-tsun.

British Officers, dangerously wounded, 1.

British non-commissioned Officers and men, killed, 1; died of sunstroke, 1; dangerously wounded, 1; severely wounded, 3; slightly wounded, 4.

Native non-commissioned Officers and men, killed, 5; dangerously wounded, 3; severely wounded, 6; slightly wounded, 20.

Total: killed, 6; died of sunstroke, 1; dangerously wounded, 5; severely wounded, 9; slightly wounded, 24.

- - -

Annexure D.
Casualties from 8th to 14th August.

8th August, native non-commissioned Officers and men, died, 1; accidently drowned.

At He-hsi-wu, 9th August, native non-commissioned Officers and men, slightly wounded, 2.

At Peking, 14th August, British non-commissioned Officers and men, died, 1, heart disease.

Native non-commissioned Officers and men, severely wounded, 2; slightly wounded, 1; missing, 1.

Total, died, 2; severely wounded, 2; slightly wounded, 3; missing, 1.

- - -

* * * * *

THE LONDON GAZETTE - TUESDAY, DECEMBER 11, 1900.

Admiralty, December 10, 1900.

DESPATCHES, of which the following are copies, have been received from the Commander-in-Chief on the China Station, relative to the siege of the Legations at Peking:-

Enclosures in China Letters Nos. 573, 605, and 613 of 5th, 17th and 18th September, 1900, respectively.

H.B.M. Legation, Peking.

Saturday, August 18, 1900.

SIR,

I HAVE the honour to forward to you this, my report of the guard of Royal Marine Light Infantry which did duty in this Legation and in the defence of the Legations Settlement in Peking during the late siege.

The guard was under the command of Captain B.M. Strouts, and left Tientsin the 31st May, arriving here the same night. Trouble began with the Boxers in the city the 13th June. An ultimatum to quit the city within 24 hours was received by the Ministers from the Chinese Government. It was decided to remain, and hostilities began the night of the 20th. The active siege continued until the 17th July, when there was a practical cessation of firing until the 5th August, during which period the Tsungli Yamen communicated several times with the Ministers. The siege was raised the afternoon of the 14th August by the allied army.

Captain Strouts having died of his wound the 16th July, and Captain Halliday still suffering from his wound, I have been in command since that date.

I have, etc.,
EDMUND WRAY, Captain R.M.L.I.,
Commanding Guard.

The Senior Naval Officer, Her Britannic Majesty's Fleet, North China.

* * * * *

H.B.M. Legation Guard, Peking,

SIR, **August 26, 1900.**

I HAVE the honour to forward to you, this, my report of the part taken in the defence of Peking by the Royal Marine Legation Guard. I beg to state that no accurate record of all the details of duties performed by the detachment was kept, as parts of it were daily employed in reinforcing other portions of the concerted defence of the Legations, and no reports were received from the foreign officers commanding those sections of the defence.

The guard arrived in Peking on the night of the 31st May, and consisted of 3 officers, 75 Non-commissioned officers and men, 1 bugler, 1 armourer, 1 signalman, and 1 sick-berth steward, the late Captain B.M. Stouts being in command. Ordinary guard duties were performed until the 13th June, on which date some 300 Boxers entered the Tartar City near the Legation Settlement, and it was from this date that the detachment was continuously on the alert and at their posts in the defence. I beg to report the subsequent events in the form of a diary:-

13th June.-A picket of an officer and 12 men was placed and kept on the North Bridge, to prevent Boxers from attacking the Legation.

14th June.-At about 10.30 p.m., some 100 Boxers wishing to cross the North Brigade from east to west, rushed at and attacked the picket, and were repulsed, losing 4 killed and 2 wounded.

15th June.- Captain L.S.T. Halliday, with a combined force of British and German Marines, rescued several hundred Chinese Christians from the Nantung Roman Catholic Mission, who were being massacred by Boxers, some 300 of the latter being killed.

16th June.-I was sent with 20 British, 9 American, and 5 Japanese Marines to rescue a Christian family from the N.E. city. A reputed Boxer Temple, which I intended visiting on my return, was passed on the way. Hearing shrieks issuing from the temple, as of victims being tortured, and seeing signs of Boxers holding their rites, I approached the temple with some men. Bricks were hurled, and spears thrust over the walls, so I decided to force my way in. I succeeded in doing so, and killed about 45 Boxers, none of them being able to escape. The mutilated bodies of two native Christians were found. My native guide having meantime run away, I returned to the Legation, and learnt that the Christian family had come in.

17th June.-Chinese Imperial troops fired on the picket on North Bridge.

19th.-An ultimatum for all Ministers and foreigners to leave Peking within 24 hours was received by the Ministers that evening. It was decided to remain and defend the Legations.

20th June.-The German Minister was killed; the picket on North Bridge was withdrawn. It was decided that all women and children should be brought into the British Legation, which would be the last line of defence. Our sentries at the Front Gate opened fire for the first time on Imperial troops, who shot an unarmed European on North Bridge. A heavy fusillade was opened by the enemy all round the settlement during a thunderstorm that night. Captain F.G. Poole, East Yorkshire Regiment, who was in Peking studying Chinese, and who was attached to the Marine Guard in June, was given a section of the defence of the Legation to command. Captain C. Percy Smith, late of the South Staffordshire Regiment, also became attached, and commanded another section.

21st June.-At the request of all the Foreign Ministers, Sir Claude MacDonald, K.C.M.G., K.C.B., Her Britannic Majesty's Minister Plenipotentiary, took supreme command of the Legations Settlement, the Commanding Officers of each guard being in command of their several Legations.

22md June.-An unsuccessful attempt was made to burn the Legations at the south-west corner. Captain Poole with 15 Marines, reconnoitred the Hanlin. Private Scadding was killed.

23rd June.-The Hanlin was set on fire by the enemy with the object of burning Legation from the north; the wind changing in time, our front was cleared. Captain Poole, with a force of British and American Marines and Volunteers, drove out the enemy and occupies the southern part.

24th June.-Captain Halliday, with 30 Marines, was sent by Captain Strouts to drive the enemy from the houses behind First Chinese Secretary's house. He was dangerously wounded almost immediately after, killing four out of five of his assailants with his revolver, returned to the Legation, and has been disabled ever since. Captain Strouts who was on the spot, then took charge and led the force. Driving the enemy back some 100 yards, he succeeded in taking several arms and much ammunition besides burning several houses, thus clearing our front. Germans and Americans occupied South City Wall. Privates Sawyer and Goddard wounded this day.

25th June.-Captain Strouts formed and took command of a Company of 85 Volunteers of all nationalities living in the British Legation.

26th June.-Lance-Corporal Allin wounded.

27th June.- Lance-Corporal Sparkes wounded.

28th June.- Enemy opened fire with a 2-7inch Krupp gun and a "1-pr.field gun" against the South stable quarters, doing considerable damage to the building; this was silenced by rifle fire.

29th June.-I made an unsuccessful sortie at daylight to capture the Krupp gun, with a mixed force of British, German, and Russian Marines and Volunteers. It was discovered that the gun had been withdrawn. Captain Poole, with a force of British Marines and Volunteers, at the same time made an unsuccessful sortie to destroy the enemy's barricade on the Imperial Carriage Park wall near the West Hanlin. On this occasion Corporal T. Johnson showed great bravery in covering the retreat, carried out under a very heavy rifle fire. Private Phillips killed on this day.

30th June.-Privates Tickner and Horne wounded.

1st July.-The Germans, having had to abandon their barricade on the south city wall near their Legation, I was sent with a party of 12 British, 3 Americans, and 2 Russians, to try and build a barricade as near the canal as possible, so as to cover the rear of the American barricade. After working for four hours, losing 2 men wounded and being wounded myself, I was ordered to give up the attempt, so retired the force to the American barricade. Corporal D.J. Gowney showed great coolness in carrying out the retirement, and Private T.A. Myers showed great tenacity and courage in building the baricade under a heavy and accurate front and rear fire, and in spite of damaged hands. Five British Marines took part in an unsuccessful sortie made by the Japanese and Italians to capture a Krupp gun in the Suan Fu. This day, Privates King, Harden, and Heap were wounded, also Privates Deane and Buckler very slightly. Volunteers took an important part in the sortie.

3rd July.-Captain Myers, the officer commanding American Marine Guard, with a force of 15 Americans 25 British Marines under Serjeant Murphy, and 15 Russians, carried and occupied two Chinese barricades on the South City wall towards the Chun Min gate. Serjeant T. Murphy showed great courage and coolness in leading the second assault after Captain Myers had been wounded. This action was carried out at night. Corporal Gregory wounded.

5th July.-Enemy mounted four smooth-bore M.L. guns firing round shot on the Imperial City wall. They opened fire on a working party, which, with its covering force of British Marines in the Hanlin, was forced to retire into the Legation. It was during this time that Leading Signalman Swannell distinguished himself. Considerable damage was done to the buildings at north end of Legation with these guns.

8th July.- An old smooth-bore gun was found and mounted by an American gunner, assisted by Armourer Thomas, Royal Navy, who also manufactured the ammunition; the projectiles being the shells of a modern Russian field gun. In the evening the enemy opened fire at the roof of First Chinese Secretary's house with a 1-pr. Corporal D.J. Gowney showed great coolness and pluck by firing at the flash of the gun from the fort on the top of the First Chinese Secretary's roof. The enemy's gun was only 100 yards off, and was silenced by Corporal Gowney at the ninth round.

11th July.-From this date eight British Marines were sent daily to reinforce the Japanese and Italian posts in the Suan Fu. (I beg to mention here that since about the 8th July the enemy seem to have given up trying to force their way into the British Legation, but to have made the Christian converts the object of their attacks, so that henceforth their worst attacks were against the Italians, Japanese, French, and Germans.)

12th July.-The Italian Officer having been wounded, Captain Strouts allowed my services, which I had offered, to be accepted, and I took command of the Italians at their post, together with eight British Marines.

13th July.-It happened that during this day British Marines were used in reinforcing every post outside the British Legation. Lance-Serjeant T.E. Preston distinguished himself on this day. (His conduct will be mentioned leter.) Private Westbrook wounded.

16th July.-Captain Strouts was mortally wounded, and died three hours later. He was returning from visiting my post in the Suan Fu. His loss was deeply felt by all. Captain Halliday was the next in seniority, but being still unfit for duty, I took command of the Royal Marines, and was relieved from the command of the Italians by Lieutenant Von Stranck, late of the Prussian Army, and now in the Chinese Imperial Maritime Customs. Sir Claude MacDonald now took command of the British Legation, and Captain Poole took command of the Volunteers. I have been in command of the British Marines ever since. A message was received from the Chinese Government saying they would protect us, and had given orders to stop all firing. Firing on the part of the enemy actually ceased about noon on the 17th.

From the 17th July until the 4th August, except for sniping on both sides, but chiefly on the part of the Chinese opposite our western defences, there was a cessation of hostilities. This sniping gradually increased on our part of the enemy, until on the 4th severe fusillades and attacks were made on the Legation's Settlements; but, as before, the enemy never rushed in the open, but only approached behind brick barricades which they built, even under a heavy fire on our part.

2nd August.-The houses east of Mongal Market were occupied by Marines and Customs Volunteers under Lieutenant Von Stranck.

4th August.-Serjeant Murphy did great execution with the five-barrelled Nordenfeldt, mounted at the south-east corner of Imperial Carriage Park, in covering the subsequent occupation of the "Ruins" behind the Chinese Secretary's house, and the holding of the Mongul Market by us. Severe fusillades at night.

8th August.-The "Ruins" were occupied and fortified. Heavy fusillades all round the settlement, especially at night. This happened every night, more or less frequently.

9th August.-In the afternoon the enemy made three heavy attacks on the "Ruins", and the Chinese officers in their barricades only 15 yards off, were heard ordering their men to charge. But we were using our ammunition more freely than at any time during the siege, and firing volleys at their barricade, doing considerable damage to it. The last attack, and one at night, we were able to repulse by merely throwing bricks and stones.

13th August.-A note was received from the Chinese Government saying orders had been given for any Chinese soldier firing on us to be court-martialled. During a total cessation of firing in the afternoon the enemy mounted two Krupp guns on their fort in the Imperial city wall over the canal, with which they opened fire on the Legation during a heavy combined attack on the whole settlement at 7.45 p.m. They were also heard again trying to urge an attack on the "Ruins" at 3 a.m. next morning, but never came, our men, with reinforcements of volunteers, remaining at their loopholes for over two hours.

14th August.-Very heavy cannonading was heard, and from the South City walls shells were seen bursting against the gates of the Tartar City. This increased during the morning, and it was realized that relief was at hand. At 3 p.m. the allied army sent to our relief reached us; the first to enter the settlement, and two hours in advance of any others, being British native troops, one company of 1st Sikhs, followed immediately by General Sir Alfred Gaselee and his Staff.

I have the honour to bring before your notice the conduct of, and to recommend for the conspicuous gallantry medal, Lance-Serjeant T.E. Preston of Her Majesty's ship "Orlando". On the 14th July, after the enemy had been driven down from their barricade on the Imperial Carriage Park wall near the West Hanlin, by shell fire, this non-commissioned officer climbed on to the wall, some 12 feet high, with the intention of capturing a banner left on the barricade by the enemy. Finding that he could not reach it, he called for his rifle to be given him, and pushing part of the barricade he kept the enemy some 50 in number, at bay, while an American gunner, named Michell, was enabled to lay hold of the flag. Serjeant Preston then jumped down and assisted Gunner Michell in drawing the flag over with difficulty, as the enemy had laid hold of the other end. He was struck on the head at the same time by a brick, which partly stunned him.

I have the honour to bring before your notice also the conduct of Leading Signalman H. Swannell, Her Majesty's ship "Orlando", and to request that you will be pleased to recommend him for that reward which you think his action deserves. I beg to enclose from Captain Poole his account of the deed, of which he was an eye-witness.

I have the honour to bring before your notice and to recommend for promotion the following:-

Lance-Serjeant T.E. Preston, Her Majesty's ship "Orlando".

Corporal W. Gregory, Wei-Hai-Wei Detachment.

Corporal D.J. Gowney, Wei-Hai-Wei Detachment.

Acting Lance-Corporal T.R. Allen, Wei-Hai-Wei Detachment.

Also the following Naval ratings:-

Armourer T.S. Thomas, Her Majesty's ship "Orlando". This man showed great ingenuity in constructing the charges, and in utilizing the modern Russian projectiles for the muzzle loading gun. Also in making projectiles for the Italian 1-pr. field gun, as well as bullets for the German and Russian modern rifles. His services were invaluable.

Sick Berth Steward, second class, R.G. Fuller.

In conclusion, I beg to report that the behaviour of the whole detachment during a very trying time, and under fatiguing circumstances, was exemplary and deserving of all praise. As a proof of their steadiness and coolness, I beg to state that out of 18,000 rounds of Lee-Metford ammunition brought from Tientsin some 9,000 remain.

I have, etc.,
EDMUND WRAY, Captain R.M.L.I.,
Commanding British Marine Guard.

To the Senior Naval Officer,
Northern Division,
Her Majesty's China Fleet, Taku.

* * * * *

H.B.M. Legation, Peking,
July 31, 1900.

SIR,

I HAVE the honour to bring to your notice particularly the conduct of Leading Signalman H. Swannell, Her Majesty's ship "Orlando".

On the 5th instant, being in command of the Hanlin outposts, at 10.30 a.m. I heard that Mr. Oliphant, Her Britannic Manjesty's Consular Service, had just been wounded.

I ran out to the spot and found Leading Signalman Swannell attending to Mr. Oliphant who was mortally wounded, under the close and accurate fire of the enemy.

He remained with Mr. Oliphant until he was brought into a place of safety.

I have, etc.,
F.G. POOLE, Captain,
East Yorkshire Regiment.

The Officer Commanding,
Royal Marine Light Infantry Detchament,
Peking.

* * * * *

H.B.M. Legation, Peking.
August 24, 1900.

SIR,

I HAVE the honour to forward to you the enclosed letter from Dr. Wordsworth Poole, Physician to the Legation, and Medical Attendant to the Royal Marine Guard, referring to the conduct of Sick Berth Steward, Second Class, R.G. Fuller, R.N.

I beg to state that, from my own observations and experience, his behaviour and treatment of wounded and sick was beyond all description. The recommendation of Dr. Poole speaks for itself.

I have the honour to request that you will be pleased to recommend Sick Berth Steward Fuller for what reward and distinction you may think he deserves, for his exemplary behaviour during a very trying time.

I have, etc.,
EDMUND WRAY, Captain, R.M.L.I.,
Commanding British Legation Guard.

The Senior Naval Officer,
Northern Division China Fleet, Taku.

* * * * *

H.B.M. Legation, Peking.
August 24, 1900.

SIR,

I HAVE the honour to bring before your notice the conduct of Richard G. Fuller, Sick Berth Steward of Her Majesty's ship "Orlando", who worked under me in the International Hospital during the siege of Peking. The work was excessively arduous, and he proved himself an invaluable assistant. He was indefatigable at his work, of which he has an excellent knowledge. He managed the sick of eight different nationalities with great tact. Both myself and my colleague, Dr. Velde, formed a very high opinion of his capabilities. In fact it would be impossible to overpraise his conduct.

I have, etc.,
WORDSWORTH POOLE,
Physician to the Legation.

Captain E. Wray, Royal Marines,
Commanding British Legation Guard,
Peking.

* * * * *

British Legation, Peking.
September 7, 1900.

SIR,

I HAVE the honour to bring to your notice the conduct of the detachment of Royal Marine Light Infantry commanded by the late Captain Strouts, which your Excellency was good enough to send as a guard in this Legation of the 31st May.

I cannot speak in any other terms but those of the highest praise of the behaviour of the officers, non-commissioned officers, and men of this detachment. They were exposed night and day, for two months to the most arduous, irksome, and responsible duties, which they fulfilled with a cheerful alacrity and with a courage and endurance which excited the admiration of everybody. Their bearing under fire was quite excellent, and could not have been surpassed by the best veteran soldiers. During the entire siege I did not observe the slightest signs of liquor in any of the men, neither was a case reported to me, and this, though the facilities for obtaining drink were great. To sum up, the general good conduct, soldierly bearing, and steadiness under fire of the men of the detachment, was worthy of the highest traditions of the British Army and of the corps to which they belong.

This high state of excellence was undoubtedly in a great measure due to the officers and non-commissioned officers. Captain Strouts was an excellent soldier and a gallant gentleman. He was killed in the defence of the Legation on the 16th July, and his loss was to me, and to the detachment generally, irreparable. Had Captain Strouts lived, I should certainly have recommended him to the Lords of the Admiralty, through your Excelleny, for promotion or for the Distinguished Service Order.

Captain Halliday was dangerously wounded whilst leading a sortie on the 24th June, and his valuable services were lost for the rest of the siege. Under another cover I am recommending this officer for the Victoria Cross.

Captain Wray, who was also wounded in taking part in the defence of the Tartar City Wall, one of the most dangerous posts in the defence, commanded the detachment very efficiently until the end of the siege. This latter officer has, I understand, recommended several non-commissioned officers. Those that came under my special notice were Serjeant Murphy, Saunders, and Preston, and Corporals Gregory and Gowney, who are all worthy of the highest praise.

I have, etc.,
CLAUDE M. MACDONALD,
British Minister.

Sir Edward Seymour K.C.B.,
Commander-in-Chief,
H.B.M. Squadron in China and Japan.

* * * * *

Letter No. 605 from Commander-in-Chief, China, 17th September, 1900, to the Admiralty.

It is clear that the Marine Guard well and ably fulfilled the duties required of them under very trying circumstances, and worthily upheld the traditions of their corps. Captain Strouts, who was in command until his death on 16th July, earned the respect and admiration of all. After his death Captain Wray took command, and carried out the responsible duties successfully. Captain Halliday was severely wounded on 24th June, soon after the siege commenced.

Captain Wray brings forward the names of several men whom he considers deserving of special recognition, and I submit them for their Lordships' favourable consideration.

E.H. SEYMOUR,
Vice-Admiral.

* * * * *

INDEX

INDEX

INDEX

INDEX

www.ingramcontent.com/pod-product-compliance
Ingram Content Group UK Ltd.
Pitfield, Milton Keynes, MK11 3LW, UK
UKHW050615260726
13967UKWH00008B/2872